D0811402

The
WESTMINSTER
CORRIDOR

HISTORICAL PUBLICATIONS

Plate 1. A contemporary portrait of young King Edgar, Dunstan's colleague in the foundation of Westminster Abbey. The King is here shown presenting his charter for the re-foundation of the New Minster at Winchester, which like Westminster was dedicated to St Peter. St Peter stands with his large key on the King's right hand. Bearded here, Edgar is shown beardless on some of his coins. See page 23

The

WESTMINSTER
CORRIDOR

An Exploration
of the Anglo-Saxon history of
Westminster Abbey
and its nearby lands and people

David Sullivan

HISTORICAL PUBLICATIONS

First published 1994
by Historical Publications Ltd
32 Ellington Street, London N7 8PL
(Telephone 071 607 1628)

© **David Sullivan** 1994

ISBN 0 948667 24 9

British Library Cataloguing in Publication Data
A CIP catalogue record for this book
is available from the British Library

Typeset by Historical Publications
Printed and bound in Great Britain by
Butler & Tanner Ltd, Frome, Somerset

Contents

List of Maps in Colour   6
List of Plates and Acknowledgments   8
Other Acknowledgments and Abbreviations   10

Introduction   11

Section 1 : The Setting for an Abbey

   1. Anglo-Saxon Middlesex   15

   2. Earth, Wood and Water   25

   3. The Shire and its Hundreds   46

Section 2 : Westminster Abbey and its Corridor Lands

   4. Westminster Abbey : Foundation and Forgery   56

   5. The Abbey's Lands in Middlesex : an outline   65

   6. Westminster : the Fields West of London   79

   7. Hendon in the Northern Weald   87

   8. Hampstead on the Hill   99

   9. Paddington : between a Road and a River   112

Section 3 : The Human Condition

   10. Hampstead : People, Village and Lives   114

   11. Rural Westminster : and Service to the Abbey   135

   12. Abbey life : the Corridor contributes   149

Appendix 1 King Ethelred's Telligraph   164
Appendix 2 The Anglo-Saxon Bounds, as described in the Charters   166
Appendix 3 Useful dates   170

Bibliography   171
Index   180

List of Maps in Colour
(drawn by author : following page 64)

Map   A   The 'Corridor' Estates of the Abbey in Middlesex

B   The three main Church Estates in Middlesex, in 1086

C   The three Kingdoms : Essex, Mercia and Wessex

D   The Geology of the Corridor

E   The Geology of Hampstead

F   The Domesday Woods of Middlesex

G   The 'Fall in value' of Middlesex Estates after the Conquest

H   The Rivers of Hampstead, Highgate, Paddington and Westminster

I   The Shire, the Hundreds, and their Meeting-places

J   The Anglo-Saxon 'five-hide' Assessment for tax

K   The main Lay Estates before the Conquest

L   The main Lay Estates at Domesday

M   The two Westminster Estates

N   The four Hendon Tracts

O   Hampstead : Anglo-Saxon Boundaries and Fields

P   The mystery of Codanhlaw; with the Hampstead Woods

Note

The maps need a word of explanation, as to the patterns into which they fall and the conventions and limitations underlying them.

There are two main kinds of map: first, the eight 'county' maps (B, C, F, G, I, J, K and L), which show certain features ranging over the whole county of Middlesex, either before or at the time of Domesday. These reveal aspects of the historical or geographical setting in which the Corridor lay. Secondly there are the more 'local' maps (A, D, E, H, M, N, O and P), which show geology, rivers, and details of the boundaries and other features of individual estates within the Corridor.

Throughout the sixteen maps, boundaries have been shown for all those estates whose names and general positions are known, so that the patterns of the holdings of the landowners or the other features illustrated can be revealed by the colours. But the degree of accuracy which can be achieved in defining the precise limits of the estates varies considerably.

At one extreme, most of the Corridor lands have boundaries which were defined in considerable detail in early extant charters (and are dealt with in the appropriate parts of this book): namely, the two rural estates of Westminster, the Hampstead estate, and three of the four tracts which made up the final manor of Hendon. These can be fairly accurately described and drawn, within the limitations of the scale, even if there remain some questions of interpretation (as indicated in the text).

But for many of the other estates outside the Corridor the boundaries were not described with precision in any extant charter, either at the time of Domesday or earlier in any Anglo-Saxon period. For them, in the absence of other contemporary evidence I have in general had to rely on the earliest known *parish* boundaries (mostly shown in the parish maps of the Church Commissioners); or on the boundaries shown in the maps which appear in the various volumes of the Victoria County History for Middlesex (some based on the admirable map of Middlesex drawn by C. Greenwood in 1819); or on the boundaries shown on any later (often much later) estate maps.

In some places even those forms of evidence give out, and one has to guess intelligently, by reference to (eg.) the positions of eponymous villages or natural geographical features. In any event some very early boundaries were themselves liable to fluctuate.

Another limitation of which one should be conscious is that both at the time of Domesday and in the pre-Conquest period there were seven Middlesex estates which still cannot be identified on a map. Most of these were small, ranging from 12.5 acres to two hides; five of them were unnamed, and the other two were Stanestaple (the largest of all, being four hides, see page 18) and Nomansland (12.5 acres, see page 141). The effect is that no allowance can be made in the maps for these estates, and it must follow that if they could be identified, room would have to be found for them, and the existing boundary-lines, as shown, would h   be readjusted.

So on any view s   boundaries shown on my maps will be fallible in some
places; principally   or. However this fault should not vitiate the general
pattern and posit   r features brought out by the colours.
In the 'c   a 'corridor' between the estates of Isleworth
and Hamp   as Hounslow; a corridor said to have given
access f   es. There is no evidence that this existed at
the   eed ever. It is alleged to be shown in the
G   oe shown there, because Mr Greenwood showed
                                         aries after Hampton had become absorbed into
                                         ss-corridor to the Thames had become unnecessary.

The Maps in colour have been bound after page 96, not page 64.

*

List of Plates and Acknowledgments

Plate 1   Contemporary portrait of King Edgar (c. 970))   *Frontispiece*
*(The British Library, MS Cotton Vespasian A.viii, fol. 2v;
copy adapted from 'Reproductions from Illuminated MSS'
(Series 1), published by the Trustees of the British Museum, 1910)*

2   St. Dunstan, founder of Westminster Abbey, kneeling before Christ   64
(The Bodleian Library, Oxford; M.S. Auct. F. 4.32, fol. 1r)

3   The royal Palaces of Winchester and Westminster, c. 1064-1066   75
(Bayeux Tapestry)

4   King Edward the Confessor's new Abbey, as at c. 1065-6   76
(Bayeux Tapestry)

5   'Reconstruction' view of Westminster Abbey and Palace, c. 1100 AD   77
(Drawn by W. T. Ball, based on researches by Dr R. Gem)

6   Ruins of Jumieges Abbey, near Rouen, Normandy   78
(Photographs by author)

7   King Edgar's grant of the estate of Westminster to the Abbey, c. 971   85
(WAM V, *by courtesy of The Dean and Chapter of Westminster)*

8   The Domesday entries for Westminster, Hampstead and Hendon   86
*(Reproduced, by kind permission, from the Phillimore edition of
DOMESDAY BOOK (General Editor John Morris), volume 11
Middlesex (County Editor John Morris), published in 1975 by
Phillimore & Co. Ltd., Chichester)*

9   The Hendon weald, and view to the Brockley Hill ridge, c. 1905   97
(Postcard, Barnet Libraries Archives and Local Studies Centre)

10   The confluence of the Silk River with the Brent River & Reservoir, 1922   98
(Photograph, Barnet Libraries Archives and Local Studies Centre)

11   Record of Ethelred's grant of Hampstead to the Abbey, c. 986-988   109
*(British Library, Stowe Charters 33, reproduced from T. Barratt's
'The Annals of Hampstead', 1912, Vol. 1)*

12 Map of Sandgate and part of the northern boundary of Hampstead 110
(Extract from O.S. map, edition of 1894, Barnet Libraries Archives and Local Studies Centre)

13 The boundary ditch between Hampstead and Tottenhall, on East Heath 111
(Photographs by M. Bassett and author)

14 Scenes of agricultural life in the period before the Conquest 133
(Drawings based on scenes illustrated in Anglo-Saxon calendars at the British Library)

15 View from Hampstead churchyard, over St John's Wood to Surrey hills 134
(Extract from print by T. Baynes, 1822, Camden Local Studies and Archives Centre)

16 View of Westminster, c.1543/4, with hinterland and Hampstead ridge 147
(A. van den Wyngaerde's Panorama at the Ashmolean Museum, reproduced from photograph at The Museum of London)

17 Print of 18th century watercolour 'reconstruction' of Westminster 148
(Print by J.R. Jobbins, reproduced from J. Ridgway 'The Gem of Thorney Island', 1860)

18 The Undercroft at Westminster Abbey, designed and begun c. 1065 163
(Photograph, by courtesy of The Dean and Chapter of Westminster)

*

Other Acknowledgments

Not wishing to cause offence by inadvertently leaving out names, I extend my gratitude in gross to all who have helped me, whether they knew it or not. However I must particularly pick out and thank all the kindly and helpful staffs of the unique Institute of Historical Research at the University of London, the Muniment Room at Westminster Abbey, the Barnet Libraries Archives and Local Studies Centre and the Camden Local Studies and Archives Centre; and also the five people who (with their own special knowledge of the Westminster and greater London area) have generously given me the help of their comments and advice: namely Professor Henry Loyn, Miss Barbara Harvey, Dr. Richard Mortimer, Dr. Emma Mason and Dr. Pamela Taylor. But the form and the content of the book remain entirely my own, and none of the deficiencies in them can be attributed to anyone else. Acknowledgment is made to Nicholas Barton for the use of an extract from his large map in his admirable book *The Lost Rivers of London.* Finally my thanks also go to my wife for her patience in the face of the demand made on me by the research and writing.

Abbreviations and References

Some obvious or familiar abbreviations have been used in places in the footnotes, to conserve space: A-NS for the volumes of *Anglo-Norman Studies;* A-S for Anglo-Saxon; A-SE for the volumes of *Anglo-Saxon England;* DB and DB2 for the two volumes of *Domesday Book;* EHD for the volumes of *English Historical Documents;* EPNS for the volumes of the English Place-Name Society's county studies; Herts for Hertfordshire; Mdx for Middlesex (and other counties likewise); PN for place-names; VCH for the Victoria County Histories; WA for Westminster Abbey. The usual abbreviations for the regular historical journals have also been used.

For the individual charters, I have generally given only the numbered reference in P.H.Sawyer's invaluable Annotated List of *Anglo-Saxon Charter*s, from which the MS or printed text can be discovered.

For references to Domesday Book, I have always given a 'Phillimore reference', for easier access for the general reader, and sometimes the folio number of the original as well. The Phillimore reference is in the form (eg.) 'DB *Mdx* 4/3'. This means the 4th landholder (numbered 4, in the top-right corner of the pages in the Phillimore Middlesex volume, with its translation printed opposite, in the essential edition of Domesday Book published by Phillimore: Ed. John Morris): viz. t*he Abbot of St. Peter's, Westminster;* and his 3rd estate (numbered 3, in the left-hand margin of the page): viz. *Hampstead.*

When a book referred-to in the footnotes has two or more volumes, I have used the form of reference (eg.) '3/45' : viz. volume 3, page 45.

Introduction

Much has been written about the first records and remains of the old City of London, enclosed within its Roman and medieval walls. But a close spotlight has rarely been turned upon the early history of many of the districts lying close to the old capital, in particular those western districts which now form part of the wider city of modern London - the West End, Westminster (itself a more recent City), Chelsea, the green areas of St James's Park, Hyde Park, Green Park and Regent's Park, Knightsbridge, Holborn, Bloomsbury and the more northern hinterland, of Paddington, Hampstead and Hendon.

As parts of our greater London, many of these outlying districts are now among the most populous and built-up areas in the country. But they began their known lives unpretentiously, as sectors of the rural lands of the Saxon Abbey of St Peter at Westminster which the Abbey had received as endowments, after it had been founded in the tenth century. They formed a 'Corridor' of land stretching from Westminster itself in a north-westerly direction and centred on the line of Watling Street (the old Roman road, now the Edgware Road), extending as far as the northern limits of the 'shire' of Middlesex. Their geographical extents and settings are to be best seen in the coloured Maps A, B and D (following page 64).

The history of this 'Corridor' of land, including the area of Westminster itself and its new Abbey, during the Anglo-Saxon period is the focus of this book. That period begins with the historical sequence of events which eventually led to the establishment of the small Abbey in its narrow site on the marshy river-shore not far west of the City of London. It ends nearly a century later, with the arrival of the conquering Normans and, a further twenty years later still, their great Domesday Survey of English lands. Fortunately for us that Survey provides not only its unique information about the new Norman period, but also much retrospective evidence of the period before the Conquest.

Within that period the Abbey's overall estate grew, slowly to begin with, more quickly at the end. But most of the 'Corridor' lands were part of that estate from the first. The early charters by which the new Abbey had acquired its first lands spelt out their boundary limits, and have left us with much information as to the extent and the nature of these lands; not to mention a number of enigmatic questions. The details of these charters and the boundaries which they described are here brought together as a whole for the first time.

The advent of the Abbey in the tenth century and its acquisition of most of the 'Corridor' lands within a short space of time had been an intrusion into another long-established empire. Over the previous centuries the Bishop of London and his cathedral church of St. Paul's in the old City had been granted extensive lands, which by the tenth century virtually girdled the whole of the City. So the new Abbey of Westminster and its 'Corridor', cutting a swathe through these encircling St Paul's estates, was in effect an encroachment upon an area which the Bishop and his Canons at St Paul's cannot have failed to regard as their own ancient preserve. It was a territorial encounter which led several times in later centuries to conflicts, of an ecclesiastical kind, between the two churches.

By the time that the Anglo-Saxon period came to an end at the Norman Conquest, the small Abbey had been dramatically transformed within a century of its foundation. By then it had been substantially rebuilt in stone by King Edward the Confessor, on a unprecedented scale and in the new Romanesque manner; the number of its monks had increased many times; and it was now the chosen mausoleum of the king. Secure in its rapidly increasing countrywide estates, and destined to retain its new national eminence, it went on to become the coronation seat and the burial-place of many succeeding kings and queens.

Although the past is part of us, no history can be more than an approximation, a reaching-out towards a reality which no longer exists: and a historian, like an artist, can only allude or point to, but cannot grasp, that reality. He therefore has to peer at every facet of the stone which he seeks to polish, to see what light it will reflect. And with this in mind I have sought to open up as much as I can of the surrounding context in which the new Abbey had its beginnings; not only its historical mould, but also the geographical and geological die from which it was cast.

Nor can one claim to describe the creation and endowment of a Saxon Abbey and its lands, without also seeking to discover the people themselves who played their part in that history, and to discern the nature of their lives, so far as these can now be made out. In this, one can only try to glance through the interstices of history, at those small tapestried panels which surround the arras of greater events. In those panels the plain figures of both the village and the sanctuary come and go, for the most part silently and unknown, the personal embodiment of that timeless character of the long medieval centuries.

So in its last section about the people involved in the story, this book is designed to do no more than open doors, into a simpler but harder world, which was once real but is now remote. If the doors are small and few, and the views from them narrow, that is no more than the ruse which History, with its tantalising fragments and evasions, plays on those who by their reading or their writing seek to understand the past.

Some points of interest

While this book is intended for both the informed and the uninformed reader, the busy professional historian may wish to discover what's new in all this for him. Without seeking to summarise the complex scene which I have tried to present, I would here merely pick out one or two small features which may perhaps be allowed to contain a little interest for even the professional: - the depiction of the concentrated and very early ecclesiastical power in the area round London, a concentration made up of two great church estates, which was to be rounded off by the establishment of a third, at Westminster Abbey; the probable existence of an earlier royal zone or sector in the hinterland of London, centred on the 'Corridor' area round the strategic road, Watling Street; the ebb and flow of the fragmentation and the regrouping of estates having their main origin in that former royal sector; the slow accretion of evidence pointing perhaps to what one might be able to call a 'coinage connection' in some of those erstwhile royal lands, close to the Anglo-Saxon kings' important mint in London; the evidence that several estates round London formed 'footholds', as residences or supply-sources close to the capital, belonging to significant land-owners whose other estates were spread more widely afield; and the monks' arrangements for early land-management at Westminster Abbey, in dealing with the problems caused by the original accession to the Abbey of landed estates in the tenth century and the very rapid acceleration of that process not long before the Norman Conquest.

The more 'local' reader, for his part, may find some interest as well in the more general picture of the small but significant origins of one of our national institutions, within a pre-Norman era which was much more sophisticated than is usually believed; in the close identification of Saxon districts and boundaries now contained within our greater London; in the detection of woods and fields in some areas; in the building at Westminster of a royal palace near the Abbey, in the course of the Abbey's great reconstruction by Edward the Confessor; and in the lives of both those who lived within the Abbey sanctuary and those tenants who served them with supplies or labour within the rural district of Westminster or in the outlying areas of the 'Corridor'.

Method

The book has been designed to give the reader a choice, and for this purpose, it is written on two different 'levels'. *Firstly*, as clear and straightforward a story is told in the main text as I have found possible, in terms which seek to avoid or at least to de-mystify the jargon and detail of medieval issues. But *secondly* it is essential that in debatable areas the history should be, and should be seen to be, as authentic as research can make it. Therefore, detailed supporting footnotes are provided, with appropriate explanations of issues, points of evidence and details of the souces relied on; all placed 'on the same page' as the relevant text.

This system enables the reader to choose how much detail to absorb. In the main text he can see the wood for the trees, by not having to disentangle conclusions from the detailed grounds for those conclusions. In the footnotes he can also study, but only if he so wishes, as many or as few of the 'trees' as he may choose. The intelligent reader will find much of supplementary interest in the footnotes; and he is also provided with the means for further inquiry and reading, if he is enticed or incited to disagree with my conclusions or to pursue the issues further.

The apology for my method, if one were needed, must be that nothing is more provoking than those histories which speak ex cathedra to historians, or give no identifiable hostage to fortune and therefore invite no challenge, so that the reader is left unable either to learn with assurance or with reason to disagree.

The mesh of detailed fact and inference in this story is so interwoven that I have not hesitated to give much cross-referencing within the footnotes, in order to enable the careful reader to see how particular facts may reflect upon quite different facets of the history. And with the same object in view, I have also not shrunk from repeating some of the facts in different contexts within the book, so that their relevance to different issues may not be lost. If this irritates or is unnecessary for those whose own memory of matters once-read is perfect, so be it.

The *sixteen coloured maps* are designed to shed light where words may fail to illuminate. Eight of them provide information about the whole of Middlesex, as part of the wider matrix of the story, including much about the Domesday and pre-Domesday situations within the county. The other eight maps reveal more local detail: about the rural areas of Westminster, Paddington, Hampstead and Hendon and other surrounding districts, about their geographical and geological composition and about their boundaries as described in the Anglo-Saxon charters. The reader should consult the Note annexed to the List of the Maps on pages 6-7.

For those who wish to have a clear structure of dates to consult, Appendix 3 provides a few useful ones.

To end with a warning, this is only a first volume. The next will take the story forward another 350 years, to the end of the fourteenth century. Because History does not suddenly break off at the end of a book, I have in some places referred forward to events which will appear in the second volume.

CHAPTER 1

Anglo-Saxon Middlesex
The historical setting

Any small tracts of rural land, such as the present built-up areas of Westminster, Hampstead, Hendon and Padddington once were, are lost to us in the mists of the early Anglo-Saxon era. Even the larger region which was to be known later as 'Middlesex'[1] can be seen only as a shadow slowly emerging from those mists.

But many centuries later, by the time of the making of the Norman Domesday Survey in 1086, some of those mists had cleared, and a major part of Middlesex had already for a long time been held in three great Church estates.[2] The first belonged to the Diocese of London and was held partly by the Bishop of London and partly by the Canons of St Paul's Church in the city, where the Bishop's seat was. The holder of the second estate was the Archbishop of Canterbury, while the third was held by the Abbot of 'St. Peter's Church at Westminster', a church whose successor is now familiar to us as Westminster Abbey.

By 1086 the rural area which had long been known to the Anglo-Saxons as 'Westminster'[3] had been a well-recorded possession of the Abbey at Westminster for a hundred years and more. So also had the more remote areas of Hampstead and 'Hendon'. To see both them and the Abbey in their mutual context, and to understand the setting in which the Abbey had been founded, we need to look back briefly at the earlier history of the Anglo-Saxon kingdoms and their impact on both Middlesex and the City of London.

The Settling of the Germanic tribes
For the first Anglo-Saxon invaders and migrants into Britain, the Thames estuary had been one of three main points of entry by river during the period of 150 years between about 450 and 600 AD.[4] These early tribal migrants had established settlements in the river-valleys of

---

[1] Although one can speak, in this context, of Middlesex as a 'larger region', one should note that when at length the region came to be recognised as a shire, probably in the tenth century (see page 46-7), it was the smallest county in England; and even when the smaller county of Rutland was formally constituted in the early thirteenth century (VCH *Rutland* 1/168), Middlesex was and continued to be the second smallest county throughout the medieval period. However for tax purposes Middlesex appears generally in later centuries to have been rated more heavily than most counties, no doubt because of its close connections with the City of London, see Keene *Medieval London and its Region* London Jo. 14 (1989) 99. For the over-rating of Middlesex at the time of Domesday, see Maitland *Domesday Book and Beyond* 462, and Pinder 'Introd. to Mdx DB' in *Mdx and London Domesday* (Alecto ed.) 5. For some fiscal and areal assessment problems for the county, see pages 50-2 and 137-8 below.

[2] See **Map B**. The Church held nearly half the shire at the time of Domesday, Pinder *ibid* 10.

[3] By that time 'Westminster', as a district, had grown, to include the areas of Paddington, Knightsbridge and Westbourne, see pages 71, 113 and 138 below.

[4] Loyn *Governance of A-S England* 6. The other two were the Wash and the Humber. While it was the Saxons who entered mainly up the Thames, the Angles seem to have used the Wash as their main point of entry and settled in East Anglia, the Fens and parts of Northamptonshire. Others who entered up the Humber gravitated mainly towards the centre and north of England, to the areas which became Mercia and

the south-east. Those who, about a hundred years later, began to be named in early land-charters [5] as 'Middle Saxons' or the people of 'the province of Middlesex' appear to have settled in the area around the Thames and its tributaries.[6] The name 'Middlesex' seems to have been derived from the generic name by which the people became known, but the boundaries of the region where they lived were for several centuries ill-defined. Meanwhile many of the 'indigenous' [7] Britons had been pushed further westward or had sailed south to Brittany, and have little impact on this story.

In these early periods of settlement, the lands which the communities known as the 'Middle Saxons' occupied came to include not only the region which was becoming known as Middlesex, but possibly also the area south of the river now known to us as Surrey ('Surrige', the 'southern district').[8] They also later included other areas westwards and northwards, up to the line of the Chilterns and into parts of the area which much later became a separate shire centred on the town of Hertford. Equally it was not until a later time that the three rivers, the Thames, the Lea on the east of London and the Colne to the west near Staines, became the boundaries which defined more narrowly the region known as Middlesex.

On either side of these 'middle' river settlements, other more organised Saxon kingdoms had arisen: the East Saxons in Essex, and the West Saxons towards the south-west; while in the south-east the kingdom of Kent, with some Jutish origins, still maintained sophisticated connections with the Continent. But it seems that the obscure communities of the Middle Saxons, such as the 'Gillingas' (who had settled at the modern Ealing), the 'Gumeningas' (whose heathen sanctuary stood on Harrow Hill) and the 'Mimmas' (who had migrated into the North and South Mimms area) produced no dominant families capable of becoming independent kings of the Middlesex region.[9] So before 600 AD the more energetic Kingdom of Essex under a strong royal line had apparently absorbed some or all of the Middlesex area which lay north of the Thames,[10] and when they did so, they also occupied London, the natural hub of the river settlements.

The status and condition of London during the period after the Romans had left in the first part of the fifth century are indistinct.[11] But according to Bede, the greatest of the

---

Northumbria. See also Hills *Archaeology of A-S England* A-S England 8 (1979) 297.

[5] Sawyer *A-S Charters* Nos 65 (704 AD); 100 (716 x 757 AD); 106 (767 AD); Stenton *A-S England* 55; Bailey 'The Middle Saxons' in *A-S Kingdoms* (Ed. Basset) 111.

[6] At places such as Shepperton, Hanwell, Mitcham, Croydon, Beddington and Mucking.

[7] The Britons were themselves the descendants of earlier waves of migrants from the Continent, such as the Belgic tribes, later mixed with other invaders, e.g. the Romans and their still later Germanic mercenaries: all of whom had successively displaced even earlier cultures. For the background, see Megaw *Introd. to British Prehistory* 415-7.

[8] Stenton *A-S England* 54-5 ; Loyn *Governance* 8. However it is also argued persuasively that Surrey may not have become the 'southern' district (of some 'northern' region) until a later stage, after other kingdoms (of Essex or Mercia) had absorbed Middlesex, see Yorke *Kingdom of the East Saxons* A-S England 14 (1985) 28 ; Blair 'Origins of Surrey' in *A-S Kingdoms* (Ed. Basset) 100-2, and idem *Early Med. Surrey* 7-8; Gelling *PNs of Berks* 3/813, 820 and 840; Dumville *Britons and Anglo-Saxons* IX/21.

[9] Loyn *Governance* 7; Bailey *ibid* 115-9; Sawyer *A-S Charters* No 1783 (Gillingas); Sawyer *ibid.* No 106 and *EHD* 1/ 500 (Gumeningas); Gover (hereafter 'EPNS') *Mdx* 76. For the '-ingas' names ('people of'), see Smith *EPN Elements* xxv; Dodgson *Distribution of the PNs -ingas* Med. Arch. 10 (1966) 1-29; Gelling 'Chronology for English PNs' in *A-S Settlements* (Ed. Hooke) 72.

[10] Loyn *A-S History* 31; Stenton *A-S England* 55.

[11] Brooke and Keir *London* 60 ; Biddle 'A City in Transition 400-800' in *British Atlas of Historic Towns* (Ed. Lobel) 3/20-2; Vince *Saxon London* 7-8.

church historians, London had again become a capital city by the early eighth century : "a trading centre of many nations who visit it by land and sea".[12] A hundred years before achieving this status, the City had first become not only subject to the East Saxons, but also the focus of Kentish interests. The prominent King of Kent, Ethelbert, recently baptised as a Christian by St Augustine, was uncle to the then king of Essex and thus able to exert his influence over him as his *Bretwalda* or 'overlord'.[13] It was this Kentish king who had first set the Church on its path to great territorial power in and around London.

The Church Estates in Middlesex   **Maps B, C and K**
In 604 King Ethelbert had founded and built the first Saxon Church of St Paul in London, his nephew's principal town. The Diocese of London, after its long lapse since Roman days, was re-established briefly, with a new Bishop, Mellitus.[14] It is probable that at that time, as part of the bishopric's endowment, great estates in Middlesex - in Stepney, and in London itself, and in unnamed districts 'next to London Wall' on its northern and north-western side - were given by King Ethelbert to the new Bishop.[15] Although it was a Kentish King who had thus been instrumental in founding St Paul's, the boundaries of the new diocese appear to have coincided with the Kingdom of Essex, not the Kingdom of Kent. It included the whole of Essex itself, the area known now as Middlesex, with London itself, and at least part of the present area of Hertfordshire.[16] It may be that it was the limits of the Essex kingdom which led to the western boundary of the later shire of Middlesex being fixed on the river Colne, instead of still further west on the dip-line of the Chiltern escarpment (which became part of Buckinghamshire).[17]

In this way the first step was taken in the spread of the great Church estates in Middlesex, in which the Archbishop of Canterbury and the Abbot of Westminster were later to join. Other steps followed. A hundred years later, in about 705, the Bishop of London received another large estate in Middlesex, based on Fulham (where the Palace of a much later Bishop still stands), and a small separate grant of lands in Ealing.[18] His estate of 'Fulham' probably included or came to include not only all the areas now known to us as Ealing and Acton and later Chiswick as well, but also the comparatively remote area later

---

[12] Bede *Ecc. Hist.* ii. 3, in *EHD* 1/609. Writing in about 731, Bede said that London "is" a metropolis and a trading centre. But the implication seems to be that by that date it had been established as such for some time; and the name 'metropolis' implies the status of a 'capital' city, see Campbell 'The Church in A-S Towns' in Campbell *Essays in A-S History* 139.

[13] From an early period it was a common feature that, by means of military power or other methods of less belligerent influence, the king of one tribal region would become overlord ('Bretwalda') to one or more of the other kingdoms within the country. The practice had mutual advantages; power for one, and protection for the other.

[14] Bede *Ecc. Hist.* ii. 3. This new See of London was interrupted shortly afterwards, but was again reestablished later in the same century. Bishop Mellitus emerges later in Westminster tradition as the perhaps mythical founder of a very early church at Westminster, see page 59.

[15] Bede *Ecc Hist.* ii, 3; Davis (Ed) *Regesta* Nos 1/246 and 274; Taylor 'Estates of Bishopric of London' (London PhD Thesis) 21-6. The grant of districts next to London Wall did not even appear in any record until after the Conquest, see the *Regesta* references above, which refer to them as given to 'St Paul's'.

[16] See **Map C (1)**. As a result of the Danish disruptions it seems that even part of Suffolk came within the partial control of the See of London for a period (Hill *A-S Atlas* Map 239; Stafford *Unification and Conquest* 183; Whitelocke *A-S Wills* No 1), but this had ended by the mid-tenth century.

[17] Hill *A-S Atlas* Maps 140 and 253 ; Brooke and Keir *London* 16-7; Gelling *PNs of Berks* 3/ 841-2, and Mawer *PNs of Bucks* 2/xiv.

[18] Sawyer *A-S Charters* Nos 1785 (Fulham) and 1783 (Ealing), and Gibbs *St Paul's Chs* No J6 and J7.

known as Finchley [19] which lies to the east of Hendon, abutting the Westminster Corridor.[20]

In the succeeding centuries the Canons of St Paul's (who from a very early date had been permitted to accept and hold property independently of their Bishop[21]) received for their own benefit other lands in inner Middlesex, at Willesden, Harlesden, St Pancras, Tottenhall (i.e.Tottenham Court), Islington, Rugmere, Stoke Newington, Hoxton and Stanestaple, with Chiswick a little more distant. They thus established at an early date their own powerful hold on much of the land around the City.[22] The dates and other details of these acquisitions are unknown,[23] save that some of the lands 'next to London Wall' which the Bishop had earlier received were probably transferred by him to his Canons.

The second great group of church estates to arise in Middlesex was that of the Archbishop of Canterbury. In the eighth and ninth centuries the Archbishopric received massive tracts of land in Middlesex, at Harrow and at Hayes, the former through the royal influence of a king of Mercia.[24] For by that time the kings of Mercia, from their base-lands

---

[19] It is not known whether it was so called at that time, or only at a later stage. It is one of the oddities of the Bishop's estates that Finchley was treated during much of the Middle Ages as part of his Fulham lands, while Hornsey (known also as Harringey) immediately adjoining Finchley on its east side was treated as part of the Bishop's Stepney estate: see **Map B** and page 54. Another dramatic, but unreliable, story concerning the same neighbourhood was recounted much later, to the effect that a sizeable wedge of land in North Middlesex 'between Barnet and Londonstone', including Finchley and Hornsey, had belonged previously to the Abbey of St Albans and had been confiscated by William the Conqueror and given to the Bishop; see Madge *Records of Harringey* 31-2; Taylor 'Estates of Bishopric of London' 18-21. The boundary between Hertfordshire and Middlesex north of Finchley is an extraordinary one (see eg. **Map B**) and had probably been subject to an earlier 'reorganisation' of shires, see page 47; but perhaps it was this very strangeness which gave rise to the more dramatic myth about the Conqueror? Even if St Alban's Abbey had once owned lands reaching right down to London, it had lost them before the Norman Conquest and not after it, Taylor *Endowment of See of London* A-N Studies 14 (1991) 303-4. Doree *DB and Edmonton* 13, 25-30 also discusses this odd boundary. For the woods in both Fulham and Hornsey, see page 34 below.

[20] Taylor 'Estates of Bishopric of London' 19-21; Robins *A Note on Early Finchley* TLMAS 18 (1955) 65-7; Madge *Records of Harringey* 31.

[21] Taylor *ibid.* 47-52. Cf. page 160 below, for a similar separation of interests at Westminster.

[22] *DB Mdx* 3/14-29 (ff.127d-128b): see **Map B**, and page 107-8 below. The tract called 'Stanestaple' is a mystery; although it was an area probably close to London, it still cannot be identified. It has been variously attributed to Islington or St Pancras, discussed in Madge *Records of Haringey* 53-5. Although the Canons undoubtedly acquired the very extensive estates near London which are listed above in the text, Madge's assertion (at page 45, said to be based on Domesday Book) that the St Paul's estates formed a *continuous* belt in a semi-circle round London from the Thames at Fulham to the Thames at Stepney 'even before 1066' is inaccurate, since it ignores the complete break in that ring which, as we shall see, the Westminster estates (and one or two other lay estates) in the Corridor had made for at least 100 years before Domesday. Madge's statement might possibly have been accurate for a very much earlier period, *before* Westminster Abbey was founded, but certainly not at Domesday nor even in the century before Domesday. **Map B** shows this break in the circle at the time of Domesday.

[23] For Willesden the Canons many years later claimed that their title went back to the time of King Athelstan of Wessex (925-39); but to do so, they had to rely on a palpably forged charter, see Taylor 'Estates of Bishopric of London' 32-3 and Sawyer *A-S Charters* No 453. But in any event they probably did acquire Willesden and its neighbour Harlesden before 1000 AD: and certainly Tottenhall, which adjoins both Westminster and Hampstead, had been acquired (for St Pauls or the Bishop) before that date, see Taylor *Endowment of See of London* A-N Studies 14 (1991) 293-4. The Bishop and Canons ended up with the largest estate in Middlesex at Domesday, assessed at 162 hides. For 'hides', see pages 50-1.

[24] See **Map B**; Brooks *Church of Canterbury* 137, 141-2, 320. At Domesday the Harrow estate was assessed for tax at 100 hides, the largest in Middlesex; and Hayes (once 100, too) at 59 hides. Although Harrow was held by the Archbishop at the time of Domesday and had become an important residence for

in central England, had now emerged as overlords to both the Kentish and Essex kingdoms and so were able to influence the grant of lands within those regions.

In this way, wedges of church land were being driven into the area which had already begun to be known quite loosely as Middlesex.[25] It was often a feature of such early acquisitions by the Church (and also similar acquisitions by lay persons) at this time that they stemmed from royal grants. Indeed when Domesday Book was compiled much later, in 1086, not only were there already the three long-standing and substantial ecclesiastical estates (including by that time the lands of the Abbey at Westminster), but one finds that the Crown by then retained scarcely any land at all in Middlesex.[26]

So the stage was now set, with two of the great Church estates already founded in Middlesex. The emergence of the third estate, that of Westminster Abbey, and the first real evidence of those areas in the Corridor which became the lands of the Abbey, are dealt with separately below, in and after Chapter 4 (page 56).

But first, what was the rest of the historical context in which that Abbey came to be founded? For that we must return to pick up the story of the political and dynastic influences through which Middlesex and London had meanwhile passed. These we left with the absorption of those areas by the Kingdom of the East Saxons. But in its turn the greater power of another kingdom, the Kingdom of Mercia from the Midlands, was soon to dominate both the Middlesex and London area and the rest of the East Saxons' territory.

The Mercian Domination (c. 670 - 850)   **Maps C, D and F**
For the next two centuries a seesaw of power continued between the various kingdoms of which England was now composed. For much of this lengthy period the Mercians, from the centre and west of England, came successively to dominate, first of all, various tribal areas round the Midlands and then, further afield, the kingdoms of Essex, Wessex, Kent, Sussex and East Anglia, becoming their Bretwalda or overlord.[27]

Both Middlesex and London appear to have passed completely under Mercian control, probably in the years after 735; [28] and they remained subject to the Mercians for over 100 years. It was in the earlier period of Mercia's growing influence that Middlesex had first

---

him, there had been a comparatively short interruption in his possession of the estate *before* the Conquest (see *DB Mdx* 2/2 (f. 127a); *VCH Mdx* 1/99 and 104-5; and Clarke *A-S Harrow and Hayes* TLMAS 39 (1988)) 186. Clarke *ibid* 177 gives a detailed analysis of the Hayes and Harrow charters (eg Sawyer *ibid* Nos 132 and 1436), with much-needed discussion of the boundaries of the component areas.

[25] See **Map B**.

[26] *D.B. Mdx* 1/1-4. Indeed almost the only land still held by William I in 1086 in Middlesex was the tiny piece (12.5 acres) called 'Nomansland', for which see page 141. Under the new Norman feudal system, the king did of course have a *residual* interest as the ultimate owner of all land, from whom each 'Tenant-in-Chief' held his estates. But even as early as the eighth century, Bede had recorded that earlier A-S kings had made so many 'foolish' disposals of their land that 'it was not easy for a vacant place to be found for a new seat for a Bishop': *Opera Historica* (Ed. Plummer) 1/413. Middlesex is one of the only three counties (with Cheshire and Staffs) in which no mention of royal 'demesne' is made in DB. In Middlesex, however, it is noticeable that right up to the time of the Conquest there were still lands over which Edward the Confessor had continued to hold a degree of *control*, either directly or indirectly, through personal influence over his family and close circle, his thegns and housecarls (see page 68 below) or other 'men', see **Map K**. For the relationship between the sworn 'man' and his lord, see Roffe *Thegnage to Barony* A-N Studies 12 (1989) 157. For a 'royal' province in central Mdx, see page 70.

[27] Stenton *A-S England* ch.vii ; Loyn *Governance* 27-8.

[28] Hill *A-S Atlas* p.78. See **Map C (2)**.

come to be described as 'the province which is called *Middelseaxan* '.[29] But it is likely that the title was still used without any great geographical precision at that time.

The subservience of the Middle-Saxons and their homelands is probably illustrated during this period by one of the earliest of extant Anglo-Saxon administrative documents - the 'Tribal Hidage'.[30] This is a written list, made probably in Mercia itself, recording the names of the subject tribes which were liable to pay tribute to that kingdom. It is significant that the Middle Saxons do not appear on the list; but the East Saxons do, and their liability to pay tribute to the Mercians is expressed in far more onerous terms than even the Domesday Survey attributed to Essex as much as 200 years later. The reason probably is that Middlesex and London (and perhaps parts of e.g. the present county of Hertfordshire as well) were being treated in the 'Tribal Hidage' as part of the territory still at that time under the influence of the East Saxons: so increasing the liability, in turn, of the East Saxons to pay tribute to the Mercians as their overlords.

There seems little doubt that by the time of King 'Offa the Great' (757-96) the Mercians were exercising almost total control in Middlesex and London and other nearby places. Offa founded St Alban's Abbey in the area now called Hertfordshire in about 793, and even perhaps another church with the name St Alban in London itself.[31] He also established a new coinage in the form of the silver penny, which was minted mainly in London and at Canterbury.[32] There is overwhelming evidence that Chelsea [33] during his reign, and afterwards, contained a royal centre or place of residence, where many charters were made [34] and councils held [35] between at least the years 785 and 816, and again later in the ninth and tenth centuries. Moreover from about 750 Mercian kings were making grants of other Middlesex land as they wished,[36] without reference to the kings of Essex who had previously dispensed similar royal generosity in Middlesex.

Significantly it was in the Mercian period that a new trading centre was developed in the district between Westminster and London. Recent archaeological research has shown that at least from about 700 the area outside the western limits of the City of London, along the Strand towards Westminster, became the site of a trading settlement which constituted a substantial market and even, it is said, an international port or at least a 'beach-market'. [37]

---

[29] Sawyer *A-S Charters* No 65 (704 AD). The term 'provincia' was an ancient and (by now) inexact one.

[30] Birch *Cart. Sax.* 297 ; Loyn *Governance* 34-8 ; Hart *Tribal Hidage* TRHS 21 (1971) 133-57

[31] Brooke and Keir *London* 18, 111. But see Vince *Saxon London* 70-1.

[32] Loyn *Governance* 41. The silver penny became the principal coin used in England in medieval times ('a role of fundamental importance for 500 years', Petersson *A-S Currency* 10) and was the basic unit of the currency referred to throughout this story.

[33] At first glance it seems that Chelsea was a curious place, in view of its lowness and therefore some vulnerability to the excesses of the river Thames, see page 26. But in fact Chelsea is on the gravel, away from the alluvium, on which much of Westminster rests, see **Map D**. If the kings wanted somewhere well away from the trade etc. of London, Chelsea was the first large area which was both near the river and on the gravel. It is likely that ready access to the Thames was important, for ease of river transport. Chelsea even had an outlying area called (in OE.) 'the King's Wood', viz 'Kensal': EPNS *Mdx* 162. For the name 'Chelsea' which in its OE. form indicates a landing place, see page 59. But there is no archaeological evidence of the Chelsea site, it seems. Could the course of the river have shifted?

[34] Sawyer *A-S Charters* Nos 123, 125, 128, 130, 131, 136, 150, 151, 158, 888, 1430.

[35] eg. *A-S Chronicle* 785 AD (for 787) ; Stenton *A-S England* 218, 237, 309. Chelsea was also the place where King Alfred later planned part of the restoration of London, see page 22 below.

[36] Sawyer *ibid* Nos 100 (Yeading); 106 (part Harrow); 119 (Harmondsworth); 132 (Hayes, Yeading and Twickenham); 188 (Harlington and Hayes); 98 and 1788 (ship-tolls, London); 1783 (Ealing).

[37] Rosser *Westminster* 10-12; Tatton-Brown *A-S London* Antiq. 60 (1986) 21; Biddle 'City in

The main site appears to have run from the the present Aldwych ('the old wic') to the area of Trafalgar Square. The name *Lundenwic* which appears in many contemporary charters almost certainly refers to this trading settlement as well as the old walled city of London.[38] It seems that while most of the Middle Saxons continued to plough their furrows in the hinterlands of the river, some may at this time have begun to join in the equally pacific practices of trade and industry, but *outside* the city of London. Perhaps this was a breakaway movement of Middle Saxons from the East Saxons; or a movement of both of them away from interference by the Mercians who were now making themselves felt within London itself.

It may also be that at about this time, if not earlier,[39] the citizens of London acquired certain rather mysterious 'rights of the chase' in Middlesex. These rights were later claimed by the citizens to exist over the whole of Middlesex up to the line of the Chilterns, in Surrey and in parts of Hertfordshire, even in parts of Kent. From shortly after the Norman Conquest the citizens appear to have asserted that these rights were already of immemorial custom, and jealously claimed them throughout the Middle Ages. Before his death in 1135, Henry I who himself, even more than his father the Conqueror, "loved the stags as dearly as though he had been their father" [40] and even more loved any profits which could be made from the control of hunting privileges, was prepared to confirm by charter to the Londoners "their hunting rights as fully as their ancestors had enjoyed them in the Chilterns, Middlesex and Surrey".[41]

So these private hunting rights, as claimed by the Londoners, appear to have extended over at least the whole of Middlesex. Certainly no part of Middlesex was ever made into a *royal* forest, even though the county was well-wooded and has been misdescribed as a royal forest.[42] But the exercise of such hunting rights is curiously unrecorded for the areas west and north-west of the City. One would dearly like to know how, and how often, such rights were in fact exercised in the Corridor estates which later came to belong to Westminster Abbey; and what problems such hunting Londoners may have caused (if they did) to lords, freemen and peasants there at any time during the Middle Ages.[43]

Transition' in *British Atlas* (Ed. Lobel) 3/26-9; Milne and Goodburn *Early Med. Port of London* Antiq. 64 (1990) 629-30. 'Wic', as in Ipswich, Norwich and Hamwic (the name of old Southampton) and (on the Thames) at Woolwich, Greenwich, Chiswick, Hampton Wick and Twickenham, appears also in 'Aldwych', and in this context probably means a trading place. Although this *Lundenwic* thesis is recent, it was known from pottery finds as long ago as the 1930s that Saxons had frequented the area round Aldwych.

[38] Biddle *ibid*. 27, note 81.

[39] As suggested by Stenton *A-S England* 58, and see also his *Norman London* 24-5.

[40] *A-S Chronicle* 1086 AD.

[41] *EHD* 2/1013. But whether Henry I's famous charter in favour of the citizens of London is indeed genuine as it stands has been called in question, see Brooke, Keir and Reynolds *Henry I's Charter* JS Arch. 4 (1973) 558, and cf. Hollister 'London's first Charter' in *Monarchy, Magnates and Institutions* 191. But even if not authentic, it may however incorporate a genuine custom as regards the hunting. Certainly Henry's successors, who also by charter confirmed the citizens' rights of chase (and other rights), acted as if they regarded not only the rights as being genuine but also as if they thought that the rights had really been confirmed by Henry I; eg *EHD* 2/ 1014 (Henry II).

[42] Beginning with Stow *Survey of London* 70. See further page 36-7, below, and **Map F**.

[43] Shortly after the Conquest, Lanfranc the Norman Archbishop of Canterbury prohibited hunting without a licence in his lands at Harrow, and the Conqueror upheld his order (Davis *Regesta* 1/ No 265; Dugdale *Monasticon* 1/111). But it is not clear who was doing the hunting. The citizens continued to assert their claimed rights throughout the whole area until after the Dissolution of the monasteries, nearly 500 years after the Conquest; but as with many of the rights claimed from time to time by the

The Danes and Wessex : War and Peace (c. 850 - 1016)   **Map C**

Two main protagonists were now emerging. The *Danes* had appeared in the Thames estuary in 835, devastating the Isle of Sheppey; they put London to the slaughter in 842, and sacked the city in 851, making their first winter stay in the Isle of Thanet in that year [44] (with other attacks on Kent and coasts elsewhere). With the need for unity on the English side thus underlined, the *West Saxons* under their King Alfred, from their base-lands of Wessex in the south and south-west, began to meet the main brunt of the Danish attacks. In this role the Wessex kings sought and finally secured the overlordship over Mercia, and later became the self-styled 'kings of all England'.

After concerted attacks on various other parts of England, which had begun again in about 866, the Danes retook and occupied London in 871/2, and remained there for perhaps fifteen years, exacting great tribute and even issuing coinage.[45] It is impossible to resist the conclusion that Middlesex must have suffered dramatically at this time: in 878, it was said, 'a band of pirates gathered and took up quarters at Fulham on Thames',[46] and this tends to confirm the general inference about the fate which must have overtaken the river valley. Further, when it fell to King Alfred in 886 to recapture the Thames area and London, this was only after the 'burning of towns and the slaughter of peoples'.[47] The walls of the city had to be repaired, and some new streets were laid out.[48] The archaeological evidence also makes it clear that the trading centre at *Lundenwic* along the Strand towards Westminster ceased to operate at about this time: it seems that all or most of the inhabitants of that 'wic' must have recognised the danger and retired (or perhaps were unwillingly transplanted) within the walls of the City.

In a celebrated peace treaty [49] in about 886 with Guthrum, the Danish King from East Anglia, Alfred established (but very briefly) a boundary between the English lands north and north-west of London and the territory of the East Anglian Danes. Both London and Middlesex were safely retained within the English half, with the boundary running northwards up the River Lea, east of the City, as far as Hertford and then up the Ouse, and thereafter back to the line of Watling Street. Alfred then entrusted London and its neighbourhood and other Midland lands, which the Danes had previously overrun, to Ethelred the Ealdorman of Mercia, who was (or soon became) Alfred's son-in-law by

---

citizens, it is difficult to reconcile the theory with practice. The absence of early evidence suggests that the 'right' was little used, at least in the areas west and north-west of London. But perhaps it was these claims of the citizens of London which many centuries later provoked Henry VIII to issue his proclamation of July 1545, asserting hunting rights for himself over the whole stretch of country between his palace in Westminster northwards up to and including Hampstead Heath. As regards the region to the east of the River Lea (and so strictly outside Middlesex), Epping Forest (previously called Waltham Forest) was part of the greater Forest of Essex, which covered the whole of the present county of Essex and was made a royal forest shortly after the Conquest. As late as 1871 a right to hunt in Epping Forest was claimed by the citizens of London before the Epping Forest Commissioners, but no documentary evidence was found to support it. See also page 37.

[44] *A-S Chronicle* 835, 842 and 851 AD.

[45] *A-S Chronicle* 871 AD; Sawyer *A-S Charters* 1278 (Birch *Cart. Sax.* 533 and 534); Brooke & Keir *London* 19. But it is not clear how continuous their occupation was.

[46] *A-S Chronicle* 878 AD. Very shortly after this time there is also a vivid description of an estate in Surrey, 'stripped bare by heathen men'.

[47] Asser *Life of Alfred* 69, see *EHD* 1/183, n.2.

[48] For a detailed acount of the questions on this topic, see Dyson *Alfred and the Restoration of London* L.Jo.15: 2 (1990) 99-110 and Dyson and Schofield 'Saxon London' in *A-S Towns* (Ed. Haslam) 285 ff.

[49] *EHD* (1st Ed.) 1/380-1. See **Map C (3)**, and Dumville 'Treaty of Alfred' in *Wessex and England* 1.

marrying his formidable daughter, Aethelflaed.[50]   So the two sides were now poised facing one another, with the Danes and other Norsemen occupying most of the centre and north of the country, to which the name the 'Danelaw' was later given.

In spite of the treaty an irregular and spasmodic tide of war continued to flow backward and forward for about another 125 years (892-1016) between the Wessex kings, who were now becoming 'English' kings,[51] and the Danes and Norsemen. Protected at length [52] by a chain of recaptured and newly fortified towns north and north-west of London, the emerging English half of the nation survived and coalesced and even reabsorbed much of the Danelaw.[53] But finally the wars swung south again, enveloping London and its neighbourhood. They only ended when a triumphant, if brief, Danish dynasty, begun by King Cnut, had to be accepted by the English nation in the year 1016.

The Cradle of Westminster Abbey and the Corridor

But for our purposes one reign stands out above all others within that era of spasmodic war, and that is the reign of young King Edgar 'the Peaceable', Alfred's great-grandson, who died aged only 32 after a reign of 16 years (959-975). He was successful, and perhaps fortunate, in maintaining a rare and brief interval of comparative peace both abroad and at home; but such success was due mainly to the earlier prowess of some of his predecessors, and particularly his uncle King Athelstan, in freeing most of England, including a growing Danish population in the north and east, from external Danish control. After some initial opposition from a group of nobles, Edgar's short reign became a creative period not only of great unity but also of dramatic reform: reform in matters as divergent as monastic discipline and organisation,[54] and the sophisticated coinage which England had already enjoyed for nearly 200 years.[55] It was in the latter part of his reign, during this intermission of the Danish menace, that the Abbey at Westminster came to be founded, as one small event in the upsurge of religious enthusiasm which the monastic revival had created.[56] At about the same time, towards the end of the tenth century, the records which

---

50 *A-S Chronicle* 886 AD. The current king of Mercia had died, and the Ealdorman appears to have become his successor in fact, even if he was not always given a royal title: Stafford *Unification and Conquest* 26; Dyson *ibid* 102 and Davis *Alfred and Guthrum's Frontier* EHR 97 (1982) 809-10. By these steps Mercia was to become subject to Wessex. For Ethelred, see also Appendix 2, page 167.

51 The generic titles 'King of the Angles' and 'King of all Britain', and even more grandiloquent titles, were often assumed by the Wessex kings, sometimes prematurely, in the tenth century, see eg. Sawyer *A-S Charters* Nos 416-9 ; Banton *Monastic Reform and Unification* SCH 18 (1982) 71-2; Stafford *Unification and Conquest* 32, 35. And even Alfred had called himself 'King of the Angles' on some of his coins in the ninth century, see Woodruff *Life and Times of Alfred* 100.

52 See page 46 below.

53 This confusing flux and reflux of war, conquest and reconquest is clearly depicted in a mainly visual form in Hill *A-S Atlas* pp. 54-61 and 63-71. But except for the reign of King Edgar, embedded in that period, none of the other detail of those wars matters here. Edgar's second son, King Ethelred 'the Unready', (who later was, at the very least, unfortunate in his wars with the Danes) had other roles to play in relation to several of the Corridor estates of Westminster Abbey, see page 67 below (for his nickname); page 80 (for Westminster); and page 100 (for Hampstead). For the Danelaw, see Hart *The Danelaw*.

54 See page 57-8.

55 Loyn *Governance* 40-1 and 122. See also page 101 below. Professor Loyn has elsewhere referred to the simultaneous occurrence of these two reforms as a 'coincidence in time', but surely this is unkind to King Edgar or perhaps his advisers? See Loyn 'Progress in A-S Monetary History' in *A-S Monetary History* (Ed. Blackburn) 6.   For a contemporary picture of Edgar himself, see **Plate 1**, frontispiece.

56 I argue below in Chapter 4 that the date of the foundation was about 971 AD, not many years before

survive first bring to life the rural districts of Westminster, Hendon, Hampstead and Paddington, which all became early endowment estates of the new Abbey and its monks.

So with 'England' now emerging with a national, if not finally established, identity, the context was set for the creation of a third Church estate in Middlesex, as part of the great religious revival throughout the country. And with the first endowments of land in the hinterland of London for a new Abbey on the Thames, the circle of ecclesiastical estates around the capital was to be finally closed. These small beginnings for the new foundation were not to foretell the greater future which lay ahead.

Edgar died. While this present history focuses on the foundation and endowment of an Abbey of *enclosed* monks at Westminster, it is possible that a long time previously Westminster had been the site, not of a 'true' monastery of monks, but of an 'old minster' church, staffed entirely or partly by priests with parochial duties in the surrounding countryside. Cf. Blair 'Minster Churches in the Landscape' in *A-S Settlements* (Ed. Hooke) 35; Radford *W. Abbey before Edward the Confessor* 3-5. The possibility of this earlier history of the Abbey's site is not directly relevant to my theme, but readers may wish to be aware of such a background. Blair *ibid.* also notices an association of such minster churches with Roman sites: Westminster had indeed had a Roman past, see Black *Roman Sepulchre at WA* TLMAS 4 (1874) 63, and also pages 81-2 and 163 below. Excavation has also shown an occupation of the site of the Abbey before the mid-tenth century, see Vince *Saxon London* 66. There are also disputed copy-charters at the Abbey (eg. Sawyer *A-S Chs.* No 124) which relate to this issue. But apart from such factors and the stronger significance of the name 'West-minster', the possibility that it had had an earlier life as a minster rests more on general inference than on direct evidence. For a possible relevance of Bleccanham, in Hendon, in this connection, see page 95 below. If there had indeed been an earlier minster at Westminster, its proximity to royal centres at both London and Chelsea (see page 20) might be another illustration of the relationship between minsters and royal *tuns* also noticed by Blair *ibid* 40. It is also possible that both Chelsea and an earlier church at Westminster might perhaps have suffered destruction together at the hands of the Danes in the ninth century (see page 22), but there is no record of either such event. For recent nearby excavations, see Mills *Cromwell Green* TLMAS 31/22-5. On these piled-up hypotheses, the creation in the tenth century of an Abbey at Westminster, and of a royal centre at Chelsea (again visited by a king, Ethelred, in 996, see Hill *A-S Atlas* map 162), would reflect 'restorations' of some earlier existence, rather than entirely new creations. It is fair to say that several charters, mostly forged at Westminster, and also later histories of Westminster speak of 'restoration' of various estates to the new Abbey at Westminster in the tenth century: see, for example, the main Westminster charter (Sawyer *A-S Charters* No 670, discussed at page 79 below), which reflects the restoration-tradition in a passage which is either interpolated in an otherwise genuine document, or reflects a manifestly inaccurate but contemporary tenth century tradition. See also pages 59-60 below as regards the later histories written at Westminster. For some other thoughts about possible minster churches in Middlesex, see Vince *ibid.* 68 and his map at 64. Aston's admirable *Monasteries* 49 asserts a definite earlier foundation at Westminster by 785 AD, but several questions must remain open about this.

CHAPTER 2

Earth, Wood and Water
The geographical setting

Human agency had not been alone in creating the setting in which the small Abbey of Westminster came to be founded on the edge of the Thames. The forces of nature also, in the form of the soils, the trees and the streams, had already been shaping the lives of men in the neighbourhood of the City of London for centuries. In a north-westerly direction from Westminster, the first monks of the new monastery could look up a partly-wooded and well-watered slope, past the present Primrose Hill (then probably a wooded bluff), to the top of the Hampstead-Highgate ridge.[1] Over the top of that ridge they could not see. But on the left of the ridge, the line of the Hampstead hill fell away to the lower ground of the Middlesex plain, where Watling Streeet,[2] the old and decayed Roman road (now the Edgware Road), stretched through its greater woods in a straight line towards the north-west. That leg of the road, already nearly nine hundred years old by the tenth century, ran from the point where the Marble Arch now stands, towards the furthest ridges round Brockley Hill on the northern boundary of Middlesex.

Earth   **Maps D, E, P and M**

In the short distance of eight miles from Westminster along Watling Street, past Paddington and Hampstead and into the northern weald where Hendon lay, no less than six soil formations were, and of course still are, to be found. Each one, in its time, has created different conditions for those who settled there in rural communities.

The Thames flows now in a narrow bed. But in a distant era, long before the Ice Ages, a great river system as large as the Ganges or the Niger, flowing from the direction of the present south-west England,[3] first laid down great sheets of sandy deposits on top of the even older marine bed which is now known as the London Clay. Then, much later, it is likely that other river waters (called now by the name of the 'Proto-Thames', also flowing from the south-west across northern Middlesex and southern Hertfordshire, in the direction of what is the present East Anglian coast) stripped away much of those same sandy deposits throughout Middlesex, but leaving a few small 'islands' of lighter soils resting as hill-cappings on top of the underlying London Clay (eg. at Hampstead, Highgate, Harrow and Mill Hill). The movement of all these river systems was mainly in a north-easterly direction, towards East Anglia.[4] But, again long afterwards, the invading ice

---

[1] One of the only places from which one can still find a view of the whole ridge which (with some modification, for height) resembles the sky-line which the early monks, and later residents of Westminster, must have enjoyed (in their case, from ground level) is from the top of the West Towers of the Abbey.

[2] The name Watling was not Roman but derived from an Anglo-Saxon tribe, the Waeclingas, living round St Albans, to which the Street led. The name appears in the tenth century, see Appendix 2, page 166 and Sawyer *A-S Chs*. No 645. But 'Street' (a *via strata*) denoted a Roman origin.

[3] Cornish minerals are to be found in the sands.

[4] The Proto-Thames must also have been joined by tributaries from the direction of Surrey (before the

during the Ice Ages, bringing its own deposits with it from the north, appears to have blocked the north-eastern course of the river waters and so diverted them southwards, ultimately to flow more easterly towards the sea: as the Thames now does in the bottom of its present valley.

In this way the London Clay, it seems, became the main visible soil or 'outcrop' throughout Middlesex, capped only in a few places with various other lighter deposits. In this long process the physical contours of the hills, the valleys and their soils with which man has since had to live in Middlesex were moulded.[5]

So by these ancient waters the two main ridges of Middlesex had been first laid down and then carved out, each ridge slanted (as the rivers had been) towards the north-east. Of these, the short Hampstead-Highgate ridge, standing over 400 feet, now overlooks the valleys on each side of it: to the south, over the 'saucer' of the Thames valley in which both Westminster and London now lie; and to the north, over the flatter weald, which was 'sculptured' out of the land towards the second and northern ridge at Brockley Hill, Highwood and Mill Hill. For their part the glaciers, receding at length after their advance from the north and north-east, in turn left behind them their own deposits, mainly in Finchley. In this way the various soils in the Corridor were laid down which were to influence the choices of settlement and cultivation,[6] and we will now look at them in more detail, starting from the banks of the present Thames.

1. *Alluvium*

On the bend of the river Thames where Westminster now stands, a wide and irregular bed of muddy alluvium adjoins the modern bed of the river. This represents not only the marshy margins and flood areas of the meandering river but more particularly the sediments from its tributaries, the Tyburn and the Westbourne.[7] Large parts of the area which later became the monks' rural estate of Westminster and the adjoining low land in 'Eia' (the modern Pimlico) were composed of this alluvial soil. Within the alluvium in Westminster there was at least one 'island' of firmer gravel, on which the Abbey was later to be built.[8]

When not actually flooded the area was, at worst, marshy and impenetrable on foot, and at best was (or would later become, as drainage improved) ideal as dyke-bordered water meadows for hay and pasture,[9] or well-suited for gardens [10] and market gardens.

---

present Thames valley was formed), because rounded pebbles of chert from the Surrey Lower Greensand are to be found on Hampstead Heath.

[5] The above brief account is based principally on personal communications from Dr Eric Robinson. See also VCH *Mdx* 1/1-10 (Prof. S. Wooldridge), and cf. Taylor (Ed) *A Place in Time* 11.

[6] See **Maps D and E**. The various parts of the present London area which are formed by the different soils described below are well defined in the Geological Survey 6' Sheets for London, Edition of 1920, Sheets NV. S-W, N-W; NIV. S-E, N-E ; NI. N-W, N-E, S-W, S-E; NII. S-W, on which **Maps D and E** are based.

[7] See pages 41 and 43, below.

[8] Another island may have existed at Eia, so as to give rise to its name (see page 59), but its size or character are unknown. Possibly at an early time there was a large gravel area still visible there and surrounded by water, which has since become covered with alluvium by reason of floods or meanders. Another explanation might be that since the estate was itself bounded on three sides by the rivers Thames, Tyburn and Westbourne, it may have been regarded as an island. Darby (Ed) *DB Geog. of S.E. England : Mdx* 97, at 101 asserts that 'the DB vill of Eia was situated on an island' in a marshy area. But there is nothing in the DB entry for Eia to suggest that there was (still?) an island: there is only the name. The manor-house called 'La Neyte' in Eia which the Abbot of Westminster Abbey bought in the thirteenth century for his own country house itself stood, in one sense, on a 'island', as it had a moat all round it; but that was much later, and it may have been artificial, not natural; whichever it was, the manor-site was known as 'the Island' in the thirteenth century and after. See **Map M**.

[9] For the amount of hay and pasture recorded in Westminster in the Domesday Survey, see pages 145.

2. *River Gravels*

Further away from the river on the Westminster bend, two levels of River Terrace Gravels lie beyond the alluvium. These were laid down by even wider flows of the ever-winding Thames in an earlier and more robust life. These levels still underlie most of the modern West End of London, Bloomsbury and Holborn, southwards from a line running roughly north of the Marylebone - Euston Road. The steep shelf from the lower terrace up to the higher terrace is still clearly visible in (eg.) St James's Street, the Haymarket, Villiers Street and Arundel Street. The higher terrace then slopes more gently and more lengthily, up (eg.) Regent Street and Baker Street. The boundary between the two gravel terraces in the West End area lies very approximately on a shelf, where the Piccadilly roadway was no doubt formed to take advantage of the natural platform above the lower and steeper slope: as we will see later, a similar shelf, formed along the same boundary further to the east, provides a platform for the eastwards extension (the Strand and the present Fleet Street) of that same roadway in its approach to the City of London.[11]

Most of the soil of these terraces was light and well-drained, and in medieval times was easily ploughable,[12] save in and near the flood areas and valleys of the Tyburn and Westbourne, which cut swathes through the gravel terraces. It made good arable and tree-bearing land throughout the Middle Ages, before the later waves of 'parking' carried out by Henry VIII (in the present St James's Park, Green Park, Hyde Park and Regent's Park) in the sixteenth century and the later extensive building in the West End changed the use of much of the area.

In Kensington, westwards from the gravel terraces which underlie the modern West End, a solid band of brickearth stretches as far west as the mouth of the Brent river at Brentford, as shown on **Map D**. It helped to provide many of the bricks and tiles with which the expanding capital was later built, supplemented in the nineteenth century by bricks made from the brickearth on Hampstead Heath.

3. *London Clay*

Underlying both the alluvium and the river gravels is the deep stratum of marine London Clay, which becomes visible northwards from near the line of the present Marylebone - Euston Road. It extends massively from there as far as the northern boundary of the county, but with various 'islands' of other soils superimposed upon it here and there. The two 'islands' on top of this sea of clay, with which we are principally concerned, are the Hampstead-Highgate ridge, and the lower prominence lying to the north of that ridge, on which the main Saxon settlement of Hendon took place.[13] Many other 'islands' exist, at Harrow, Finchley and Alexandra Park, for example, and of course on the northern ridges

---

Eia, the adjoining estate, had enough meadow to feed 64 oxen, and sufficient more to produce hay worth 60 shillings. In this way the southern, riparian, belt (Pimlico) of Eia clearly provided for the ploughing of its more northern areas of Hyde and Ebury with its seven (or eight) ploughs, see **Maps D** and **M**.

[10] Even by the time of Domesday (1086) there were, unusually, 41 cottagers with 'gardens' in the Westminster area, see *DB Mdx* 4/1 and pages 139-41 below.

[11] See page 82 below. For Chelsea, also on the gravel, see page 20 above.

[12] For its extent, see **Map D**. There is evidence in the farming accounts of Eia, Knightsbridge and Westminster of the productiveness of this district, see Vol 2. Those parts of the district which were not affected by Henry VIII's 'parking' in the sixteenth century continued to be the good farm lands of Ebury, Belgravia and Mayfair which Mary Davies, the heiress of the lord of the manor (a property-owner, and a Scrivener; not an ordinary farmer, as is sometimes alleged), brought with her when in 1677, at the age of 12, she was wed to Sir Thomas Grosvenor and so laid the foundations of the Grosvenor Estate. See also the Map of the Manor of Eia in 1614 (Plate 31 in Gatty *Mary Davies and the Manor of Ebury*) and the later one of 1675 in the Crace Collection (also copied in Loftie *History of London* 103).

[13] *A Place in Time* (Ed. Taylor) 52-3, and see page 90 below.

at Mill Hill, Brockley Hill and other places which are outside the scope of this book.

So the Clay forms the bed of the depression or weald from which the ancient Thames and the glaciers have removed most of the top formations which had been laid down even earlier over the Clay. As a visible layer it covers more than half the area of Middlesex.[14]

The Clay is a heavy impermeable soil, blue in colour in the ground but becoming ochre-ish when exposed to the air (hence the colour of 'London Bricks'). Heavy woodland, by which most of Middlesex was formerly covered, thrived on such land, but such soil did not at first take easily to the ox-drawn plough. When however it had been successfully cleared and well ploughed, it formed solid arable land, the 'wheat and beans land' of later Middlesex. During the Middle Ages it also bore considerable quantities of lighter oat crops, as we shall see; and 300 years after the Dissolution of the monasteries proved also to be highly productive of the profitable hay crops which the livestock of the capital and its environs were by that time requiring.[15]

4 and 5. *The two Sandy-Beds.*
On the lower slopes of Hampstead Hill, the London Clay in its upper contour was and still is visible (in gardens) up to a level approximately just above the modern Finchley Road. Above that level, the surface soils of the hill form one of the main hill-cappings supported on top of the clay. There, two layers of these lighter soils are superimposed on top of the London Clay: first, the Claygate beds and further up the hill, the Bagshot sands. Both of these extend along the ridge eastwards to Highgate and Alexandra Park. The same two layers now appear together in only one other 'island' in the sea of London Clay, namely on Harrow Hill.[16] Both layers had been originally laid down as *continuous* sheets over the whole of Middlesex and other areas, stretching north east from Hampshire and Surrey (from where indeed both the Bagshot and the Claygate[17] beds get their names).

As a soil, the Claygate is both loamy and sandy, with a residue of clay. On its edges, deposits of brickearth suitable for making tiles and bricks were present, and were particularly used for these purposes in a circle round the slopes of Hampstead Hill, where the Claygate bed outcropped above the London Clay.[18] Being comparatively light, it was easily worked and fertile for the growing of the lighter crops such as oats. The Bagshot is an even lighter sandy less-productive soil; being restricted to the higher slopes of the hill, it was less suitable for the growing of crops by reason also of some of the steeper contours.

Both the Claygate and the Bagshot soils could, and still can, sustain a heath association of plants (furze, heather, broom, heath grasses); but equally in some places each has had no difficulty in bearing trees, including beeches, oaks[19], and lighter varieties

---

[14] See **Map D**.

[15] Middleton *Agriculture of Mdx* (1807) 284-91; *Report from Sel. Cttee on Agriculture* H.C. 612 (1833) V. 545-52; Thompson *Hampstead : Building a Borough* 10-13. See also page 145.

[16] The Claygate beds, without the Bagshot sands but with other pebble deposits on top, appear in considerable quantities in other hill-cappings, at Mill Hill, Highwood, Brockley and Elstree, all of them on or near the northern boundary of the county.

[17] The Claygate deposits are named from the area in Surrey where, coincidentally, the manor of Claygate from not later than 1086 was also owned by the monks of Westminster Abbey; see Harmer, *A-S Writs* 303-6

[18] Eg. at Childs Hill; at the 'East Park' estate (now in the middle of Hampstead East Heath); at Belsize. See **Map E**. These were intermittent deposits. The main brickearth deposits near Westminster were those at Kensington, see **Map D**.

[19] A large oak wood grew on the Bagshot bed in the Frognal-Childs Hill area in the fifteenth century and probably for centuries before, see page 127, and **Map P**. See also the present northern Hampstead Heath (i.e. 'West Heath' and 'Sandy Heath') which is now over-prolific with oaks and other large varieties such as the intrusive sycamores. Moreover on present showing even the East Heath will look like the

such as birches and willows. In prehistoric times these soils were even dominated by the great lime woodlands [20], before the beech, oak and lighter varieties, with which the heath plants appear to have shared the area since at least the thirteenth century,[21] took over.

6. *The Glacier Deposits*

The other 'island' with which we are principally concerned is the small area of high ground on which the church and centre of Hendon stand. This rises to only 280 feet in height, but is (or at least must have been in the past) a significantly visible prominence in the weald, with a steep dip slope towards the north. The top soil of this 'island' is a *gravel* deposit left in the area by the melt-waters of the glaciers which had come from the north east, after the London Clay had been uncovered by the waters of the Proto-Thames.

The other main deposit left in some places on top of the Clay by the glaciers, when they retreated, was *boulder clay*. While the gravel alone was left where Hendon stands, both the gravel and boulder clay on top of it were deposited nearby at Finchley, forming there an extensive plateau. It was no doubt the added height given to the underlying Clay by the gravel from the glaciers which led to Hendon being chosen for its early Saxon settlement by at least the ninth century, if not much earlier.[22] It is at least possible that an outlier of this glacial gravel at Temple Fortune may have formed a similar site for the settlement of 'Bleccanham', one of the four estates which comprised Hendon,[23] but there is no hard evidence for this, as yet.

****

Wood   **Maps E, F, G, L and P**

To early settlers, woodland is both a provider and a barrier. For the hunter it provides meat; and for the home, it provides wood for housing, warmth and cooking. But for the agricultural pioneer, it means hard work, the work of clearance and then heavy ploughing. In an Anglo-Saxon poem it was the ploughman who was called 'the ancient enemy of the wood',[24] but the feeling between them must have been mutual.

For the Middlesex settlers, there was certainly plenty of woodland. It is not surprising that throughout the later centuries of the Middle Ages one of the staple products of the Abbey's manors in Middlesex [25] continued to be an endless flow of wood: cartloads of wood for burning, on which the Abbey's kitchen, brewhouse, bakehouse and hearths

---

present Sandy and West Heaths in fifty years time. The birches in medieval times seem to have favoured the area towards the eastern boundary of Hampstead, i.e the East Park area, but there was heavier woodland south of those birch woods, where the weightier clay surfaced, see page 127.

[20] See Taylor (Ed) *A Place in Time* 25. The ancient lime was the small-leaved lime, not the more modern common lime, see Rackham *History of the Countryside* 67. It covered almost all of lowland England, Rackham *ibid.* 69-70.

[21] The earliest documentary reference to furze or heather on the 'Heath' is in the late thirteenth century, but the heath plants were probably there for ages before that. The fact that the great prehistoric small-leaved lime-woodlands were overtaken by other species did not mean that the small-leaved lime faded out altogether; it still survives as one indicator of ancient woodland, Rackham *ibid.* 108. Present limes on the 'Heath', however, are all common limes and mostly imported.

[22] For Hendon, see page 90 below. For settlement at Finchley, see Taylor (Ed) *A Place in Time* 24, 26, 57-9.

[23] I owe this suggestion to Dr Pamela Taylor. For Bleccanham, see page 94, below.

[24] The Exeter Book (Ed. Mackie) EETS Riddle No 21.

[25] See Vol. 2.

depended; of timber needed both for the construction and repair of the buildings in the manors themselves and for the more sophisticated buildings of which both the Abbey and the Palace at Westminster were composed; and of wood available for sale by the Abbey to local purchasers, including purchasers from the City of London.[26] But what kinds of woodland were these in Middlesex, and how were they distributed ?

The main evidence as to the extent and nature of the early Middlesex woodlands appears in the Domesday Survey, made in 1086, more than 100 years after the Abbey had been founded (c. 971). The following review of the Domesday record of the Middlesex woods, particularly in the areas near London and Westminster, cannot recreate with any precision the situation in that previous century, but it can at least provide some clues as to the wooded character of the neighbourhood into which the Abbey was introduced.

One of the questions, to which the Circuit Commissioners who were appointed to collect the material for Domesday Book had to obtain answers, was *Quantum silvae?* [27] How much wood ? For all its curt phrases and its omissions, the Survey reveals a fair amount of information as to the extent of the woodlands in 1086 AD, and since established woods cannot have sprung up overnight, the woodland which still existed at the time of Domesday must have been of some antiquity and should represent a *minimum* extent for the woodland which had existed during the century since the foundation of the Abbey.[28]

The usual method used by the Domesday Commissioners for Middlesex (and for the other four counties in their Circuit, Buckinghamshire, Hertfordshire, Bedfordshire and Cambridgeshire [29]) was to assess and record the number of domestic pigs which the woods in any manor could support, in the form 'Wood for (100) pigs.[30] The medieval pig was a wilder,[31] thinner and blacker creature than the modern pig, and was turned out loose into the woods in autumn to feed on the acorns and beechmast. 'Wood' (*silva*) therefore in Domesday Book, it seems, meant woods in which oak or beech prevailed, not those composed of lighter varieties, such as birch, hazelwood or hawthorn, nor varieties such as hornbeam or ash, which would have been of less interest to your medieval pig. In many places, woodland would often have been of a mixed kind; but it seems likely that the pig assessors would have disregarded those areas which were principally composed of other tree varieties or were 'waste' areas, ie. where scrub or bushes predominated, without affording much food for pigs.

So the basis of the Domesday figures for the extent of woodland in Middlesex was the amount of what one can call 'pigwood'. It does not follow that all the pigs assessed for an estate were actually there. The object of the assessment was not to count the extent of the

---

[26] Galloway and Murphy *Feeding the City* London Jo.16 (1991) 4, 8.

[27] In the *Inquisitio Eliensis,* a twelfth century document copied by the Abbey of Ely from an earlier document which had itself been compiled probably from original circuit returns for the Domesday Survey, there is the list of questions which were probably the questions to be answered for the purposes of the Survey, see Galbraith *The making of DB* 36-8 ; Frearson *DB:The Evidence Reviewed* History 71 (1986) 384; Darby *Domesday England* 4-5.

[28] While it is possible that in some places the woods might have actually *increased* during that century, the overall picture must surely have been one of gradual decrease, particularly nearer a city like London.

[29] It now appears to be generally accepted that these five counties were surveyed together, in 'Circuit 3', see eg. Frearson *ibid.* 392. It was one of the first areas recorded and 'returned' in the Survey.

[30] The same formula was used in the survey of the three East Anglian counties, in the second (and smaller) volume of Domesday, the 'Little Domesday'. But in most other counties the more usual method was to express the woodland in either linear dimensions or in acres, see Darby *Domesday England* 176. However, in general, DB is very irregular and inconsistent in its records of woods, see Darby 'DB and the Geographer' in *DB Studies* (Ed Holt) 104-5, 107, 111.

[31] But medieval records generally distinguish between the real wild pig (*aper*), which was hunted, and the domestic pig (*porcus*), see Rackham *History of the Countryside* 36

existing pig herd belonging to the lord of the manor, still less the pigs belonging to his tenants.   The actual number of the pigs present within a manor would depend both on the nature of the estate's management at that time, and of course on the particular preferences or needs of the inhabitants.   But the object was to estimate how much wood there was. The number of pigs actually present in a manor would obviously provide a 'floor' for reaching such an estimate, but would not necessarily give the *potential* of the 'pigwoods' for supporting pigs.

On the Domesday figures possibly about 30% of Middlesex was covered with 'pigwood'.[32]   Compared with many other parts of the country this was quite a high percentage; but the context is that (contrary to popular belief) England overall was far from being a heavily wooded country.[33] The findings of the Survey, so far as they go, reveal that only about 15% of the recorded land of England was covered with 'pigwood' and other semi-wooded areas where animals could be pastured. Even allowing for substantial omissions, the figure is not a great one. And within Middlesex itself there were widely differing extents of woodland, a feature which has considerable significance for all issues relating to the extent and the nature of the human settlement within the county.

In the northern half of the county, including the weald which lay north of the Hampstead-Highgate ridge, heavy woodland prevailed : -

Table 1   :   The well-wooded areas of Middlesex [34]

Manor	No of pigs	'Size' in Hides [35]	Pigs per Hide [36]
Enfield	2000	30	67
Edmonton	2000	35	57
Tottenham	500	5	100
Hendon	1000	20	50
The Stanmores	1600	18	89
Kingsbury	1200	10	120
Willesden	500	15	33
Harrow	2000	100	20 [x]

[32] Rackham *ibid.* 78.

[33] Rackham *ibid.* 16 and 76.

[34] See **Map F**. Fulham and Stepney have deliberately been omitted from this Table and Table 2, because of their complicated holdings and uncertain boundaries. See also Note 42 below. Hooke *Pre-Conquest Woodland* Ag.HR 37 (1989) 114 notes that big boundaries were sometimes heavily wooded, for perhaps political reasons: the wooded and convoluted Herts/Mdx boundary had probably had a political past in the course of some fairly dramatic 'reorganisation' of estates and shires, see page 18.

[35] For this purpose it is (artificially) assumed that the number of 'hides' assigned by Domesday Book to a manor has some relationship to the actual size of the manor. But the assumption has to be an artificial one, because factors other than size were much more significant in the assessment of an estate's 'hidage'. For the problems of the 'hide', see pages 50 and 137-8 below.

[36] An average per hide is obviously an inexact tool, since it does not take account of the different areas *within* each manor. But since one cannot at this range of time pinpoint the exact location of most of the wooded areas *within* the manors (though for Hampstead, see page 126-8, and for Paddington, see page 112-113), some such tool has to be used. The average over the whole county was about 24 pigs per hide. Apart from its curious result in Harrow (see next Notes), such a tool is probably the best we have.

[x] Though it had one of the largest assessments of 'pigwood', Harrow's equally large hidage results in a very low average. But if (as seems likely) the 'pigwood' was concentrated mostly in the north of the manor, the average in that part would rise appreciably and more in line with all the other northern manors which had large pig assessments. The very size of this (the largest) manor in Middlesex would make the actual location of the woods within its area more significant than in the smaller manors. From Williams and Cunnington *Fryent Country Park* 6, it appears that there may not have been much heavy woodland in that Park (i.e. in the south-east corner of the Harrow estate, adjoining Kingsbury); or maybe

Ruislip	1500	30	50
Hillingdon	1000	4	250
Harefield	1200	5	240 y

In contrast with the heavily wooded regions, there were two areas (shown on **Map F**) where no 'pigwood' at all was recorded: -

> (a) a large area in the far south-west of the county bordering the River Thames, where the soil was almost entirely composed of river terrace gravels. On this soil, it seems, no heavy woods had grown, or if they had, had been cut down by the time of Domesday. But another sneaking suspicion must also remain: that since the area is so compact, some policy or failure in recording on the part of the Domesday Commissioners was responsible for it in that area; and
> (b) a group of estates which appear to be on or near the road leading northwards out of the City of London, the old Roman Ermine Street,[37] later called Kingsland Road in its southern stretches. The absence of 'pigwood' on these estates is not surprising, because clearly the region was one where trees would have long been removed, owing to the vicinity of the city and its large population, the importance of the road after it left the city gates and the need to prevent surprise attacks on the city.[38]

Between these two extremes, the area west and north-west of the City of London was comparatively lightly covered with 'pigwood', as one might expect of a neighbourhood which was nearer both the river and the city, and therefore likely to be already more developed with settlements, however small they may have been. At least parts of such an area were more adaptable for human cultivation by reason of their lighter gravelly soil, on which paradoxically most of the present urban West End of London is now situated. The whole of this region lying to the west and north-west of the old city contained several of the early endowment-estates of the Abbey: namely the estates of Westminster (which by the time of Domesday also included the districts of Knightsbridge, Westbourne and Paddington) and Hampstead.

---

if there had been, it must have been cleared very early.

y. There is obviously a wide variation in the above averages, but (with some adjustment, as above, for Harrow) one can take the figure of 50+ as the lower limit of the range of averages for these more heavily wooded areas. By way of contrast, see the lower range of averages below in Table 2 for the less-wooded estates, with which we are principally concerned.   24 is about the average for the whole of Middlesex.

[37] In the so-called *Laws of Edward the Confessor* (retrospectively compiled between 1115 and 1150) four great roads were confirmed as being protected by the 'King's Peace', which had been a very early concept (in one sense preceding the concept of a centralised criminal law), such that any breach of the 'King's Peace' on any of those roads gave rise to special penalties: Liebermann *Die Gesetze der A-S* 1/637-8 and 510-1. As to assault on the King's highway, see Wormald 'Aethelred the Lawgiver' in *Ethelred the Unready* (Hill Ed.) BAR 59 (1978) 65-6. The four roads included both Watling Street and Ermine Street, described as running 'the length of the kingdom'. The other two roads were the Foss Way and Icknield Way, described as running the 'width of the kingdom': see Hill *A-S Atlas* Map 199. As to the origin of the *Laws*, see Barlow *Edward the Confessor* 266 and Campbell *The Church in A-S Towns* 16 SCH 129. It does not follow from this 'legal' provision that other roads did not also share in the King's Peace.

[38] Within the Bishop's great estate of Stepney there were at least five other small holdings (held, in effect, by sub-tenants from the Bishop) in which there was no woodland, see DB *Mdx* 3/5-9 (f. 127c). But in his main Stepney manor the Bishop himself had woodland (DB *Mdx* 3/1, 500 pigs), probably where Victoria Park now is (I owe this attribution to Diane Bolton). For the significance of woods in relation to Watling Street, see page 37-8.

Table 2 : The more lightly-wooded areas near the City and Westminster.

Manor	No of pigs	No of Hides	Pigs per Hide
Clerkenwell	60	5	12
Barnsbury	150	5	30
Tollington	60	2	30
Tottenhall	150	5	30
St Pancras	-	5	-
Tyburn	50	5	10
Rugmere	-	2	-
Hampstead	100	5	20
Westminster	200	16.5. z	12
Eia (Eye)	-	10	-
Lileston	100	5	20
Chelsea	60	2	30
Kensington	200	10	20

If this was the position in 1086 AD, can one assume that it would have been much the same during the period of a hundred years before the Norman Conquest? Would the first monks at Westminster have seen approximately the same amount of woodland around them in Westminster and across the slopes leading in an arc, north to northwest, up to the Hampstead-Highgate ridge ?

One of the factors which might have affected the degree of woodland in this area during that century was the progress of William I's army in Middlesex, as he approached London in his conquering marches after winning the battle of Hastings. The detail of the Domesday Survey shows quite clearly that the values put on the various estates in Middlesex (a) immediately before the Conquest, (b) after the Conquest, when each estate was distributed, and (c) twenty years later in 1086 reveal a dramatic fall in value in almost all the Middlesex estates immediately after the Conquest, a fall which in general still existed at the time when the Domesday Commissioners were still doing their job twenty years later.[39] In some places the pre-Conquest value was even three or more times greater than the post-Conquest value. This has generally been ascribed either to devastation caused by William's army as it circled round to the north of the City of London, or to subsequent subjugation by the Normans in the Middlesex neighbourhood. The details of this loss of value, as recorded in Domesday Book, are set out in **Map G**.

If it is right that it was William's army which caused the fall in value, it is certainly possible that the devastation included the burning or other destruction of woodlands. Two of the areas which suffered the greatest falls in value were in the northern part of the county where the woods were thickest, near the big roads, Watling Street and Ermine Street, down which military contingents would have marched. So it may be the case that before the Conquest, and even more so a hundred years before that, the woods had been greater than in 1086. But it is likely that the destruction of woodland may have been only a small factor in the causation of the great fall in value, since the wasting of woods may have brought benefits as well as disadvantages: clearance could mean a higher value, because where the

---

[z] Although the original five-hide estate of Westminster had been enlarged to include other areas (see pages 71, 113 and 165), it was still known as 'Westminster' or the 'Westminster Liberty'. See page 166.

[39] There is no doubt that in the counties on the south-west, west and north of Middlesex there were also consistent falls of value. For further discussion, see page 121-2 and **Map G**.

woods were excessive, the destruction of some of them was at least a first necessary step in the process of clearance for the purpose of cultivation.

If one jumps forward in time nearly a hundred years after Domesday, one finds an exuberant admirer of London, William FitzStephen [40] a monk of Canterbury, describing in about 1174 the position in his day. Having spoken of the sparkling streams and mills north of London at that time, he continues : "Very near lies a great forest with woodland pastures in which there are the lairs of wild animals, stags and fallow deer, wild boars and bulls".[41] Unless the woods to the *north-west* of London had by then dramatically increased since Domesday (which seems unlikely), the contrast which FitzStephen was making was probably the contrast with the heavily pigwooded area up the *eastern* side of the county (and particularly to the *north* of the City, in Tottenham, Edmonton and Enfield, and possibly Hornsey [42] as well). This is also consistent with a much earlier record made in the Anglo-Saxon Chronicle of a successful English counter-attack made in 1016 AD against the Danes who were at that time besieging London and encamped round it on the north side. In order to surprise them King Edmund marched towards London from the west, "keeping north of the Thames all the time and coming out through the wooded slopes" of Tottenham.[43] It looks as if he took advantage of the heavier cover all along the northern half of the county, and emerged suddenly into the open spaces along the old Ermine Street just north of the City,[44] where the Danes were encamped.

So FitzStephen's allusion to the 'great forest' could hardly have been a reference to the more lightly wooded areas which lay to the *north-west* of the City, below the Hampstead-Highgate ridge. In that direction it was not until one reached Hendon, Willesden and Kingsbury in the northern weald that the real woods began, see the above Tables and **Map G.** For its part Hampstead, with its 100 pigs, had not been heavily 'pigwooded' at the time of Domesday. Nor would it be right to regard the long slope from Westminster up to the ridge as being heavily wooded with 'pigwood': there was certainly some such wood there (as shown in Table 2), but nothing like the concentrations in the more heavily wooded part of the county. In St Pancras and Rugmere, respectively east and south of Hampstead, as well as (more distantly) in two parts of Stepney and in Cranford, no pigs at all were assessed: instead 'wood for fences' (indicating some coppicing?) was recorded.

So far Domesday has dealt with the heavier oak and beech woodlands. Our English word 'woodland' is of course an inexact term, since it includes both the concentrated forms of wood, and the sparser kinds of treed area, where either the trees are of the lighter

---

[40] FitzStephen was one of the monks who had actually been present at the murder of Thomas Becket. He was a Londoner by birth, and his enthusiastic description of London and its immediate neighbourhood is strongly prejudiced and overblown in favour of his birthplace, but it is nevertheless a vivid and invaluable record.

[41] The variation in the translations which have been ascribed to these words is extraordinary. See *EHD* 2/1025 ; Darby *D/B Geog. of S.E. England* 123 ; *VCH Mdx* 2/224 ; Brooke & Keir *London* 115.

[42] For the anomalous position of Hornsey (and Finchley) among the estates of the Bishop of London, see page 18 above. Neither Hornsey nor Finchley appeared by name in Domesday Book. The wood in Stepney and Fulham were assessed at 500 pigs and 1000 pigs respectively; and it is probable that much of this pig assessment related to Hornsey and Finchley, which lay in the northern part of the county where other assessments were higher than in the south. Perhaps they were 'denns', detached swine-pastures, as in Kent? see Everitt *Landscape & Community* 77-81. But within Fulham the names of both Acton (oak town) and Hanger Lane (cf. page 106) indicate substantial woodland. For Finchley, see also VCH *Mdx* 6/58.

[43] *A-S Chronicle* 1016. The estate of Tottenham (see eg. **Map B**) is not itself mentioned, but a place which has been identified as being in Tottenham is referred to, see Stenton *A-S England* 391.

[44] For the open space 70 years later in DB, see page 32 above.

varieties such as hazel or birch,[45] or where there are broken clumps or stands of single trees interspersed between tracts of rough grass, scrub and tangles of small shrubs.[46] Those areas which were devoted by Anglo-Saxon kings (and Abbots) to their own hunting,[47] or were subsequently designated as 'royal forests' under Forest Law by the Norman kings, contained much of this kind of woodland. Indeed a hunting 'forest' had to contain wide areas of open space, to allow the royal sport to be a sufficiently attractive and energetic activity.[48]

Much of the broken form of scrubland (when not incorporated into some royal forest) came to be called 'waste'. It performed the valuable function of providing rough pasture for domestic livestock as well as for game. Even without evidence, one would expect there to be much of this kind of more open 'woodland' in any region where neither the tree population nor the human population covered the whole area. For many of the Middlesex manors it so happens that Domesday is particularly rich in its references to something called 'pasture for the village livestock'.[49] To the modern mind, the term 'pasture' suggests pleasant fields providing fresh grass for the stock. But in a less sophisticated form, pasturing can be quite different : it may include grazing on cultivated land after the end of a harvest, and it can also mean (and no doubt principally meant in 1086) grazing on unfenced land, among scrubby bushes and low trees, often common land or 'waste', where the livestock has to find its food, whether grass, weeds or leaves, wherever it can. This Domesday phrase clearly meant common rights of pasturing of this kind.

But there is one unusual feature about this Middlesex 'pasture'. If one plots its Domesday references on a map,[50] it emerges that there are two quite large blocks of land where no such pasture is recorded at all. One block almost exactly coincides with the Ermine Street area, just north of the City walls, where there was also no record of 'pigwood'. This means in effect that apparently not only the 'pigwood' but also that any more open form of woodland had been cleared, as one might expect on the outskirts of the City and also near to so important a road.

But the other main area where no 'pasture for the village livestock' is recorded is a block of ten estates in the centre of the county, of which both Hampstead and Hendon form

---

[45] For example, in Hampstead the 'East Park' area on the present 'East Heath' (towards its north-eastern boundary, see **Map E**: recently it has become more heavily wooded) was a sandy place where, it seems, birch woods grew for (unusually) centuries. In 1312 it was undoubtedly the 'Wytebirche' wood, which was named in the Hampstead survey made by the monks in that year, a name which it retained into the eighteenth century, see page 126; and it is a matter of conjecture as to how long it had already had the name Whitebirch before 1312. It is however possible that the name had survived after the original birches had long gone: in general the birch is not a long-surviving tree, see Rackham *History of the Countryside* 111-2, and is usually followed fairly quickly by the oak, as the Heath record elsewhere shows. Still for all we know, by reason of the favourable soils in that region the birches may have survived there for a long time before 1312.

[46] Again parts of Hampstead Heath at the present time have this kind of character. Other parts (eg. Sandy Heath) are now largely 'pigwood': unfortunately without the pigs.

[47] For example King Cnut's Laws (about 1023 AD): 'everyone is to avoid trespassing on my hunting whenever I wish it to be preserved'; but also,'every man is to be entitled to his hunting in wood and field on his own land': *EHD* 1/467. Cf. Hooke *Pre-Conquest Woodland* Ag.HR 37 (1989) 122-3.

[48] Hatfield Forest in Essex is perhaps the best surviving relic of the medieval hunting forest, with the open spaces which were so necessary.

[49] In two other counties both in the same Circuit as Middlesex this kind of pasture was recorded fairly consistently, namely in Cambridgeshire and Hertfordshire. Geographically they lie in a band, from the Thames northwards, virtually as far as the Wash. See Darby *Domesday England* 149-50.

[50] See **Map L**. Owing to the scale, only the second block of land can be plotted, with a green symbol.

a part, as shown in the following Table : -

Table 3 : Middlesex estates without 'pasture'

Manor	Holder	(Pigs)
Hampstead	Westminster Abbey	100
Hendon	Westminster Abbey	1000
Kingsbury (2)	A. de Hesdin; and Westminster Abbey	1200
Harlesden	Canons of St Pauls	100
Rugmere	1 Canon of St Pauls	-
Tottenhall	Canons of St Pauls	150
Twyfords (2)	2 (separate) Canons of St Pauls	150
Willesden	Canons of St Pauls	500

It can hardly be an error on the part of the scribe or the editor of the Domesday book material which accounts for this feature. All the manors in question lie together and form one block geographically, but there are three different Tenants in Chief concerned : the Abbey, the Canons, and Arnulf de Hesdin, one of the Conqueror's magnates. But the Domesday Survey was organised to show the complete, and often scattered, holdings (within a county) of each of William's Tenants-in-Chief in turn, rather than to follow a geographical course describing the county from one end to the other. It follows that the above manors appear in three quite different places in Domesday Book; but when assembled *geographically*, they form a block in the middle of the county. Like the Ermine Street manors, these estates too lie on or at least near one of the principal roads, Watling Street : but this could not account for the absence of pasture in all of them (eg. Twyford), still less in all parts of all of them. Together the ten manors account for 'pigwoods' sufficient to support over 3000 pigs, and it is strange that such estates should have (in total) a fair amount of 'pigwood' but no waste woodland or other pasture land. It is difficult to see what the explanation could be. A correlation with small estates of five hides or less has been suggested,[51] but Hendon, Kingsbury or Willesden were considerably larger.

The 'Forest of Middlesex'.

A later myth about the so-called 'Forest of Middlesex' has sometimes contributed to the impression that also in the Anglo-Saxon period the woods were even greater than they in fact were. The Middlesex woods have frequently been claimed [52] to have been designated a royal forest under the later Norman kings, and to have been 'disafforested' in the thirteenth century by Henry lll.[53] It seems clear however that no part of the main woodlands of Middlesex was ever subject to royal reserve and Forest Law.[54] Indeed it is doubtful

---

[51] Pinder *Mdx and London Domesday* (Alecto Ed.) 7

[52] Barratt *Annals of Hampstead* 1/24; Montague Sharpe *Forest of Middlesex* 95-6; Bazeley *Extent of English Forest* TRHS (4th) 4 (1921) 152.

[53] A limited royal 'warren' in an area in the southwest of the county, between Staines and Hounslow, was created in about 1160 by Henry II, but was disowned (ie. de-warrened), after some doubts, by his grandson Henry III in 1227: *Cal.Ch.Rolls* 1/56; *Rot. Litt. Cl.* ii/181b and 197b.   But this was in a place where in any case the woods were (or at least had been) much thinner or non-existent, see page 32: and rights of warren were restricted to certain animals or birds (eg. rabbits, hares, foxes, pheasants, partridges etc.) which were not 'beasts of the forest' and were usually limited to land which was outside a royal forest, Young *Royal Forests* 46, 97. In due course even the warren of Staines became promoted in popular talk to the 'Forest of Staines', see eg. Montague-Sharpe *ibid.* 98-99. This Staines warren seems to have been the source of the myth of the 'royal Forest of Middlesex', which Stow in his *Survey of London* later initiated.

[54] See *VCH Mdx* 2/224 .

whether they even achieved the grand and rather empty title of 'The Forest of Middlesex', until at a much later date the concept of a 'Forest' had become a remote and romantic one, instead of (as it would have in fact been under royal Forest Law) a very practical and sometimes brutal matter of fact. And little early evidence which can be relied on has emerged of other private hunting rights actually being practised, even by the citizens of London,[55] in the area west or north-west of the City of London during the Middle Ages.[56]

Woods and Roads

The woods were undoubtedly significant in relation to the safety and the maintenance of the roads. The surprise attack from the Tottenham woods in 1016 AD had demonstrated the vulnerability of lands adjoining such woods : no doubt the Kingsland estates just north of the City had since been fully cleared of all forms of trees in order to prevent the City itself being similarly vulnerable, and this was reflected in the Domesday record. The northern stretch of Watling Street, within Middlesex, must have been encompassed by the heavy pigwoods of Kingsbury, Hendon and the two Stanmores.[57] For its part, the more southerly stretch of Watling Street (bordering Hampstead, Willesden and Paddington) probably ran through a mixture of light and heavy woods, since the pigwood there at the time of Domesday was apparently less extensive than it was further north.

The steps necessary to keep the roads clear of the woods are shown by the improvements said to have been made to parts of Watling Street by Abbot Leofstan of the Abbey of St Albans in about 1050 during Edward the Confessor's reign. According to early records of that Abbey edited much later by Matthew Paris,[58] the Abbot caused the deep woods surrounding the road to be cut down, followed by other improvements, the building of bridges and the levelling of the roughnesses in the road itself.[59] This took

---

[55] See pages 21-2 above.

[56] Save possibly the indirect claim of unlawful hunting by unknown persons, when a prohibition was imposed just after the Conquest in relation to Harrow, see page 21-2. In about 1174 William Fitzstephen was boldly asserting, "many of the citizens take pleasure in sporting with birds of the air, with hawks, falcons and such like, and with hounds that hunt their prey in the woods. The citizens have the right of chase in Middlesex, Hertfordshire, all the Chiltern country and in Kent as far as the river Cray", but he does not say where or how far afield this took place. Many centuries later there was also a story of the Lord Mayor and Aldermen in 1562 (after the Dissolution and after Henry VIII was well out of the way) dining at the Mayor's Banqueting House built on about the site of Stratford Place on Oxford Street, having chased and killed a hare before dinner and then after dinner, hunting and eventually killing a fox at St Giles with great blowing of horns, Stow *Survey of London* (Strype Ed) 1/25. It is also clear that, in that period in the sixteenth century after Henry VIII was gone, the City did keep its own hounds and huntsmen, and that some hunting was done in St James Park and Marylebone Park, Masters *Chamber Accounts* 14, 46, 129; but this was both late and limited to the parks, so far as one can tell. As late as Charles I's reign, the (nominal) office of 'the keeping of our games of hares, partridges, pheasants, herons, red deer, fallow deer and all other wild fowls...' over 27 districts which included Paddington, Knightsbridge, Hampstead Heath, Hendon and Westminster was still being granted by the king, PRO. C 66/2891. M13. But such evidence is largely anecdotal, and is also post-Middle Ages.

[57] Edgware was not referred to by name in Domesday, and there are various theories as to the reason for its absence : see Baylis *Omission of Edgware* 17 TLMAS 62 and VCH *Mdx* 4/155. Probably parts of it were treated as belonging to Little Stanmore and Kingsbury. The Edgware area was probably untouched forest for the most part, see Baylis *ibid*. 66, and may have fed much of the large population of pigs which Kingsbury must have had. For Kingsbury woods, see Appendix 2, page 167-8 below.

[58] About 200 years after Abbot Leofstan's time Matthew, the monk-historian of the abbey of St Albans, wrote up certain earlier records of the Abbey: Vaughan *Matthew Paris* 182-3. It is difficult to believe that his story was all invention, but it gives some impression of embroidery and anachronism; and Matthew was inclined to gossip.

[59] Paris *Gesta Abbatum* 28 RS. 39-40. In Nottingham, anyone who later at the time of Domesday ploughed or made a ditch within two perches of the king's road to York had to pay a fine of £8, but it is

place "from the borders of Ciltria (i.e. the Chilterns area) almost as far as London". In fact the Abbot's jurisdiction would not have extended further south than the southern limits of Hertfordshire, or perhaps Stanmore,[60] and probably most of his clearance works took place further up the road, to the northwest of St Albans. It was in that area in Hertfordshire that he is also said to have granted an estate at Flamstead, which in fact lies exactly across the road, to three 'knights' (i.e. Anglo-Saxon thegns, or other 'men' of that Abbey), on condition that they kept the road free of wild beasts and robbers. We do not know what precise source Matthew was using for this story, but it gives us at least an impression of the problems which might be faced in travelling along Watling Street. Matthew also followed William FitzStephen in describing 'spreading woods, dense and abundant' around the road, in which all manner of wild beasts, robbers and fugitives lived.

****

Water : the ridge-streams   **Maps E, H, M and O**

For a village as much as for a city, water comes before everything.[61] So it is one of the nice accidents of nature that the Hampstead-Highgate ridge possessed the right combination of features to satisfy all or some of the water-wants of both village and city at the same time. In addition, and even more importantly, the three streams which flowed south from the ridge served, for most of the medieval period, as important boundaries [62] for parts of the rural estates of Hampstead, Paddington, Westbourne, Knightsbridge, Lileston, Tyburn, Westminster and its neighbour, Eia, not to mention the City of London itself.

While a hill may provide protection for the early settler, its height generally spells a lack of water. Fortunately on the Hampstead hill the soils are so arranged that water was (and still is) plentiful even near the very top; and when it was allowed to do so, it flowed visibly in abundance in every direction.[63] The water sinks through the sands and gravel until it reaches a clay layer below, and by that barrier is diverted sideways to emerge on the slopes of the hill wherever the junction of the two layers is exposed.[64] The combination of both height and water suggests that the ridge, and particularly the Hampstead end of it, must have been an obvious site for very early settlement by the Saxons.[65]

Looking upwards from the Thames, an observer in the Westminster area could see the visible effects of the waters flowing down from the hills. Two centuries after the foundation of the Abbey at Westminster, William FitzStephen, the enthusiastic admirer of

---

not clear if this was a local custom or a general ordinance, or even an old one: DB *Notts* f. 280a.

[60] It is clear that Stanmore had belonged to the Abbey of St Albans at an early date (mid-tenth century), see the charter evidence in Appendix 2 at page 167, and EPNS *Mdx* 219 ; VCH *Mdx* 5/9. But part of it was then lost to the Abbey before the Norman Conquest: it was then recovered by 1106, see VCH *ibid*. After further adventures it was back again in the fold by Matthew's time.

[61] cf. Parker *The Common Stream* 15-6. For this section, see **Map H**.

[62] Nearly all the 'lost rivers' flowing to or near London formed boundaries of estates in Anglo-Saxon times, and the line of some are still important boundaries, see Barton *Lost Rivers of London* 63.

[63] To this day the source streams under the built-up areas flow down ceaselessly, but now sheltered in deep culverts. At several public (and private) places their unending flow can still be witnessed with the aid of a torch or an acute ear. Some of the streams begin very near the top of the hill, suggesting that the sand layer is very shallow in some places, with the clay close underneath. If not, there is artesian action.

[64] For the position of the contour near which these exposures occur, see **Map E**.

[65] But there is no hard evidence of Saxon settlement before the tenth century, see page 100. The Saxons however certainly went over, or round, the ridge and settled on the lower hill at Hendon, see page 90.

London, could still write that the fields north of the City of London were threaded with flowing streams and (by then) whirring mills, 'with moreover excellent wells[66] in the suburbs with sweet, wholesome and clear water which flows rippling over the bright stones'.[67] While the detail may have been perhaps a little less dazzling, the general picture is probably substantially accurate, *for his day.* In pre-Conquest days, the scene of highly-ordered cultivation and industry which FitzStephen later evokes would probably have been premature, certainly for the area north and north-west of Westminster which was more remote from the City of London.[68] At or before the time of the Domesday Survey there is not even one record of any mill at work in the area north of the Abbey. But the lushness of the region watered by the streams descending from the ridge (a lushness which in part was still apparent as late as the nineteenth century), and perhaps the glint of the streams themselves between the trees, were visible to any monk who lifted up his eyes from the precinct of his Abbey in the Anglo-Saxon period.

The story of these streams took several significant turns during the later Middle Ages, and since these subsequent changes of fortune give one some idea of the size, sources and effects of the streams, and of the importance which they must have had in the earlier and more primitive period of Anglo-Saxon settlement of the Westminster area, the record of such later and therefore out-of-sequence changes is included here.

1. The Holebourne, or Fleet.   Maps E, H and M

One of the streams which descended from the ridge and became known, in its lower reaches, as the Holebourne [69] ('the stream in the hollow'), and also the Fleet,[70] rose from

---

[66] Eg. Clerkenwell, Bagnigge Wells, Faggeswell etc: Barton *Lost Rivers* 69.

[67] *EHD* 2/1025. For FitzStephen, see page 34.

[68] The nearest mill to the Abbey, as recorded in Domesday Book, is the mill (at that time only *water-mills* existed) said to have been in the manor of Barnsbury (Hugh de Berners' estate, part of the Bishop's Stepney estate), a large and valuable mill which brought in as much as 66/8d annually; see *D.B.Mdx 3/2* (f.127b). On geographical grounds it seems unlikely that such a watermill could have existed in Barnsbury. If this is right, it would mean that either the identification of Hugh's estate is wrong (contrary to the evidence, see VCH *Mdx* 8/51, 72-3), or that his estate had some distant outlier on the River Lea or even on the Thames itself. Of these possiblities, the latter would seem more likely: we know that Hugh was up to no good in at least one other Stepney manor, see DB *Mdx* 15/1 (f. 130b). According to the Domesday record there were six other mills east of Barnsbury, all of them in the Bishop of London's extensive lands in Stepney, which bordered on both the Thames and the Lea, some of them even larger than the so-called Barnsbury one: but of these, one had been built in the twenty years between the Conquest and the Domesday Survey. See VCH *Middlesex* 1/96 and McDonnell *Medieval London Suburbs 15.* Only fifteen of the 62 Middlesex settlements referred to in DB are recorded as having mills, see Darby (Ed) DB *Geog.of S.E.England* 129-31, in spite of the county's abundance of water. Hendon (in spite of the large Brent river) had no record of one. Kingsbury, alone of estates adjoining the Corridor, had one, presumably on the Silk Stream above its confluence with the Brent, see **Map N**. In Battersea, across the Thames, WA had seven massive mills of its own at Domesday, yielding over £42.

[69] The earliest authentic record of this name is in Domesday Book, see DB *Mdx* 1/3 (f.127a), but it was clearly older than that. See also Sawyer *A-S. Charters* No 1450, a late compilation (made at Westminster) of earlier charters, in which the word 'Holeburne' has been added, probably in the twelfth century, to the original form of the boundaries for Westminster which had been described in charter No 670, see page 79 below and Appendix 2, page 166. The 'hollow' was the valley which the river created, mainly in its lower reaches eg. where Farringdon Road and Street now are. The modern car drives along the river bed, past both Newgate and Ludgate, a historic 'underwater' route, creating yet another pollution for the old 'river'.

[70] The OE 'fleet' meant a creek or inlet, and when first used, the name Fleet appears to have been limited at first to the lowest reaches of the river, and much later became the name of the whole river. Both its two names seem to have been used at first for its lower waters. The Holebourne or Fleet may well have been nameless in its upper reaches for a long time, as one suspects the Westbourne was in its lower

two main sources: from the spring-fed marshes, which used to exist at the sites of the modern Vale of Health, the Viaduct Pond and the Hampstead Ponds on Hampstead Heath; and from the marshes which lay in the next valley to the east, below Highgate Hill, where the Highgate Ponds are now embanked. From there the stream flowed down past Kentish Town [71] to the outskirts of the City of London. In its lowest reach, stretching down the deep valley (the 'hollow') of the modern Farringdon Street, it became in due course the boundary between the City of London and the Westminster estate of the early Abbey; to end, as it had begun, surrounded by yet another marsh, called London Fen,[72], at its outflow to the Thames.

In these lower reaches which were tidal, the Fleet was wide enough for boats, and although later from at least the thirteenth century it was constantly being contaminated and indeed choked by sewage and industrial rubbish,[73] it carried much cargo traffic by boat from at least the eleventh century.[74] But having regard to its situation alone, it is impossible to believe that the river's mouth and lower reaches had not played a significant, if unrecorded, part in very early settlement and trading in the area, at least from the *Lundenwic* era in the eighth century.[75]

Before *Lundenwic* had been abandoned in the ninth century, the river had served also to separate the established City from its neighbouring commercial suburb. But in addition to its subsequent role as the boundary between London and the first estate of Westminster, the river had an ever-increasing importance as one of the principal sources of drinking and washing-water for the citizens of London. When it became polluted and inadequate in quantity, the citizens (particularly as their City grew in size, and demand for ever more water rose) were driven on a number of occasions, from the thirteenth century onwards, to look further west and north for different, cleaner sources of water, with consequent effect upon the other available waters both in and around Westminster and also much later in Hampstead itself. A centuries-long competition between London and Westminster began.

The spring waters still available in the Westminster area for the citizen of London were dependent on the two other Hampstead streams: the Tyburn and the Westbourne.

*

---

reaches, see page 43.

[71] Various explanations have been proposed for the name Kentish Town. A connection with the county Kent was put forward by Ekwall *Dict. of E.P. Names* 272, viz. the tun or settlement of the Kentishmen. A similar theory is that it means 'the settlement where the people (or family) *called* Kentish live'. Another theory is that it is possibly derived from an even earlier word for the river Fleet: this word, 'kent or cant' has even been said to have given its name perhaps to the county Kent, and also to Kenwood as one source of the river Fleet; see Draper *Kenwood and Kentish Town* LTR 22 (1965) 27-8. But the name 'Kent' has a very ancient origin, long pre-dating the Saxons, see Brooks 'Kingdom of Kent' in *A-S Kingdoms* (Ed. Bassett) 57. And 'Kenwood' is also said to be derived from the Norman French 'keynes en le bois' (oaks in the wood), see Lovell *Highgate* Survey of London 17/126. You can take your choice. For the Fleet's course through Kentish Town, see **Map H** and Waller *The Holebourne* TLMAS 4 (1874) 97.

[72] See the charter which described the boundaries of Westminster in the Anglo-Saxon period , page 79 below and Appendix 2; and Honeybourne *The Fleet* LTR 19 (1947) 14. The marsh at the entrance to the Thames was probably about 600 feet across and extended over the area south of St Bride's church.

[73] Much later, from at least 1307 AD, Commissions of Inquiry to investigate and resolve the obstructions and other nuisances in the river were frequently appointed,. The first such inquiry was ordered in that year by Edward 1 to be held by Sir Roger Brabazon, his Chief Justice, who had a house at Belsize in Hampstead, *Cal.P.R.* 1301-7 p. 548 ; and see Vol. 2.

[74] See Barton *Lost Rivers* 74-5 ; Honeybourne *The Fleet* ibid. 52; Flower (Ed) *Public Works* Selden Soc. 40 (1923) 32-6.

[75] See pages 20-1 and 55.

2. The Tyburn   Maps E, H and M

For its part, the Tyburn flowed down from a source at the later-named Shepherds' Well, in the fields which lay at the top of the present Fitzjohns Avenue, and from a second main source in the Belsize area.[76] It passed near the area which is now Swiss Cottage and then through the Regents Park locality, across the equally rural districts of the present Marylebone Road and Oxford Street, and finally through the woods and fields which lay in Mayfair and Green Park,[77] towards the site of Westminster Abbey. In doing so, after leaving the bounds of the Abbey's Hampstead estate (near the northern line of Regents Park), it formed the boundary between the two adjoining estates of Lileston (the Lisson Grove area) and Tyburn (now Marylebone and Regents Park), and further south still, the boundary between the next two adjoining estates of Westminster and Eia (part of Mayfair down to Pimlico).

In its closer approach to the Thames, the original Tyburn appears to have divided:[78] one arm flowing eastwards from near the present Buckingham Palace towards Westminster Abbey, the other continuing southwards somewhat disjointedly through marshy ground to join the Thames west of the present Vauxhall Bridge.[79] Near the Abbey, the first arm further sub-divided into other small streams, so as to form at least one large island out of the gravel platform on which the Abbey was to stand, and also to create, roundabout, a small estuary.

There seems little doubt that the Tyburn was a comparatively small stream when measured against the Fleet and the Westbourne. In spite of its nearness to the Abbey, to which it was closer than either of those two other rivers, there is no surviving record of the Tyburn having been used as a water source for the monks for drinking and washing purposes. It may perhaps have ended in such swamps and marshes as to be unsuitable for at least drinking purposes.[80] On the other hand there was such a virtually universal practice[81] of building monasteries on the edge of streams (for very obvious domestic and sanitary reasons) that it is impossible to believe that in at least the early days of the Abbey (in and after Edgar's reign in the tenth century) some use for these purposes was not made of the Tyburn, so close to which the new Abbey had been built. Certainly an arm of the Tyburn became used later for the purpose of driving the Abbey mill at the point where the stream entered the Thames. However by the time of Edward the Confessor's reign (1042-1066), shortly before the Norman Conquest, it seems that it was the Westbourne, not the Tyburn, which had become the source of domestic water for the monks: see below.

---

[76] By its very descent down a long slope it also must have picked up drainage water at all contours.

[77] The present very noticeable dip in Piccadilly and the Green Park still shows the course of the old stream, and the site of an old pool there.

[78] There have been considerable arguments as to whether the Tyburn did so divide, and if not, in which direction the stream reached the Thames. These are described (though not entirely accurately) in Barton *Lost Rivers* 31-6 and the sources cited by him. The geological and archaeological evidence seems to be conclusive that there was such a division, and that further subdivisions took place. See in particular the Geol. Survey Sheet NV SW (pub.1936); Barton *ibid.* 34; Honeybourne *The Fleet* LTR 19 (1947) 317; Mills *Excavations at Westminster* TLMAS 33 (1982) 350-2. It may be that there were early changes in the stream's bed, just as there were later ones when the higher waters were diverted, as described in the text.

[79] See discussion in Barton *ibid.* 33-4.

[80] As suggested by Barton *ibid.* 36.

[81] This can be observed at almost every surviving site of a monastery, whatever the state of the buildings. The practice is well illustrated in some of the names which have been given to monasteries, eg. in France, by the names Fontevrault, Fontgombault, Fontenay and Fontfroide; or Fountains and Brinkburn, in England.

The name 'Tyburn' took the Anglo-Saxon form 'Teoburne' in the first record made of it in a charter, by which King Edgar granted the rural land of Westminster to the new Abbey. Probably this meant 'boundary stream'. [82] The southern part of the stream which did mark the boundary between Westminster and Eia began to lose its old name in later centuries and became known sometimes as the Aye Brook.[83] Upstream the Tyburn, in about the fifteenth century, was sometimes called the Maribone, after the name of Maryburne which the manor of Tyburn acquired much later when a new church dedicated to St Mary the Virgin was built there in about 1400.

Even if the monks and other residents of Westminster tended later to overlook their own stream for their domestic purposes, the City had no such qualms in later centuries. At the point where Stratford Place stands, on the north side of Oxford Street, and near where the Tyburn used to cross the 'broad military road' [84] (Oxford Street) which led out of London, the gravels on either side of the stream contained ample water. It was therefore an area for many springs and wells, one of the western equivalents of the wells-area north of the City of London which William FitzStephen described in about 1174. By 1236 the main sources of the water supply for London (the Thames, the Fleet and the Walbrook) had become so polluted or inadequate that the citizens had sought other places from which to draw water for the City. In 1237, with the help of King Henry III, the City Mayor Henry Waleys obtained from the holder of the manor of Tyburn, Gilbert de Sanford,[85] the grant of a right to bring the waters from those wells in 'the town of Teyborne' in his manor, by a conduit and system of pipes leading to the City.[86] A Conduit House was built ('the Great Conduit') on the north side of Oxford Street, and an elaborate pipe system was constructed, leading down to the present Charing Cross via the St James area and then along the Strand to the Fleet and so to Cheapside.[87]

The result was that the Tyburn from that time onwards seems to have been greatly diminished in its lower reaches, as the waters in the surrounding gravels near the present Oxford Street were diverted for City use. Ultimately after a further diversion of other waters in the same neighbourhood in 1354, again for the domestic benefit of the citizens of London, the lower Tyburn - at least in its arm which flowed towards the Abbey - became even further reduced.[88] Even so, it was not the last London raid on the waters in the west.

*

3. The Westbourne   Maps E, H and M

Rising from a cluster of springs on the western side of the Hampstead Hill - at Frognal, and the present Branch Hill and Telegraph Hill (the summit of 'Childs Hill'[89]) - various tributaries of a river flowed down through the areas of West End and West Hampstead, to meet and form one united stream at Watling Street. It was first of all known as the

---

[82] Ekwall *English River Names* 424. Gelling *PNs in the Landscape* 18. For the dispute as to the reliability of place-names, see Gelling 'Towards a Chronology' in *A-S Settlements* (Ed. Hooke) 59.

[83] Rutton *Manor of Eia* Archaeologia 62 (1910) 41, 48. And there is an Aybrook Street still in Marylebone.

[84] See page 79 and **Map M.**

[85] Gilbert at that time held the manor from the Abbey of Barking. He was the Chamberlain to Eleanor of Provence, Henry III's Queen. For more about him, see Vol 2.   The name was also spelt 'Sandford'.

[86] Sharpe *Cal.Letter Book A.* p.14; Morley Davies *First Conduit* TLMAS 8 (1913) 36.

[87] Dickinson *Water Supply* 8-9; Morley Davies *ibid.* 43-50. See a later conduit in **Plate 17**, page 148.

[88] See Barton *Lost Rivers* 34-5. On the other hand it is noticeable that on the Elizabethan maps many watercourses are shown still in the Westminster and St James's area.

[89] See page 93.

'Kilbourne',[90] and gave its name to that area. It then crossed Watling Street and passed through the districts of Paddington and Westbourne into the present park district of Kensington Gardens and Hyde Park. The modern Serpentine Lake is the former marsh area made by the stream, which then crossed into the present Belgravia, to flow down a line just east of Sloane Street and Sloane Square, and so to reach the Thames in the gardens of the Chelsea Hospital.[91]

The name 'Westbourne' or 'Westburne' is a recent one for the river itself. The latter form of the name, 'Westburne', was first used from a comparatively early date (at least the thirteenth century) for the *district* which lay on to the west of the river. It meant probably no more than 'west of the river'. Although the first surviving record of the use of this name for the district west of the river goes back only to the thirteenth century, its Old English form suggests that its origin is much older than that. But the river had certainly been known as the 'Kilbourne' in its higher reaches (east of Watling Street), and in its lower reaches seems to have lacked any specific or abiding name, until in the seventeenth century it became named the 'Bayswater' rivulet and, later in the nineteenth century, then became known as the Westbourne.[92]

Like the Tyburn, the Westbourne river in its passage to the Thames performed also the function of being the boundary between various estates through which it flowed. One of its sources, the one which rose on the south-east slope of Telegraph Hill, acted for part of its length as the old Anglo-Saxon boundary between Hampstead and the area probably then called Codanhlaw, at that time part of Hendon.[93] After crossing Watling Street the river divided Paddington from the Westbourne area; and south of the old westbound Roman road (Bayswater Road) it became the boundary between the estate of Eia on one side and Knightsbridge and Chelsea (and perhaps another part of the Westbourne estate) on the other.

For reasons given earlier, it is more than likely that in the earliest days of the Abbey, after its foundation, the water-supply for the monks was taken from its adjoining river, the Tyburn. But it seems clear that, within a comparatively short space of time, it was the Westbourne which was harnessed to provide water. Probably this change took place during the reign of Edward the Confessor, shortly before the Norman Conquest, and was part of the works of restoration and improvement of the Abbey which that King undertook.[94] Much later, in 1285, a lease granted by the Abbey of land in the area of or near the present Hyde Park, refers to the existence of an 'underground aqueduct' [95] (i.e. a piping system, probably built of hollowed-out elm trunks,[96] pottery or lead) which carried the water from the Hyde area down to the Abbey; but one cannot say what the method of

---

[90]Meaning perhaps 'royal stream' or "cows' stream"; more likely the latter: EPNS *Mdx* 112-3; Mills *English PNs* 195. Or 'Cylla's stream'? Gelling in *PNs in the Landscape* thinks it all 'uncertain'.

[91] See **Maps H and M**. The stream passes through Sloane Street Station on the London Underground, in a large overhead 'box' (for illustration, see Barton *ibid.*, Plate 26).

[92] Gelling *PNs in the Landscape* 18; EPNS *Mdx* 8; Barton *ibid.* 37; Prideaux *N & Q* (9th) Vol. 8/517 and 10/16.

[93] See pages 92-6.

[94] This is based on general probabilities, not on specific evidence. Ormsby *London on the Thames* 88 asserts it as a fact: although that book is an interesting but rarely quoted authority, no evidence for the assertion is given.

[95] WAM 4875. The land so let was in 'Cressewellfeld', and it may be right to think that the name indicates that watercress grew in or around the river or the no-doubt wet areas where the surrounding springs lay. The exact location of the field within the Hyde Park or perhaps Paddington areas is not as-yet known. See also the much later map *Principle Head of W.Abby Main* (sic), BL. K. Top. xxi. 1-3.

[96] See Rackham *History of the Countryside* 237.

bringing this water supply to the Abbey might have been in Edward the Confessor's time. Whenever the monks subsequently granted any rights over land in the vicinity of Hyde Park, they took particular care to preserve for themselves both the sources there of the water on which they depended and their legal right to carry out repairs and cleansing operations on their 'aqueduct' and its supporting equipment (such as conduit heads and cisterns).[97]

To deal with the water when it arrived in the Abbey itself, no doubt an internal system of cisterns and piping had to be built from the earliest times, to feed all the essential buildings. There are no very early documents at Westminster which record the system: but for Christ Church, the Cathedral at Canterbury (then a monastery), there have survived two unique and detailed engineering plans from the twelfth century,[98] each showing the elaborate waterworks system of that monastery, which brought the water from a water 'tower' in the fields, through the vineyard and the apple-orchard of the monastery (with settling tanks and standpipes at appropriate intervals), under the city wall and the monastery wall, to feed the bathhouse, the dormitory, the infirmary, the bakery, the brewhouse, the cloister, the privy, the herb-garden, the kitchen, the refectory, a large cistern in the 'new hall' and the fish-pond of the monastery. At Westminster the water system certainly grew to be an impressive one, with piped water to all the main offices; but this evidence all relates to a much later period.[99] There had been at least two cisterns there for filtering purposes in the fourteenth century,[100] and probably these were themselves ancient or had replaced earlier cisterns, with some form of hydraulic system to feed them.

However the needs of the Abbey were not the only call to be made upon the Westbourne river. The main demands of the City for further water, which we have already seen in relation to the Tyburn, seem to have arisen regularly about every hundred years. By 1439, the need for even more water had grown so much that the citizens had to seek further supplies, this time from even further afield. In Paddington, adjoining the Westbourne at a point near the modern Paddington Station there was another area in which (as at the crossing of the Tyburn over the military road, the present Oxford Street) the river gravels contained water which fed many springs and wells.[101] In that year, 1439, at the request of the City Mayor, Robert Large, the Abbot and Convent of Westminster gave the citizens the right to erect a fountain-head in that area and to pipe the water to the City, for an annual fee of two pounds of pepper. It was however essential that the Abbey's source of water from their wells (also adjoining the Westbourne) in the 'Manor of Hyde'[102] should not be interfered with, and accordingly the Abbot's grant provided that the City's pipe should not pass through that manor, and that 'if the intended work should draw the water from the ancient wells in the manor of Hida, then the grant should cease and become

---

[97] See eg. the lease to the City of London in 1439, referred to in the text below. When the monastery was dissolved, it was necessary to preserve the (by then Protestant) Abbey's water rights; and again after the area of Hyde (part of the old manor of Eia) had been absorbed into Henry VIII's greater hunting Park, see WAM 18265 and Ormsby *London on the Thames* 88 (but see Barton *Lost Rivers* 31). In 1650, a survey of 'three conduit heads' in Hyde Park was carried out, see WAM 25200.

[98] The plans were drawn up as early as 1165 AD by the engineers who designed and built the system, see Willis *The Conventual Buildings Of Christ Church, Canterbury* Arch. Cantiana 7, pages 3ff and 158ff, and copy plans and Appendix 1, page 174. The original plans are bound into the Great Psalter at Trinity College, Cambridge, replacing certain missing pages, a device adopted surely to ensure that these unique documents were not lost. Aston *Monasteries* 20 is illuminating about monastic water-needs and supply.

[99] See Harvey *Living and Dying* 78.

[100] See eg. Micklethwaite *A filtering cistern at WA* Archaeologia 53 (1892) 161.

[101] The present names Brook Street and Conduit Place still record the water sources in this area.

[102] The present Hyde Park area, which had become a sub-manor of the old and larger manor of Eia, see page 84.

entirely void'. The pipeline was completed after a delay of 32 years, and it supplied water to a 'faire water conduite' in Fleet Street, and from there to the present Ludgate Circus where it crossed the stinking river Fleet by the Fleet Bridge, and so on to Cheapside.[103]

The City's next major demand on the Hampstead streams takes us even further forward, beyond even the end of the Middle Ages. But there is a certain irony in the fact that this time it had the effect of draining much of the flow of the City's own river, the Fleet itself. Because the City's water supplies were by 1543 'sore decayed, diminished and abated, and dayly be lyke to [dis]appeire and fayle ', the new City Corporation obtained an Act of Parliament [104] to allow the conveyance of water to the City from 'dyvers great and plentyfull sprynges' at Hampstead Heath, Marylebone, Hackney, Muswell Hill and other places within five miles of the City.[105] But it was not until 1589-90 that the Act was put into part-execution so far as Hampstead was concerned, by the embankment of two reservoirs of water near the modern South End Green (known earlier as 'the Pond Street area') and the building of two main water pipes each with a bore of seven inches, to carry water from Hampstead down to St Giles, the area just west of the capital.[106] And so the Fleet suffered the same fate as the Tyburn had done 300 years before: one of its main water supplies was cut off and its flow reduced. Its pollution later became even worse, as other Hampstead ponds and the Highgate ponds were created. Finally it only remained for the great Victorian High, Middle and Low-level Sewers to carry off most of the remaining volume of the old rural streams; and the progressive canalisation below ground of their residue was completed.

The binding threads of water
So from the earliest times, and indeed until after the end of the Middle Ages, Westminster and the Hampstead/Highgate ridge were bound closely together by the threads of these three streams. When estates were first carved out by the Anglo-Saxon kings in the hinterland on the north side of the Thames, almost invariably it was the streams, on their way down to the big river, which were used as the main physical features to define the boundaries of those holdings. And when in the tenth century the new Abbey came to be founded in Westminster, the long-lasting competition, between the City and its hinterland, for the life-giving waters of the streams had only just begun.

---

[103] Morley Davies *ibid* 25-7; Dickinson *ibid.* 11; Stow *Survey of London* (1633) 278 and 431.

[104] The London Conduit Act, 35 Henry VIII c. 10, after a bad drought in 1539 and a plague in 1543.

[105] See Park *Topography of Hampstead* 71-4. At that date the inhabitants of Hampstead had 'springes at the foote of the hyll of the heath...nowe closed in with bricke', which were at least one of their sources of water and the Corporation were forbidden to meddle with them. For the whole topic of water for Hampstead itself, see Potter *Hampstead Wells* 6-22 and *Random Recollections* 20-2.

[106] Maitland *London* 2/1267

CHAPTER 3

The Shire and its Hundreds
The administrative setting

In **Map B** we have already seen the early concentration of Church estates around the London and Westminster area, even before the Abbey at Westminster came to be founded. But, in turn, around the church and its estates lay the world of secular government, both national and local. The framework of this secular power from the tenth century onwards was twofold: the power of the King and his officers on the national level, and the power of the local communities, working through the 'shires' and the smaller districts (the 'hundreds') into which the shires were divided. In our case, it was the Shire of Middlesex, and (principally) the Hundreds of Ossulston and Gore.

The Shire   **Maps C and I**

During the early Anglo-Saxon centuries the region of Middlesex, into which the monastery at Westminster was later to be introduced, had progressively become a more recognisable unit. Since before 700 AD the names of 'Middlesex' and the 'Middle-Saxons' had been in recognised use, as the charters show; but there is no evidence that the area round London, which was eventually to become the 'Shire' of Middlesex, was regarded as a single administrative district, when it was subject to the kingdoms of either Essex or Mercia. But after about 910, with the Wessex kings at last in the ascendant, the position was to change. By then King Alfred's son, Edward, was carrying on the work which his father had already begun,[1] in again driving the Danish threat northwards away from the Midlands and the Thames valley, and eventually within fifteen years bringing some degree of unity to all England south of the Humber. The results for the area round London were both military and administrative.

After taking back into his own control both London and Oxford 'and all the lands which belonged thereto',[2] King Edward then successively recaptured from the Danes a group of key towns in a wide arc north and north-west of the capital. Where their walls needed rebuilding, these towns were refortified as defensible 'burhs' or boroughs. Together with other towns, the 'burhs' of Colchester, Hertford, Buckingham, Bedford, Cambridge and Huntingdon now formed a protective barrier for the south, including London.[3] At about the same time it is probable that a network of 'shires' was introduced into these districts, each shire centred on one of the new 'burhs'.[4] This network was an

---

[1] See page 23.

[2] *A-S Chronicle* 911-2. This must, at the least, have included the region of Middlesex, and have extended further afield as well, to include presumably the area between London and Oxford, ie. at least, all the lower Thames valley.

[3] For the above towns, see respectively *A-S Chronicle* 920, 912-3, 917, 918, 920, 920. A similar reconquest was achieved further to the west and north-west by Edward's sister Aethelflaed, and other protective burhs were established there.

[4] Loyn *Governance* 135-6 ; Sayles *Medieval Foundations* 180-1. New shires also in the Midlands and in the West also formed part of the same chain of administration.

import from Wessex, which was now the driving-force in the emerging English state.[5]

London was itself a 'burh' for the area round it. It became *Lundenburh';* and the name *'Lundenwic'* which had included the Aldwych suburb disappeared. Middlesex became a 'shire', centred on London, in probably the first part of the tenth century, at the same time as other new shires in the Home Counties and the Midlands. Three of the Middlesex boundaries were now rivers: the Thames, the Lea and the Colne. But in the creation of this more formal territory, it is likely that some of the land to the north which until that time had loosely been regarded as Middle-Saxon territory was lost and became incorporated in another newly reorganised shire, Hertfordshire.[6]

Certainly in the *second* half of that century (shortly before the foundation of Westminster Abbey), when young King Edgar soon after his accession issued two sets of Laws in the period 959-963, the pattern of most of the shires and their 'shire-courts' seemed already to have become established. Both the 'shire' and the 'shire-court' (together with the 'borough' and the 'borough-court') were referred to in Edgar's Laws in such a way that there is no doubt that each was an institution with which everyone in at least the English half of the country would already be familiar:[7] eg."And the borough-court is to be held thrice a year, and the shire-court twice". In fact a 'shire' as a unit of local administration had already appeared in even earlier legislation, when Edgar's uncle, King Athelstan, at some date about 935 had promoted a peace-keeping Ordinance [8] setting up a self-help 'peace-guild' among the people of both London and surrounding areas, designed for dealing (among other things) with cattle-thieves who were chased out of one 'shire' (probably a smaller unit, at that time) into another.

The main administrative purposes for which this shire organisation had been created were threefold : financial, military and judicial, i.e. to facilitate both the collection of taxes and the mustering of armed forces, and to provide a forum, through the shire-court, for the resolution of significant local disputes.

The shire-court was a popular assembly, at which all freemen as 'suitors' to the court were entitled and, in early days, were bound both to attend and, presided over at first by the 'Ealdorman' of the shire and the Bishop, to give their opinion on all administrative, judicial or ecclesiastical issues which were brought before them. It little resembled a modern 'court'; but it did deliver 'judgments', given by various forms of 'signals' of assent or dissent, on one side or the other of any question which was raised. It was in effect a folk-meeting or moot, held together by its 'presidents'.[9] In each shire the King's

---

[5] For example, from well before 850 the peoples of the areas now known as Wiltshire, Dorset and Somerset had been recognised as separate territorial groups, each centred on a royal estate which gave its name to the area; and each under its own Ealdorman and therefore with its own 'scir' (shire), meaning the Ealdorman's 'share' of territory or lordship: *A-S Chronicle* 802, 840, 845, 851 at *EHD* 1/ 183-8; Stenton *A-S England* 336-7. In fact the concept of a 'scir' in Wessex went back more than a hundred years even before that, see *Laws of (King) Ine* (688-694 AD) EHD 1/ 403.

[6] See Taylor *Endow. of See of London* A-N Studies 14 (1991) 301 and **Map C (1)**.

[7] *Laws of Edgar (III and IV)*, EHD 1/ 433 and 435.

[8] *Ordinance of the Bishops and Reeves of London* para 8.4., *EHD* 1/423. Although the Ordinance has that title, it was an instrument which (a) the King had clearly promoted and had agreed to enforce with his own declared sanction, and (b) it extended to an area much wider than just London, probably to the whole area of the Diocese of London and also of Surrey and Kent. See also Athelstan's *Laws at Grately EHD* 1/419. For the extent of the Diocese, see **Map C (1)**. For the extent of the Shire, see **Map I**.

[9] In one case in or just after Edgar's reign those who were summoned to act as the judges and give their judgment were called the 'better and wiser people' of the relevant village: *Liber Eliensis* (Ed. Blake) Camden (3rd) 92 (1962) xv and 89.

special interests (such as his taxes and his estates) were looked after by his own reeve, the 'Shire-Reeve', who carried out within that shire any orders from the King communicated to him by brief 'writs' or by other means. In due course the 'Shire-Reeve' became known as the 'Sheriff', and as the King's representative, came to be the chief executive and presiding officer in each shire, taking over many of the former functions of the Ealdorman.

It seems therefore that when Westminster Abbey was founded, Middlesex was already an established Shire, with no doubt its own shire-court. The place where the Middlesex court met at that time is not known for certain : the nearest that we can get to it is in about 1296 (that is, 300 and more years later) when the court, by then usually known as the Court of the County, possessed of a more professional procedure, was sitting in a circuit of three different places: at Brentford; at the crossroads where the Marble Arch now stands, near the 'Speakers' Corner'; and in the 'Strand' road leading from London towards Charing and Westminster.[10]

Of these three places Brentford, lying in a central position along the twisting coils of the Middlesex bank of the Thames, had also been an ancient meeting place for a number of different purposes in earlier Anglo-Saxon times, dating back to at least 705.[11] For its part, the site near the Speakers' Corner had also had a very old history, starting from at least Roman times, since it lay at the crossroads made by the north-bound leg of Watling Street and the other, westbound, Roman road (now Oxford Street and Bayswater).[12] At the Marble Arch a Roman 'geometric stone' apparently still stood as recently as 1870, now sadly lost.[13] Such a place, where there was a crossroads or some traditional feature, eg. a well-known tree, stone or barrow, was often the chosen site for open-air public meetings in both Anglo-Saxon and later medieval times. For example in Middlesex itself two of the other 'Hundreds' (Elthorne and Spelthorne) had names which indicate that the meeting place of each of them was at or near a well-known (haw)thorn tree.[14] With this sort of history for the Marble Arch area, is it mere coincidence that the Speakers' Corner is still the site for open-air gatherings? For the choice of this place for the original shire-moot, it may also be significant that the estate of Eia, at the corner of which the place lay, remained

---

[10] Palmer *The County Courts of Medieval England* 9.

[11] Birch *Cart. Sax.* 115 (a political meeting to try to settle disputes between the East Saxons and the West Saxons); Chaplais 'The letter from Bishop Wealdhere of London' in *Medieval Scribes* (Ed. Parkes and Watson) 3 or in his own *Essays* XIV.   Brentford had also had a Roman past, being the site of both the famous ford over the Thames which the army of Julius Caesar may have used in 55 BC, and a Romano-British settlement, before it was abandoned in the fifth century, see Vince *Saxon London* 131. It had later become a central site for religious synods and national councils in Saxon times.

[12] This place was also the meeting place of the Hundred of Ossulton, which is dealt with below in the text. For the view that Watling Street in Roman times had continued south from the present Marble Arch to Westminster, see page 81-2.

[13] See Black *The Roman Sepulchre at WA* TLMAS 4 (1874) 63 and his petition No 6870 (H.C.Committee on Public Petitions, Report 1869) to the House of Commons to preserve such 'ancient monuments'; a petition which seems to have sunk without result. That stone (described as 'uninscribed') must have survived for up to 1800 years; and perhaps still exists somewhere unrecognised? When last seen in 1869/70, it was actually leaning against the Marble Arch, having been dug up, see VCH *Mdx* 6/1. Rocque's larger-scale map (of London, 1746, not the 'Environs',1745) records a 'Mile Stone' at the site of Marble Arch; and some distance away (beneath the so-called 'Tyburn' gallows) it says 'Where soldiers are shot' . That map's record is not 'Stone where soldiers are shot', as is sometimes alleged: that version would wrongly suggest that the stone was in some way particularly significant to the shooting of (presumably) deserters. The true inference from the map is that soldiers were shot, not hung.

[14] EPNS *Mdx* 31 and 11; Anderson *English Hundred-Names* 55-6.

under *royal* family control as late as the Conquest.[15]

The Strand meeting place for the later Middlesex court had probably had no long history from Anglo-Saxon times. It may have dated only from some point of time after the Norman King William Rufus is said (by what is clearly a later, and inaccurate, tradition [16]) to have erected a Stone Cross in the road near the site of the present church of St Mary le Strand. The 'Stone Cross', or later the Bishop of Coventry's house nearby, thereafter became a recognised site for meetings, including the Middlesex courts of the royal justices sitting 'in eyre' in and after the twelfth and thirteenth century. In view of its later provenance, it seems unlikely that the Cross was the site where the shire-court sat in any period before the Conquest. So we are left with Brentford or Marble Arch as the probable site of the early court : or more probably the court was held on a circuit (but only between those two places), as the same court did between the three sites in succeeding centuries.

The Hundreds   **Maps I, J and M**

More important for most local inhabitants than the shire and its court were the territorial 'hundreds', into which a shire was divided, each with its own court which, like the shire-court, was a folk-court. From shortly before the time when Westminster Abbey was founded, Middlesex was divided into hundreds: perhaps six hundreds as shown in **Map I**, or maybe four, see below. Assuming that there were six, we can see that both Westminster itself and all the rest of the Corridor estates, except Hendon, fell within the Hundred of Ossulston; while Hendon alone lay in Gore Hundred. These six hundreds (if there were in fact six from the outset) survived in very much the same form for many centuries, except that Hounslow as a Hundred was renamed Isleworth not long after the Norman Conquest, and after about another hundred years lost the manor of Hampton, when Hampton was absorbed into the adjoining Hundred of Spelthorne.

The name 'Hundred' does not appear in any surviving record until it emerges in the tenth century, again shortly before Edgar came to the throne in 959. But the idea of a smaller district, carved out of the larger shire, had apparently had some forerunners, in the form of loose territorial units, which had been used in earlier periods both for tax assessments and for other purposes, such as the provision of justice.[17] Yet again it was King Edgar who, as with the shire-court, provided a more detailed method of working for the hundred-court, which had already come into existence shortly before his time.[18] In the

---

[15] See page 84 and **Map I**. Did a royal reeve preside from an early date?

[16] *Cal. Inquist. Misc. (Ch)* ii/26 (1311 AD). '...erected by King William Rufus in devotion to the Holy Cross and for the health of the souls of himself and his mother Queen Matilda whose body rested there while being carried to Westminster for burial...'. However in fact his mother's body was not buried at Westminster, but at Caen in Normandy, and could not have rested in the Strand on such a journey (I owe this point to Dr Emma Mason). So either the reason given for the journey is wrong; or perhaps it was Henry 1 (whose wife, also a Queen Matilda, *was* buried at Westminster in 1118) who erected the Stone Cross. Later, there was a small bridge in the Strand ('Strand Bridge') over a stream which flowed down Catherine Street on its way to the Thames: the Stone Cross stood just to the west of the bridge. By 1600 it had lost its top, and a maypole took its place. See further Somerville *The Savoy* 154, 223 and 229.

[17] Loyn *Governance* 140-2. The 'hundreds' also served, it seems, as units of military organisation, Loyn 'Hundreds in the tenth and eleventh centuries' in *British Government and Administration* (Eds. Hearder and Loyn) 1-15.

[18] *III Edmund* 2 ; *The Hundred Ordinance* EHD 1/429, by which a close predecessor of Edgar (or possibly Edgar himself) had laid down the basic operation of the hundred and its court against cattle-thieving. There is something of a 'wild-west' atmosphere about England at this time, with its distinct emphasis in both shire and hundred courts on cattle thieving, which necessitated pursuits ranging over different

same set of Laws [19] in which he decreed (or repeated earlier decrees?) that 'the hundred court is to be attended as it was previously established' (ie. once every four weeks[20]), one finds his detailed instructions about legal principles and procedures in all the existing local courts : these included the important and overriding principle, "It is my will that every man, whether poor or rich, is to be entitled to the benefit of the common law, and just judgments are to be judged for him". All this was clearly directed to each of the local courts, because the King added significantly, "And no one is to apply to the King in any suit, unless he may not be entitled to right or cannot obtain justice at home".

But why was the name 'Hundred' used for these territorial divisions of the shire ? Since the summary answer to this is that in *theory* the Hundred was at first composed of a hundred 'hides', it is necessary to pause and consider briefly what a 'hide' was.

The word is simple, but it is one weighed down by its own long history. As an Anglo-Saxon land-measurement, which was later retained by the Normans, the 'hide' was used unfortunately for at least two quite different purposes, often confused and always confusing. Firstly it was a measurement of the tax-liability at which a tract of land came to be assessed by the Anglo-Saxon kings. Secondly in some contexts it was intended, or at least was regarded, as a measurement of area; and the 'virgate', which meant a quarter of a hide, was similarly used. Much ink and spleen has flowed in the historical debate as to which meaning the 'hide' carried in the various contexts in which the word appeared; particularly in the later Domesday Survey. Indeed as long ago as the last century the 'hide' was already labelled a "dreary old question" by one famous historian, while for another it had become "somewhat tiresome".

So let us side-step that debate, and reach out for some conclusions, in the form of working-guidelines which will be useful in the search for some of the Middlesex lands. Firstly, the number of hides ascribed to any 'shire', 'hundred' or whole estate almost invariably reflected the amount of the tax-liability of that particular tract of land (a liability which sometimes seems also to have denoted its value, at roughly the rate of £1 per hide). It did not directly reflect the physical size of the tract (even if size was one of the factors). One can see this illustrated in the respective sizes of many estates in Middlesex. For example Hampstead (a central estate) and Harefield (a peripheral and highly-wooded estate in the north-west) can be compared not only visually (on **Map J**), but also numerically: Their physical sizes can be shown to have been about 1900 and 4600 acres (one much more than double the other), but each was assessed at the same figure of 5 hides.[21]

On the other hand, the descriptions in Domesday Book of the smaller holdings of the villagers within the various estates in Middlesex look much more like measurements of

---

'shires' and thereby giving rise to the need for cooperation and the avoidance of disputes about authority and jurisdiction in the different areas.

[19] Edgar's *Code at Andover* EHD 1/ 433. Further instructions were given in his later *Code* (perhaps drafted by Dunstan, the founder of Westminster Abbey) at EHD 1/434-7: the effect of all these seems to be even more extensive than the dictates of *The Hundred Ordinance* ibid.

[20] See *The Hundred Ordinance,* ibid. In important cases the courts of neighbouring hundreds might meet together, see *Liber Eliensis* (Ed. Blake) Camden (3rd) 92 (1962) 90.

[21] See Bailey *Hidation of Middlesex* TLMAS 39 (1988) 172. On Hampstead's size, see page 125. Harefield also had more land actually available for cultivation, and more equipment (ploughs), than Hampstead. Like any tax-liabilities, these land-assessments were not fixed for all time, although there was somewhat more constancy about them than we are now accustomed to. Many factors may have influenced such assessments: size itself was one, but fertility or poverty of soil, resources, woodland, value, and royal favour or disfavour may all have played their part in differing contexts.

actual areas of land.[22] Middlesex was almost unique both in that respect, and also in the large amount of *detail* given about its villagers' holdings by the Domesday Survey. The equations used for this purpose appear to have been that a 'hide', when used as a physical measurement (in Middlesex, but not everywhere) was 120 acres, and a virgate, 30 acres.

There is little doubt that in those parts north of the Thames where the new shires were being shaped in the tenth century by Alfred's son, the *theory* was that each hundred in a shire was to be of such a character as to merit an assessment at a round figure of one hundred 'hides',[23] being a proportion of its shire's total assessment for tax expressed as a multiple of a 100 hides.[24] This system of shires and hundreds was imported into the midland areas as an off-shoot of a much more ancient (and by that time, distorted) pattern of territorial units which had prevailed in Wessex in the south and south-west of the country. But by Domesday, a hundred and fifty years later, only relics of a 'hundred hide' pattern were still visible in most of the counties, and the assessments for the hundreds were little related to the figure '100'. Middlesex may have retained some small vestiges of it.

The hides assessed at Domesday for the six Hundreds are (totalled and rounded off) : -

Hundred	Hides
Ossulston	220
Elthorne	225
Spelthorne	110
Hounslow	105
Gore	150
Edmonton	70
	880

It is clear that any precise 'hundred' figures have by this time disappeared, but it can be seen that if one adds each of the second and third couples shown above (Spelthorne with

---

[22] The correlations (and inconsistencies) between the tax-assessments of the Middlesex estates and these (factual?) details of the tenants' holdings within those estates are dealt with in Maitland *DB and Beyond* 477; Vinogradoff *English Society* 167-76 and App. IV. 490; VCH *Mdx* 1/85-90 and 130; Campbell 'Middlesex' in *DB Geography of S.E.England* (Ed. Darby)107-8; Bailey *Hidation of Mdx* TLMAS 39 (1988) 165; and see the statistical evidence in Abels *Bookland and Fyrd-Service* A-N Studies 7 (1985) 15-7 and 21; McDonald and Snooks *Were Assessments of DB England artificial?* Ec.HR 38 (1985) 352 and iidem, *Domesday Economy* 72-4 (but none of this last evidence relates to Middlesex). One returns in full circle, as usual, to Maitland's appropriately tentative conclusion: "it seems possible that in these Middlesex 'particulars' [of the tenants' holdings] we do at last touch real agrarian arrangements", *ibid.* 478, ie. figures of estimated area and value, see Lennard *Rural England* 341.

[23] More rarely there were 'double-hundreds' of 200 hides (see next page); or 'half-hundreds' of 50 hides (eg. Edmonton: it was so styled, though with a different name. It may have once made a full 'hundred' with the adjoining half-hundred of Waltham in Essex, just over the River Lea).

[24] See eg. Maitland *DB and Beyond* 455-60 and the round figures of the later *County Hidage* (an assessment list of the eleventh century, but before the Conquest), tabled by Maitland. For example, Bedfordshire and Worcestershire each had twelve 'hundreds' in the DB Survey, and had each been assessed in the *County Hidage* at 1200 hides for the whole county. But it is unfortunate that the *County Hidage* is itself irregular in its patterns, and relates to only thirteen counties, of which only one (Wiltshire) came from the old Wessex heartland: if there had been more Wessex counties, we might have been able to extract more information about the old Wessex territorial units, in the same way as Maitland did for the other counties in the *County Hidage*. As it is, Wiltshire by itself gives at least some appearance of an existing 'hundred' system, even if not consistently: but it is only one sample. One or two clues from the *Burghal Hidage* (a list made not later than the early years of the tenth century) also support the theory that some shires were assessed on a round multiple of a hundred hides, and that each 'hundred' represented a hundred hides. For a detailed analysis of the Mdx 'hidation', see Bailey *Hidation of Mdx* TLMAS 39 (1988) 165 ff; and for Cambs, see Hart *Hidation of Cambridgeshire* 32.

Hounslow; and, separately, Gore with Edmonton), there is still some symmetry about the figures, perhaps reflecting an original total of 800.[25] One possibility is that there may once have been four *double* 'hundreds', each with a total of 200 hides, and that later two of those larger hundreds may have been split unevenly. Another rearrangement of them shows that they can be divided into two groups, east and west, each with 440 hides: Ossulston, Gore and Edmonton forming an eastern bloc, and Elthorne, Spelthorne and Hounslow a western one.

Another interesting and more visible feature of the Domesday assessments in Middlesex is that there are many estates (each with at least one settlement as a focal point; or more) assessed in round figures in *five* or a multiple of *five* hides.[26] Many more than half of the Middlesex places which were actually named in the Survey were assessed in this way: no other shire relatively had so many. It is certain that this five-hide method of assessment for the purpose of taxation was much older than Domesday Book: it probably dated back at least to the time when the shires and hundreds were being formed in the early tenth century, and it may reflect the way in which earlier and larger estates were broken up and smaller units were distributed as rewards to loyal followers. Moreover the system may be linked with the obligation which existed before the Conquest that each five-hide area was to supply one, and only one, soldier (accompanied by food and resources) for the army, when required; an obligation which by a lucky chance happens to have been recorded in one place in Domesday Book.[27] The five-hide form created a strong pattern in the western and north-western neighbourhood of London, and it extended strongly to most of the Corridor estates of Westminster Abbey, see **Map J**.

The two Hundreds with which we are most concerned are Ossulston and Gore. The name Ossulston meant Oswulf's (or Oswald's) Stone;[28] but we do not know who he was, save that he clearly was an Anglo-Saxon. His stone may well have been the much older Roman geometric stone, already referred to, which stood at the present site of the Marble Arch until the nineteenth century. At least there is now little doubt that, just as the shire-

---

[25] See VCH *Mdx* 1/ 83-4; Baring *Hidation of Southern Counties* EHR 14 (1899) 290; Corbett *The Tribal Hidage* TRHS NS 14 (1900) 218; Davies *DB Hidation of Mdx* Home Counties Mag. 3 (1901) 232. For other possibilities, see Bailey *ibid*.180-2. One intriguing suggestion is that Mdx might have had 1200 hides, if parts had not been hived off to help form Herts or Bucks, see page 47 above.

[26] Round *Feudal England* 66-7. See **Map J**. In some cases the five-hide assessment for a village is concealed by the Survey's method of recording manors in groups, listing the group *held by each landholder in* turn (i.e. all his manors in different parts of the shire), and *not* following a geographical course within the shire. In such cases, in order to discover the total assessment of a *village* and its 'area' (the basis of early parishes?), one has to find the various manors which make up the village (when held by more than one landholders) and add up their separate assessments. For example Westminster Abbey were entitled to an estate of two and a half hides in Kingsbury (fronting Watling Street), while a baron, Arnulf of Hesdin, held seven and a half hides also in Kingsbury (DB *Mdx* 4/11 and 10/2; ff 128d and 130a). St Andrew's was the single (and possibly ancient, see page 66-7) church for the one settlement there at that time, which apparently extended over both estates and had been assessed at ten hides. There are other more complicated examples, see eg. Ickenham on **Map J**.

[27] DB *Berks* f.56b. Another significance of a five-hide holding under the Anglo-Saxons is that apparently a 'ceorl' (see page 114; hence 'churl', even if a ceorl was 'free') who acquired five hides was entitled to the rights of a thegn, Liebermann *Gesetze* 1/456-8; *EHD* 1/468. This is often stated without qualification, but it is clear from that source that another of the essential requirements was that he had to have 'a seat and a special office in the King's hall' as well. So not any jumped-up ceorl could qualify, even if he did obtain the necessary five hides. See also a requirement of holding a private church, Godfrey *The Church in A-S England* 320; and *Wulfstan's Wergelds* EHD 1/468. For a full discussion of the Mdx 'five- hide' estates, see Bailey *Hidation of Mdx* TLMAS 39 (1988) 168-76.

[28] EPNS *Mdx* 81 (Oswulf); VCH (RB.Pugh) *Mdx* 6/1 (Oswald). For its position, see **Map I**.

court perhaps did during the Anglo-Saxon period, so also the hundred-court met in the open at that same site, where the two great roads provided reasonable access for suitors who may have been living a considerable distance away within the extensive boundaries of Ossulston Hundred. It was a point about as near the centre of the Hundred as the awkward shape and geography of the Hundred allowed. At some later stage the site for the hundred meeting seems to have been moved about half a mile down the road which is now known to us as Park Lane, to its junction with South Street. There, in a field shown in a Grosvenor Estate map of 1614, an oval circle within an enclosure which was probably an open-air site still for meetings is shown, with the name 'Osolston' against it.[29] It is possible that this move took place because (at some stage unknown to us, but before 1341) a settlement arose at the Marble Arch site [30] and it was more convenient to hold the meetings away from that settlement. Or again, it may be that a move became necessary in order to avoid clashes between dates for the meetings of the two courts. There are a number of surviving records of the court's meetings at Ossulston, which continued in that area until after 1750, well after the end of the Middle Ages.

As in Ossulston, so in Gore the meeting place of the Hundred (ie. its court) was at a meeting of roads;[31] and in this case near the dead-centre of the Hundred. The site was at the junction of Honeypot Lane (formerly 'Wicstrete', see **Map N**) and the Kingsbury-Harrow road, near Oxendon Hill, and its raised area of about two and a half acres was still visible as recently as 1948. Nearby stood 'Gore Farm' which was demolished as recently as 1937.[32] At that point, the meeting place was nearly central to the four constituent churches of the Hundred, at Harrow, Hendon, Kingsbury and Stanmore.

Within the Hundreds   **Maps I, M, N and P**

As can be seen from **Map I** and the Table on page 51, the hundreds of Middlesex varied greatly at the time of Domesday in their size; but they also varied in the numbers of the estates within them. One can contrast Gore with its six estates against Ossulston with at least 26: a contrast which might reflect the fragmenting influence of a nearby large city on the pattern of royal grants.[33] There were even sharper contrasts elsewhere in the county, such as Hounslow with but two estates, against Spelthorne (rated nearly the same) with at least 14, where that influence can have played less of a part. But it is now well-recognised that, as one would indeed expect, a process of the 're-forming' of estates, by amalgamation

---

[29] Gatty *Mary Davies and Ebury Manor* 1/ 56-7. In the eighteenth century that area was still being called in legal deeds 'a common or waste...called Ossulton Common', Sheppard (ed) *Grosvenor Estate,* Survey of London 39/ 2. The name Ossulston was spelt variously at different times. For the new site's position, see **Map M**. Thorn, 'Hundreds and Wapentakes' in *Mdx and London Domesday* 39 says that the Hundred moot was "probably in Westminster" at DB, but gives no reason. Neither of these sites was a Westminster estate, and I see no reason why a Westminster site should have been chosen for Ossulton.

[30] VCH *Mdx* 6/1; WAM 4875, 4834, 4786 and 17164.

[31] Braun *Hundred of Gore* TLMAS 13 (1937) 218-28; Davenport *Two Mdx. Hundred Moots* TLMAS 16 (1948-51) 145-9; VCH *Mdx* 4/ 149-51. For its position, see **Map I**. Even as late as 1445 there was a *Motehegg,* 'the moot-hedge', nearby. A 'gore' was a wedge-shaped piece of land. It is to be noticed that five out of the six hundreds in Mdx (ie. all except Edmonton) had names derived from their meeting-places, not from any estate contained in them, as was frequent elsewhere. This may have been due to frequent re-forming of estates within the shire and therefore their more transitory significance.

[32] VCH *Mdx* 1/83.

[33] But Bailey *Hidation of Mdx* TLMAS 39 (1988) 177-8 also shows clearly how most larger Mdx estates were granted to churches before 850; and the smaller estates to laymen after 900, often as rewards.

or break-up, took place quite frequently during the Anglo-Saxon centuries;[34] and perhaps Domesday Book's contrasts would not have been so evident at much earlier times.

For example, as shown below, there were in Hendon four separate estates at earlier points of time, instead of the one large manor recorded at the time of Domesday.[35] The beginning of a process of amalgamation into one unit is clearly evident as the monks of Westminster were successively granted these four estates; and the completion of the process probably took place well before the Conquest. Conversely it may be that the anomalous inclusion of the areas of Finchley and Hornsey within the Bishop of London's distant estates of, respectively, Fulham and Stepney[36] may be explicable on the grounds that Finchley and Hornsey were perhaps lone components left over from the break-up of unknown larger estates at some much earlier time.

The amalgamation in Anglo-Saxon times of those estates which eventually formed the Norman manor of Hendon serves to conceal the fact that within the resulting manor there were clearly more settlements than one. There can be little doubt that each of the four component estates must have contained at least one settlement of its own : in Lotheresleage, perhaps at the Hale (an OE. name) or at Mill Hill; in the 'smaller Hendon',[37] on the central hill where the present church of St Mary stands (and the earlier church must have stood), a place which became the primary centre of the subsequent unitary estate; in Bleccanham, probably on the smaller hill known now as Temple Fortune';[38] and in Codanhlaw, probably round the green in Fortune Green.[39] Even as early as Anglo-Saxon times there may have been others (such as the 'old tunstall or `farmstead' site [40] on Watling Street in Lotheresleage?), as there were later.

Hampstead on the other hand, so far as our evidence goes, begins and ends as a single estate; but this does not rule out the possibilities that at some period earlier than the tenth century it may have formed part of a larger estate, later to be divided-up by the process of royal grants;[41] or that in at least the tenth and eleventh centuries it contained one or more settlements in addition to its main one on the hill-top, as it did in later medieval times: at West End, Kilburn (that part of Kilburn which lay east of Watling Street), the Pond Street area and North End, each of which was a well-watered site and suitable for settlement. If, as roughly estimated below,[42] it is right that there may have been as many as 75 people living in Hampstead in the period before the Conquest, it seems highly unlikely that in such

---

[34] See eg. Hooke 'Early med. Estate and Settlement Patterns' in *Rural Settlements* (Ed. Aston, Austin and Dyer) 14; and Blair *Early Med. Surrey*.

[35] See Chapter 7 below, at page 87 ff.

[36] See page 18 above. Equally the Herts/Mdx shire-reorganisation in the early tenth century (or any later one) would have led to a reforming of estates around the boundary: cf. Doree *DB and Edmonton* 25-30. And similarly Staines seems to have had an important minster church at an early time, owning much land, which later became broken up into smaller units, as shown by DB: Bailey *ibid* 173.

[37] See pages 90-1.

[38] See pages 29 and 94.

[39] See page 96 and **Map P.**

[40] See **Map N** and the bounds in Sawyer *A-S Charters* No 1451, translated in Appendix 2, page 168.

[41] See Bailey 'The Middle Saxons' in *A-S Kingdoms* (Ed. Basset) 122. One can contrast the large size of some very early grants to religious persons (Harrow, Hayes, Fulham, Stepney, see pages 17-8) with the comparative smallness of almost all later grants (including those to WA), which suggests considerable fragmentation; and see also **Map B.** For the Hundred of Edmonton, it is argued that the large (by the standards of DB Mdx) estates of Enfield and Edmonton were themselves 'fragments' of even larger earlier estates overlapping into 'Essex' and 'Herts' (Doree *DB and Edmonton* 13-4, 29; cf 18).

[42] See pages 121-2 below.

an area there would have been merely one 'nucleated' village containing them all. The hill-slopes, variety of soils and the woods suggest small outlying knots of occupation, and even a few isolated small-holdings, as well of course as a core-group near the hill-top.

In the rural district of Westminster (which was to extend as far as the Fleet river), the presence of a new Abbey, after its foundation in the tenth century, created the right incentives for the development of a village of servants and suppliers around the Abbey to support the monks.[43] But there were several other places within the area where earlier settlements are known to have previously arisen.

As we have seen, a large commercial settlement had existed much earlier in the region of the Strand, the area called *Lundenwic*.[44] While those who had traded there had retreated within the walls of London when the Danes threatened in the ninth century, it is likely that scattered pockets of population had remained in the neighbourhood of the Strand. Thus it is noticeable that by about 1005 the area of Charing was already known by the separate name of *Cyrringe* in one of the Westminster charters,[45] which suggests that at that time it may still have been an inhabited junction of the west-bound Roman road and the approach road to the new Abbey at Westminster. A second early settlement must also have been established well before 970 round the 'old church' of St Andrew,[46] which stood in Holborn on the Westminster side of the river Fleet just opposite one of the gates (Newgate) of London. It seems improbable that this was merely part of the *Lundenwic* trading area: it may have been a waterside community served by the Fleet. Thirdly the excavations of St Bride's church near Fleet Street have also shown that there were underlying burials there, pre-dating the eleventh-century church, so it seems that there must already have been a separate settlement there, possibly at one time a component of *Lundenwic*. but a survivor after its demise.[47] Fourthly the dedications of St Dunstan's in the West and St Clement Danes, both churches close to one another in the Strand, each suggest that they were neighbourhoods which were settled in or shortly after the tenth century.[48]

So it would be wrong to think that only one settlement was to be found in each estate, even as early as Anglo-Saxon times. The scarcity of evidence relating to the pre-Conquest period unquestionably prevents us seeing the full picture, but there is no doubt that many communities were spread here and there in each of these estates near London.

---

[43] See pages 139-41 below. If there had been an earlier church at Westminster (as questioned above on page 24), the formation of such a community would have taken place considerably earlier than the tenth century, but no doubt on a smaller scale.

[44] See page 20-1 above.

[45] Meaning a 'turning' (in the road), see page 82-3, below and Appendix 2, page 167.

[46] See page 80 and Appendix 2, page 166. See also Barron *Parish of St Andrew, Holborn* 8.

[47] Vince *Saxon London* 63.

[48] No other firm evidence of these foundations has been found, see Cowie, 'Gazetteer of Middle Saxon Sites' *TLMAS* 39 (1988) 39. St Clement's church 'of the Danes' has some interesting legends attached to it, but in the absence of real evidence they may be no more than later rationalisations of an older name.

CHAPTER 4

Westminster Abbey : Foundation and Forgery

The new Abbey   **Maps B, D and M**

Material prosperity and power are hardly fit measures for evaluating the true worth of a monastery. But the fact remains that more than four centuries before its eventual dissolution in 1540, the Abbey of St Peter at Westminster had already become one of the most powerful and indeed 'fashionable' in England. Moreover it ended its days as the second richest religious house in England, second only to Glastonbury Abbey.[1] Unlike other, smaller, houses it owned estates which at the Dissolution were spread over at least nineteen counties, ranging from North Lincolnshire to Sussex and from Essex to Worcestershire.[2] Even at Domesday it had held land in fifteeen counties.

The 'Rule' of St Benedict - the code of observance laid down by Benedict, the Abbot of Monte Cassino for his monks in the sixth century - had forbidden them the personal ownership of any property; even indeed the ownership of their bodies.[3] But it did not prohibit *corporate* property, that is the ownership of material assets by the community in which the monk lived.[4] Those who later committed their lives to St Benedict's 'Rule' and lived in an 'enclosed' community had to depend, for their own sustenance and the support of their church, on food and money derived by their community from land and alms. So it is that the possession of land figures powerfully in the histories of such houses. Indeed if it were not for the charters and other records relating to their estates, the histories of the monastic churches themselves and their personnel would be significantly the poorer.

In about 1050 AD, nearly 500 years before its dissolution, the condition of "the church dedicated to St Peter, lying beyond the walls of London, above the river Thames" had been in marked contrast with its later affluence. The Abbey could be described (by two nearly contemporary chroniclers) as having been a "monasteriolum", a *little* monastery; "insignificant in buildings and numbers", with only a small community of twelve monks, whose endowments were "slender" and "provided no more than their daily bread".[5] By

---

[1] Harvey *Estates of WA* 26 . Even at the much earlier date of the Norman Conquest, its estates were more widely spread (in fifteen counties) than those of any other monastery, see Knowles *Monastic Order* 102; Ayton and Davis *Ecc.Wealth* SCH 24 (1987) 58-9.

[2] Harvey *ibid*. Map 2, at page 472.

[3] *The Rule*, Ch. 33. For the text in Latin and early English, see Logeman *Rule of St Benet (Benedict)* E.E.Text Soc. Vol 90 p.63-4. "Monks are not allowed to have even their own bodies or their own wills at their own disposal..."; Dom Bolton (trans)*The Rule* 41-2.

[4] No major restriction on *communal* ownership was imposed on monks for about five centuries, until *corporate poverty* became a tenet of the reforming disciplines, such as the Cistercian order of monks in the twelfth century and later the Friars.

[5] Barlow *Vita Edw.Regis* 67; Wm. of Malmesbury *De Gestis Pontificum* 52 RS 178. The *Vita*, which contains most of this description, was written only about twenty years after the time when the Abbey was said to have been so insignificant, and it can probably be relied on for accuracy. But one cannot rule out entirely the possibility that since Edward the Confessor had proposed to rebuild the church in a new and magnificent style (see page 68 below), his biographer may have chosen to play down the character

that time it had been in existence for less than 80 years. Its "slender endowments" of land in 1050 were no more, or at least little more, than those which it had been given in the period just after it was founded. So the Abbey's condition at the time of its foundation must also have been fairly fragile. But in the early stages of those 80 years of existence it had also passed through fraught periods of yet more Danish wars spreading over the London and Midlesex area, and yet, as far as we know, it had survived with its endowments intact.

So the Abbey's first period of existence had, it seems, been frugal and replete with danger. Its foundation as a monastery at the start of that period can probably be dated to the period 970 - 975,[6] nearly a century before the Norman Conquest, during the latter part of the reign of King Edgar. And it is from about that time that we first learn authentically of some of the lands in Middlesex with which it was endowed.

The founder of the new monastery was Dunstan, Edgar's Archbishop of Canterbury, who as the King's close confidante and counsellor was able to secure lands from him for the purpose: see **Plate 2**, page 64, for a drawing of him. The age was a strongly reformist one. More than four centuries had passed since St Benedict had first formulated his 'Rule', and in that period both on the continent and particularly in England the early vigorous monastic life had since subsided into decline and then virtual extinction, due in great part to the Danish and Norse attacks since the ninth century.[7] In those attacks, both on our coasts and inland, many of the old religious houses, such as Lindisfarne, Peterborough, Abingdon and Evesham,[8] had been totally destroyed or had had to be abandoned.

On the Continent, in the early part of the tenth century, revival and restoration had begun in earnest. In England also the first ripples of reviving interest began to be seen,[9]

---

and style of the Abbey's previous establishment in order to underline the new magnificence. For his part, William of Malmesbury's reference to the early Westminster Abbey was written about 75 years after the Confessor had begun his rebuilding. Other monasteries also (eg. Worcester and Evesham) had only small numbers of monks at the same time, see Knowles *Monastic Order* 425, and Farmer 'Progress of the monastic revival' in *Tenth Century Studies* (Ed. Parsons) 16.

[6] The exact date, within the wider bracket of the whole of Edgar's reign (959-975), has been much debated. But the programme of monastic foundations in the 'Mercian' part of the kingdom as well as in Wessex, initiated by Edgar in 970 at a great Easter meeting, referred to below in the main text, has been persuasively described (see Banton *Monastic Reform and Unification* SCH.18 (1982) 74 ff), and this fits well (as Banton suggests) with the creation of a small new monastery at Westminster, and also with the date of 971 suggested long ago by Napier and Stevenson *Crawford Charters* 90, 97 for the foundation of the Abbey. See also page 79 ff, where the relevant charters are dealt with. It seems also that the years 959-964, within which the foundation of the Abbey is usually ascribed, were years in which Edgar was slow to adopt a reforming mantle, Stafford *Unification and Conquest* 52. The other dates which have been proposed are 958-9 (Brooke and Keir *London* 296); 959 (Harvey *WA Estates* 23); and 960 or after (Rosser *Westminster* 13). See also Harmer *AS Writs* 287; Widmore *Enquiry* 8-9; VCH *London* 1/433; Robinson *Flete* 12-13; Wm of Malmesbury *Gest. Pont.* 178; Whitelock *Hist., Law and Lit.*II/22; Brooks 'Career of Dunstan', in *St Dunstan* (Ramsay et al.) 22. Nothing in this grand array seems convincing as to the probabilities. For a possible even-earlier history for Westminster, see pages 24 and 59-60.

[7] Asser *Life of Alfred* EHD 1/273 ; Fleming *Monastic lands* EHR 100 (1985) 248; Knowles *Monastic Order* App.1, p.695. John *Orbis Britanniae* 154-5 disputes the part played by the Vikings in the decline.

[8] The list is a long one. Those nearest to Middlesex were Barking, a house of nuns east of London, where the nuns were said to have been burnt by the Danes in their priory in about 870: for the part of their later successors in this story, see pages 73-4 and 142 below; and Chertsey, in Surrey, just across the Thames opposite the south-west corner of Middlesex: for their sites, see **Map B**.

[9] Before the time of the Danish onslaughts in the ninth century, Abbots had been sufficiently respected and involved in the exercise of power to have been regular attenders and advisers at royal courts and witnesses to their kings' charters. This practice had then lapsed, but in the tenth century the Abbots reappear as witnesses in many of the royal charters, see Banton *ibid.* 72-3.

but it was in the second part of that century that monks began to wield great influence again. A triumvirate of English Bishops, Dunstan, Ethelwold and Oswald,[10] instigated (with the King's help) an organised resurgence of monasticism, so 'changing the face of English ecclesiastical geography'.[11]

The culmination of this revival appears to have been a great meeting at Easter 970, when the King in the presence of his Bishops and Abbots is said to have ordered the foundation of forty new monasteries.[12] At about the same time, with guidance from the restored monasteries on the continent, a fresh English code of observance for monks,[13] based on St Benedict's 'Rule' and called the *Regularis Concordia,* was drawn up. In some of the surviving churches, such as Evesham, Malmesbury and the Old Minster, Winchester, which had previously been served by chapters of priests and canons, Benedictine monks had already been or were now introduced in their place. Other new monasteries were established in new places. Some of the former derelict houses (such as Abingdon and Ely) had already been refounded, and now a further group were to be restored. More lands, drawn in part from those estates which had reverted to the ownership of past kings when older monasteries had been destroyed by the Danes, were found for the support of both the new and the restored houses.[14]

That was the context in which the foundation of a new monastery at Westminster took place. Significantly the biographers of Dunstan [15] do not even mention the foundation as one of the achievements of the Archbishop. Probably that was a reflection of the Abbey's small scale and of its relative unimportance at that time, in the context of the great restorations and other new foundations then taking place. Or perhaps it merely underlines the limitations of early biography.

The site chosen by the Archbishop for the small monastery was an 'island', later called Thorneia or Thorney Island, which he bought from the King together with the surrounding land in rural Westminster. The island was an oval tract of gravel, little more than 450 yards[16] in length, set in a profusion of silt on the edge of the wide and ever-shifting Thames. No doubt the island was covered with thorny thickets, like many of the present

---

[10] All three were *monks* as well as bishops, and each of them was canonised after his death. 'Cathedral monasteries', where it was monks who performed the offices in the cathedral and a 'monk-bishop' who took the place of an Abbot, were virtually unique to England, see Knowles *Monastic Order* 619. If Dunstan (a puzzling, eccentric man) is to be seen as the leader of the revival (Dales 'Spirit of the Reg. Concordia.' in *St. D., his Life, Times and Cult* Eds. Ramsay, Sparks and Tatton-Brown 49), it was Ethelwold who became the dynamo which supplied the energy and drive behind the *Concordia.*

[11] Loyn 'Progress in A-S monetary history' in *A-S Monetary History* (Ed. Blackburn) 6.

[12] See Banton *ibid.*74. The last five years of Edgar's reign were marked by a spectacular sense of pageantry. The Easter meeting of 970 must itself have been a dramatic occasion. Then in 973, when he reached the age of 30, the King underwent a solemn and ceremonial coronation at Bath, 14 years after his accession. And shortly afterwards he made a triumphal voyage round the coast of Wales to Chester, where he received the submission of eight Celtic kings from various kingdoms in the north and west: Hill *A-S Atlas* p.61-2; Stenton *A-S England* 368-70. For Ethelwold's own view of a pliant Edgar, see *EHD* 1/921.

[13] Symons (Ed) *The Regularis Concordia.* For the effect of some relevant parts of the Concordia, see pages 158-9 and 161 below. The Rule of St Benedict was itself translated from the Latin into OE. by Bishop Ethelwold, commissioned by King Edgar and his Queen; Wulfstan *Life of St Ethelwold* (Eds. Lapidge and Winterbottom) p. liv. The name meant "The Accord as to the 'Rule' ".

[14] See Gransden *Abbey of Bury St Edmunds* EHR 100 (1985) 1; Fleming *Monastic Lands* EHR 100 (1985) 245: (but the geography suggested in the latter for Harrow in Middlesex at p.261 is curiously misplaced).

[15] Stubbs (Ed) *Memorials of St Dunstan* 63 RS. For Dunstan's appearance, see **Plate 2**, page 64.

[16] Bardwell *Westminster Improvements* (1839). For the site, see **Maps D** and **M.**

'eyots' or 'aits' still left higher up the Thames.[17] Into the Thames near this place the small tributary, the river Tyburn, flowed in an estuary, at the end of its passage through the woods and countryside from its sources on the Hampstead hill.

Surrounded by marshes, the gravelly Thorney Island was liable to regular, not to say irregular, flooding. Throughout the whole medieval period (and indeed far beyond it, into quite recent times[18]) floodings of the Thames round or near the Abbey have been recorded. Over the course of time, river-walls had to be built to protect the Abbey,[19] and the recurring duty to carry out the repair of the walls (the *reparatio wallorum*) became reserved to the Abbot himself as a special and expensive duty. The word-ending '*-eia*' is still preserved close by, in other erstwhile 'islands', at Battersea and Bermondsey, and also in the island-words already mentioned, 'eyots' and 'aits'. But more particularly it was also used for the estate of Eia, immediately adjoining Westminster to the south, part of which was known in later centuries as Eye or Ebury.[20]

In a seemingly early, but probably spurious, Anglo-Saxon charter,[21] which purports to relate to an even more remote period, the site of the Abbey was, for the first of several times, called a '*terribilis locus*', a place to strike 'terror' into you. This is now regarded as a description of its numinous or awe-inspiring quality, arising from its religious connections and some of the foundation-myths which became attached to the Abbey. But that early setting, the bleakness of the surrounding marshes, the site's vulnerability to the uncontrollable river movements,[22] and its obvious defencelessness against Danish attacks on London and Middlesex make it easy to regard the description as a realistic one as well.

While it is certain that the monastery - as a monastery - was founded in King Edgar's reign, there were later strong traditions at Westminster, and indeed some evidence,[23] that a church had previously existed on Thorney Island for very many years, at least until its possible destruction at the hands of the Danes. The details of these engaging traditions do not matter here, but like many of the traditions of Westminster they were perpetuated later in writing, to their own cost, by dubious charters and unevidenced histories.[24] The trail of

---

[17] Barton *Lost rivers of London* 32

[18] Eg. in 1928, see Barton *ibid.*

[19] Just as they had to be built to prevent flooding of the similar alluvial plain in Stepney which lay east of the City of London, on its opposite flank, see McDonnell *Medieval London Suburbs* 64-7. For its part, the City itself had a wall (in various states of condition) on the river side since Roman times, but this was for military defence, not against the river.

[20] Some of the residents in Eia received the locative name 'de Insula' (as residents in the Isle of Wight also did). For Eia generally, see page 84. But -eia is apparently not responsible for the ending of 'Chelsea', the OE name for which, Cealchithe, indicates that there was a landing place for boats there: other nearby 'hithes' are also to be seen in the names Lambeth and Putney, (Gelling *PNs in the Landscape* 76-7) reflecting the vital importance of the river for local traffic in this area. For the Abbots' country house in Eia in and after the thirteenth century, see page 26 above.

[21] Sawyer *A-S Charters* No 124 ; Harmer *A-S Writs* 501 ; see also WAM II and III.

[22] See page 26.

[23] See page 24 above. The original traditions are to be found in the Abbey's history written by Sulcard, a monk who was the first historian of the Abbey, writing shortly after the Conquest in the period 1076-1081 (see Scholz *Sulcard* Traditio 20 (1964) 59 ff and Goscelin *Life of Bishop Mellitus*, written before 1099 AD). See also Mason *The Site of King-Making* SCH (Subsidia) 9 (1991) 63-5 and Radford *WA before Edward the Confessor* 1-4. Mellitus, the first authentic Bishop of London in c. 604 (see page 17), was due, so the story goes, to reconsecrate an earlier church at the Westminster site, only to be forestalled by St Peter himself who, unasked, had already done the job.

[24] Miss Harvey in her major book *Estates of WA* 18 has elegantly called them 'the exotic tradition of historiography at Westminster'. Although we need not be concerned at this point with any details of

reliable written evidence is now so obscured that it is probably impossible to follow it, except with an overdeveloped enthusiasm for legend. At all events neither the legend nor the evidence cast light upon the later Abbey.

The foundation of any new monastery involved at least four stages for its founders:[25] the formation of a new community of monks; the building of a church; the dedication of the church; and the endowment of the monks with lands for their support. We do not surely know where the monks for the new establishment at Westminster were drawn from, but it seems likely that they were from Glastonbury or from Canterbury, with which Dunstan had the closest connection. The Abbey church was certainly built (or rebuilt, if we believe the traditions of an even earlier Westminster), and presumably it was dedicated by Dunstan. So finally we are left with the question of the endowments granted to the new Abbey : and with endowments, we move into the world of charters and other early documents relating to land, a world in which one can sense now long-forgotten struggles and discern dimly the motives of those who chose to bend the truth in order to protect or benefit their church and themselves.

The Lure of Forgery

Since the word 'spurious' has already occurred at least twice and must re-occur throughout any telling of the early history of Westminster Abbey and its original estates, one should perhaps pause to consider the nature of monastic forgery. This takes us into some rather later history, but the excuse for this must be that anyone who approaches the early history of the Abbey has to be forewarned of the implications of this delicate but intriguing subject.

From an early time the Abbey became (and for historical purposes, remains) famous, and indeed notorious, for its extensive fabrication of documents of title. Such fabrication took place in cases both where no title had ever existed and, more commonly, where a good title could no longer be proved by other means. The Abbey was far from being alone in this practice, but it excelled all others, at least in England, and in this capacity has even been described as a "factory" and "the forger's headquarters".[26] A Westminster forgery which, as far as we know, was the first to have been *recognised* as such, by being already labelled a "*falsum breve*" (a false writ), received that dubious salute as early as Domesday Book itself in 1086;[27] but there may well have been others recognised by contemporary people before that.

The Westminster forgeries seem to have been made in possibly two waves : some of them in the period before or around 1071 when Edwin, the last Anglo-Saxon Abbot of the

---

these forged charters from Westminster, they emerge as relevant factors in connection with Hendon, see Chapter 7 starting at page 87.

[25] Gransden *Abbey of Bury St Edmunds* EHR 100 (1985) 1.

[26] See Brooke and Keir *London* 295 and Heslop 'Twelfth Century Forgeries' in *St D., Life Times and Cult* (Ed Ramsay) 309. More generally, see Brooke *Approaches to Med. Forgery* J.S. Archiv. 3 (1968) 377, and the further discussion in Chaplais *Essays in Medieval Diplomacy* XV/1-3

[27] 'This land [Fanton Hall] was claimed for the King's use, because it had come to the Church [WA] by a false writ', *DB2 Essex* 6/4 (f.14a); Harmer *A-S Writs* 105. It is fair to record that the later Westminster forgers took their cue and some of their methods from other even earlier forgers on the Continent, eg. those at the great Abbey of St Denis outside Paris (which as a 'royal' Abbey also played the same role for the French King as Westminster Abbey did later for Edward the Confessor, see Mason *Site of King-Making* ibid 58 and 67-8, and page 68 below). The Westminster monks used the French charters for copying purposes; see Scholz *Two forged charters from WA* EHR 76 (1961) 466-78. Such forgery had had an even greater and earlier precedent in the forgeries which during early centuries had been made of new and unauthorised 'Canons' of church law and papal decrees, and had reached a climax on the continent in the ninth century, see *The Canon Law of the Church of England* SPCK 13-4.

Abbey who had survived the Norman Conquest, died, to be followed by Norman Abbots; and the second and most important wave in the next century between about 1130 and 1160 AD. During the first of these periods, the monks may have remodelled in lengthy Latin some of their more pithy Anglo-Saxon documents, so that they might seem more intelligible, reliable and weighty to the Normans.[28]

During the second period, for many of the forgeries there was a single perpetrator, namely one of the Priors of the Abbey, Osbert de Clare, whose obsessive purposes in creating them must have overridden any scruples which he may have felt. One of Osbert's main objects was to procure, by fair or unfair means, the canonisation of the long-dead King Edward the Confessor, who had patronised the Abbey and had been the architect of its greatness. Under Osbert's supervision a flood of forged documents, many in the Confessor's name and pretending to show how the Abbey had acquired its early estates and how important it had become under the Confessor, were created in a design to impress those in Rome by whom petitions for canonisation were determined.[29] There is no doubt however that behind Osbert's forgeries there existed certain strong traditions at Westminster about the manner in which the early possessions of the Abbey had been acquired, and that in the main the forgeries probably reflected those traditions, whether or not those traditions themselves were accurate.

Why did monks and priests find it necessary to resort to forgery in this way? Paper did not exist in the West until the twelfth century; and both before that time and indeed for many centuries after the introduction of paper from the Far East, the effective way of making a lasting record of an event such as a grant of land was on parchment. But for a long time even the parchment record of a grant was not regarded as the legal grant itself, in the way in which a modern conveyance is. The act constituting an early medieval 'grant' was some physical or otherwise overt act, eg. at least the use of identifiable oral words (such as 'I grant.....'), spoken before witnesses who while alive could be later called upon to prove, if necessary, that a grant had been made.[30] The words making the grant might be accompanied by some other act, such as the handing over of a symbolic object, again before the same witnesses.[31]

But witnesses die, and a record made on parchment therefore became more and more important. However in the poor storage conditions of very early times, parchment records became damaged, or lost, or were eaten by rats or insects; and the Danes destroyed massive amounts of them, when they overran the monasteries. Monks (and others, including lay

---

[28] Robinson *Crispin* 40; Harmer *A-S Writs* 338. It may be that these views have now been superseded, (see eg. Chaplais 'Original Charters' in *A Medieval Miscellany* (Ed.Barnes and Slade) PRS. NS. 36 (1962) 89 ff (also *Essays* XVIII); and Heslop *Twelfth Cent. Forgs.* 309), and that all (or all but a very few of) the forgeries are now to be relegated to the second period. But to sort this out here is not necessary.

[29] On an embassy to Rome between 1139 and 1142 Osbert failed to achieve this purpose, in spite of all his forged documents. But the canonisation of the Confessor did eventually come in 1161, nearly 20 years later, after Osbert's death; and none of the glory reflected on him, see Robinson *'Westminster in the Twelfth Century: Osbert de Clare'* 354-6; Mason *Site of King-making* 72-3; Brooke & Keir *London* 306-9 . In the course of his chequered and frustrated life, in which he fought hard with two successive Abbots, one incidental part which Osbert played was in connection with the foundation of the small nunnery at Kilburn in Hampstead, see Vol. 2.

[30] Clanchy *From memory to written word* 203 ff

[31] The best known example relates to a Middlesex estate, but not one belonging to Westminster. In granting the manor of Harmondsworth to the Abbey of the Holy Trinity in Rouen, William the Conqueror who was not a man given much to jesting managed to make a sardonic joke, by pretending to stab the Abbot's hand with the dagger with which the grant was symbolically being made, saying at the same time, "Thus ought land to be granted": Pollock and Maitland *History of English Law* II. 87.

owners of land) were faced with the real problem of *proving* their rights, particularly after their losses at the hands of the Danes and the reversion of their rightful lands to the Crown, followed perhaps by regrants to other persons.[32]

Where a monastery had already been in possession of land for a long time, but had no witnesses still alive or any extant written record to establish its right, the creator of a *new* document may have wished only to be able to prove an entitlement which was ostensibly good. But where land had been lost, or was merely *believed* to have been lost many years before, there was ample reason, if not excuse, for the creation of documents which (if one is to judge by their language) were almost as deceptive to those who created them as to those who read them. And where there were quite other powerful motives at play, such as those of Osbert's, the area for deception grew even greater.

Any such forger ran the risk that if his forgery were revealed, or even suspected (as most of them have now been), it might be assumed by all his readers, particularly in more modern times, that his rights were necessarily invalid. But historically one has to guard against such an assumption. Even when a forged document has been created to bolster up a claim, it does not follow that the claim itself must be bad. But the later Westminster historians themselves acknowledged the risk which their earlier forgers had run, of positively harming the very claims which they aimed to uphold, by using means which destroyed (as one of them presciently foretold) the 'Certainty of History'.[33]

Because of the vulnerability of documents, it was found that copies of charters and other records were essential, and to ensure their survival, it became an Anglo-Saxon practice to ensure that copies of a valuable document were even deposited in different places.[34] But copying often extended the opportunity for forgery. A contemporary copy, such as one half of a 'chirograph' (an agreement written out in duplicate and cut into two parts, so that the two halves could be matched) could generally be expected to be an exact copy of the other half. But an Abbey like Westminster, which had a proficient scriptorium or writing department [35] and was often required by the King or other benefactors to make out or copy original charters recording gifts to the Abbey, sometimes kept another copy ; or they might choose to make 'copies' at some subsequent time, maybe many years later.[36]

---

[32] See Fleming *Monastic Lands* EHR 100 (1985) at 250 ff.

[33] Widmore *Enquiry* 11; Harvey *WA Estates* 22.

[34] Clanchy *From Memory to Written Word* 128.

[35] Other no doubt grateful monasteries, such as Coventry, Battle and Ramsey, made use of the forging centre at Westminster, see Bishop and Chaplais *Facsimiles of Writs* xxii and *The Chronicle of Battle Abbey* (Ed. Searle) 22,196. (Lay beneficiaries found this role more difficult, because they did not command the same literate facilities, see Chaplais 'The Royal A-S Chancery revisited' in *Studies in Medieval History,* Eds. Mayr-Harting and Moore, 6). After the Conquest, the monks of Westminster even lent a matrix, for forging a seal, to other monasteries, see Searle *Battle Abbey* EHR 83 (1968) 458-9, 465, 473ff. Yet other monasteries, however, such as Chertsey, Abingdon and Evesham, used their own similarly creative initiatives; while the Canons of St Pauls forged their own charters and even a papal Bull, to substantiate their possession of numerous ancient estates, including those round London, see page 18 above. Not only charters but histories too were fabricated. So widespread was the practice and so arguable is the justification of it in *some* cases, in the special circumstances of the era, that the comments have been made that at least in that early setting "forgery was hardly a crime" (Galbraith *Studies in the Public Records* 49) and that until the mid-twelfth century "forgery was an entirely respectable activity", even if it was a crime (Brooke *Approaches to Med. Forgery* J.Soc. Archiv. 3 (1968) 377). See also the apology for it in *The Canon Law of the Church of England* SPCK 13-4.

[36] The most pertinent example for our purposes is the great Cartulary or register of charters and other documents, called the 'Westminster Abbey Domesday', written up from originals and other copies at the beginning of the fourteenth century, with additions up to 1445; see Robinson *MSS of Westminster Abbey* 93-102. Its 655 pages contain many spurious 'copies'.

When this happened, the opportunity was there for the copyist (or his superior) to include, in the so-called 'copy', new matters which inconveniently were not in the original; and to exclude other unwanted matters.[37] If the original and earlier copies have since been lost (as most of them were), and the new 'copy' alone has survived to this day, we are left now with a hybrid version containing two strands of information, one genuine and the other false. The danger with such documents is that if the latter strand can then be seen to be bogus and the document is condemned outright, the genuine information may be unwittingly discarded too : the wheat goes out with the chaff. We have one very good example of such a document which is directly pertinent to this story.

While many of the Westminster monks' records which relate to their lands in the Corridor are entirely spurious (even if they were based on a 'tradition' which may, or may not, have been accurate) there is one document of great significance for us, which falls into this category, being almost certainly partly fabricated and partly derived from genuine material.[38] It is (or purports to be) a document created by King Ethelred, the second son of King Edgar, the founder of the Abbey, and it plays an important role in revealing or confirming some of the very early history of the Abbey's growth into the Corridor north of the Abbey. It has become known as the 'Telligraph of Ethelred' [39] (by which name it will be called later on in this book). While the form of the surviving copy is highly suspicious, the details of the circumstantial facts which it contains about the different parts of Hendon, about Hampstead and also Paddington, in addition to other estates in Middlesex and one or two elsewhere, are such that it is difficult to believe that so much factual detail is invented. Moreover some of this detail is itself consistent with other material from different sources. But there is no doubt that other more wordy parts of the document are spurious,[40] and the problem in such cases is always to distinguish the false from the true. This is only one of the 'uncertainties of history' which the forgers created for themselves and posterity.

---

[37] Many varieties of falsity were available. As Brooke *ibid.* 379 says, documents might be "badly copied, tendentiously copied, or deliberately altered, improved or brought up to date". Chaplais *Essays* XV/1 rightly recommends the pursuit of a 'graded authenticity', rather than a 'black or white' decision.

[38] Sawyer *A-S Charters* No 894. It has survived only in a late copy in the register called the 'Westminster Abbey Domesday' (see note 36 above), which is enough to put anyone on their guard. But its *factual* detail, which is important for other areas in Middlesex as well as many of the Corridor estates, is such that I give a translation of that detail in Appendix 1, page 164-5 below. See also pages 88, 89, 90, 94 (for Hendon) and 99 and 100 (for Hampstead) below. For its general significance, see Harvey *WA Estates* 22 and Korhammer *Bosworth Psalter* ASE 2 (1973) 184. See also Gelling *Early Chs. of Thames Valley* No 231, giving some of the details contained in the document.

[39] A 'Telligraph' is a 'charter of lands with a description of bounds' (OED). But in fact the Telligraph of Ethelred has no descriptions of bounds in it at all, although it does have a detailed and apparently factual list of lands already acquired by or earmarked for the Abbey, with their provenances. Nor is it a charter granting anything. It is a record in the form of a list of past events. By chance another Ethelred document which is important to this story (a recently authenticated document relating to Hampstead, see page 100) is similarly a *subsequent* record, rather than a contemporaneous substantive grant.

[40] Keynes *Diplomas of Aethelred* 108, 112, 122, 237, 256; Korhammer *ibid.* 183. Although it contains various inconsistent material, the Telligraph was apparently modelled on a genuine charter (viz. Sawyer *A-S Charters* 895, see Keynes *ibid.* 256).

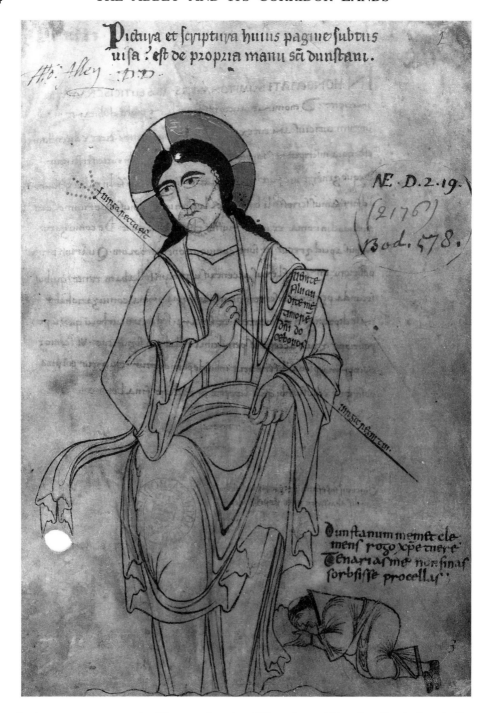

Plate 2. A contemporary portrait of Dunstan, founder of Westminster Abbey, kneeling before the figure of Christ. Dunstan himself almost certainly wrote the four lines of script written above his kneeling figure and embellished both them and his own figure with red lead pigment. The script begins "I beg thee, merciful Christ, to watch over me, Dunstan....".

See page 57

CHAPTER 5

The Abbey's Lands in Middlesex : an outline

Land, and the need to live

The estates which the new monastery at Westminster received, both by royal grants and from other benefactors, in the century between its foundation in about 971 and the Norman Conquest, came in two separate clusters. First of all, a young religious house needed immediate endowments, if its personnel were to survive. Lands meant not only influence, but more importantly food, and rents which were probably received at that time also in the form of food.[1]   So it was that, in that first cluster, a number of estates, most of them in Middlesex, soon came into the Abbey's hands; one of them immediately, and the rest in stages during the period of about 35 years after the foundation, between 971 and 1005.

While some Abbeys were supported not only by religious patrons, but also by patriarchal lay benefactors [2] who lavished their properties and financial assistance upon the monasteries of their choice, at Westminster Abbey most of the lands which the monks were granted during the years immediately after the foundation of the Abbey came to them from or through the influence of their religious patron, Dunstan the Archbishop of Canterbury. Dunstan's interest in the Westminster site may have stemmed from the fact that before he had become Archbishop in late 959 or 960, he had been the Bishop of London,[3] and so had connections with the City of London and its environs, where many of the St Paul's estates already were. As King Edgar's nominee for Canterbury, he had the King behind him in his monastic initiatives,[4] and since money was always necessary to kings, it was fortunate for both of them that Dunstan had been entrusted with the disposal of the great wealth of an Anglo-Saxon lady called Aethelflaed, who had been a patron and friend of his.[5] Accordingly the form of Dunstan's and Edgar's collaboration in support of the new

---

[1] For some early Westminster food renders from its manors shortly *after* the Conquest, see page 151; and pages 156-7, for a Hendon render.

[2] For example, one of the great benefactors of Ramsey Abbey, which was founded in the Fens in 974, a few years after Westminster, was Earl Aethelwine, the Ealdorman of East Anglia. For details of his munificent gifts to Ramsey Abbey, see Raftis *Estates of Ramsey Abbey* 6-7.

[3] In fact Dunstan continued to be Bishop of London (and of Worcester), even after becoming Archbishop, Brooks *The Church of Canterbury* 243 and 247. Such 'pluralism' was not unknown, although forbidden by Canon Law.   D. was "one of the most remarkable pluralists of the tenth century".

[4] Brooks *ibid.* 247-8; Stubbs (Ed) *Memorials of St Dunstan* RS 63. page cv-cvi.

[5] The lady has also been given the name of Aelfgifu, but probably wrongly, see Stubbs *ibid* 85-9. There were several Aethelflaeds at about that time, but this one, who was perhaps the widowed niece of the former King Athelstan, was very attached to Dunstan who in turn 'cared for her as if she were his own mother', and on her death near Glastonbury Abbey, where she had lived possibly as a hermit, she left all her assets to God, entrusting them to Dunstan to effect that purpose, Dales *Dunstan* 23; Stubbs *ibid* lxxv-ix; Symons (Ed) *Reg. Concordia* page xx. Dunstan (who was much supported by such aristocratic widows) is said to have reserved part of the riches for founding five monasteries, Stubbs *ibid.* 89, 178, 301. Dunstan spent 390 'mancuses' of gold (at 30 silver pennies per mancus) and 152 pounds of silver (a little over £200 in all) in his shopping for lands for the new WA: see Harvey *WA Estates* 23.

Abbey was that while the King appears to have supplied some of the lands, Dunstan provided the money and, in effect, bought the lands from the King (and from other lay owners [6]), for the purpose of their bestowal on the Abbey.

It is not clear whether King Edgar himself took a particularly close personal interest in the new Abbey at Westminster. It was the Archbishop's foundation; and as such, the King was clearly prepared to assist it with small grants of land. In return he received useful amounts of money. But there is little sign that he wished to help it to become an elaborate or well-endowed foundation, and it seems that he did not establish any strong personal connection with it in the form of a residence for himself nearby, as later successors did. Indeed little evidence exists that until Edward the Confessor paid very close attention to the Abbey about 80 years later, it had had great importance in royal eyes before him.[7]

1. *The first cluster*   **Maps A, M, N and O**
The first estates [8] which the Westminster monks were given in Middlesex included *eight* tracts of land situated in the Corridor which lay between the Abbey and the northern limits of the county :

> (i) the rural area of Westminster itself around the monastery.[9] This was composed of two tracts, granted separately to the Abbey and at different times: one by King Edgar (after suitable payment by Dunstan) and the other by his second son, King Ethelred (again after adequate recompense);

> (ii) the four territories - Lotheresleage, Hendon ('the smaller'), Bleccanham and Codanhlaw - which, when later combined together at some point of time before the Conquest, constituted the larger Manor of Hendon recorded in the Domesday Survey;[10]

> (iii) Hampstead, an estate which from Anglo-Saxon times seems to have corresponded closely in size with both the later Norman Manor of Hampstead and the still later Parish of St Mary's, Hampstead;[11]

---

[6] For example, he bought Hanwell in Middlesex (in effect through a foreclosed mortgage) from a 'minister' of the King, and Sunbury from a 'dux', an Ealdorman and as such one of the King's military-leaders: see Thorpe *Dipl.Ang.Aev.Sax.* 297-8 (Sawyer *A-S Charters* 894). He also bought parts of Hendon from persons other than the King and gave them to the Abbey, see pages 90-1, and App. 1.

[7] The only indications of any 'special relationship' are (a) that King Cnut (1016-1035) is said to have consulted and been very fond of Abbot Wulnoth, the third Abbot, whose election he had influenced (see page 159) and for that reason to have visited the Abbey many times and to have given many holy relics to it: *Flete* (Ed. Robinson) 70 and 81; Lawson *Cnut* 135,155; and (b) that, for reasons which remain obscure, King Harold Harefoot the possibly illegitimate son and immediate successor of Cnut was buried at Westminster; whence he was forcibly disinterred by his brother who succeeded him: *A-S Chronicle* 1040; Stafford *Unification and Conquest* 76-7.

[8] See **Map A**.

[9] See further page 79, **Map M**; and (for Dunstan's purchase from King Edgar) Appendix 1, page 164.

[10] See further page 87, and **Map N**.

[11] See further page 99, and **Map O**. Until probably the twelfth century Hampstead seems to have had not even a chapel, still less a church of its own: and then for two centuries it had only a chapel, annexed to its mother-church at Hendon; but the chapel (like its mother-church) was dedicated to St Mary (the Virgin). Of all the earliest churches in Middlesex (over 60 of them), more than half were originally dedicated to St Mary, see the Church Commissioners' Parish Maps. The only surviving church in Middlesex which may date (even in small part) from *before* the Conquest is not a St Mary church, but the now sadly-disused church of St Andrew (the 'old church'), lying just west of the present Brent Reservoir in the intriguingly-named estate of 'Kingsbury' (previously 'Tunworth'). It had the same eponymous name as the A-S church by the Fleet in Holborn, see page 80 and Appendix 2. In the past it has had many

(iv) a tract in Paddington.[12]

These eight areas were the Corridor lands which (together with a few other estates in Middlesex and elsewhere [13]) were bestowed upon the Abbey in the first period between its foundation and 1005. The total hideage of all these first endowments of the Abbey is about 65 hides, a very small amount of land compared with the initial grants which some other houses appear to have received.[14] This accords with the denigrating description given to the small Abbey by the chroniclers, before Edward the Confessor started his great enlargement of it.

2. *The second cluster*   **Map B**

The second cluster of acquisitions began to accrue to the Westminster monks about 40 years later.

That interval of about 40 years between these two periods of endowment was a chequered one for English history. The Danes had already renewed their attacks again within five years of Edgar's death in 975, and wars between them and the English continued until 1016, when the Danish King, Cnut, was finally accepted as the King of both the English and the Danes in England.[15] During that period London and its neighbourhood had been the centre of hostilities on many occasions; in 982 when the City was burnt, in 994 when it withstood attack, in 1013 when it submitted briefly to the Danes, and again in 1016 when it resisted multiple attacks and sieges. Although there can be no doubt that with the Danish army present the countryside must have suffered terribly, it seems that the Abbey at Westminster survived; at least there is no evidence of destruction: perhaps because it had little to offer to the plunderers? When the wars ended, the Danish dynasty beginning with King Cnut came to power and reigned for 26 years from 1016,

---

supporters as at least a part-Saxon church, but Pevsner is tepid if not chilly about this (*Buildings of England, Mdx* 120), and Vince *Saxon London* 68 dismisses it outright as having no early features. This issue should be resolved. The site was a Roman one, and the church has two significant remaining sarsen corner stones, and may have had four. If it does have any Saxon elements, it probably was built originally and owned by a thegn: two of Edward the Confessor's thegns occupied the two parts of Kingsbury immediately before the Conquest, and it had been thegn-land even before King Edgar's day (see pages 87-9 below). Such private building of churches was quite usual before the Conquest (cf. Blair *Early Med. Surrey* 115-9), although churchmen had long striven to wrest control of them and hand them to the bishops: Godfrey *The Church in A-S England* 319 and 329-30. Kingsbury also contained the site of the Gore Hundred-court. Or could the church (or nearby Hendon, see page 90) have been another 'old minster', see Blair 'Secular Minster Churches in DB' in *DB: A Reassessment* (Ed. Sawyer) 118?

[12] See further page 112 below.

[13] See further pages 70-1.

[14] For example, Westminster's contemporary, Ramsey Abbey, one of a great ring of Abbeys founded in the Fens, received many times more lands (incidentally with a little help from both Dunstan and King Edgar), see Raftis *Estates of Ramsey Abbey* 6-9. And there are many other even greater examples; Worcester, with a quarter of its whole county; Barking and Chertsey, much earlier, with their 300 hides apiece; and Bury St Edmunds, later, with a third of its own county, Suffolk.

[15] These were the wars with which the unfortunate King Ethelred, the second son of King Edgar, had to deal, earning himself the well-known nickname 'the Unready'. In fact the nickname is a misleading adaptation of the OE word which became applied to him, in a verbal play upon his own name, 'Ethelred' which meant 'well-advised'. As he was unfortunate, to say the least, in his wars and other dealings with both the Danes and his own dissident nobles, he became dubbed 'Unraed', as a sardonic joke, which really meant 'ill-advised' or 'ill-served', see Abels *Lordship and Military Obligation* 93-4 and Barlow *Edward the Confessor* 4-5. Ethelred's main interest for us is that he was the (ostensible) maker of the important 'charter' which records much about the early estates of the Abbey (his 'Telligraph', see page 63 and Appendix 1), and also that it was he who gave Hampstead to the Abbey (see page 100).

until in 1042 the throne was again occupied by an Englishman [16] with the accession of Edward the Confessor.

Under Edward, Westminster Abbey was again reborn. He not only patronised and rebuilt the Abbey in a new and exciting style to serve as his own mausoleum,[17] but also appears to have moved his 'palace' from Aldermanbury in the City of London to the banks of the Thames, on the narrow site between the Abbey and the river.[18] Starting as 'a little monastery' with insignificant buildings,[19] the Abbey now emerged as the prototype (with the Abbey of Jumieges, rebuilt inside a great ox-bow meander of the river Seine, near Rouen in Normandy) of the new Norman form of Romanesque building.[20] It was the first such building in England, and may even have preceded Jumieges [21] in the design of its nave : it constituted the focus of Edward's 'new capital' and was intended to symbolise his own majesty.[22] In length it eclipsed all other Norman and French churches of the time.

During this second endowment period in Edward's reign, the growth of the Abbey's empire 'outwards' into the more distant counties was enormous.[23] But also in the more central counties its prestige and honours doubled. The many gifts of lands which the Abbey received during this period came not only from the King, but also from his thegns and housecarls,[24] who followed the King's lead [25] in honouring the new royal 'private

---

[16] Edward, as the son of Ethelred the Unready, was in fact the great-grandson's grandson of King Alfred (see page 22-3), so his credentials were impeccable. But in exile for 26 years in Normandy during the Danish dynasty's rule in England, he had cultivated Norman loyalties which were to lead ultimately to William the Conqueror's claim to be his heir to the throne of England and so to the Norman Conquest.

[17] *Vita Aedw.Reg.* (Barlow Ed.) 44; Barlow *Edward the Confessor* 229-31

[18] Brooke & Keir *London* 297-8; Rosser *Westminster* 14; Mason *Norman Kingship* 10; Brooke 'Central Middle Ages' in *British Atlas of Historic Towns* (Ed. Lobel) 3/37; Dyson and Schofield 'Saxon London' in *Saxon Towns* (Ed. Haslam) 307-8. The evidence is not as clear as one might expect for such a significant move. Probably the best evidence is in the Bayeux Tapestry (made before 1082, Wilson *B. Tapestry* 212) which shows King Edward twice in his palace immediately alongside the Abbey. See **Plate 3**, page 75. Also his body, after his death, was recorded as being moved from his 'palace home' apparently straight to the Abbey, Barlow *Life of K. Edw.* 125. And on general grounds, one can say that during the process of building the new Abbey (it probably lasted fifteen years or more), Edward's close personal part in the project may well have made the establishment next door of a residence essential. Domesday Book itself may also have some indirect (and perhaps hitherto unnoticed) evidence for the existence of a royal residence there in Edward's time: see my suggestion on page 141 on this issue.

[19] See page 56. For the new Abbey (old and modern perceptions), see **Plates 4** and **5**, pages 76 & 77.

[20] Gem *Romanesque rebuilding of WA* A-N Studies (1980) 33; Colvin *King's Works* 1/ 14-17. English masons were used on Norman work. About 60 years later, the monk-historian William of Malmesbury called it 'a style which now almost all attempt to rival, at vast expense', *De Gestis Regum* RS. i. 280.

[21] See Gem *ibid.* Much of the Abbey of Jumieges, which had earlier been destroyed by the Vikings and was being rebuilt at much the same time as Westminster Abbey, still stands and is well worth visiting, both for its own sake and for the impression which it conveys of the probable nature of parts of Edward's rebuilding at Westminster. For photographs of Jumieges, see **Plate 6**, page 78.

[22] Mason *The Site of King-Making* SCH (Subsidia) 9 (1991) 59. See Gem *ibid.* 44-6 for its size.

[23] A good deal of the Abbey's expansion into the West Country, where its expansion was extensive, was at the expense of another Abbey, Pershore, in Worcestershire: Mason *Beauchamp Cart.* xvii.

[24] The housecarls were a highly organised military body, with Danish origins, united by loyalty to the Danish kings of England. They formed the king's household troops, and since the Danes were a sea-going people, the housecarls had a close connection with the Danish navy in England. They survived into Edward the Confessor's reign. The thegns were, by contrast, the native 'king's servants' or 'ministers', who had formed an elite class in Anglo-Saxon society, see Loyn *Governance* 166 and *Gesiths and Thegns* EHR 70 (1955) 529-49; and Abels *Lordship and Military Obligation* 141-2 : though usually of noble blood, they were not necessarily so, and could include eg. the King's huntsmen,

monastery' (as in effect the Abbey had become).

It was also probably during this period that part of Westminster itself (that is, the village area near the Abbey which was slowly to graduate to a small town [26]) started in a simple way on its second career, as a secular as well as a religious centre. With the likely establishment of a royal residence at Westminster, the administrative arrangements which had to be made for even the temporary residence of an itinerant [27] king must have now been as necessary at Westminster as they were at the older residences which the ever mobile kings had previously set up on their own royal estates in other parts of the country.[28] It would probably be too early to see the setting-up at Westminster of an organised royal secretariat or exchequer at this time, such as was later centred there.[29] But the building of the new Abbey alone must have called for a complicated local administration; and the location of a new royal residence at Westminster (perhaps needed for that very purpose) can only have added to the secular business executed there.

The detailed stages of the Abbey's growth :   Maps A, B, I, K, L and N
Let us now look at these two periods of endowment in more detail.

1. *The first cluster* (971 - c.1005 AD)
Within the whole of Middlesex [30] it seems that, in total, twelve estates were given to or bespoken for the Westminster monks during that first period. Of these, eight were the Corridor lands referred to above. The remaining four fell into two categories. One was in the centre of the county, the strategically placed estate of *Hanwell;* and the others were grouped in the southwest, each of them lying on a river boundary (the Thames, and the Colne), namely *Sunbury, Shepperton* and *Cowley Peachey.*

---

purveyors and even artisans (see *DB Wilts* 2/74-8). Interestingly one finds both titles surviving as ordinary surnames in later centuries: eg. 'Huscarl' was to be found in Stepney at least 400 years later and had even become the name of a manor there, McDonnell *Medieval London Suburbs* 157. For a clear analysis of the 'men', thegns, huscarls and lay-estates recorded in *Mdx DB*, see *VCH* (TG Pinder) 1/98 ff.

[25] Eg. in Middlesex, the King gave Staines, and his nobles gave Greenford and Chalkhill, see below, pages 71-2. In other counties the king's lead was much more generous, and had been demonstrated early in his reign. As regards gifts from the King's vassals, one of Osbert de Clare's later forged charters, made in the name of Edward the Confessor (Sawyer *A-S Charters* No 1043), has an impressive list of 13 'optimates' (magnates) who gave named estates to the Abbey; but even this was not complete.

[26] See Chapter 11, page 135.

[27] For the journeys made by Edward the Confessor in England, see Hill *A-S Atlas* page 94-5. It is noticeable that his journeys centred mainly on Gloucester and London and did not take in nearly so many distant parts of the kingdom as some of his predecessors' travels had done; cf. Hill *ibid* pages 83-4, 87 and 91.

[28] Eg. at Winchester, Wilton or Cheddar. In Middlesex, it is clear that there had been a royal meeting place and presumably a residence at Chelsea more than 200 years before, see page 20.

[29] There is now a very arguable case that (in addition to the use made by the kings of the writing skills practised in the *scriptoria* of religious houses, including Westminster) the later Anglo-Saxon kings had developed some form of secretariat within their own Household, see the important discussions in Loyn *Governance* 106-18 and Keynes *Diplomas of Aethelred* 39ff and 134ff; though see Clanchy *From Memory to Written Record* 17; Bishop and Chaplais *English Royal Writs* p.xii; Chaplais 'The Royal A-S Chancery revisited' in *Studies in Med. Hist.* (Eds. Mayr-Harting and Moore) 41. But if any permanent secretariat existed before the Conquest, it would have been at Winchester, where the kings kept their treasury and some financial staff, and there is nothing which would link it with Westminster. For some thoughts about personnel available in Westminster at the time of Domesday, see page 139-44 below.

[30] See **Map B,** (but the separate estates *within* Westminster and Hendon are not shown there).

The pattern formed by all these early grants to Westminster Abbey is an interesting one. We see the *Westminster* estate lying along the whole of the east-west leg of Watling Street (the present Oxford Street and Holborn); the *Paddington-Hampstead-Hendon* lands lying alongside the north-south leg of Watling Street (the modern Edgware Road); *Hanwell*, lying across each of the main westbound roads to Bath and Oxford, and bordering, for the whole length of the estate, on the river Brent in its lowest reaches, and fronting the Thames and its substantial ford at Brentford; and finally, in the south-west, *Sunbury and Shepperton* lying alongside a length of the Staines-Kingston road and fronting a long stretch of the Thames. *Cowley* lay separately on the River Colne, the western boundary.

It may of course be no more than a coincidence which gives to this pattern the appearance of a careful selection of reasonably strategic areas, for bestowal on an ecclesiastical house which owed both its very existence, and all its motives for loyalty, to a patronage which had close connections with the King. On the other hand it may be that since Middlesex is and was small and, being close to the City of London and its port, contained a network of various means of communication, it was very likely that any new monastery would be endowed with strategic estates, if any of its lands were to be chosen from Middlesex. Another possibility is that these areas were given to Westminster simply for the purpose of the *maintenance* of the important roads and waterways.

Whatever the explanation, and whether the pattern of the new Abbey's earliest lands was deliberate, coincidental or inevitable, it did mean that shortly after its foundationn the Abbey found itself in control of areas in Middlesex which must have been of considerable significance to the King, whether in times of peace or even more in times of war when the Danes were again on the attack (as indeed they soon were [31]).

Even if there were no significance at all in the strategic character of the Abbey's acquisition of these early Corridor lands, the *source* from which they came to the Abbey may itself be suggestive of their even earlier importance. That source was largely a royal one.[32] As will be seen later, Westminster, Lotheresleage, Bleccanham and Hampstead came to the Abbey directly from kings. Hendon ('the smaller'), Codanhlaw and possibly Paddington had been in the hands of men close and sworn to the king. This suggests that these lands, clustered round Watling Street, formed in some period before the Abbey was founded a royal zone or 'sector' (or at least part of a wider 'province'), held by kings for probably strategic reasons, and perhaps for those reasons retained in royal hands longer than other parts of Middlesex. The adjoining estate of 'Kingsbury', undoubtedly a royal estate in origin (with its own 'king's wood') and itself also bordering on Watling Street, fits into this same pattern. Similar reasoning may also explain why the northern boundary of Hendon was apparently called 'the king's boundary' in the tenth century.[33]

But it was not only in Middlesex that the Abbey received its early endowments. In each of Hertfordshire, Essex and Sussex it was bequeathed single estates under the wills of three nobles:[34] and there are several other more questionable 'grants' which have been

---

[31] See page 67, above. For an early road-protection contract, see page 38 above.

[32] See Appendices 1 and 2, and Chapters 6, 7, 8 and 9.

[33] For the Kingsbury wood and Hendon boundary, see Appendix 2, page 168. Kensal ('king's wood'), in Kensington, a lay estate still held by a king's man before 1066, is also consistent with this notion.

[34] The apparently authentic grants relate to Brickendon (Herts); part of Kelvedon & nearby Markshall (Essex); and 'Chollington' (Sussex), see Sawyer *A-S. Ch.* 1487, 1522 & 894. I have included 'Chollington', because of Harvey *WA Estates* 359 and Bugden *Chollington in Eastbourne* Sussex Arch. Coll. 62 (1921) 122 ff. But Gelling *Early Charters* 114 makes it 'Sullington'; and Sawyer *A-S Charters*

ascribed to this period.[35] But none of these lie within the range of this book.

2. *The second cluster* (1042 - 1066 AD)

An enormous growth of Westminster Abbey's power and possessions took place during this period. Over 50 grants of land to the monks can be verified, ranging for the first time over many 'outer' counties, such as Hampshire, Northamptonshire, Oxfordshire, the region which later became the county of Rutland, Staffordshire, Lincolnshire, Gloucestershire, Warwickshire and Worcestershire; as well as the 'inner' counties such as Middlesex, Hertfordshire, Essex, Surrey, Buckinghamshire, Bedfordshire and Kent.

But in Middlesex itself, the Abbey's acquisitions in this period were few. Their general localities were virtually identical with those given in the first cluster : -

(a) Near the Abbey's main existing Westminster estate, Knightsbridge was probably received by the monks at this time.[36] As with Westminster, part of it lay directly on one of the two roads leading to the west from London. Being on that road, it had probably already become the nucleus of a 'vill' (a village or town, including outlying settlements), and it already was important enough to have a bridge over the river now known as the Westbourne. It also probably included at that time the larger district known also as Westbourne, which undoubtedly became Abbey property at an early stage.[37] After acquisition, Knightsbridge (together with Paddington) was apparently seen as part of the Westminster estate, but later was sometimes classed with Paddington as a separate manor.

(b) Either adjoining their Hendon land on the west side of Watling Street, or perhaps immediately adjoining Watling Street itself, a tract of land called Chalkhill within Kingsbury (see **Map A**) was given in about 1044-6 to the monks by one of King Edward's housecarls, Thurstan.[38] For reasons which are not certain but no doubt

---

894, 'Sillington', which Sawyer interprets as 'Chiltington', Sussex. And Robinson *Crispin* 46-8 makes a spirited case for it as (the modern) 'Chillenden' in Kent; and indeed its donor Aelfwine had a Kent connection. Because it is irrelevant to my present theme, I have not gone further into the issue, which has everyone at odds. For the text of Sawyer *A-S Chs.* No 894, see Appendix 1, page 164.

[35] There are at least seven other estates whose acquisition has been ascribed to this period, mainly by the charters forged about 140 years later (see page 61); Harvey *Estates of WA* 24 and Appendix 1 thereto. My tentative view is that the ascription is doubtful in some of these cases, but the subject is too detailed for further discussion here.

[36] The first and only reference to Knightsbridge in the early charters is in Sawyer *A-S Charters* 1039 (part-printed in Robinson *Crispin* 40 and nowhere else; a part-forged but probably part-genuine record).

[37] The reason for this supposition is that in Sawyer No 1039 Knightsbridge is assessed at four hides, which seems far too high for just the small area which was known later as Knightsbridge (see **Map A**).

[38] *Regesta* i. 89 and ii.p.392; Sawyer *A-S Charters* No 1121; Harmer *A-S Writs* No 77 and page 308 and 497. In the Domesday Survey it was recorded as having been occupied (under a mortgage) by Alwin Horne, one of Edward's thegns (see *VCH Mdx* 1/103-4), immediately before the Conquest, and held in 1086 by William, the Chamberlain of the Conqueror, 'under' the Abbot of Westminster. It sounds as if the Chamberlain must have claimed some rights to the land through Alwin, while the mortgagor (a 'man' of WA) or WA itself claimed to have redeemed the mortgage. If indeed there was a legal dispute at that time, it all came right later in the same century when William the Chamberlain gave it up to the Abbey (see Harvey *WA Estates 39;* Mason *WA Charters* No 11 and Robinson *Crispin* 130) and so earned for himself the right of 'confraternity' with the monks,which gave him various spiritual benefits, including the singing of masses for him after his death. William had had estates in seven counties at the time of Domesday, including Middlesex, where he held a vineyard which probably lay in Holborn and a small estate near Crouch End in Hornsey, as well as Chalkhill. He had clearly been well in favour shortly after the Conquest, because he had been invested with the Manor of Eia, next door to Westminster, in fee from Queen Edith (Edward the Confessor's widow), but had been ousted from it in favour of the greater baron,

reflected legal disputes, it seems that the monks did not receive undisputed possession of the land, until at least well after the Conquest.

(c) In the centre of the shire, and adjoining the already-held Hanwell, the Abbey received (with King Edward's blessing) an estate at Greenford, from a man called Ailric, probably another of Edward's thegns.[39] Like Hanwell, it too fronted onto the river Brent. It had earlier contained a flourishing settlement, which had already been described more than 200 years before as 'the famous vill of Greenford'.[40]

(d) In the southwest, another large estate, at Staines, together with four other unnamed dependent tracts nearby,[41] called 'Berewics', and also some property in London itself, were apparently granted to the monks by King Edward, probably shortly before his death in 1066.[42] Of this land, it seems that the monks did not obtain possession, or having received possession they then lost it, until some point of time between the Conquest and the Domesday Survey.[43]

So whether by design or coincidence it looks as if the geographical pattern of the grants in Middlesex which the Abbey had received during its previous foundation period was again reproduced during the later reign of Edward the Confessor, but on a smaller scale. The gifts to the Abbey of lands in Middlesex, made by King Edward and also by his housecarls, were very small in scope and number, when measured against the more substantial grants, at that time, of lands in other counties. Probably the reason for this was that by the time of King Edward there was less room within Middlesex for either royal or lay generosity than there had been in earlier centuries, and the scope for such generosity was greater in the counties further afield where there was more geographical elbow-room.

There appears to be no evidence that Westminster Abbey, or indeed any other estate-owner in Middlesex, ever received a grant of what has become known as a 'private Hundred', i.e. full jurisdictional and fiscal control over any block of territory forming one complete 'hundred' (or indeed more than one) within a county.[44] Nor, it seems, did the Abbey receive such a block of land even in any other of the more distant counties, in spite of the fact that the grants in those counties to the Abbey were geographically much larger than those in Middlesex. By way of contrast, one finds that in about 1044 King Edward himself was conferring on the Abbey of Bury St Edmunds (recently founded by King Cnut in about 1020) a large block of territory, with full jurisdictional rights, in its surrounding county of Suffolk, a block consisting of eight and a half 'hundreds' in that county. And during the same monastic revival as that in which Westminster Abbey had been founded in

---

Geoffrey de Mandeville, four years before the Survey, see *DB Mdx* 9/1 (f.129c). For Geoffrey, see pages 84 and 137.

[39] Sawyer *A-S Charters* No 1132 ; Harmer *A-S Writs* No 88 and p. 320 and 510 ; *VCH Mdx* 1/ 109.

[40] Birch *Cart.Sax.* No 448 (Sawyer *A-S Charters* No 1194)

[41] Identified as Ashford, Laleham, Halliford and Teddington estates; with possibly a fifth not referred to, at Yeoveney; according to *VCH Mdx* 1/109 and 3/18. For the term 'Berewic', see page 80.

[42] Sawyer *A-S Charters* No 1142; Sanders *O.S.Facs.* Westm. vol. ii , No. 10; Harmer *A-S Writs* Nos 97 and 98 and pp.328-30; Mason *WA Charters* No 38.

[43] According to Harmer *ibid.* p.327-9, relying on DB *Mdx* 4/5 (f. 128c). But it is questionable.

[44] For the six Hundreds in Middlesex, see **Map I** and page 49. On the issue of private hundreds in Middlesex, see further Taylor *London Endowment* A-N. Studies14 (1991) 301-2. For whole Hundreds elsewhere in England which became in effect 'private hundreds', see Cam 'The Private Hundred', in *Studies presented to Jenkinson,* (Ed. Davies) 50-7. But even the physical possession of an area which happened to coincide with or contain a whole Hundred did not of itself give the right to carry out fiscal and judicial functions within that Hundred. Such rights required a special grant, of what is called the 'hundredal soke', the right to exercise full powers in the Hundred to the exclusion of even the King's sheriff.

Edgar's reign, the Abbey at Worcester had been given jurisdictional control by the King over three 'hundreds' in Worcestershire through the influence of its founder, Bishop Oswald, (an area which appropriately became known as 'Oswaldslaw'). Possibly as a result of a royal policy not to allow the creation of an independent 'empire' in so strategic an area as Middlesex, and to retain some control over such small estates as were granted to dependent laymen,[45] no private Hundred was (it seems) granted in this county.[46]

In addition to all the lands which it now held in the more distant counties and in the outer sectors of Middlesex itself, the Abbey remained in possession immediately before the Norman Conquest of its original band of Corridor estates, augmented now by Knightsbridge. These ran from Westminster up to the northern limits of Hendon: but there was one principal break in the Corridor, and it is worth pausing to look at that break, which still prevented the Abbey's holdings from forming a solid block of territory (see **Map A**). Two estates there were held by other tenants, a lay man and a church; and they continued to be held by others during the whole of the medieval period: -

(a) The *first* estate was the 'corner' estate of Lileston (from which the present 'Lisson Grove' was derived), held during the period before the Conquest by the Anglo-Saxon (or Danish?) lay man, Edward son of Suein. It was clearly an estate which held an important position not far from the City, in the corner formed by the two legs of the road which were each known as Watling Street. We will see that after the Conquest it had an interesting history as the land of Otto, the Conqueror's Goldsmith and also his Die-cutter, and his successors in that office within his own family; as well as being the subject of transactions connected with the estate of Hampstead onto which it bordered. The suggestion has been made that even before the Conquest Edward son of Suein had also been a royal officer, a cutter of the metal dies necessary for the job of making coins in the minting of the coinage, which both Anglo-Saxon and later kings had learnt to keep firmly under their own control.[47] It is clear that the office was a crucial one for this royal purpose, and that at least from the Conquest the estate was made available for successive holders of that office.

(b) The *second* estate was Tyburn, held by the ancient Abbey of Barking in Essex, a house of nuns during the tenth and eleventh centuries. The Abbey had been founded in the seventh century as a double-monastery of monks and nuns,[48]

---

[45] For the A-S estates existing in Middlesex before the Conquest, see **Map K**.

[46] But see Thorn 'Hundreds and Wapentakes' in *The Mdx Domesday* (Alecto) 37. The whole Hundred of Hounslow (which was later renamed Isleworth and lost the manor of Hampton to Spelthorne) had been held in Edward the Confessor's time by Earl Aelfgar, (an adventurous man, who had held each of the earldoms of East Anglia and Mercia in his time, as well as having rebelled twice against the King). After the Conquest the whole Hundred was kept intact and given by the Conqueror to one of his supporters, Walter de St Valery (who had embarked with him at St Valery-sur-Somme); see **Map L**. But neither at that time nor earlier does there appear to be any evidence that any jurisdictional rights were held by either of these men. The fact that the Archbishop of Canterbury's large estate at Harrow was 100 hides in its assessment did not mean that any jurisdictional rights went with it; it was merely one (major) part of Gore Hundred, whose total assessment was about 150 hides, see page 51 above.

[47] VCH *Mdx* 1/118. On Lileston, and one of its connections with Hampstead, see further pages 103-4 and 137 below. Such a close royal connection with Lileston may also support the suggestion made on page 70 above that the Corridor lands may reflect an earlier strategic royal sector in that area.

[48] The Abbeys of Barking, to the east of London, and Chertsey, to the west, were both founded at about the same time by Eorcenwald, later the Bishop of London who also called himself "Bishop of the East-

only to be burnt down by the Danes in 870 and restored again in the tenth century. It is not known how long the nuns had already held Tyburn. The estate had not been part of their original, very early, endowments. It may have been granted to them in the tenth century, when the Abbey was restored in the monastic revival; or later by Edward the Confessor. At all events the manor remained theirs after the Conquest (see **Map B**),[49] and until the dissolution of their Abbey in 1539 continued to be held in chief by them, through at first their great tenants, the de Veres (who later became the Earls of Oxford), and then through other tenants. The river Tyburn, which gave its own name to the estate, at all known times formed its western boundary, separating it from the adjoining Lileston.

Saxons". This was during the period of East-Saxon ascendancy, see pages 16-7 above.

[49] Barking Abbey seems to have had a special relationship with the Conqueror, who after his Coronation at Westminster Abbey went to stay at Barking with the nuns, until his first building programme at the Tower of London was completed, Brooke and Keir *London* 30; and later he granted them freedom from any obligation to provide soldiers under his new feudal system (a freedom which was frequently challenged thereafter), Chew *Ecc.Tenants in Chief* 8,13; VCH *Essex* 2/119 and 3/257. See also pages 137 and 142 below. It was from the springs in this manor of Tyburn that the citizens of London were permitted to draw extra water for their needs in and after 1237, see page 42 above.

Plate 3. King Edward the Confessor in his two main palaces, as depicted in the Bayeux Tapestry. The top one is probably his Winchester palace, his principal seat, with the King instructing Harold to visit Duke William in Normandy. The bottom one is his less elaborate Westminster palace, standing close to the new Abbey, with Harold reporting back to the King the results of his flawed embassy.   See pages 68-9

Plate 4. Anglo-Saxon Westminster Abbey, rebuilt by Edward the Confessor, as depicted in the nearly contemporary Bayeux Tapestry. The heavenly hand, with pointed finger, denotes its consecration; and the final weathercock has just been fixed on its perch. For the architecture, compare the 'reconstruction' drawing on page 77, and the ruins of Jumièges Abbey in Normandy on page 78.

See page 68

Plate 5. A 'reconstruction' of the Westminster scene about 35 years after the Norman Conquest, drawn by W.T. Ball and based on the researches of Dr Richard Gem. The main parts of the Abbey which had not been completed *before* the Conquest were the west end of the nave (shown 'opened-up' here), the west towers and most of the monastic buildings. The palace, shown behind, had probably been less impressive before the Conquest : compare page 75. See page 68

Plate 6. The ruins of Jumieges Abbey, which stood within a meander of the River Seine, not far from Rouen. Rebuilt contemporaneously in the new Romanesque style, Jumieges and Westminster Abbeys had certain architectural links, although Westminster was much longer than Jumieges. The nave piers, middle storey and clerestory at Jumieges are used as a model in the drawing on page 77.   See page 68

CHAPTER 6

Westminster : The Fields West of London

There are two charters which tell us the boundaries of the original Westminster districts which the new Abbey received: the first and main estate purchased by Archbishop Dunstan from King Edgar and given to the monks; the second and subsidiary estate, purchased later by the Abbey itself from Edgar's second son, King Ethelred.

The main Estate, between three Rivers   **Maps M, A and H**
On three sides of the gravel island chosen for the site of the monastery itself, the 'famous place called Westminster' (as it is described in the charters[1]) stretched north, west and south. As we have seen, the alluvial area inland from the river was fairly flat until it reached the first of the two ridges of river gravel which lay above the immediate basin of the river. These gravel ridges now form, first, the hill up the present Haymarket and St James's Street, followed by the shallower incline of Regent Street and Baker Street. The two levels, both the flat alluvium and the raised gravel shelves, formed the first and main estate of Westminster (at that time assessed at only five hides) with which the monks were endowed at the time when their church was founded in about 971.

The boundaries of this rural estate formed a rough triangle. They began at the estuary of the southern arm of the Tyburn river (near the present Vauxhall Bridge), and ranged northwards along the Tyburn to the line of the modern Oxford Street; then eastwards along that street, past the present St Giles and Holborn to the bed of the river Fleet; from there a short distance southwards along that river (now the hollow of Farringdon Street and New Bridge Street) to the mouth of the Fleet, where it entered the Thames; and so south-westwards along the curving bed of the Thames back to the southern mouth of the Tyburn.

These bounds are well-authenticated and reasonably identifiable, being described originally in an Anglo-Saxon text contained within a Latin charter ostensibly made at Glastonbury by King Edgar in about 971.[2] Already by that time the line of Oxford Street

---

[1] This formula is common to both genuine and forged charters. The extent of the boundaries of both the Westminster estates is shown on **Map M**. See Appendix 2, pages 166-7, for their translated texts.

[2] Sawyer *A-S Charters* No 670 and 1450; and see also No 894, the Telligraph of Ethelred (see page 63 and Appendix 1). For the full text of the A-S bounds and some other translations, see Appendix 2 and Robinson *Crispin* 170; Gelling *Boundaries of the WA Charters* TLMAS 17 (1954) Pt.3. 101-4. The main points of reference in the Bounds are described in the text above and **Map M**. Charter No 670 is probably an early copy (with additions) of a lost document (contrast Brooks 'Career of St D.' in Ramsay *St D., Life, Times and Cult* 22). However it is dated 951, a date which is not possible for Edgar (959-975). Wrong dating (often added in later copies) of apparently genuine material was not uncommon. Usually the date 959 has been proposed as the correct date (eg. Harvey *WA Estates* 23); or 960 or after (Rosser *Westminster* 13). But there seem to be reasonable grounds now for dating the foundation and charter to about 971 (see above, page 57). The charter however has other problems as well, eg. a long (interpolated?) reference to an 'ancient charter' and also to King Offa (whether of Essex or Mercia) and Archbishop Wulfred as contemporaries, which they were not; and an absence of witnesses. See **Plate 7**, page 85. Another clearly 'forged' copy of No 670 was later made at Westminster (as part of Sawyer *ibid.* No 1450), which has a further added embellishment and other alterations (see eg. page 39, as to the later

and Holborn was apparently known as the 'broad military-road',[3] an important route no doubt used for moving troops quickly either to or from the west, or up or down Watling Street to or from St Albans in the north. In Holborn, at the entrance to the City of London, there was the 'old wooden church of St Andrew',[4] probably where the modern church of St Andrew stands near Holborn Circus.

Where both the two tributaries, the Fleet and the Tyburn (in its southern arm), entered the third river, the Thames, there were fens or marshy areas. At the mouth of the Fleet, the wide marsh was known as 'London Fen',[5] the Fleet being at that time the boundary where Westminster ended and the City began. At the south-western corner of the estate where the southern mouth of the Tyburn reached the Thames, a marsh, at that time called the 'Bulunga Fen', lay in the area which after considerable drainage became the 'Tothill Fields', south-west of the Abbey. Apparently through this Fen ran the 'boundary stream' (ie. the southern arm of the Tyburn, see **Maps H and M**). Along the Thames itself, the boundary ran along the mid-line of the wide-spreading river, so that the monks had the fishing and other rights over the nearer half of the river. Finally there was a ford called the 'Cowford' probably at the point at which the Tyburn crossed the road which was on or near the line of the present Piccadilly (or possibly even a road on about the line of the present Mall). The Piccadilly road was already by then a second west-bound highway, linking up with the line of the present Strand, which unexpectedly was called 'Akeman Street' at that time, as we see from the second charter described below.

The 'Berewic', across Watling Street   Maps H, M and B

To complete the Westminster boundaries, one has to break the chronological sequence and jump about 30 years ahead from the date of the Abbey's foundation. In 1002, with Edgar dead and his second son Ethelred [6] on the throne, the monks purchased from that King [7] another small estate of two 'mansae' (probably hides) of land called the 'Berewic' (a name meaning an outlying farm or croft) which lay, it seems, to the north of the 'broad military road' (High Holborn), and therefore on the opposite side of that road from their existing Westminster land. Again detailed Anglo-Saxon bounds are provided in this Ethelred charter, but not just for the Berewic itself; instead they were bounds for the whole

---

interpolatation of 'Holeburne'), together with a list of 'witnesses'. As to the effect of some of these witnesses, see Napier & Stevenson *Crawford Charters* 85. As to Ch. No 1450, see also page 92 below.

[3] The OE. noun for 'military road' was 'herestraet'. By an analysis of its use in all the A-S charters, Rackham *History of Countryside* 259 shows that this does mean an A-class road (for that time), wide enough for an army to use. Ekwall *Dict. of EPN* 236 and 449 suggests that 'straet' meant a Roman road, or a paved road (of some other origin). The width of Roman roads varied, with a norm of about 20-24 feet for a goodish road, but for a specifically 'broad' road it could go as high as 30 feet: no doubt, like the rest of Watling Street, it had suffered in the centuries since the Romans had left, but there is no doubt that the Anglo-Saxons could travel remarkably quickly. Both kings, with or without their courts, and armies could move with extraordinary speed (witness Harold from Stamford Bridge, before Hastings).

[4] Stone, as a material for Anglo-Saxon churches in or before the tenth century, was limited, but several examples still survive, see Taylor 'Tenth century Church building' in *Tenth Century Studies* (Ed. Parsons) 141-68; Jackson and Fletcher 'The Priory Church of Deerhurst' in their *Collected Papers on A-S Churches*. Wood was plentiful and commonly used for such churches (cf. Greenstead in Essex).

[5] See its description in Honeybourne *The Fleet LTR* 19 (1947) 14-5; Barton *Lost Rivers* 29, and page 40 above.

[6] For Ethelred, see pages 67 and 100.

[7] Sawyer *A-S Charters* No 903. For the full text of this grant by Ethelred and some translations, see Robinson *Crispin* 167-9, and Gelling *Boundaries* 17 (1954) 101-4. Keynes *Diplomas of Aethelred* 143 says that No 903 is 'probably authentic'. For the boundaries themselves, see Appendix 2, page 166.

Westminster estate including the new Berewic. There seems little doubt that this comparatively small area of the Berewic (later increased to three mansae [8]) lay to the north of High Holborn, in the present Bloomsbury area, probably in the district where much of the later St Giles parish lay and where the British Museum and the University now stand, and extending eastwards to the river Fleet.[9]

In other respects the Anglo-Saxon bounds given in the Ethelred charter follow broadly the same outline as that given in the earlier Edgar charter.[10] But although more puzzling in some ways, they contain a number of interesting additions. *Firstly* they begin, and end, by referring to a 'hlaw' (which was a hill or mound) in what is probably the Tothill Fields area, which was otherwise flat or marshy. A mound there must have been an artificial one, perhaps for look-out purposes [11] and is probably commemorated by the Tothill name itself. *Secondly*, the bounds go on to show that the modern Oxford Street-Holborn road was at that time called not only the 'broad military road', but also 'Watling Street', as an *eastward* extension (as far as the City gate [12]) of the road which was more familiarly known as

---

[8] *DB Mdx* 4/2 (f. 128b); Sawyer *ibid* No 1039 (if the charter can be relied on in this respect). See also Robinson *Crispin* 40; Harmer *Three Westminster Writs* EHR 51 (1936) 99. After the Conquest (indeed just before the Domesday Survey) this piece of land which by then had certainly become three hides was granted by the Abbey to a Norman baron, William Baynard, as a knight's fee, see pages 136 and 142. In the period before the Conquest the Berewic seems to have been assessed at a high value, £6 p.a., if one compares it with, say, the main Westminster estate of the Abbey, which with its (by then) 13.5 hides was worth only £12. If it is right that the DB assessments took account of the economic potential of estates (see Macdonald and Snooks *Were DB Assessments artificial?* Ec.HR 38 (1985) 352 in relation to Essex) and if the same were true of Middlesex, it would be clear that the Berewic was an unusually valuable estate. Standing at or near the gates of London, it suffered a six-fold loss of value due to the Conquest, although it had recovered to half its old value by the time of DB: see page 121 for the reason.

[9] The geography is considered in Davis *University Site* LTR 17 (1936)19 ff; EPNS *Mdx* 222-3 ; and in the text and map in Gelling *Boundaries* TLMAS 17 (1954) Pt.3, 101-4. There must be a strong probability (having regard to the importance of all the local rivers as boundaries at these early times) that the Fleet's feeder-stream which ran in part along Gt Ormond Street (as shown on the main map in Barton *Lost rivers*; see also my **Maps H and M**) and the Fleet itself formed boundaries of the eastern half of the Berewic. Robinson *Crispin* 41 and Harvey *WA Estates* 73 and 75 and Mason *WA Charters* No 236 all appear to locate the Berewic in the area just south of the Abbey itself, on the grounds that 'Totenhala' (referred to in the charter to William Baynard, printed by Robinson *ibid* 38) could be 'Tothill' (which gave its name to Tothill Street and Tothill Fields near the Abbey, see text below); but the premise for all this (started by Robinson) is probably wrong. It is likely that the reference to a mysterious 'Tatewell' which appears in Sawyer *A-S Charters* No 1039 *is* a reference to Tothill; but 'Totenhala' is surely Tottenhall, the area-name also used for the adjoining estate (later, Tottenham Court) of the Canons of St Pauls, see **Map B** and page 18 above.

[10] However EPNS *Mdx* 223 and Honeybourne *The Fleet* LTR 19 (1947) 16-7 have suggested that the eastern boundary of Westminster in the Ethelred charter was different from that in the Edgar charter, sloping down to where the present City boundary lies (near eg. the Temple). I doubt this. It rests on assumptions, and does not reflect the inferences to be drawn from the 'old gallows' and the great Arbitration in 1222 (see below, page 83). For the bounds themselves, see Appendix 2.

[11] Built because of the new Danish attacks? see page 67. For another *hlaw*, see page 95; and for the meaning, see discussion in Gelling *PNs in the Landscape* 162-3.

[12] Although there is still a surviving part of a street within the City itself which has been called 'Watling Street' since at least the thirteenth century, this is *not* an extension of the Holborn stretch of the real Watling Street referred-to in the text above. But it is clear that, whatever it was called within the City, the line of the real Watling Street ran (through Newgate) straight to the Roman Second Forum within the City, and thence southwards to the old Roman bridge over the Thames, see the maps at the end of Lobel *British Atlas* (vol.3): *London* ; Grimes *Roman and Med. London* 45. However there is good reason, including archaeological evidence, to think that in even earlier Roman times (and perhaps pre-Roman times?) the *main* leg of the road which became known as Watling Street (now the Edgware Road) had continued its path from the present Marble Arch *southwards* (via the present Park Lane, which had

Watling Street (i.e. the present Edgware Road). So by about 1002 the monks already held land along the southern edge of that *eastward* extension of Watling Street; and towards the furthest end of that extension, at Holborn, they also held land on the northern side of the road.

Thirdly, instead of using the Thames mid-line as the eastern boundary of the Westminster estate, the Ethelred charter uses the line of the strand-road (the line of the modern Fleet Street and Strand), calling it Akeman Street,[13] namely the road which led to Acemannes Ceaster, the Anglo-Saxon name for Bath, and on its way passed through Brentford and Staines (both to become Westminster properties). There is considerable sense in describing this part of the boundary by reference to the road, rather than to the wide-spreading, unreliable and marshy river, whose waters in any case came up to at least the bottom of the gravel ridge itself, at the lower end of Villiers Street and Arundel Street; if indeed not higher still, i.e. not far short of the well-defined 'strand' road itself along the top of the gravel slope.[14]

Fourthly the Ethelred bounds of Westminster show that a settlement continued to exist (or had revived) on the line of Akeman Street, at 'Charing' (approximately the site of the present-day Trafalgar Square [15]), where part of the early *Lundenwic* development had

---

become known as Westminster Lane and then Tyburn Lane at later dates) to a ford over the Thames at Westminster and from there had linked up with the main route leading from Dover towards the London area, via Canterbury, Shooters Hill and Blackheath, VCH *London* 1/28-31; Morris *Londinium* 80, 83, 101; Higden, *Polychronicon* RS ii.46; Morley Davies *First Conduit* TLMAS. 8 (1913) 55-7. Certainly the route along Westminster Lane/Tyburn Lane must have continued to be open for local traffic, since it alone was the access to the Abbey which (from at least the twelfth century onwards) carts carrying timber from Paddington, Hendon and Hampstead and plying down Watling Street could use. But with the later development of London by the Romans, well to the east of Westminster, and the building of the wooden Roman London Bridge, it is likely that that part of Watling Street which led from the present Marble Arch southwards towards Westminster was abandoned as a main route, and the eastwards leg of the present Oxford Street and Holborn became the new route towards the City, and became also known as 'Watling Street', as the Ethelred charter establishes (with then the further road-link through the City to the Forum and so to cross the river over the then newly built bridge) see VCH *London* 1/34 and 133; Honeybourne 'Pre-Norman Bridge of London' in *Studies in London History* (Ed. Hollaender and Kellaway) 17 ff.; Merrifield *Roman City of London* 116-7, 124-5.

[13] This makes two Akeman Streets, since the old (former Roman) road from St Albans to Bath via Alchester was also, and more familiarly, known by that name.

[14] Gelling *Boundaries* TLMAS 17 (1954) Pt 3, 102. See also the position of the later Buckingham Water Gate still standing in the Embankment gardens, at the bottom of the slope near the lower end of Villiers Street; and the waterfront excavated near Charing, Vince *Saxon London* 11. The bounds in the Ethelred charter omit the mid-river rights referred to in the bounds in Edgar's charter.

[15] The street apparently took a bend northwestwards at about this point, up the slope in the area where the Haymarket now is, to join up with the line of the present Piccadilly, continuing westwards from there. The bend is probably reflected in the name Charing, which in OE. ('cyrring' or 'cerring') means a bend in a road: Mills *EPN* 71-2. But cf. Robinson *Crispin* 169. The more direct route would have been to continue westwards from the Strand on the line of either the present Pall Mall or the Mall (between which the Leper Hospital of St James was later to stand, from at least Henry II's reign), but beyond that, there were probably marshes and a pond on the line of the Tyburn in the modern Green Park area (see page 41) which would have prevented access that way to Knightsbridge. So the higher level of the first river gravel terrace which ran just below the line of the present Piccadilly, which probably had its 'cow-ford' through the Tyburn, was to be preferred for the Bath road, even if it did mean an ascent up or perhaps *across* the steep Haymarket slope. However it seems likely that some road or track must have led towards and through (say) the present Buckingham Palace site, and so on towards Chelsea (and possibly Fulham?), to which access was needed even in the earliest times; see Vince *Saxon London* 124 and **Map M**, but also see page 59 above for the importance (predominance?) of river traffic in those times.

taken place in the eighth century before being 'rehoused' in King Alfred's time.[16] *Fifthly*, the charter establishes that 'old gallows' (suggesting 'new gallows' also existed?) stood at or near the gateway into the City from Holborn. In this position these must surely have been City gallows, rather than Westminster gallows, and no doubt they were the precursor of the later practice whereby the heads of criminals were exhibited on Newgate. *Sixthly* we learn from the charter that the City boundary (on the Fleet river) was known as 'the alderman's boundary', probably named after an earlier Ethelred, King Alfred's son-in-law who was the Ealdorman of Mercia and to whom Alfred had entrusted the City.[17]

In summary therefore the Abbey now held land in Westminster which (like Middlesex itself, on its larger scale) was bounded by three rivers : in this instance, the Tyburn, the Thames and the Fleet. The fourth Westminster boundary, on the north, was a well-defined military road, except at its eastern end where the Westminster lands actually extended across that road. For a period of 250 years or more the monks continued to hold jurisdiction over all this land,[18] through the present districts of Mayfair (in part), Piccadilly, Soho, Covent Garden, Holborn, the Temple and Fleet Street, as far as the City boundary on the Fleet river. All the above area also became the Parish of St Margaret's, when that church was later built as the local Parish church of Westminster alongside the Abbey itself, probably during the reign of Edward the Confessor (1042-1066).[19]

The later changes to the Eastern boundary

As a result of much later disputes between the Abbey and the Bishops of London as to the limits of their respective jurisdictions and the proper boundaries of the Parish of St Margaret's, the monks of Westminster in 1222 were held to have lost the eastern end of this Westminster territory. The district so excluded stretched from the Fleet river westwards to the western limits of St Giles' parish, and to the church which is now St Mary-le-Strand (its predecessor named at that time the 'Church of the Holy Innocents'). Thereby the Abbey lost the parishes of that church and St Clement Danes; with those parts of the parishes of St Giles and St Andrew, Holborn which they had previously held, and the Savoy. This reduction of territory occurred as a result of a decision [20] in an arbitration which had been sought by both the Bishop and the Abbot in order to resolve their disputes, a decision made by five Papal judges appointed by Pope Honorius III.[21]

---

[16] See page 22 above.

[17] See page 23 above, and Appendix 2, page 167.

[18] Initially subject, in the case of the Berewic, to the tenancy of the military Baynard family: see Robinson *Crispin* 38- 40, and Note 8 above.

[19] Mason *A Truth Universally Acknowledged* SCH 16 (1979)178 ; Rosser *Westminster* 251-2. It is possible that St Margarets was built with the intention on the part of that King (who was elevating the status of the Abbey) of freeing the Abbey monks from their duties on behalf of local Westminster parishioners who had had to use the north transept or aisle of the Abbey as a parish church, and so leaving the monks and particularly the monk-priests among them undisturbed by such 'secular' distractions. ('Secular' priests were those who were concerned with the 'care of souls' and who administered to the laymen of a parish: while monks were 'regulars', i.e. followers of a 'regula' or Rule, and usually had no or few parish duties; but see Chibnall *Monks and Pastoral Work* J.Ecc.H.18 (1967) 165-72). The Abbey monks were granted the 'rectory' of the new parish church, and so were entitled to the great tithes of the parish, which for about 300 years were worth up to £20 p.a., see Rosser *ibid* 253.

[20] *WAM* 12753; *Acta S. Langtoni* (Ed. Major) Cant. and York Soc. 50 (1950) 69. See Rosser ibid. 229.

[21] The extensive Parish of St Margaret's was reduced to the same boundary, on the east, as that to which the monks' lay powers were limited; and it was later reduced still further in about 1250, when the earlier church of St Martin's in the Fields (in the present Trafalgar Square) was given an extension of its parish, and the land in the former St Margaret's parish which lay to the north of Charing was assigned to the

The further limits of the Corridor

As already noticed, the separate ownerships of the estates of Lileston and Tyburn had always prevented the monks' original endowments in the Corridor from forming a solid block of land. In addition, their Westminster estate at its outset did not include the land immediately to its west, between the rivers Tyburn and Westbourne, i.e. the present Pimlico, Ebury and Hyde Park districts. That area was the separate estate known as Eia, probably then still royal land. Later, before the Conquest, it came into the hands of Earl Ralph, Edward the Confessor's nephew, and in that way was still kept under indirect royal control.[22] After the Conquest it was granted by the Conqueror to Geoffrey of Mandeville, one of his magnates, who became the Sheriff of London and Middlesex [23] and was not only a powerful next-door neighbour but also fortunately a supporter of the Abbey. Not until after the Domesday Survey (i.e. more than a hundred years after the Abbey's foundation) were the monks at last given this territory, when Geoffrey before his death granted it to them in 1100 in return for burial rights in the Abbey.[24] When they did in this way receive the Eia estate, the monks held for the first time a contiguous strip of territory (although not a solid block) from the Abbey to the northern limits of Middlesex, through Westminster, Eia, Knightsbridge, Westbourne, Paddington, Hampstead and Hendon: see **Map A**. Before this gift of Eia in 1100, the Abbey's estate in Westminster had remained separated (save by the public roads) from the other Corridor lands which the monks had received in the Abbey's earlier years. To their acquisition of those other lands we can now turn.

---

parish of St Martin. Although the decision in 1222 entailed some loss for the monks of part of their rights in favour of the Bishop of London, Eustace de Fauconberg, its overall effect was a victory for them, since once and for all it freed all the rest of their Westminster estate so that it was officially recognised as 'exempt' from the claims of the Bishop of London. This included the three 'vills of Knightsbridge, Paddington and Westbourne', which were expressly recognised as lying within the parish of St Margaret's by the Papal judges in their decree of 1222: this position seems to have continued even after the later increase in the size of the parish of St Martin's and the corresponding reduction for St Margaret's. 'Exemption' meant that the local Bishop could not exercise his usual episcopal rights over the monastery, such as the right to 'visit' it with all due formality, and to order corrections of any practices in it, or to excommunicate any of its monks, or to summon the Abbot to attend a Diocesan Synod, etc., see Knowles *Growth of Exemption* Downside Rev. 50 (1932) 201-8, 415-20, and *Monastic Order* 585-6; Cheney *Episcopal Visitation* 39 and 42. Although thus freed from control by its local bishop, an exempt monastery became thereby directly subject to the Pope: but the Pope was a more distant danger and might not trouble the monks so easily (but if he did, could be worse). Only five or six other monasteries in England acquired such exemption (and that at different periods).

[22] After Earl Ralph's death, Eia was held by his young son, for whom Edward the Confessor's widow Queen Edith was acting as guardian at the time of the Conquest. See *DB Mdx* 9/1 (f.129c); Stenton *A-S England* 569; VCH *Mdx* 1/100. Since much of Earl Ralph's time had been spent in the western Marches (where he was an ingenious deviser of castle systems against the Welsh) and he held no other land in Middlesex, his solitary tenure of Eia so close to the City and Westminster appears to be a classic case of a 'foothold', granted and kept for the purpose of visits to the centre of power.

[23] See discussion in Brooke & Keir *London* 191-2, 194-7; and Hollister 'Misfortunes of the Mandevilles' in *Monarchy, Magnates and Institutions* 118; Round *G. de Mandeville* 37-8.

[24] Mason *WA Charters* No 436; Harvey *WA Estates* 38, 373. Geoffrey called Eia a 'maneriolum', a little manor. Although it was rated at 10 hides (which was quite large compared with many of the estates round Westminster and London), it was small compared with some of his large possessions in Essex and eleven other counties, including Edmonton and Enfield in Middlesex; VCH *Mdx.*1/111, and Doree *DB and Edmonton Hundred* 7-10. See also Mason *ibid.* No 462 (gift by Geoffrey to the Abbey, on the advice of his second wife who perhaps knew best what his soul really needed, of the church at Hurley, Berks, which later became a Priory dependent on the Abbey); Robinson *Crispin* 32-3. The Mandevilles were the only noble family which showed an interest in the Abbey for a period of several generations: Mason *Donors of WA Chs* MP 8: 2 (1987) 28 and 33. For the Westminster DB entry, see **Plate 7**, p. 86.

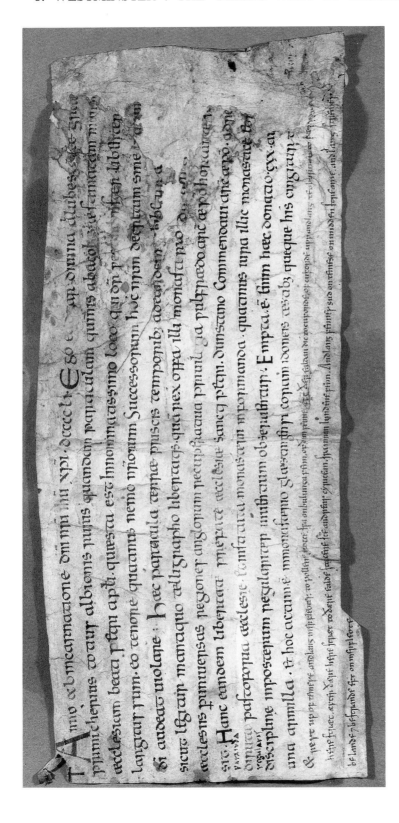

Plate 7. An early 'copy' of the grant by King Edgar of the five-hide district of Westminster to the 'church of the blessed Peter'. The main text (in the large letters) is in Latin, with forged interpolations, but the clearly genuine 'bounds' of Westminster appear in Old English in the small script at the bottom. The 'bounds' are translated in Appendix 2 at page 166.

See page 79

TERRA SCI PETRI WESTMON *In Osvlvestane*

In Villa ubi fedet æccla S PETRI. tenet abb ejdē
loci. xiii. hið 7 dim. Tra. ē ad xi. car. Ad dnium
ptiñ. ix. hidæ 7 i. uirg. 7 ibi fuꝗ. iiii. car. Villi hñt. vi.
car. 7 i. car plus poꞇ fieri. Ibi. ix. uilti ꝗſꝗ de. i. uirg.
7 i. uilts de. i. hida. 7 ix. uilti ꝗſꝗ de dim uirg. 7 i. coꞇ
de. v. ac. 7 xl. i. coꞇ ꝗ reddꞇ ꝑ anñ. xl. ſoꞇ ꝑ ortis ſuis.
Ptū. xi. car. Paſta ad pecuñ uillæ. Silua. c porĉ.
7 xxv. dom militū abbis 7 alioꝛ hōum. qui reddꞇ
viii. ſoꞇ ꝑ annū. In totis ualent uaꞇ. x. lib. Qdo
receꝓ. fimiliꞇ. T.R.E. xii. lib. Hoc ᴍ fuit 7 eſt
in dnio æcclæ S PETRI. Weſtmonaſterij.

In ead uilla teñ Bainiarð. iii. hið de abbe. Tra. ē
ad. ii. car. 7 ibi fuꝗ in dnio. 7 i. coꞇ. Silua. c porĉ.
Paſta ad pecuñ. Ibi. iiii. arpenni uineæ. nouiꞇ plant.
In totis ualent uaꞇ. lx. ſoꞇ. Qdo receꝓ. xx. ſoꞇ. T R E.
vi. lib. H tra jacuit 7 jacet in æccla S PETRI.

HAMESTEDE teñ abb S PEꝜI. iiii. hið. Tra. iii.
car. Ad dñiū ptiñ. iii. hið 7 dim. 7 ibi. ē. i. car. Villi
hñt. i. car. 7 alia poꞇ fieri. Ibi. i. uilt de. i. uirg. 7 v.
borð de. i. uirg. 7 i. ſeru. Silua. c porĉ. Int totū
uaꞇ. l. ſoꞇ. Qdo receꝓ. fimiꞇ. T.R.E. c. ſoꞇ.

In ead uilla teñ Rañ peurel ſub abbe. i. hidā
de tra uilloꝛ. Tra dim car. 7 ibi eſt. H tra ualuit
7 uaꞇ. v. ſoliꝺ. Hoc ᴍ totū fimul jacuit 7 jacet in dnio
æcclæ S PETRI.

HANDONE. teñ abb S PETRI. ꝑ xx. hið ſe defenð.
Tra. xvi. car. Ad dñiū ptiñ. x. hide. 7 ibi fuꝗ. iii.
car. Villi hñt. viii. car. 7 ꝟ adhuc poſſ fieri. Ibi
pbr hꞇ. i. uirg. 7 iii. uilti ꝗſꝗ dim ħ. 7 vii. uilti
ꝗſꝗ. i. uirg. 7 xvi. uilti. ꝗſꝗ dim uirg. 7 xii. borð
ꝗ teneꝗ dim hið. 7 vi. coꞇ 7 i. ſeru. Ptū. ii. boū.
Silua. mille porĉ. 7 x. ſoꞇ. In totis ualent uaꞇ. viii.
lib. Qdo receꝓ. fimiliꞇ. T.R.E. xii. lib. Hoc ᴍ
jacuit 7 jacet in dnio eccle S PETRI.

LAND OF ST. PETER'S OF WESTMINSTER

In OSSULSTONE Hundred

1 M. In the village where St. Peter's Church stands the Abbot of that
monastery holds 13½ hides. The land is for 11 ploughs. 9 hides
and 1 virgate belong to the lordship; 4 ploughs there. The
villagers have 6 ploughs; 1 more plough possible.
    9 villagers with 1 virgate each; 1 villager with 1 hide;
       9 villagers with ½ virgate each; 1 cottager with 5 acres;
       41 cottagers, who pay 40s a year for their gardens.
    Meadow for 11 ploughs; pasture for the village livestock;
    woodland, 100 pigs; 25 houses of the Abbot's men-at-arms
    and other men, who pay 8s a year.
Total value £10; when acquired the same; before 1066 £12.
    This manor was and is in the lordship of St. Peter's
Church, Westminster.

In the same village Baynard holds 3 hides from the Abbot.
The land is for 2 ploughs; they are there, in lordship.
    1 cottager.
    Woodland, 100 pigs; pasture for the livestock;
       4 *arpents* of newly planted vines.
Total value 60s; when acquired 20s; before 1066 £6.
    This land lay and lies in (the lands of) St. Peter's Church.

The Abbot of St. Peter's holds HAMPSTEAD. 4 hides. Land for 3
ploughs. 3½ hides belong to the lordship; 1 plough there.
The villagers have 1 plough; another possible.
    1 villager with 1 virgate; 5 smallholders with 1 virgate; 1 slave.
    Woodland, 100 pigs.
In total, value 50s; when acquired the same; before 1066, 100s.

In the same village Ranulf Peverel holds under the Abbot 1 hide
of villagers' land. Land for ½ plough; it is there.
    The value of this land was and is 5s.
    The whole of this manor lay and lies in the lordship of
St. Peter's Church.

The Abbot of St. Peter's holds HENDON. It answers for 20 hides.
Land for 16 ploughs. 10 hides belong to the lordship; 3 ploughs
there. The villagers have 8 ploughs; a further 5 possible.
    A priest has 1 virgate; 3 villagers, ½ hide each; 7 villagers,
       1 virgate each; 16 villagers, ½ virgate each; 12 smallholders
       who hold ½ hide; 6 cottagers; 1 slave.
    Meadow for 2 oxen; woodland, 1000 pigs, and 10s too.
Total value £8; when acquired the same; before 1066 £12.
    This manor lay and lies in the lordship of St. Peter's Church.

Plate 8. The Domesday Book entries for Westminster, Hampstead and Hendon. The estates held by the two
Normans, William Baynard in Westminster and Ranulf Peverel in Hampstead, are shown as separate entries.
The 13½ hides in Westminster at this date (1086) included the areas now known as Knightsbridge, Westbourne
and Paddington. Note the detailed villagers' holdings.   See pages 84, 87 and 118-9

CHAPTER 7

Hendon in the Northern Weald

For the new monks of Westminster, the first five 'hides' of land around their Abbey were not enough. Their next endowments were four separate tracts in the Hendon area.

The weald which lies north of the Hampstead ridge and fronts onto Watling Street had clearly been divided into a number of different estates before the middle of the tenth century. It only became unified again in the next century, probably well before the Norman Conquest. Certainly by the time of Domesday in 1086 there was only one recognised unit, namely the large Norman 'manor of Hendon', which was assessed at 20 hides,[1] and had been formed (as we now know) from the various smaller tracts which had been firmly in the possession of the Abbey since long before the Conquest. One can identify the four component parts of the whole district before about 1000 AD, each held as a separate estate with its own name and with most of its boundaries reasonably identifiable.

The area covered by these four tracts ranged (in a northwards direction) from the borders of Hampstead at the northern end of the present Hampstead Heath, where the ground drops away steeply from the shelf on which the hamlet of North End now sits, to a boundary as far north as Deans Brook and Hendon Wood beyond the steep escarpment of Highwood and Holcombe Hills.[2] Each of the four estates is named and (in whole or in parts) identified in one or more genuine records: and even though some of the more peripheral charters are spurious in whole or in part, one can be fairly certain that this overall picture of a district having four constituent tracts is correct. These four tracts were named Lotheresleage, 'Hendon' (which I will call 'the smaller'),[3] Bleccanham and Codanhlaw. Some of the details of their historical geography are complicated, but the outline is clear.

(i)   Lotheresleage   Maps N and B

Although it has sometimes been wrongly dismissed as a lost and unidentifiable tract, Lotheresleage clearly occupied the northern quarter of the later manor and parish of Hendon. It first emerges in about 957, when King Eadwig (Edgar's elder brother and predecessor) granted two areas of land, in 'Loceresleage' (sic) and in his adjoining royal estate at 'Tunworthe' (later known as 'Kingsbury', on the *western* side of Watling Street) to his 'faithful *minister*' called Lyfing.[4]   The bounds of these lands are described in Old

---

[1] For the Hendon record in Domesday Book (*Mdx* 4/12; f.128d), see **Plate 8** opposite.

[2] See **Map N**. For the texts of the various 'Bounds' in the charters, see Appendix 2, page 166.

[3] This 'smaller Hendon' in the tenth century must be distinguished from the larger Hendon which constituted the full Norman manor in the eleventh century, as described in Domesday Book. It is not known when the four constituent parts of the larger Hendon were assembled to form the one unit, but it seems certain that this occurred *before* the Conquest: the form of the Hendon entry in Domesday Book indicates this, since it refers to the larger 'Hendon' in the period immediately *before* the Conquest as though it was one whole unit even at that time. The forged charters created in the twelfth century (see pages 60-1) cannot be relied on for this purpose, although they support the thesis; but there seems to be no other reliable evidence on this issue during the first half of the eleventh century.

[4] Sawyer *A-S Charters* No 645; Gelling *Early Charters of Thames Valley* No 220. It is not known who

English, within a genuine Latin charter, and as interpreted by the English Place Names Society are shown (somewhat tentatively) on **Map N**.[5]

But within about twenty years later the monks of Westminster received from Archbishop Dunstan two areas of land, both at Lotheresleage : one whose size or assessment is described as six 'cassati' (also the same as 'hides'), which the Archbishop had earlier bought from King Edgar for 70 gold shillings; and another tract of three cassati, which the Archbishop had later bought from Edgar's first son and immediate successor, King Edward 'the Martyr', for 30 pounds of silver. Although these two purchases by the Archbishop were made at widely differing times, he seems (on one interpretation) to have given them together in one grant to the monks of Westminster.[6] This gift by Dunstan was said to have been made in 977-978, the second or third years of King Edward's reign. Again certain boundaries (for either the whole area covered in this gift, or more likely for just the second of the two tracts) are described in Old English in the 'charter' which records Dunstan's gift, and the effect of these, based again on the English Place Names Society's interpretation, is also attempted in **Map N**.[7]

It is clear from **Map N** that the lands given to Lyfing and the lands given to the Abbey (*in so far as* they are described in the bounds in the second 'charter') are not identical or even overlapping, but contiguous. It is probably impossible to answer or reconcile the conflicting issues of either history or geography [8] which this result gives rise to, but the

---

the thegn Lyfing was. The total area granted was nine 'mansae', including the Tunworth tract. We have already met the 'mansa' as an measurement (whether of area or fiscal liability) in connection with the Westminster Berewic: it is to be equated with the hide, see note 6 below. *Leah* (-leage) means woodland with glades or a clearing in woodland, which tends to confirm the nature of the main feature of this wooded area. The full name Lotheresleage may mean the *leah* of 'Hlothere', a Kentish personal name (cf. Gelling *PNs in the Countryside* 99 and 296) and also a royal one; or (more romantically) the *leah* of 'robbers'! For the Weald as it still was a thousand years later, see **Plate 9**, page 97.

[5] The bounds have been interpreted in the EPNS's volume, Gover *PN Mdx.* 219-20. They are very difficult to unravel, and no blame can be attached to any unsuccessful attempt to make sense of them. After examination of the ground and maps, I am sceptical of several aspects of that interpretation, but I would find it hard to put forward reliable alternative solutions of the many problems in them. On the other hand there is a vitriolic attack (almost worthy of J.H.Round) on the EPNS authors and their interpretation, made by Mr Holliday (Grange Museum, Brent; Holliday Papers), but his own solutions, although backed by much local knowledge, seem to me to be equally, if not more, vulnerable. Unfortunately Mr H. is dead, or he could have further explained his own interpretation. I have sought to reproduce on **Map N** the arguable interpretations made by the EPNS: but I retain several doubts.

[6] Sawyer *A-S Charters* Nos 1451 and 894. The latter charter (the Ethelred Telligraph again, see page 63 and Appendix 1) refers to no more than the three cassati (in fact calling them 'mansae', so equating the two terms), but says that they were, not '*at*' Lotheresleage, but '*next to*' (iuxta) Lotheresleage; which is odd. It is also arguable, on the wording of Sawyer *A-S Chs.* No 1451, that the two areas (of six cassati and three cassati) were given *separately* to the Abbey by Dunstan. Dunstan's predecessor Bryhtmer in the three cassati is said to have been a (royal?) huntsman, which again seems to emphasise the woods in this area, see Appendix 1, page 164. But where meanwhile had Lyfing's title got to?

[7] See EPNS *PN Mdx.* 220, in relation to the bounds in Sawyer *ibid.* No 1451. But I find it difficult to see how the bounds in the two grants can relate to areas which are 'clearly the same', as the authors seem to assert, since on their interpretation (if I have understood them right) the areas are, when one works them out, adjacent and therefore must be different. See again **Map N**. In view of what I say below, it would make more sense to regard the two *grants*, but not the two sets of *bounds*, as relating to the same land. The *bounds* in the Westminster grant do not appear to relate to the whole of the land granted.

[8] Eg. Did the monks in fact receive the whole Lyfing land initially? Do the A-S bounds in Sawyer No 1451 relate to the area of the whole six-plus-three tracts, or only the final three? Were the bounds in that charter defective? How does one explain the fact that the 'Hendon boundary' which is actually referred to in the charter granting the land to Westminster (Sawyer *ibid.* No 1451) appears to be on the *north* side of the Lotheresleage tract in the Lyfing charter (as interpreted in **Map N**)?

general conclusion seems to be fairly clear: it is likely that the region was known loosely as Lotheresleage and that by at least 988 the monks had received, on at least the east side of Watling Street, the whole of this northern part of the later manor of Hendon.[9]

It may be significant that Lyfing had been given not only land on the *east* side of Watling Street, but also considerable land (in 'Tunworthe' or Kingsbury) on the *west* side of the Street, and that later the Norman manor of Hendon also included an enclave (albeit much smaller by then) on that west side of the road: see **Map A**. This enclave was an important piece of land since it lay on either side of both the Brent river and its substantial tributary the Silk stream, and included part of the confluence of those rivers (now the Brent Reservoir or 'Welsh Harp'). It was unusual for an early estate boundary to cross such an obvious boundary-line as the great road, so as to feature on both sides of the road: no other estate along the whole length of Watling Street, on its northern 'leg' within Middlesex, did as much.[10] Since we have no other explanation about the process by which the monks must have obtained that western enclave, it seems possible that this gift by Dunstan (or even other gifts) extended to all the land which had been previously given to Lyfing, including all his land on the west side of the road, and that the Abbey subsequently lost all but that important enclave.[11] There is no indication that Lyfing or any successor of his laid claim to any part of the area, either then or at any later time. One can only assume that perhaps Lyfing voluntarily surrendered or was made to surrender all the land which had been given to him, or that he died, and that then the land was free for further disposal.

At all events Lotheresleage clearly appears among the monks' earliest possessions. Apart from the charters which contain authentic material, there is the confirmation that when one comes to the great series of forged charters [12] about 130 years later, based on the 'tradition' at that time at Westminster, in some of them Lotheresleage (with Bleccanham as well, see below) is listed as one of the first-named possessions of the monks in Middlesex, after their main Westminster estate.

(ii) 'Hendon' (the 'smaller')   Map N

There is no doubt that south of Lotheresleage there was an early estate called Hendon, a smaller tract than the later manor which received the same name. Almost certainly it filled

---

[9] If anyone is still interested in the problem, the best (but still questionable) solution which I can suggest is that the two estates (the Lyfing one and the Westminster one) *were in fact the same* (contrary to the EPNS interpretation of the Lyfing bounds, but in *accordance* with the authors' statement as to their similarity). See further Note 11 below. A step leading to this conclusion is the inference that the OE. bounds in the Westminster grant relate only to the three cassati, and that the boundaries of the six cassati (which the monks also clearly received) were not defined in any surviving document. But this still leaves the question as to the exact position of the 'Hendon boundary' (see Note 8 above); as to which the only apparent possibility is that the EPNS identification of the two streams at Burnt Oak and Colindeep is the wrong way round. But that in turn gives rise to yet other seemingly unresolvable problems.

[10] But whether Edgware could be another exception is not clear (see page 61). For the confluence of the Brent and Silk rivers, see **Plate 10**, page 98.

[11] It is a necessary condition of this hypothesis that the description contained in the OE bounds in the document (Sawyer *A-S Chs.* No 1451) recording Dunstan's gift of the two areas applies only to the second of the lands so given, i.e. the three cassati only. This may be more likely in any event, having regard to the wording of the document. It is of course noticeable that it was nine mansae which were given to Lyfing, and nine cassati later to the Abbey.

[12] i.e. the ones forged by Prior Osbert de Clare, see page 61 above. Sawyer *A-S Charters* Nos 1293 and 774 are two such charters, in which Lotheresleage appears very high on the list. It also appears first, after Westminster, in No 894 (the Ethelred 'Telligraph', see page 63 above and Appendix 1, page 164).

the space between the boundary of Lotheresleage [13] and the curving path of the River Brent. It is fortunate for us that the Anglo-Saxon bounds [14] of the lands at Lotheresleage which were given to the Abbey by Dunstan in 977 refer specifically to the 'Hendon boundary', so recognising that there was already such a territory with that name. This is the only reference at that time to the name, and it is noticeable that the name does not recur in any authentic source until it reappears in Domesday Book in 1086 as the name of the much larger Norman manor.[15] Apart from this indirect reference to a Hendon boundary on its northern side, there are no Anglo-Saxon bounds for the 'smaller' Hendon in any surviving charter. But its southern and eastern limits were clearly established by Nature, in the form of rivers (as so often in this part of Middlesex), which separated this smaller Hendon area from the next estate of Bleccanham (see below).

However both the name of Hendon and the associated archaeological evidence establish quite clearly that there was indeed an early settlement in the central Hendon area, in the very place where one would expect it, namely the natural hill where the Parish Church was built. The name 'Hendon', meaning in Old English 'high hill',[16] has a form which suggests that a settlement was made there even before 800; and black handmade pottery in fair quantities has been found at a site close to the Parish Church, of a type which is dated to the sixth to ninth centuries.[17]

The connection between this early settlement and the monks of Westminster in the tenth century is probably confirmed by other charter evidence, even though that evidence does not refer to the name Hendon. The Ethelred 'Telligraph' (see page 63 and Appendix 1) lists the lands with which the monks had been endowed, in the following order:- the monastery itself; the land round the monastery; Lotheresleage; Hampstead; two *unnamed estates;* Codanhlaw... .[18] It seems likely from this positioning that the two unnamed estates were associated with or close to those named round them in the list. The Archbishop, Dunstan, is said by the charter to have bought these two estates separately, from respectively his reformist colleague,[19] Bishop Ethelwold of Winchester (an estate amounting to ten mansae) and from 'a royal soldier' called Wulfnoth [20] (another ten mansae), for a sum totalling 80 pounds of proved silver, and to have then given the two

---

[13] Wherever that boundary in fact lay, see above and particularly Note 9 and **Map N**.

[14] In Sawyer *A-S Charters* No 1451; EPNS *PN Mdx* 220. For their terms, see Appendix 2, page 168.

[15] The name 'Hendon' appears of course in some of the retrospective charters forged by Osbert de Clare, because by his day (the twelfth century) 'Hendon' was widely known and used as a name. One can see that Osbert, in forging the two so-called Great Charters of Dunstan and of Edgar (Sawyer Nos 1293 and 774), seems to confirm the theory that there were four component parts of this whole area in the tenth century ; and in those other charters which he attributed to King Edward the Confessor and which happen to contain lists of the Abbey estates (Nos 1043 and 1040), Hendon has become one single unit (i.e. the complete area of all four components, but without any mention of their names). In No 1039 (an unprinted charter attributed to the Confessor, which seems not to have been one of Osbert's, but is probably spurious though with some authentic material in it) one finds the description 'Hendon with its territories Bleccanham, Codenhlawe and Lothereslege', see Robinson *Crispin* 40: if the charter is aiming to be logical, the 'Hendon' here should be the original component Hendon, not the larger unit composed of all four components.

[16] In OE, 'Heah' means high; 'dun' means hill. The form of the ending is particularly common in central Middlesex, with Willesden, Neasden, Uxendon and Horsedon in addition to Hendon.

[17] Gelling *Place Names in the Landscape* 152; Taylor (Ed) *A Place in Time* 52-3, 57.

[18] Sawyer *ibid.* No 894.

[19] Associated with him in the great monastic reformation during Edgar's reign, see page 58 above. But the reputed size of these estates (20 mansae, in total) is difficult to reconcile.

[20] King Edgar had a 'faithful minister' of this name, see Sawyer *A-S Charters* No 722.

tracts to the monks of Westminster. It is almost certain that at least one, but more probably both, of these unnamed estates constituted the earlier and smaller area then called Hendon. This inference was certainly the one which became enshrined in the later Westminster 'tradition', because when the so-called Great Charter of Dunstan [21] was forged about 130 years later by Osbert de Clare, it was specifically stated in that charter that *both* of these estates were 'in the place called Hendon'.

Since at the time of Domesday [22] there was a priest present in Hendon (meaning the full Norman manor), one can with assurance infer that there was already an early church there. If so, it would certainly have been at the hill-site of the later Parish Church, where the earlier Anglo-Saxon settlement lay. It is noticeable that the Domesday Survey records four separate priests in Gore Hundred, where all the four constituent tracts of Hendon lay and where there were only three other main settlements and five manors at the time of Domesday, This means that each of the four settlements in Gore (Harrow, Kingsbury, Stanmore and Hendon) already had its own priest and presumably its own church.[23] This contrasts completely with the adjoining Hundred of Ossulston, where there were no less than 23 settlements referred to, but only one priest mentioned in the whole of that Hundred. Since most of Ossulston was held by the Church (the Bishop, the Canons of St Paul's, and the Abbot of Westminster Abbey), it is likely that most of the priestly ministration to the lay people in those areas was done by visiting priests or priest-monks from St Paul's and the Abbey.[24]

(iii) Bleccanham   Maps E, N and P

The land south of the River Brent, stretching towards the Hampstead border at the present North End was called Bleccanham (in various spellings). The name is said to mean 'Blaecca's homestead', presumably the name of a remote inhabitant.[25] There is no doubt

---

[21] Sawyer *ibid* No 1293. Both that charter and another spurious one, No 1295 (relating only to the gift of the smaller Hendon by Dunstan to Westminster Abbey), which has not been attributed to Osbert de Clare, also confirm or at least repeat the story that Dunstan bought the two estates from Ethelwold and Wulfnoth, and then gave them, to the Abbey, see *O.S.Facs*. ii. Westminster 5.

[22] DB *Mdx* 4/12 (f. 128d). The earliest structures surviving in the present Hendon Church are in the chancel, dating from the mid-12th century. The spectacular Norman-style font has been dated to the second half of that century, see Taylor (Ed.) *A Place in Time* 70. No church in Mdx is actually referred to in DB, although 18 priests are.

[23] But there are no surviving A-S. structures, save perhaps at the 'old church' of St Andrew at Kingsbury, see pages 66-7 above.

[24] See eg. **Map B**. In general individual priests were not always resident on church lands in A-S times, see Page *Churches of DB Survey* Archaeologia 66 (1915) 62, because the monks, monk-priests or priests of the relevant religious house served the outlying communities, sometimes at the house itself or in the settlements (see Dudley 'The Monastic Priest' in *Monastic Studies II,* Ed. Loades, 186). But in contrast we have seen that in Gore Hundred both Hendon and Harrow were Church lands and yet had their resident priests by the time of Domesday. In counties like Suffolk and Surrey there was a church and a priest in almost every village, according to DB, see Blair 'Local Churches in DB and before' in *DB Studies* (Ed. Holt)265. According to Godfrey *The Church in A-S England* 322, DB only recorded a church when it was significant for the purposes of revenue, but with that as a hypothesis, it is difficult to see why there were so many omissions in Middlesex. For Hampstead's dependence on the Hendon church, see page 99. Perhaps Hendon Church had earlier been either one of the A-S minster churches, or one of the second wave of churches in substantial vills, which took their place, see Mason 'WA and its Parishes' in *Monastic Studies* II (Ed. J. Loades) 44; Blair 'From Minster to Parish Church' in *Minsters and P. Churches* (Ed. Blair); Blair 'Minster Churches in the Landscape' in *A-S Settlements* (Ed. Hooke) 35.

[25] EPNS *PN Mdx* 57. Other more enthusiastic local historians have read this name as meaning 'a blackened or burnt homestead', with suitably sensational effects, see Hitchin-Kemp *Notes on a Survey of*

that it belonged to the monks from an early date. We know both the name and and the probable extent of the estate from a description of the Anglo-Saxon bounds which are included in a short Latin grant contained within a composite set of charters.[26] The grant is undated, but by it King Edgar gives, or purports to give, *five mansiunculi* (again hides, but little ones this time) in Bleccanham to the Abbey. Its date therefore is before 975. Most of the boundaries (shown on **Map N**) are quite clear : Watling Street; the river Brent; the stream now called the Mutton Brook; the Finchley boundary; and finally on the south, the stretch of land from 'Sandgate' [27] (the clearly identifiable place where the three boundaries of the estates of Hampstead and Finchley met Bleccanham, near the sharp corner of the present Wildwood Road) towards North End and then the Sandy Road (the northern edge of the West Heath, facing now into Golders Hill Park).

But from the Sandy Road westwards a doubt arises. On the one hand, the verbal description given in the charter bounds is quite clear: the line follows "the Hampstead boundary to the boundary-stream". The 'boundary-stream' is almost certainly the northern arm of the many sources of the Kilbourne-Westbourne stream, as shown on **Map P**.[28] This rises on the *south* side of the hill which became known later as 'Child's Hill' [29]

Hendon 160, 172.

[26] Sawyer *A-S Charters* No 1450: the main version of this document is a compilation made (or at least copied) in the twelfth century, of 'charters' relating to four different areas, Westminster, Bleccanham, Lotheresleage and Hampstead. The Sawyer description of the document is inadequate. Although Edgar is identified in the Bleccanham passage as the King who gave (or rather 'restored') five tracts in Bleccanham to the monks, there can be no assurance that the probably genuine bounds expressed in Anglo-Saxon were correct *at that time,* as opposed to some earlier period. There was possibly a much earlier history for Bleccanham, see text under 'Codanhlaw' at page 95, below. Keynes *Diplomas of Aethelred* 109, 143, 245-6 speaks of Sawyer No 1450 being suspicious, but it is not clear which parts are being referred to. Parts of Sawyer 1450 are *more* than 'suspicious'. Other parts are undoubtedly genuine copies of genuine material; e.g. there is a separate and authenticated document (the Ethelred charter for Hampstead, see page 100 below) which is copied into Sawyer 1450, so to that extent alone there can be no argument but that Sawyer 1450 is accurate and (as a copy) genuine. If one is not careful, it could be a classic case of the wheat blowing away with the chaff (see page 63 above). For the text of the bounds, see Appendix 2, page 166.

[27] The 'Sandgate' is a precisely apt description. This is exactly the point at which the Claygate beds meet the London Clay (see page 28 and **Map E**): with resulting springs breaking out just inside the southern border of the present Hampstead Heath Extension. See **Plate 12**, page 110. The same 'springing' occurred a little to the west at North End, where one of the old wells of Hampstead used to exist (but no longer), see Evans *Geology of Hampstead* Hampstead Annual (1904-5) 77, and further westwards in Golders Hill Park, where it still flows; and again at Blacket's or (by an early spoonerism?) Placket's Well, near the present junction of Platt's Lane and West Heath Road; etc.

[28] EPNS *PN Mdx* 8, 221. But see VCH Mdx 9/3. The map in Waller's article on the *Tybourne and Westbourne* in TLMAS 6 (1890) 244, at page 272 is a map personally drawn by Mr Waller and is probably the best surviving factual evidence of the old 'boundary stream'; it was also accepted by Barton in his map in *Lost Rivers,* inside back cover. However the frontispiece map by Newton in Park *Topog. of Hampstead* (1814) shows a quite different line for a Kilbourne-Westbourne source in the West End area (and incidentally only *from* West End, not in the region leading *to* West End from Child's Hill). Why is this? It seems (suspiciously) to follow roughly the same line as appears in Rocque's Environs map of 1745 (shown conveniently in Barratt *Annals of Hampstead* 1/72-3). Rocque's map is a masterpiece in its general effects, but notoriously unreliable as regards local detail. But in any case the Rocque/Newton line appears to be a very different feeder-stream from the 'boundary stream', and one which Barton has also shown partially in his map in addition to the real 'boundary stream'. There are other reasons as well why the Waller line is clearly more reliable as first-hand evidence, even though it is considerably later than the others. Unfortunately the first OS. map of 1822 gives little away.

[29] The name 'Child's Hill' can be deceptive. The settlement known by that name (only since the sixteenth century, so far as is known for certain, but since the Child family went back at least to the

(named subsequently after a family farming near there in the fourteenth century [30]). On the other hand all later boundaries, for both parishes and local authorities, appear to skirt round and away from the top section of Child's Hill on its *northwestern* side and not to circle right round the hill or link up with that stream : instead, they have diverged towards the west, as shown on **Map P**.   However, as already stated, the Anglo-Saxon bounds are very clear in stating that the boundary joined and followed the stream. This surely must mean that the boundary went *right round the apex of the hill*, on one side or the other, in order to link up with the stream.[31] For reasons given below in the text about 'Codanhlaw', it seems more likely that the Anglo-Saxon boundary passed round Child's Hill on its *east* side, rather than on the *north and west* sides.

The effect would be that the top of the hill, instead of being within Hampstead (as it later was), would have been within a Hendon component tract in the tenth century. This is perhaps confirmed by the fact that much later in the early fourteenth century there was definitely a continuing dispute as to where the Hampstead-Hendon boundary near this point really was.[32]   That dispute may well reflect doubts which had arisen because of an earlier change of the boundary round the hill, when the line of the 'boundary stream' was abandoned (as it seems to have been) in favour of a more northerly (and modern) line, as

---

early fourteenth century and probably before, the name is likely to have been used for the settlement well before the sixteenth) lay towards the *bottom* of the hill and has always been within the area of Hendon (manor and parish). But the hill itself at first climbed steeply up into (as I argue below) 'Codanhlaw', which became part of the Norman Hendon; and then, after some early change of boundary between Hampstead and Hendon at this point, I suggest that the *top end* of the hill became part of Hampstead; so that its summit is still Hampstead's 'Telegraph Hill' (famous for its telegraph from the end of the seventeenth century, but now lost to view among the houses above the top end of Platts Lane).

[30] Eg. Richard Child in 1312, see Vol. 2.

[31] One of the relevant pieces of evidence about the position of this boundary is a reference in one of the Hampstead charters to a cucking pool in the northwestern corner of the Hampstead estate, see page 108 below. Although this is probably to be located on or near the Kilbourne-Westbourne stream, it is ironic that the very first Ordnance Survey map of this area shows another pool (on the *west* side of Watling Street) actually level with the *modern* boundary between Hampstead and Hendon. It is (as marked) the source of the small stream called the Slade which used to flow (but no longer, see *VCH Mdx 9/3*) *westwards* from Shooters Hill to join the Brent (see **Map N**). But does the existence of that pool at that point mean that the original Anglo-Saxon boundary was in the same position as the modern Hampstead/Hendon boundary? But there is no evidence of any stream flowing from the area *east of the road* along or near the modern boundary, as both the Bleccanham charter and one of the Hampstead charters (see page 105) would require. (An existing *northwards-flowing* stream, from the Childs Hill/Golders Hill area on its way to the Brent, is irrelevant for this purpose). It is true that the fields on the *eastern* side of Watling Street, in the northwest corner of the Hampstead estate, were still called (800 years later, in the 1762 Hampstead Manor Map) 'the Slads', which appears to link them with the Slade stream or its source pool. But this was probably because the *westward-bound* Slade began there, not because there was any Slade stream running *eastwards* (as the Bleccanham, and also Hampstead, bounds would require) on the *east* side of the road. One important confirmation that the 'boundary stream' of the charters was indeed the western source stream of the Westbourne, and not the westwards-flowing Slade, is the fact that the whole of the south-eastern boundary of the later Templars' northern estate in Hampstead appears to follow fairly closely the line of the source stream as drawn by Mr Waller, see **Map P** and the excellent map at VCH *Mdx* 9/94. This seems to confirm that this stream was and no doubt had previously been a significant boundary, since the near-equivalence of these two lines cannot be dismissed as a mere coincidence.

[32] The dispute related to the questions whether certain tenants of the Abbey (including the Child family referred to above) should be regarded as being entirely within Hendon or partly within Hampstead, and to which manor they should pay rent. It sounds as if the dispute was a very old one. The evidence for all this is contained in detailed surveys made by the monks of their manors of Hampstead and Hendon in 1312 and 1321 AD respectively: see Vol. 2.

shown on **Map P.**[33]

No obvious place for a Saxon settlement in 'Bleccanham' has been identified, and the name itself later became lost, except as a locative name for a well-known local family [34] in the early thirteenth and fourteenth centuries (and no doubt earlier). Since on any view 'Bleccanham' was an early name, one might expect the settlement to have been on a raised site, as for example Harrow, Hampstead and Hendon were. Within the area south of the Brent river and its tributary the present Mutton Brook, the low hill at Temple Fortune is the most likely candidate.[35] But no archaeological evidence of this supposition has yet been discovered, so far as is known.

The date when Bleccanham may have *first* become associated with the Abbey is discussed immediately below, under 'Codanhlaw'.

(iv)   Codanhlaw   Maps N and P

Even an estate which has been 'lost' for a thousand years can sometimes be found.

There can be little doubt that an estate (of three 'cassati') called Codanhlaw was granted to the monks by Archbishop Dunstan [36] before 988 (when the Archbishop died). Its name however, in that form, later completely died out, except in Westminster 'tradition'. Both its position in the list of estates mentioned in the important charter called King Ethelred's Telligraph,[37] and the strong later Westminster tradition about it,[38] suggest that this estate was emphatically regarded as being in the Hendon area. But if it was indeed within the region of Hendon, the question must arise, Where was it? The three other areas nearby, namely Lotheresleage, the 'smaller' Hendon, and Bleccanham, appear by their bounds to cover the whole of the area which became known later as the Manor of Hendon at the time of the Domesday Survey: that is, from the Edgware boundary in the north to the Hampstead boundary in the south. So where is there room for Codanhlaw ? Of course it may be that Codanhlaw was somewhere quite different, nowhere near Hendon. That would dispose of the problem *within* the Hendon region, but still leave the even more difficult questions, Where then was it *outside* the Hendon region?, and Why were the Westminster monks in the twelfth century so mistaken about the whereabouts of the small estate (not a matter for forgery), when they were about 850 years nearer the problem than we are?

Working on the hypothesis that it must indeed have been within the neighbourhood of Hendon in the period before 988, one can look to see if there is any way in which the apparent absence of a named locality for it could be explained. Clearly if there is no such possible way, then that would be fairly persuasive in favour of the view that Codanhlaw must have been somewhere quite different, well away from the Hendon area, whatever evidence or tradition there was that it was part of the Norman manor of Hendon.

---

[33] See under 'Codanhlaw' below.

[34] The earliest known reference is probably Thomas de Blechenham in 1226, Hardy and Page *Lon. & Mdx Fines* 1/59.

[35] See page 29 above.

[36] Dunstan had apparently bought it from another of Edgar's 'ministers' called Eadnoth, in order presumably to bestow it on the monks, see Sawyer *A-S Charters* No 894 (Ethelred's Telligraph), Appendix 1 below, and No 1039 ('Edward the Confessor's Telligraph', Note 15 above).

[37] See Note immediately above. For Codanhlaw's *position* in the list in Ethelred's Telligraph, directly following the smaller Hendon, and preceding those other estates in Middlesex which were outside the Corridor, such as Hanwell, Sunbury etc., see page 90 above and Appendix 1, page 164.

[38] Eg. Sawyer *ibid.* Nos 1293 (one of Osbert's) and 1039 (partly spurious, but probably recording some accurate material: see also Note 15 above).

Now it is a curious fact that Bleccanham was regarded later by some as having been a named possession (and indeed probably the very first estate) of a church at Westminster even long *before* the monastery was founded by King Edgar. For example the first historian of the Abbey, Sulcard, who was a monk writing in the period shortly after the Norman Conquest, stated that Offa, the King of Essex in the early eighth century, gave Bleccanham to an early church at Westminster.[39] If that had indeed been the case, it is at least possible that the Anglo-Saxon text which describes the Bleccanham boundary reflected an even earlier state of affairs, rather than the tenth century situation. Indeed the form of the charter which refers to Bleccanham rather suggests this, since by it Edgar is pictured as giving that estate to the Abbey 'as it was dedicated long ago'.[40]

Since we know that a later dispute arose over a change in the boundary near Child's Hill (see above under 'Bleccanham'), one needs to look closely again at that area. The land round the bottom slopes of Child's Hill was later known as Cowhouse from at least the thirteenth century; and the farm of Cowhouse (with its name changed at different times to Dickers Farm and finally the more pedestrian Avenue Farm) was still in existence 700 years later, in the present century.[41] Cowhouse Lane (now roughly Cricklewood Lane), near which Cowhouse Farm stood, led from the Child's Hill hamlet to Watling Street, and indeed became one of the principal ways of taking produce from the southern parts of Hendon and (unexpectedly) also from Hampstead [42] to the Abbey and to London. Equally the two farms of Cowhouse and Hodford (the latter near the present Golders Green Station, see **Map N**) became a separate unit, treated in and after the thirteenth century (if not earlier) as a sub-manor of the larger Manor of Hendon.[43] Cowhouse as an area has sometimes been suggested to be the old area of Codanhlaw, although without any real evidence for this. But there is no doubt that the component 'hlaw' certainly meant either a (burial) mound or a natural hill.[44] There is also no doubt that 'Child's Hill' was (and, even under its present concealment of urban housing, still is) a most impressive natural hill, whether or not it also had a burial mound on it : so much so that on some of the first comprehensively-attempted maps of Middlesex in the eighteenth and nineteenth centuries, Child's Hill appears as though it were an Alp. There is no other worthy candidate for the 'hill' referred to by the 'hlaw' in 'Codanhlaw'. If the boundary with Hampstead led *eastwards* round the hill's summit (now called Telegraph Hill) to link up with the northern

---

[39] Scholz *Sulcard* Traditio 20 (1964) 59. The name used by Sulcard for the estate so granted was 'Blekenham', which has been read as referring to our Bleccanham. Scholz however thought that this was Blakenham in Northants, but this is clearly wrong (there is no reference to Northants, and the boundaries given in Birch *BCS* No 1351 (Sawyer *ibid*. No 1450) which Scholz cites as authority show clearly that Bleccanham is, instead, our Hendon tract). For further details about the estate, see Napier and Stevenson *Crawford Charters* 96-7.

[40] Sawyer *ibid* No 1450; for text, see Birch *Cart.Sax.* No 1351.

[41] The farm house itself and its older barns (old, but not 700 years old) were finally pulled down in 1931-2, after earlier reductions of the farm itself since the first World War, see article *The Times* 13th June 1931 and note at TLMAS 6 NS (1929) 683.

[42] See WAM 6623-4 ('Couhouselane in Hendon leading from Hampstead to London', which appears to be going the wrong way, as indeed it was in part). But for carts it was probably easier to go partly northwards from at least some parts of Hampstead, in order to use Watling Street via Cowhouse Lane (in spite of having to face the steepness of Child's Hill and the notorious defects in the big road), than to go down the direct southwards track through Belsize and Chalcots, which involved some equally steep bits and possibly marsh as well.

[43] See Vol 2.

[44] Gelling *Place Names in the Landscape* 162-3; Smith (EPNS) *PN Elements* 248-9. The name probably meant 'Codda's hill (or mound)'; cf. EPNS *PN Wilts* 164.

source of the Westbourne stream ('the boundary stream': see above, under *Bleccanham*), one would expect this very prominent hill to be the dominant feature for any naming or renaming process for the land *north* of that ~~stream~~.

As we have seen, Hampstead ended at the 'boundary stream', at an early period. This means that all the present Fortune Green area [45] could not have been part of Hampstead *at that time*, but subsequently must have been subtracted from the larger Hendon and added to Hampstead, where it has ever since been. The processes by which this happened are not known, but it is not impossible that after an earlier church at Westminster, holding Bleccanham, had itself suffered destruction at the hands of the Danes, as so many other churches had done, with the consequent loss or abandonment of Bleccanham, a smaller estate was later carved out of the land in that area; and both it, under the name Codanhlaw, and the rest of the Bleccanham lands (under their old name) were 'restored'[46] to the new Abbey in the tenth century by King Edgar as part of the endowments for the new foundation. This would make sense of the wording of the written record relating to Bleccanham, and would account for the undoubted presence of Codanhlaw as part of the Hendon region both in the Telligraph of King Ethelred and in later traditions at Westminster. Equally the subsequent subtraction of the present Fortune Green area (as shown, appropriately, in green on **Map P**) from Hendon and the adding of that area to the estate of Hampstead would account for the change in the boundary (which must on any view have taken place) and for the subsequent dispute, which appears to have lasted until at least the fourteenth century,[47] about where that boundary really should be.

So while this supposition is not totally conclusive of the question, it does show that there was a place where Codanhlaw could have been; and that one cannot rule out the likelihood, which accords with the Ethelred Telligraph and with Westminster traditions, that Codanhlaw had been a component tract of the eventual Norman manor of Hendon. It would also explain in a persuasive way the 'hlaw' element in the name. And it is at least consistent with later evidence that the Cowhouse land is known to have been treated in subsequent centuries as an independent tract which, with the adjoining Hodford farmlands in the erstwhile Bleccanham area, formed a 'sub-manor' of the manor of Hendon. So the probability is that from the beginning of its known history Codanhlaw had always been regarded as a separate estate in the Hendon area, which like the other three tracts was swept up into a larger composite estate of 'Hendon' before the Conquest, and that it then continued to retain an individual identity *within* that larger estate until some much later period, when (after disputes) it was subtracted from Hendon and added to the adjoining estate of Hampstead.

---

[45] This is a rough description : see **Map P** for the full extent of the area in question. 'Fortune' is recorded only very late. Its derivation has not been pronounced upon; but it may be much earlier than the records reveal: 'tune' perhaps based on 'tun', a farm, and/or 'for' based on a ford on the 'boundary stream' ?

[46] 'Restoration', by Edgar and Dunstan, of something previously lost (as opposed to first-time giving) was a strong theme in later Westminster tradition, see the forged and so-called 'Great Charters' of Edgar and of Dunstan, Sawyer *ibid* Nos 774 and 1293. See page 24 above for an 'earlier church' at Westminster.

[47] See Note 32 above.

Main ref : page 11, and throughout

HERTS

ESSEX

SURREY

THE "CORRIDOR" ESTATES OF THE ABBEY IN MIDDLESEX

1. <u>From the Endowment period</u>   (971-1005 AD)
   Westminster   (acquired in two parts)
   Hendon   (acquired in several parts)
   Hampstead
   Paddington   (shown as " PAD <u>N</u> " on map)

2. <u>From the reign of Edward the Confessor</u>   (1042-1066)
   Knightsbridge   (shown as " KNB " on map)
   Westbourne   (shown as " WEST <u>NE</u> " on map)
   Chalkhill   (in Kingsbury)

3. <u>Within 30 years of the Domesday Survey</u>   (after 1086)
   Eia   (both shown striped on map)
   Chelsea

MAP A

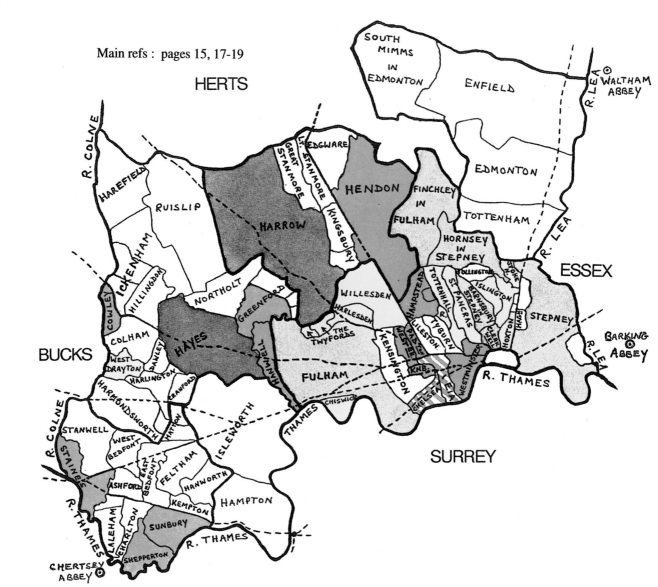

Main refs : pages 15, 17-19

THE THREE MAIN CHURCH ESTATES
IN MIDDLESEX, AT DOMESDAY (1086)

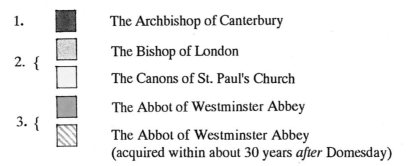

1. ▪ The Archbishop of Canterbury

2. { ▨ The Bishop of London

    ☐ The Canons of St. Paul's Church

3. { ▨ The Abbot of Westminster Abbey

    ▨ The Abbot of Westminster Abbey
    (acquired within about 30 years *after* Domesday)

[In addition to the three main estates, there were three other small church holdings in
Middlesex: of which, Tyburn, held by the Abbess of Barking, also has a part in this story]

MAP B

THE THREE KINGDOMS : ESSEX, MERCIA AND WESSEX

Main refs : pages 17-23

C.1

Middlesex dominated by Essex : c.600 - 750 AD

- The Kingdom of Essex
- The Diocese of London
- Areas possibly included in the Kingdom and Diocese
- The later boundary between the Shires

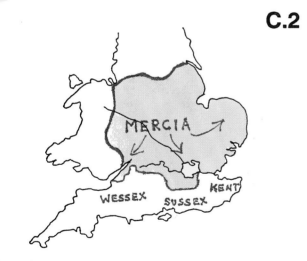

C.2

Middlesex dominated by Mercia
c.750 - 850 AD

[After about 750, Mercia also went on to absorb Wessex, Sussex and Kent as well]

C.3

Middlesex dominated by Wessex
c.850 - 950 AD

- Alfred's boundary with the Danes, in 886.

- The Wessex boundary by about 925.

By 959 when Edgar became king, the Wesssex boundary had been pushed even further north, and Wessex had in name become "England".

MAP C

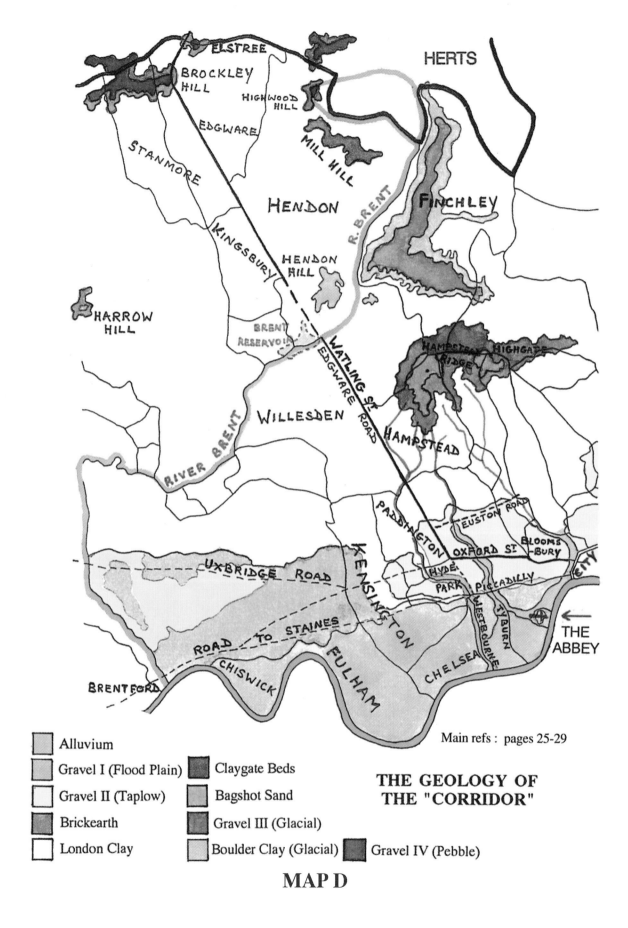

THE GEOLOGY OF
THE "CORRIDOR"

Main refs : pages 25-29

Alluvium

Gravel I (Flood Plain)

Gravel II (Taplow)

Brickearth

London Clay

Claygate Beds

Bagshot Sand

Gravel III (Glacial)

Boulder Clay (Glacial)

Gravel IV (Pebble)

MAP D

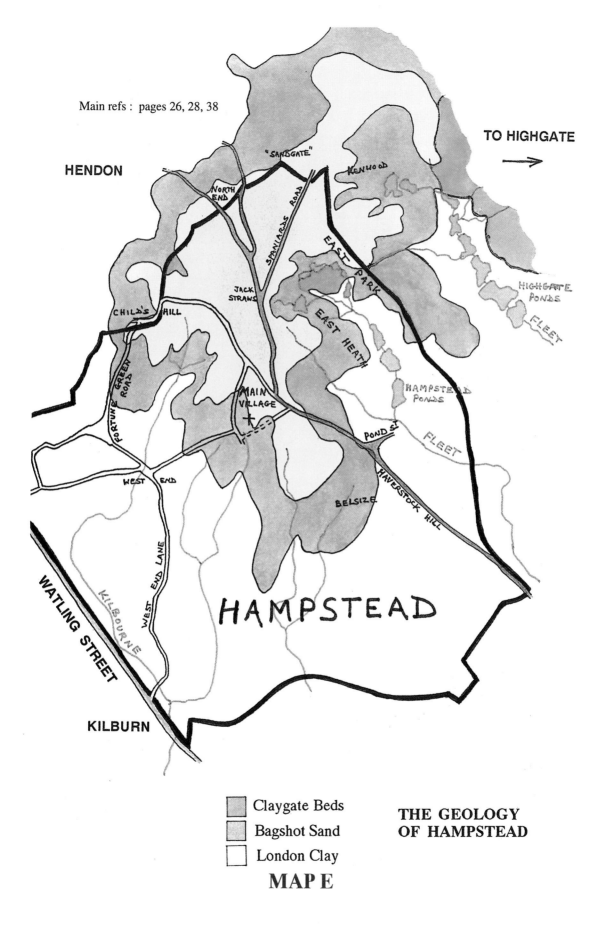

Main refs : pages 26, 28, 38

HENDON

TO HIGHGATE

"SANDGATE"

NORTH END

KENWOOD

SPANIARDS ROAD

EAST PARK

HIGHGATE PONDS

FLEET

JACK STRAWS

CHILD'S HILL

EAST HEATH

FORTUNE GREEN ROAD

MAIN VILLAGE

HAMPSTEAD PONDS

POND St

FLEET

WEST END

HAVERSTOCK HILL

BELSIZE

WATLING STREET

KILBOURNE

WEST END LANE

HAMPSTEAD

KILBURN

Claygate Beds

Bagshot Sand

London Clay

**THE GEOLOGY
OF HAMPSTEAD**

MAP E

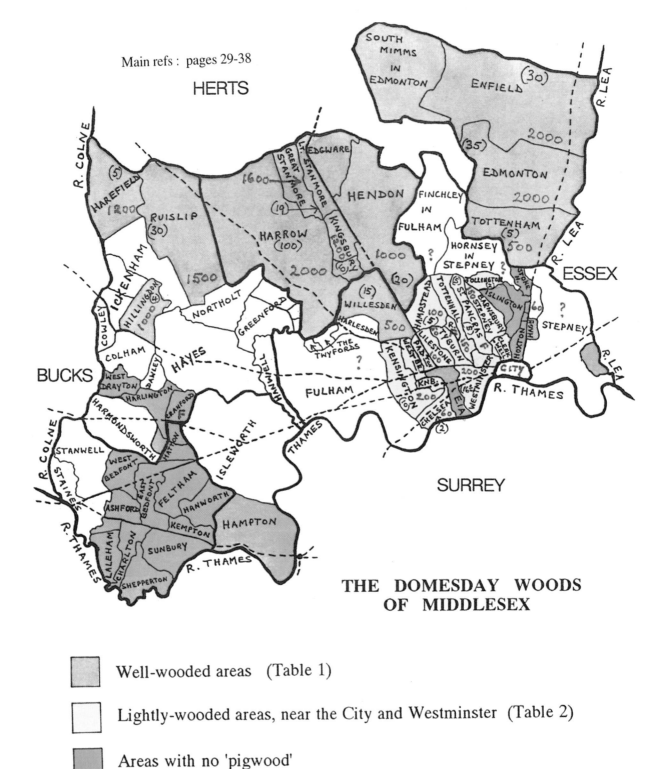

Main refs : pages 29-38

HERTS

SOUTH MIMMS IN EDMONTON

ENFIELD (30)

R. LEA

(35)

EDMONTON 2000

2000

R. COLNE

(5)
HAREFIELD 1200

RUISLIP (30)

1600

GREAT STANMORE

EDGWARE

LT. STANMORE

HENDON

FINCHLEY IN FULHAM

TOTTENHAM (5)

500

(19)

KINGSBURY

1000

HORNSEY IN STEPNEY

?

ESSEX

HARROW (100)

1500

2000

(5)

(20)

?

R. LEA

ICKENHAM

COWLEY

HILLINGDON (4) 1000

NORTHOLT

GREENFORD

WILLESDEN (15)

HARLESDEN

500

HAMPSTEAD 100

TOLLINGTON

ST. PANCRAS

ISLINGTON

STOKE

60

?

STEPNEY

COLHAM

HAYES

THE TWYFORDS ?

KENSINGTON 200

TYBURN

CLERK

HOXTON

HAGE

R. LEA

BUCKS

WEST DRAYTON

DAWLEY

HANWELL

FULHAM

WESTBOURNE

LILESTONE

PADDINGTON

WESTMINSTER

CITY

HARLINGTON

CRANFORD

KNB.

ETA 100

R. THAMES

HARMONDSWORTH

HATTON

ISLEWORTH

THAMES

CHELSEA 60

200

(2)

R. COLNE

STANWELL

WEST BEDFONT

EAST BEDFONT

FELTHAM

HANWORTH

HAMPTON

SURREY

STAINES

ASHFORD

KEMPTON

R. THAMES

LALEHAM

CHARLTON

SUNBURY

R. THAMES

SHEPPERTON

THE DOMESDAY WOODS
OF MIDDLESEX

Well-wooded areas   (Table 1)

Lightly-wooded areas, near the City and Westminster   (Table 2)

Areas with no 'pigwood'

Notes   1. Fulham and Stepney have been omitted because of their complicated holdings.
2. The other 'white' areas are also omitted as they are not significant for the present purpose.
3. Red figures = pig numbers.   Red "F" = "wood for fences".   Black figures, in brackets, = hides.

MAP F

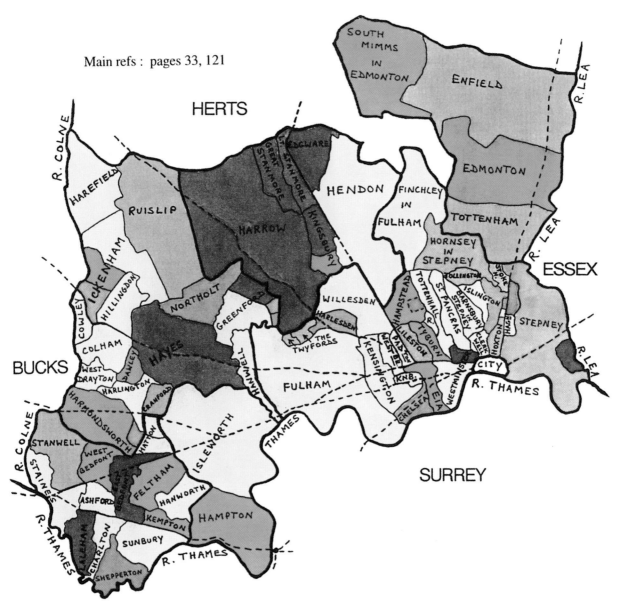

Main refs : pages 33, 121

THE "FALL IN VALUE" OF ESTATES
AFTER THE CONQUEST

Fall in value, three times or more

Fall in value, more than two but less than three times

Fall in value, two times

Fall in value, more than one but less than two times

Same value as before the Conquest

Rise in value

MAP G

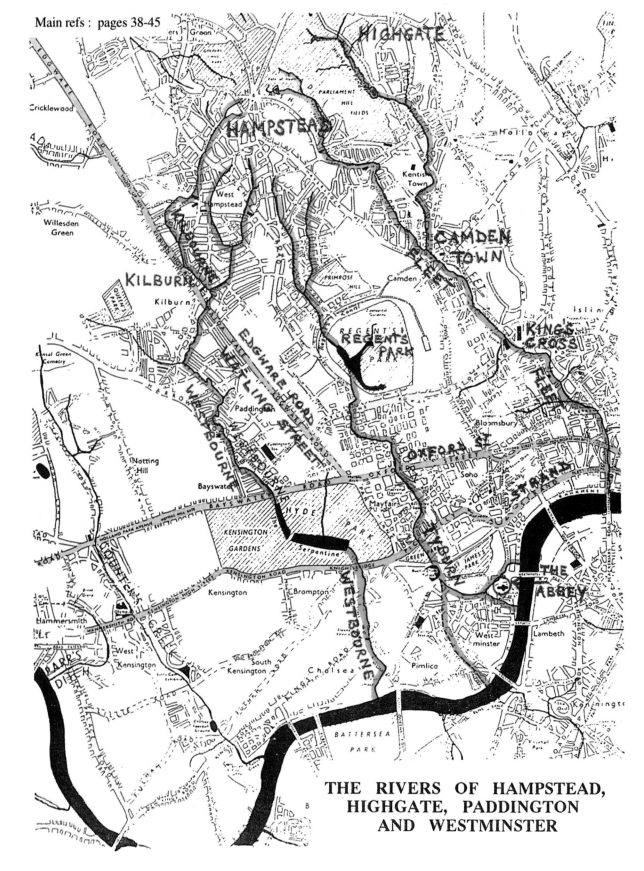

THE RIVERS OF HAMPSTEAD,
HIGHGATE, PADDINGTON
AND WESTMINSTER

MAP H

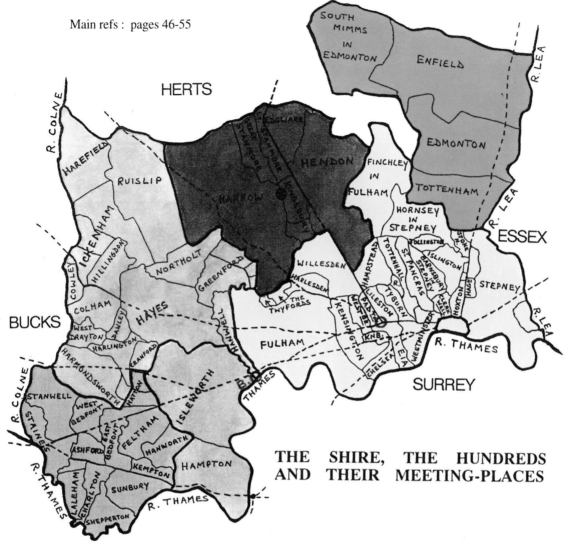

Main refs : pages 46-55

HERTS

SOUTH MIMMS IN EDMONTON

ENFIELD

EDMONTON

R. COLNE

HAREFIELD

RUISLIP

HENDON

FINCHLEY IN FULHAM

TOTTENHAM

R. LEA

ICKENHAM

HILLINGDON

NORTHOLT

GREENFORD

WILLESDEN

HORNSEY IN STEPNEY

ESSEX

COWLEY

COLHAM

HAYES

HARLESDEN

THE TWYFORDS

HAMPSTEAD

TOTTENHALL

ST. PANCRAS

ISLINGTON

HOXTON

HAGG

STEPNEY

BUCKS

WEST DRAYTON

DAWLEY

HARLINGTON

CRANFORD

HANWELL

FULHAM

KENSINGTON

CHELSEA

WESTMINSTER

R. THAMES

R. LEA

R. COLNE

HARMONDSWORTH

STANWELL

WEST BEDFONT

EAST BEDFONT

HATTON

FELTHAM

ISLEWORTH

B.

R. THAMES

SURREY

STAINES

ASHFORD

HANWORTH

KEMPTON

HAMPTON

THE SHIRE, THE HUNDREDS AND THEIR MEETING-PLACES

R. THAMES

LALEHAM

CHARLTON

SUNBURY

R. THAMES

SHEPPERTON

The Meeting-places

○ The "elbow" of Watling Street (at Marble Arch): -
(a) the meeting-place of the Ossulton Hundred Court, probably from the tenth century or before;

(b) one of the meeting-places of the Middlesex Shire Court, from at least the thirteenth and probably from the tenth century or before.

B.○ Brentford, another of the meeting-places of the Middlesex Shire Court.

⊗ The Gore Hundred Court's meeting-place, at the junction of Honeypot Lane and the present Harrow-Kingsbury road: possibly from the tenth century or before.

The Hundreds

☐ Ossulston
■ Gore
▨ Edmonton
▨ Elthorne
▨ Spelthorne
▨ Hounslow
(later Isleworth)

MAP I

Main ref : page 52

HERTS

BUCKS

ESSEX

SURREY

SOUTH MIMMS IN EDMONTON
30.
ENFIELD
35.
EDMONTON
R. LEA
TOTTENHAM
HAREFIELD
5.
R. COLNE
RUISLIP
GREAT STANMORE
LT. STANMORE
EDGWARE
KINGSBURY 7½+7½
9½
HENDON
FINCHLEY IN FULHAM (40)
HORNSEY IN STEPNEY
5.
ICKENHAM 2½+3½+9½
HARROW 100.
15.
WILLESDEN
15.
20.
HAMPSTEAD
TOLLINGTON
STOKE
STONE
HILLINGDON
COWLEY
30.
NORTHOLT
GREENFORD
11½+3½+1
HARLESDEN 5.
TOTTENHALL 5.
ST. PANCRAS 5.
ISLINGTON 2½+2½+¼
BARNSBURY
KENTISH
HOXTON
STEPNEY
COLHAM
HAYES
40.
THE TWYFORDS 5.
ACTON
KENSINGTON
ST. PAUL
PADD.
LILESTON 5.
STYBURN 5.
10.
WEST DRAYTON 10.
DAWLEY
HARLINGTON 5.
HANWELL
59.
FULHAM
KNB.
10.
WESTMINSTER
EIA
5 Hides in Tenth Century.
CRANFORD 10.
CHISWICK 5.
CHELSEA
HARMONDSWORTH
15.
30.
HATTON
ISLEWORTH 70.
THAMES
R. THAMES
STANWELL
STAINES
R. COLNE
ASHFORD
FELTHAM 5.
HANWORTH
KEMPTON 5.
HAMPTON 35.
19+
LALEHAM 8
CHARLTON 5
SUNBURY 7
SHEPPERTON 8
R. THAMES

THE ANGLO-SAXON "FIVE-HIDE"
ASSESSMENT, STILL VISIBLE
IN THE DOMESDAY SURVEY

5 Hides

10 Hides

15-20 Hides

30 or more Hides

Linked pairs, making a multiple of five Hides

Estates once part of the Five-Hide assessment?

MAP J

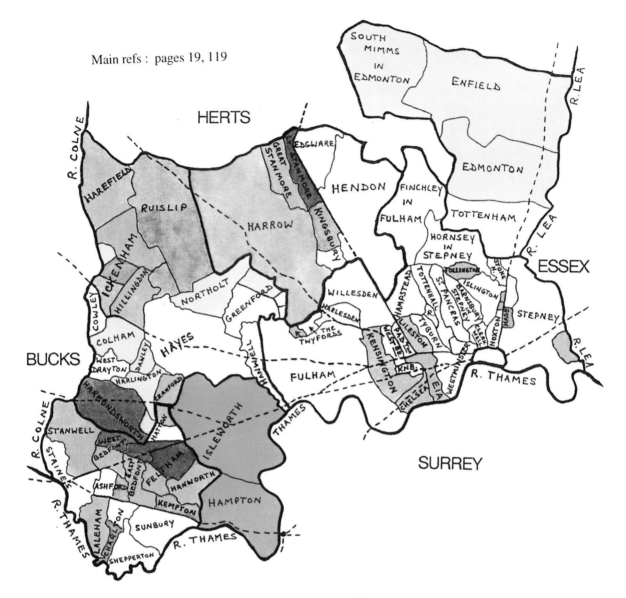

Main refs : pages 19, 119

SOUTH MIMMS IN EDMONTON

ENFIELD

R. LEA

HERTS

EDGWARE

GREAT STANMORE

STANMORE IN KINGSBURY

HENDON

EDMONTON

FINCHLEY IN FULHAM

TOTTENHAM

R. COLNE

HAREFIELD

RUISLIP

HARROW

KINGSBURY

HORNSEY IN STEPNEY

R. LEA

ICKENHAM

HILLINGDON

NORTHOLT

GREENFORD

WILLESDEN

TOLLINGTON

STOKE N.

HAMPSTEAD

TOTTENHALL

ST. PANCRAS

ISLINGTON

BARNSBURY STEPNEY

CLERK.

ESSEX

STEPNEY

COWLEY

HARLESDEN

LILESTON

TYBURN

HOXTON

COLHAM

THE TWYFORDS

KENSINGTON

WESTB

RAD'TE

R. LEA

WEST DRAYTON

DAWLEY

HAYES

HANWELL

FULHAM

KNB.

WESTMINSTER

STEPNEY

BUCKS

HARLINGTON

CRANFORD

CHELSEA

EIA

R. THAMES

HAREMONDSWORTH

HATTON

ISLEWORTH

THAMES

R. COLNE

STANWELL

WEST BEDFONT

FELTHAM

SURREY

STAINES

EAST BEDFONT

HANWORTH

ASHFORD

KEMPTON

HAMPTON

R. THAMES

LALEHAM

CHARLTON

SUNBURY

SHEPPERTON

R. THAMES

THE MAIN LAY ESTATES
BEFORE THE CONQUEST

Earl Leofwine (brother of King Harold)

Ansgar (the "Staller", a royal adviser and officer)

Earl Aelfgar (of Mercia)

King Harold

King Edward the Confessor's family (at Eia and Harefield), and some of his thanes or "men"

Wulfward Wight (large land-owner and thane of King Edward)

Wigot (probably Wigot of Wallingford, thane and kinsman of King Edward)

MAP K

HERTS

R. COLNE

HAREFIELD

RUISLIP

ICKENHAM

HILLINGDON

NORTHOLT

COWLEY

COLHAM

WEST
DRAYTON

BAYLEY

HARLINGTON

HAYES

CRANFORD

GREENFORD

HARROW

L. STANMORE

GREAT
STANMORE

EDGWARE

KINGSBURY

HENDON

WILLESDEN

HARLESDEN

THE
TWYFORDS

FINCHLEY
IN
FULHAM

HORNSEY
IN
STEPNEY

TOTTENHAM

TOLLINGTON

HAMPSTEAD

TOTTENHALL

ST PANCRAS

ISLINGTON

BARNSBURY
STEPNEY

STONE

CLERK
ENWELL

HOXTON

HAGG

STEPNEY

KENSINGTON

LILESTON

TYBURN

RADST

WESTBE

KNB.

WESTMINSTER

CHELSEA

EIA

R. THAMES

R. LEA

ESSEX

R. LEA

SOUTH
MIMMS
IN
EDMONTON

ENFIELD

EDMONTON

HARMONDSWORTH

HANWELL

FULHAM

STANWELL

STAINES

R. COLNE

ASHFORD

LALEHAM

CHARLTON

SHEPPERTON

R. THAMES

SUNBURY

KEMPTON

HANWORTH

FELTHAM

ISLEWORTH

HAMPTON

THAMES

R. THAMES

SURREY

⊘ : No pasture,
See pages 35-36.

BUCKS

**THE MAIN LAY ESTATES
AT DOMESDAY**

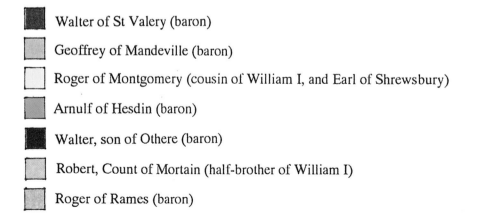

Walter of St Valery (baron)

Geoffrey of Mandeville (baron)

Roger of Montgomery (cousin of William I, and Earl of Shrewsbury)

Arnulf of Hesdin (baron)

Walter, son of Othere (baron)

Robert, Count of Mortain (half-brother of William I)

Roger of Rames (baron)

MAP L

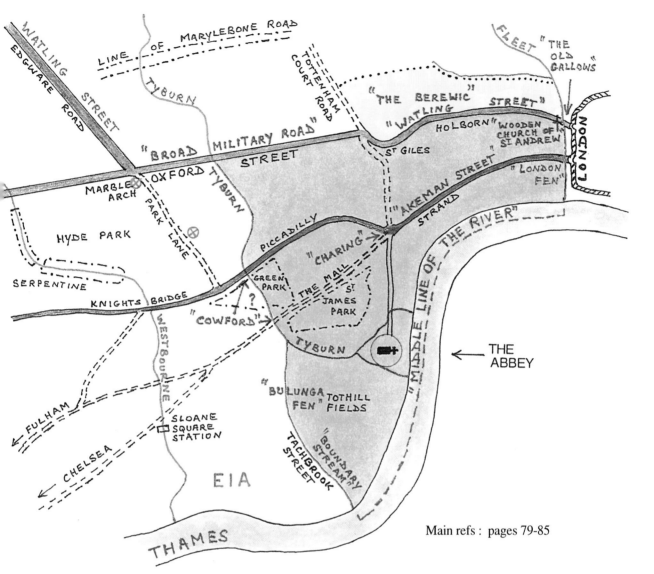

**THE TWO
WESTMINSTER ESTATES**

Dunstan's gift of the main estate, c. 971

The Berewic, bought from King Ethelred, c. 1002

Notes : (1) Identifiable features from the charters are in RED.
(2) Modern names and places, to give location, are in BLACK.
(3) Some conjectural roads or tracks are shown dotted.
(4) Original and later sites for the Ossulston Hundred Court.
(5) The River Thames is here shown as it would be on a modern
    sketch-map, but it was much wider in the tenth century,
    closer for example to Akeman Street along the "strand".

MAP M

THE FOUR TRACTS OF HENDON
(Lotheresleage, Hendon, Bleccanham and Codanhlaw)

Main refs : pages 87-98

Notes : (1) Main boundary-names (in OE.) from the charters are in RED.
      (2) Translations of the boundary-names are in (BLACK), with brackets.
      (3) Later place-names, to give location, are in BLACK, without brackets.

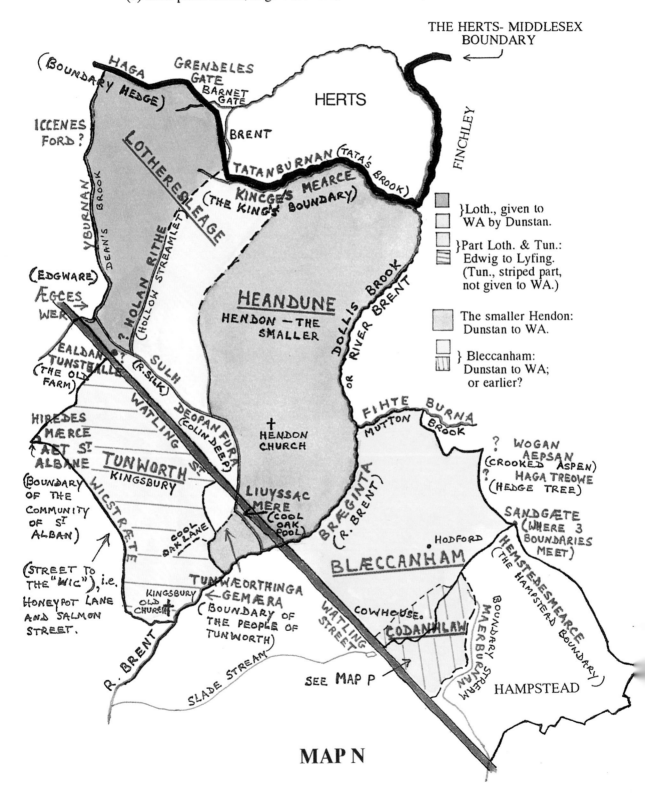

THE HERTS- MIDDLESEX BOUNDARY

(BOUNDARY HEDGE)   HAGA

GRENDELES GATE
BARNET GATE

HERTS

ICCENES FORD ?

BRENT

FINCHLEY

LOTHERESLEAGE

TATANBURNAN (TATA'S BROOK)

KINCGES MEARCE (THE KING'S BOUNDARY)

YBURNAN   DEAN'S BROOK

? HOLAN RITHE (HOLLOW STREAMLET)

}Loth., given to WA by Dunstan.

}Part Loth. & Tun.: Edwig to Lyfing. (Tun., striped part, not given to WA.)

HEANDUNE
HENDON — THE SMALLER

DOLLIS BROOK OR RIVER BRENT

The smaller Hendon: Dunstan to WA.

} Bleccanham: Dunstan to WA; or earlier?

(EDGWARE) ÆGCES WER

EALDAN ?
TUNSTEALLE (THE OLD FARM)

(R. SILK)

SULH

DEOPAN FURA (COLIN DEEP)

HENDON CHURCH

FIHTE BURNA

MUTTON BROOK

? WOGAN AEPSAN (CROOKED ASPEN)
? HAGA TREOWE (HEDGE TREE)

HIREDES MEARCE AET ST. ALBANE

(BOUNDARY OF THE COMMUNITY OF ST ALBAN)

TUNWORTH
KINGSBURY

WATLING ST.

LIUYSSAC MERE (COOL OAK POOL)

BRÆGINTA (R. BRENT)

SANDGÆTE (WHERE 3 BOUNDARIES MEET)

HEMSTEDESMEARCE (THE HAMPSTEAD BOUNDARY)

(STREET TO THE "WIC"), i.e. HONEYPOT LANE AND SALMON STREET.

WICSTRÆTE

COOL OAK LANE

HODFORD

BLÆCCANHAM

KINGSBURY OLD CHURCH

TUNWÆORTHINGA GEMÆRA (BOUNDARY OF THE PEOPLE OF TUNWORTH)

COWHOUSE.

CODANHLAW

BOUNDARY MAERBURNAM

HAMPSTEAD

R. BRENT

WATLING STREET

SLADE STREAM

SEE MAP P

MAP N

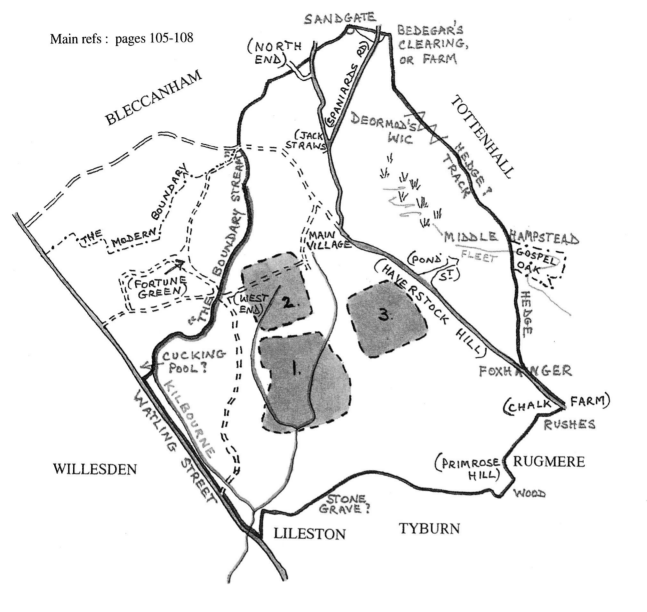

Main refs : pages 105-108

HAMPSTEAD : ANGLO-SAXON BOUNDARIES AND FIELDS

Notes: (1) Boundary-names (translated) from the charters are in RED.
(2) Later names, to give location, are in (BLACK), in brackets.

 Probable sites of the three main fields, which were identified by name in 1312 AD: -
1. "Somerlese" (part still "Summer Leys" 450 years later, in 1762)
2. "Homefeld"
3. "Pyrlegh" (parts still "Purloins" in 1762)

MAP O

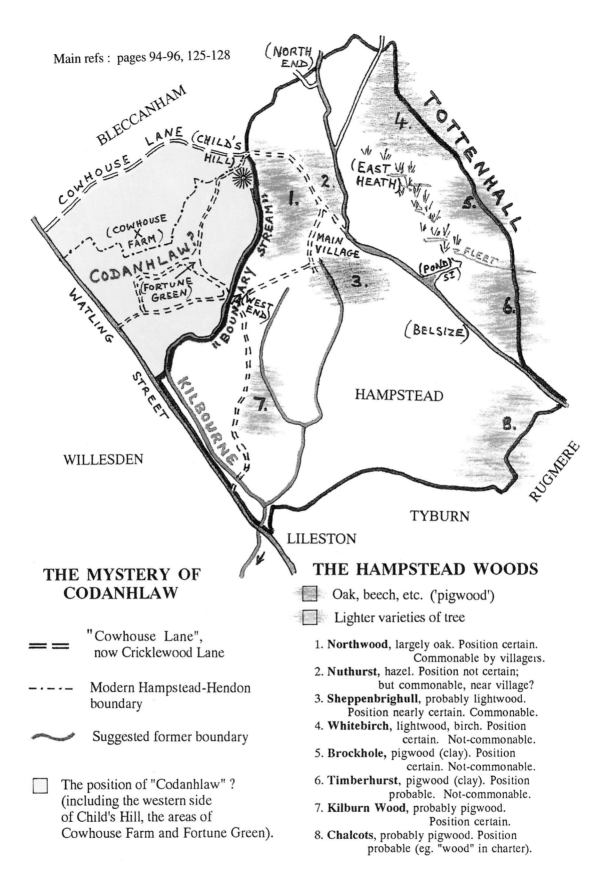

Main refs : pages 94-96, 125-128

(NORTH END)

BLECCANHAM

COWHOUSE LANE (CHILD'S HILL)

TOTTENHALL

4.

(EAST HEATH)

2.

1.

5.

(COWHOUSE X FARM)

CODANHLAW?

(FORTUNE GREEN)

MAIN VILLAGE

"BOUNDARY STREAM"

FLEET

(POND) ST

3.

WATLING

WEST END

(BELSIZE)

6.

STREET

KILBOURNE

7.

HAMPSTEAD

8.

WILLESDEN

RUGMERE

TYBURN

LILESTON

THE MYSTERY OF CODANHLAW

══   "Cowhouse Lane", now Cricklewood Lane

─·─·─   Modern Hampstead-Hendon boundary

〜   Suggested former boundary

☐   The position of "Codanhlaw" ? (including the western side of Child's Hill, the areas of Cowhouse Farm and Fortune Green).

THE HAMPSTEAD WOODS

☐ Oak, beech, etc. ('pigwood')

☐ Lighter varieties of tree

1. **Northwood**, largely oak. Position certain. Commonable by villagers.
2. **Nuthurst**, hazel. Position not certain; but commonable, near village?
3. **Sheppenbrighull**, probably lightwood. Position nearly certain. Commonable.
4. **Whitebirch**, lightwood, birch. Position certain. Not-commonable.
5. **Brockhole**, pigwood (clay). Position certain. Not-commonable.
6. **Timberhurst**, pigwood (clay). Position probable. Not-commonable.
7. **Kilburn Wood**, probably pigwood. Position certain.
8. **Chalcots**, probably pigwood. Position probable (eg. "wood" in charter).

MAP P

Plate 9. The view along Hall Road, now Aerodrome Road, in Hendon, in c.1905, showing part of the weald north of Hendon Hill, with above it the line of the Brockley Hill ridge on the Middlesex/Hertfordshire boundary. This area, heavily wooded, was part of Lotheresleage and the smaller 'Hendon' in the tenth century. See pages 88-91

Plate 10. Even as late as 1922 the Silk River still ran, meandering, through fields on its way to join the Brent River, now flowing through the Brent Reservoir. For centuries this confluence of the two rivers had formed a marshy area, which was drained partly by the making of the reservoir in the 1830s and by later drainage works. The foreground was part of the Saxon and Norman Hendon. See page 89

CHAPTER 8

Hampstead on the Hill

Compared with the complicated history of the Hendon area before the Norman Conquest, early Hampstead fortunately presents a fairly straightforward picture.

The two estates of Hendon and Hampstead, being contiguous neighbours and each being reasonably close to the Abbey, were clearly associated with one another in the minds of the monks. In the earliest charter-lists of the Abbey's possessions, the name of Hampstead is generally recorded immediately after the names of the component tracts which eventually made up the later Norman manor of Hendon; and in one charter the name even appears encircled by the names of the Hendon tracts. Moreover both estates 'in tandem' were usually named immediately *after* the very first endowment estate of Westminster in those lists.[1] More important to their inter-dependence is the fact that, from the earliest time when any system of parishes can be detected, the church [2] at Hendon was the parish church for Hampstead as well, and this seems to have continued until after 1478. From some early date before 1248, Hampstead had only a chapel [3] (with a chaplain who later was sometimes called a parish priest) which was annexed to Hendon Church; and the tithes of Hampstead were paid to the Rector of Hendon for the time being. On the secular side, when surviving documents in later centuries begin to tell us more about the course of daily life in the manors, it becomes clear that there was often quite a close liaison between the officers of the two manors, closer than that with other neighbouring estates.[4]

Apart from prehistoric finds on Hampstead Heath,[5] no reliable archaeological evidence

---

[1] This is true not only of the forged charters, but also of the genuine material, see eg. Sawyer *A-S Charters* Nos 1043, 1040 and 1293 (forgeries); and No 894 (part genuine material: this is where the Hampstead name appears encircled, see page 90 above and Appendix 1; this may have given rise to the once-held belief that Hampstead was formerly part of Hendon).

[2] There was already a priest in Hendon by 1086, since he was specifically referred to in Domesday Book, see *DB Mdx* 4/12 (f. 128d), and therefore probably an existing church. See further page 91 above.

[3] It is unlikely that any chapel was provided in Hampstead until the twelfth century at the earliest, and then probably only for the convenience of the first main tenant of the manor from the Abbey (Richard de Balta, see Vol. 2) and his family, rather than for the benefit of the other parishioners. It may not have been until the thirteenth century, since the earliest reference to the chapel is in 1244-8 (VCH *Mdx* 9/145). The grant of a licence to have a chapel was often a convenience (at a price) for a landowner, and as an example we can see this convenience being studied in Westminster itself by the grant by the Abbot of such a licence to Robert Mauduit in c.1195-1200, to have his own chapel in Westminster, even though the parish church of Westminster, St Margaret's, was (by that time) close at hand; Mason *The Mauduits* BIHR. 49 (1976) 19. The fact that, on the secular level, Hendon was in Gore Hundred and Hampstead in Ossulston Hundred does not seem to have affected the dependence of Hampstead on Hendon. The earliest *record* of tithes being paid from Hampstead to Hendon does not appear until the thirteenth century; but it is clear that already from the tenth century some tithe system was in operation in England, see *Edgar's Laws at Andover* (959-63) EHD 1/ 431. Like Hendon Church (and very many others), the Hampstead chapel was dedicated to St Mary the Virgin: see page 66.

[4] See Vol. 2.

[5] Summarised in Taylor (Ed) *A Place in Time* 20-4. The finding of a later Roman urn or urns and other pottery in the Wells area in 1774 and subsequently of certain coins has not been regarded as proof of any

has been found to identify any very early settlement in Hampstead, such as the Saxon pottery of the sixth-ninth centuries found in Hendon. But both the position of Hampstead on its ridge, and its boundaries which were already fixed by the tenth century, argue that it too must have been settled by earlier Saxons. However, with the chance of archaeological evidence becoming more and more remote in the built-up areas, it seems unlikely that we shall ever know for certain (unless the Heath again produces something).[6] The name Hampstead is a common one in Old English, composed of the two early elements 'ham' and 'stede' and meaning 'homestead', which apparently could denote either a single or a multiple settlement as its origin, more commonly the latter.[7]

The Hampstead Charters

In its physical relationship with the monks after the Abbey at Westminster had been founded in the tenth century, one must remember that Hampstead's wooded hill was well within their view. It must have been an abiding presence for those who (unlike modern Westminster residents) could then still choose to lift their eyes up to the hills. Nevertheless the Abbey was not given any land in Hampstead until after King Edgar was dead. As far as one can tell, the grant of an estate there to the Abbey came not from Edgar or Dunstan, but from the second of Edgar's sons, Ethelred (the 'Unready' [8]).

The reason why Edgar had no land in Hampstead to spare for a grant to the Abbey was that, as we shall see, he had already granted the estate to one of his 'faithful Ministers'. Like Westminster, the settlement at Hampstead is unusual in having two apparently genuine documents recording at least part of its early history and including two descriptions in Anglo-Saxon of its boundaries. It is the second of these which shows that Hampstead's association with the Abbey began in 986, when King Ethelred bestowed on the monastery 'five little mansae... in the place which is called Hamstede'.[9]

The document recording the grant is not itself a charter, but a subsequent record of the grant, a record made very soon afterwards, probably in 987-988. It has recently been endorsed as authentic,[10] which has removed certain doubts which had earlier existed about its form. It is an interesting document for other reasons as well, because in its preface or 'proem' it also bears well-dramatised witness to the troubles ('the dreadful events, the disasters and stormy tribulations') which arose in the kingdom, when King Edgar's premature death in 975 had brought sixteen years of peace and religious patronage to an end. That unexpected death unleashed a secular reaction by certain nobles against the effects of the monastic reforms in which Edgar had played so prominent a role,[11] a period

---

specifically Roman settlement in the neighbourhood: see Park *Topog. of Hampstead* 4; Barratt *Annals of Hampstead* 11; Farmer *Hampstead Heath* 148.

[6] I am hopeful that part of the 'boundary ditch' on Hampstead East Heath (see page 105 below) will be excavated this year (1994) by the Hendon and District Archaeological Society, to learn its possible date.

[7] Smith (EPNS) *PN Elements* 1/226, 232; 2/148; Gelling *Place Names in the Landscape* 284

[8] See page 67 above.

[9] BL *Stowe Ch*.33, Sanders *O.S. Facs* vol. iii. No. 34; Sawyer *A-S Charters* No 1450, see page 92 above; the same gift by Ethelred is also recorded in his Telligraph, see Appendix 1 below. See also Ramsay et al. *St Dunstan* 146.   For the Stowe charter recording the grant to Hampstead, see **Plate 11**, page 109.

[10] By Dr P.Chaplais, see VCH *Mdx*. 9/92. Its style may be a Middlesex example of the 'hermeneutic style' vividly described in Lapidge *The Hermeneutic Style* A-S England 4 (1975) 67, which does not unfortunately refer to Middlesex charters. Dunstan who died in 988 witnessed it, hence my dating.

[11] Fisher *Anti-monastic reaction* CHJ 10 (1952) 255; Stenton *A-S England* 372-3; Williams 'Aelfhere, Ealdorman of Mercia' in *A-S England* 10 (1982) 143; *Councils and Synods* I (Eds. Whitelock, Brett and Brooke 142-54. For Edgar's reforms, see page 58 above.

which in its turn was to be followed by renewed onslaughts by the Danes and the 'burning of towns'.

But, like Lotheresleage in Hendon, Hampstead too had had its own even earlier secular history which is documented. At one time among the muniments at Westminster Abbey there existed a charter which recorded an earlier grant by King Edgar of five tracts in Hampstead to his 'faithful *minister,* Mangoda', who is also described as 'noble'. This charter was subsequently lost in unknown circumstances in the eighteenth century, but fortunately in 1702 before the loss, the historian Thomas Madox who had examined and recorded it published a printed copy of it.[12] So the printed version of the charter has come down to us, but not the manuscript itself. The loss poses the problem of authenticity acutely, in that no one can now examine the handwriting. However the form of the published text, the nature of the language used and the details of the witnesses can still be compared with other genuine, and other forged, charters in Edgar's reign. On such a comparison, it seems likely that the charter is indeed a genuine one.[13] In any case there could have been little incentive for anyone to have forged such a charter, and the likelihood is that as part of the very recent history of the estate the charter or a copy of it was lodged at Westminster when the same estate was later regranted to the Abbey.

No less than 60 written grants by King Edgar to various 'faithful *ministers*' and other royal officers have survived, most of them genuine documents.[14] So 'Mangoda' is only one of many. Hitherto no candidate for his identity has been put forward. Indeed the historian John James Park in his *Topography of Hampstead* in 1814 suggested that the name Mangoda might be a generic or symbolic type of name, an inverted 'Goodman'. But in fact the name is clearly an unusual one, of a continental pedigree, and there is at least one likely candidate for its owner : interestingly, a candidate connected with the coinage of the period.

By the middle of the tenth century England already enjoyed one of the most advanced currencies in Europe, possibly because it was one of the most taxable of countries.[15] At that time the making of the coinage was not carried out in one central mint, but was farmed out at many different mints throughout the country. Within those towns at which coins were minted, a moneyer or moneyers were in charge of the minting processes: they were

---

[12] Madox *Formulare* 283. See also Park *Topog. of Hampstead* App.1, where the Latin text is printed.

[13] Park *ibid* at p. 84-5 expressed many objections to this charter. But in the present state of knowledge, none of his objections seems now to be valid. It is true that the date added at the bottom of the charter is wrong, but it seems to have been a later addition; and a wrong date is not necessarily fatal. Each of the witnesses can be verified as contemporary persons; and most of the formulae used in the text appear word for word in other genuine documents of the time, eg. Sawyer *ibid* No 794. The probable date of the charter is 970-5 (i.e. fairly late in Edgar's reign and therefore about contemporaneous with the foundation of the Abbey), because one of the witnesses is Oslac, a *Dux* (Ealdorman and military leader) from Northumbria who, as Banton *Monastic Reform* SCH 18 (1982) 78-9 has shown, was introduced as a regular witness to royal charters in those years. All the four '*Duces* ' who witnessed the Mangoda charter were precisely the four named by Banton as the regular 'ducal' witnesses in the period 970-5.

[14] Edgar's three immediate predecessors had made even many more lay grants, which indicates the rate at which lands held by the kings were being distributed at this time, with the corresponding rise in lay dynasties during the period; see Stafford *Unification and Conquest* 37-8. But only five of these charters recorded grants to laymen (rest to the church) in Middlesex, see Bailey *Hidation of Middlesex* TLMAS 39 (1988) 177, who tables four but not the Mangoda one, which is a fifth. Incidentally Bailey points out (page 175) that laymen with property in Middlesex before the Conquest included very few Londoners.

[15] England was a rich country, richer than most neighbouring parts of the Continent, and it was this wealth which attracted the attacks made by the Danes and Northmen: Runciman *Accelerating Social Mobility* P. and P. 104 (1984) 8-9. It was also conveniently small.

appointed by the King, and were generally men of substance, from the class of the royal thegns. Edgar's uncle, King Athelstan (924 - 939) had decreed that thenceforward there was to be only one coinage throughout the realm; that each 'burh', or fortified town, was to have its own mint,[16] and that the number of the moneyers should be limited. Edgar in turn, in 973, followed that example with a reform of the whole coinage, in which the types of the silver penny, the basic current coin since the eighth century, were standardised, but with regular changes of the types, probably at six yearly intervals (at that time). Moreover as a standard practice (instead of the previous irregular practice) the penny had now to include on its reverse the name of both the moneyer and his mint:[17] perhaps the most permanent of all ways of achieving immortality.[18]

In the south-west of the country, the mint at Exeter in Athelstan's time had already had two moneyers in charge of it. During Edgar's reign one of the two moneyers at Exeter was called Mangod, a name of Germanic origin. He was a continental specialist in the field of coinage, whose foreign name is to be seen on his coins minted in Exeter, together with his mint's name. Such immigrant continental moneyers had become prominent in England since the end of the ninth century.[19] Indeed the name 'Mangod(a)' does not appear to be known in any context other than coinage. Equally it seems that a 'Mangod' (the same man, or same family?) had been working during the reign of Edgar's predecessor at Southampton, and another at Winchester.[20]

As a moneyer he (or each of them) was probably a thegn; as the Mangoda of the Hampstead charter, the King's 'noble' and 'faithful *minister*', undoubtedly was. But, it may be asked, what could a moneyer from Exeter (or other mint) be doing with a small estate in Middlesex? Although the minting was carried out in many centres, the common factor to them all was the metal 'die', with which the coin was actually struck. While it was royal policy to farm out the minting itself in many different places, after the middle of the tenth century the kings maintained their control of the coinage by restricting the cutting of the dies to one or two centres. In the tenth century London became the principal centre for the die-cutting, even if later there were some regional centres too.[21] All moneyers had

---

[16] *Athelstan's Laws at Grately,* at *EHD* l/420. Canterbury, Rochester, London, Winchester, Lewes, Hastings, Chichester, Southampton, Wareham, Dorchester, Exeter and Shaftesbury were named, with between two and eight moneyers each; while all other burhs were to have one each. But probably even Athelstan's decree was not the first law to that effect, but was a renewal of an earlier code: Metcalf 'Monetary history of England in the Tenth century' in *Anglo-Saxon Monetary History* (Ed. Blackburn) 140.

[17] Loyn *Governance* 123-4 ; Dolley and Metcalf 'Reform of English Coinage under Edgar' in *Anglo-Saxon Coins* (Ed. Dolley) 136-8.

[18] Loyn 'Progress in A-S Mon. Hist.' in *A-S Monetary History* 5. Moneyers' names had been used on at least some coins since the seventh century, and continued to be used until Edward I radically reorganised the coinage in the early fourteenth century: Smart *Moneyers' Names* Nomina 3 (1979) 20-22.

[19] See Feilitzer and Blunt 'Personal Names on Coinage of Edgar' in *England before the Conquest* (Ed. Clemoes) 201, 208; and Smart 'Scandinavians, Celts and Germans' in *A-S Monetary History* (Ed. Blackburn) 175-6. For facsimiles of the Exeter Mangod's coins, see Blunt, Stewart and Lyon *Coinage in Tenth Century England* Plate 15 (no 24) and Plate 21 (No 251); and see also *ibid.* pp. 261 and 302 There appears to have been something of a Mangod dynasty, since the name is to be seen not only on coins from about 950 but also until at least 1010 (see Thompson *Ashmolean Mus. A-S Pennies* Plate xx, No 523; also from Exeter), 35 years after Edgar's death. By the latter date the continental moneyers were on their way out, Smart *ibid* 177; but nevertheless the name Mangod recurs yet again at the Bedford mint during Cnut's reign, Grueber and Keary *English coins in the BM* 2/246. It seems to have appeared exclusively in a coinage context.

[20] Archibald and Blunt *BM: A-S Coins* Plate xxxv (No 806) and Plate xxxvi (No 817).

[21] See Loyn 'Boroughs and Mints' in *A-S Coins* (Ed. Dolley) 124-5; Blackburn and Lyon 'Regional die-

to collect their metal dies (and to pay for them) at a cutting centre: during Edgar's reign a moneyer in Exeter may well have had to visit London for new dies.[22] But even if he had no reason to come to London in order to collect dies, a royal officer had another reason for coming to London, namely that he might on occasions have to attend upon the king when the itinerant court happened to be in London. For such a person who had to visit London, a 'foothold'[23] on an estate near London would have been important, if only for the advantage of making use of his own produce or food-rents, while attending there.

So there are several factors which tend to indicate that the Hampstead Mangoda may well have been the Exeter moneyer. Any other explanation would entail the premise that there happened to be another thegn closely connected with the king at the same time, with the same unusual and specifically Germanic name. Another small pointer may be the date given in the copy of the charter, as published by Thomas Madox. That date was 978, which is an impossible date for Edgar, who died in 975. The '8', written in Roman numbers, was 'VIII'. Often the transcriptions of such dates in early charters were inaccurate [24] because of illegibility or human error, without necessarily being fatal to the authenticity of the charters. If the 'V' were a misreading or a miswriting of another 'I', the resulting date of 974 might be a significant one, since it was in 973 that Edgar was carrying through his coinage reforms, which in turn must have involved other steps connected with the countrywide network of moneyers (including the Exeter Mangod) who had to implement such reforms.[25]

It may also be coincidence, but there are a curious number of features which appear to link this area outside London with the coinage of the realm. As mentioned above,[26] the immediately adjacent estate to the south of Hampstead, namely Lileston, was held - certainly from early Norman times after the time of Domesday, and possibly earlier in Anglo-Saxon times - by men who possessed the hereditary office of the king's Die-cutter and whose attendance in London was essential.[27] Indeed the office of Die-cutter seems to

---

production in Cnut's Quatrefoil issue' in *A-S Monetary History* (Ed. Blackburn) 223-4. Stafford *Unification and Conquest* 142 says that all the die-cutting was at Winchester, but without giving authority for this opinion which seems to conflict with other views.

[22] Brooke & Keir *London* 93 ; Loyn *Governance* 125. See also at the time of Domesday, about 100 years later, *DB (Worcestershire)* f. 172 ('each moneyer must pay 20/- at London for the coin-dies in accordance with the custom of King Edward')

[23] This is a possible illustration of the 'foothold factor' referred to in the Introduction, page 13. Other examples are probably to be seen in Ranulf Peverel, also in Hampstead (see page 119-20); William Baynard in the Westminster Berewic (see page 155); Edward, son of Suein, and Otto the Goldsmith at Lileston (see page 73); Earl Ralph or his son, at Eia (see page 84); Robert, Count of Mortain, whose house at Bermondsey is actually recorded in DB, see *DB Surrey* 17/2 (f. 34b) and Golding *Robert of Mortain* A-N Studies 13 (1990) 131. To revert to Mangoda, it is also noticeable how far-flung the lands of individual Anglo-Saxon thegns often were, so that it would not be surprising to find a thegn in the ordinary course of events owning lands as separated as land in the southwest and in Middlesex, whether or not he had special practical motives for owning them.

[24] We may be dealing here with at least a copy of a copy (a copy by Madox of a copy by a Westminster scribe) of perhaps yet some other copy.

[25] The organisation needed for such a network for the making, issuing and regulating of the coinage makes one realise the scale of the administrative skills which must have been required even in the tenth century, let alone the more sophisticated eleventh. By about 1000 AD the number of mints had grown to over 60 throughout the country, Metcalf *ibid.* 134.

[26] See page 73 above.

[27] The Norman family began (in England) with Otto Fitz William, the Conqueror's Goldsmith, who also was or became a Cuneator or Die-cutter. Otto may have been only one of several Die-cutters during the Conqueror's reign (see Nightingale *Some London Moneyers* NC 142 (1982) 40-1), but by about 1100 his

have been or to have become 'appurtenant' to that estate itself. It may even be that the Anglo-Saxon 'Edward, son of Suein' who had held the same estate *before* the Conquest had filled the office of Die-cutter under the Anglo-Saxon kings.[28] There was of course nearly a century between Mangoda in Hampstead and Edward in Lileston, and there may be no more than a coincidence of possibilities here. However the office of Die-cutter remained appurtenant to Lileston for 170 years *after* the Conquest, and it could be that the office had previously been attached to the estate in that way for long before the Conquest as well. In view of the sophisticated coinage of Anglo-Saxon England a senior Die-cutter would have been an essential officer for the king to have in or near London.

And then by perhaps another coincidence (but a strange one) Hampstead itself throws up another name which has possible connections with the Anglo-Saxon coinage, namely 'Deormod'. This is contained in the place-name 'Deormodswic', which appears in the Anglo-Saxon bounds contained in the record of King Ethelred's grant of Hampstead to Westminster Abbey, see below. A 'wic' in this context was probably a dwelling or farm, and the place-name therefore meant the dwelling of Deormod, presumably a past or present holder of the land. No one can now establish with any certainty who this Deormod was or had been, but it is not unreasonable to believe that he was or had been at least a person of some consequence, commemorated in this way. It so happens that another moneyer [29] and a royal '*minister*'[30] with that name had lived about 50-75 years earlier, in the reign of Edward the Elder (Alfred's son, 899 - 924). It is not known exactly where Deormod's mint was, but it certainly was somewhere in Wessex in the south-west, where Mangod's was later. Whether there is any connection between this earlier moneyer and Hampstead's Deormod one cannot say, but if there is not, it is odd that the elements of both the coinage and a royal office recur as multiple coincidences in the two Hampstead names and in the immediately adjoining estate of Lileston.

To return to Mangoda himself one can say that, whoever he was, he does not appear to have held Hampstead for long, if indeed he entered into possession at all. Although by the terms of the charter he was entitled to bequeath the estate to any heir whom he chose, it may be that the estate (which seems to have been granted to him in the period 970-5) soon reverted to royal control for some reason, to be regranted in due course to the monks of Westminster by King Ethelred in 986. Or it may be that the estate was granted to him merely so that *he* could be seen to bestow it on the new Abbey, a not unusual practice : in that event Ethelred's action would have been a royal confirmation of Mangoda's own (now lost) grant of the estate to the Abbey.

The Boundaries   Maps O, N, A, E and P

The two sets of bounds for Hampstead, given in Mangoda's and the monks' charters, correspond in their general effect, although the monks' version is more elaborate and specific. An interpretation of the places or other geographical points contained in the two texts is given in **Map O**. Reversing the order of those geographical points, one can say

---

family had acquired a monopoly and the office then remained with that family for more than another 200 years. But most of the manor of Lileston (including, it seems, some land in Hampstead into which the holding extended) was sold to the Knights Templars in about 1237, with the office excluded, see Vol. 2.

[28] As suggested in VCH *Mdx* 1/118. Eideva, Edward's widow, married again after the time of Domesday, this time to Otto the Goldsmith. So she was able to stay on her first husband's estate of Lileston, which she took with her when she moved from perhaps one Die-cutter (English) to the next (Norman).

[29] Grueber and Keary *English coins in the B.M.* 2/99 and Plate VIII (No. 12); Blunt *Coinage in Tenth Century England* 291.

[30] See Sawyer *A-S Charters* No 1443.

that, firstly, the northern boundary, starting from the 'boundary stream' which leads up from Watling Street towards the present Childs Hill (i.e. the same one as discussed above under 'Codanhlaw') and ending at Sandgate, appears to match closely the line of the boundary given in the Bleccanham bounds, as discussed above and shown on **Maps N and P**.[31] In effect Hampstead at that time did not include the Fortune Green area. Secondly, the whole of the western boundary of the estate, formed by Watling Street, is another fixed datum. So that leaves only the eastern and southern boundaries to resolve.

Both geography and history combine to identify at least part of the eastern side of the estate. Since Sandgate is firmly fixed as the place where the three estates (Bleccanham, Finchley and Hampstead) met,[32] it is clear that the boundary must begin from there. And then the ridge of high ground which runs southwards across the middle of the East Heath section of the present Hampstead Heath, acting as a watershed with streams and marshes in the valley on either side (see **Map E**), is an obvious natural feature for a boundary. So indeed it became historically, for both the manors and the parishes [33] on either side of it, for more than a thousand years. To this day, the line of a medieval boundary-ditch [34] (see **Plate 13**, page 111) which ran and still runs along that ridge (and in which many of the later boundary stones of the two parishes still stand) can be traced across East Heath; and even the relics of a hedge such as that which accompanied the ditch [35] can be seen.

But the beginning of that ridge only becomes visible some way south of Sandgate, and so there is a gap to fill between Sandgate and the start of the natural ridge. That gap is filled by the boundary details supplied by the charter which granted Hampstead to Westminster. The charter says that the line starts by going *eastwards* from Sandgate, to the "wood-clearing (farmstead?) [36] of Bedegar". If one could still go eastwards from

---

[31] It is also significant that these Hampstead bounds too mention the 'boundary stream' in the vicinity of Watling Street, in the same way as the Bleccanham bounds do. This tends to confirm the identification of the stream with the northern source of the Westbourne river, see pages 92-3 above.

[32] See page 92 above. For the bounds, see Appendix 2, page 169, and map on **Plate 12**, page 110.

[33] The manors and the parishes were not identical. The manors were Hampstead and Tottenhall, but the parishes were Hampstead and St Pancras. See **Maps A and O**.

[34] No record of the ditch before 1226/7 AD has survived, but the ditch clearly predated that time; see Davis *University Site* LTR.17 (1936) 118; Farmer *Hampstead Heath* 37. The ditch was part of an encirclement of ditches which in 1226/7 surrounded the whole of an estate at the present Kenwood.

[35] The existing relics of a hedge are of course comparatively recent, some of the oak trees being only up to 200 years old, and the old hawthorns much younger. But whether or not there was a ditch there as early as Anglo-Saxon times (and it is fair to say no *ditch* is referred to in the early charters), there certainly was a hedge (see Text), possibly the whole length of the boundary from the beginning of the ridge or at least from a point level with the present South End area, southwards to Chalk Farm. In the monks' charter the 'hedge' is only mentioned in relation to the latter (southern) portion of the boundary, but (subject to the position of the woods in that area, see pages 127 and **Map P**) there seems little reason why it should not have run along the crest of the more northerly ridge as well. It is pointed out by Hooke *Pre-Conquest Woodland* Ag.HR 37 (1989) 123 and 128 that a '*haga*' (the term used in the charter for a hedge) often was an important boundary, accompanied by a ditch and bank. Since this boundary marked the line between the Westminster Corridor and the extensive St Paul's lands north of London, it was clearly important. See Appendix 2, page 168 for another very significant '*haga* ' on the shire boundary with Hertfordshire.

[36] Each of the surviving copies of the monks' charter (O.S.Facs iii. 34; WAM Vl; WAD f.76) has a slightly different and difficult reading to describe Bedegar's grounds. The position of the site is further confirmed by all the later maps (eg. in 1762) and by descriptions of the furthest limit of the Hampstead manor and parish below the site of the present Spaniards Inn (known much later as Park Gate, i.e. one entrance to the Bishop of London's great park in the present Bishop's Avenue area, then in the manor of Hornsey. It was approached by 'the Bishop's Way', within the boundaries of Hampstead, in the fourteenth century. The Bishop's other, and main, 'Park Gate' was near the present East Finchley station).

Sandgate, that meeting-place of the three estates or parishes, one would come to a position at or near the former 'Kenwood Dairy Farm', which stands (as one can see to this day) at the very northern end of the boundary-ditch which then runs south to the watershed ridge. So Bedegar, whoever he was, seems to have lived (at that time or earlier) near the dairy farm.

Then the line ran, according to the same charter, to the (as yet, unidentified) "dwelling of Deormod", whom we have already mentioned as a possible moneyer; and then to "middle Hampstead", and so "along the hedge to the rush field". There is no doubt that the present Pond Street-South Hill Park area was a place of settlement by the thirteenth century. It had plenty of water, with some of the source-waters of the river Fleet gathering off the heath, and it is likely that the area may have been settled much earlier and could have qualified as "middle Hampstead".[37] So a "hedge" ran, if not down the whole length of the ridge already described, at least from the present Pond Street-South Hill Park area down to the undoubtedly wet parts of Chalk Farm at the very bottom of the long Hampstead hill, where apparently rushes grew in a marshy area. Along the latter stretch it is likely that the woodland later called *'Timberhurst'* grew (see **Map P** and page 127), and it may be that the hedge formed the eastern boundary of that wood or that, accompanied by the 'track' mentioned below and possibly a continuation of the ditch and a bank,[38] it ran through areas kept open within the wood.

Two other pointers are given by the other charter, the grant to Mangoda, (which incidentally is much more terse than the Westminster one). It speaks only of a 'track' on this eastern boundary. The watershed ridge was a natural choice for such a track, leading from the central heights (near the present Spaniards Inn, above Sandgate) down alongside or through the woods [39] to join the other and no doubt larger track on the present Haverstock Hill which must have led from the main settlement in Hampstead in the direction of Westminster. That smaller 'track' along the eastern ridge came down, the charter says, to 'Foxhanger'. A hanger meant a wood on a steepish hill,[40] and one of the steepest slopes of all on the long Hampstead Hill, where the 'Load of Hay' pub now stands, comes just before the Chalk Farm bottom. While none of this is entirely conclusive, the consistency of all the features is very persuasive. At almost every point along this eastern border, the established boundary of the Manor eight centuries later, in 1762, as shown in the Manor Map of that date, tends to confirm the directions given by the Anglo-Saxon charter about 800 years before.[41]

Outside the whole length of this eastern boundary of Hampstead lay the even older

[37] The main settlement being higher up the hill, on the southwest side of the hill, see page 123 below.

[38] See Note 34 above.

[39] See page 127.

[40] Shorter OED. See also Gelling *PNs in the Landscape* 194-6.

[41] SCL *Manor Map* 1762. The only qualification to this is that the 1762 boundary broke the natural line by including within the Hampstead borders a field (from, in effect, the erstwhile Tottenhall estate next door) which included the site of the 'Gospel Oak', as marked on **Map O**. It has been suggested that 'middle Hampstead' may instead have been near the Gospel Oak in Anglo-Saxon times (see EPNS *PN Mdx* 221), which if correct might imply that that area round the Oak was already part of the Hampstead estate. In support of this, one can see that the Fleet river forms a neat loop round the Gospel Oak site itself, see **Map O** and the map in Waller *The Holebourne* TLMAS 4 (1870) 97. This suggestion could be right, but on balance it seems more likely that the appropriation of the Gospel Oak field would have taken place at some later and unknown time and that originally the boundary ran unbroken in its gentle curve down to the Chalk Farm area, instead of being diverted round the Gospel Oak area by a river which it had not otherwise followed.

Tottenhall estate of the Canons of St Paul's. Tottenhall and the adjoining estate of St Pancras, which also belonged to the Canons, stretched in two elongated strips northwards from the present Bloomsbury and Holborn area (the Westminster 'Berewic'), see **Map A.** The way in which they were acquired by the Canons is not known, but it had been at an early date and may have arisen as part of a mutual partition of the Cathedral estates between the Bishop of London and the Canons.

From the wet bottom of that last steep slope the boundary swung roughly westwards, as both charters assert, and made for Watling Street, so completing the circuit of the estate. On its way it passed a 'wood',[42] and then a 'stony thicket' (or grave?)'. But the exact line of that southern boundary now defies any accurate identification,[43] and later in the medieval period it seems to have been subject to fluctuation.[44] After the marsh, it probably skirted round the south of Primrose Hill (which may have had the 'wood' on and near it); and then formed an elusive boundary with the woods of the later-named St John's Wood area. In later centuries it seems to have been a shifting line between cultivated fields and the forested belt, which at times became the recognised hiding place of robbers and other criminals. This southern region of Hampstead was probably one where much assarting [45] was carried out, as the lower slopes of the Hampstead Hill were cleared of trees and scrub, and the line of cultivation was pushed slowly forward up the hill.

So the southern boundary came at last to Watling Street. There it turned north-west and followed up the line of the Street, thus completing the 'circle' of Hampstead at the point where the Street met the 'boundary-stream' which had descended from the top of Child's Hill (see **Maps H and P**)

None of the estates outside the southern boundary of Hampstead was held by the monks of Westminster at any time. As already indicated, the estate of Rugmere at the time of Domesday was held by one of the Canons of St Paul's, called Ralph; the estate of Tyburn by the nuns of Barking Abbey,[46] and the estate of Lileston by the widow of Edward, son of Suein. Outside the western boundary of Hampstead, formed by Watling Street, another of the St Paul's estates lay : there Willesden, a heavily wooded area, was held by the Canons collectively, and at some time before (probably well before) the Conquest it had been earmarked to provide part [47] of the food which the Canons needed for

---

[42] EPNS *PN Mdx* 111: the OE. word 'baeru(w)e' in the text of the bounds, which apparently has given rise to the name Barrow Hill near Primrose Hill, in fact means a wood and not a barrow. Another reading has suggested a 'marsh' *before* the wood: it would fit the locality, but it is doubtful.

[43] Hales *Charters of Hampstead* TLMAS 6 (1890) 569 seeks to pinpoint a 'stone-grave', but it is guesswork, since there are no other identification signs; and the meaning is unclear anyway.

[44] This was the mainly wooded boundary with both the later St John's Wood area (contained in the estates of Lileston and Tyburn, see pages 73 and 103-4 above) and the small estate of Rugmere which, like its larger adjoining estates of Tottenhall and St Pancras, was held by the Canons of St Paul's. Rugmere disappeared subsequently many centuries later when Henry VIII acquired part of it (named, as it then was, Rugmoor) in 1540, for inclusion in his new Marylebone Park. But it seems that about the same time one of the remaining fields of Rugmoor was tacked onto the southern boundary of Hampstead (which with its sub-manor Belsize had also in 1540 been surrendered to the King in the course of the dissolution of the monasteries), in the form of an appendage (rather like the Gospel Oak enclosure already mentioned), see **Map O**, and the Manor Map of 1762. This field, now the lower slopes of Primrose Hill with visible stones still marking the old boundary, was apparently not needed by the King for his Marylebone Park. See also Lovell & Marcham *Old St Pancras* Survey of London 19/1.

[45] This was the term used during the the medieval period for the practice of clearing a part of a wood, fen, heathland or waste land in order to convert it to cultivation.

[46] See pages 73-4 above.

[47] Willesden was not unique in Middlesex in serving this purpose. Other estates of the Canons which

their maintenance.[48] It has not proved possible to date the acquisition of any of these estates by their holders, and one cannot say whether the details given in Domesday Book about the position at or immediately before the Conquest reflected as well the state of affairs (say) a hundred years before, in the tenth century.

One other geographical point of interest (which appears in the Mangoda charter, but not in the Westminster one) is the reference to a 'cucking pool',[49] on or near Watling Street in the north-western corner of the estate. There is no surviving evidence that the northern 'boundary stream', between Hampstead and Codanhlaw, actually joined Watling Street. As far as one can tell, it turned round a bend before reaching the road and then flowed roughly parallel to it at all known times.[50] One is left to infer that there was such a pool, probably a static field-pool used by animals, somewhere close by the road in the corner of the estate.[51] If this is indeed a tenth century mention of a cucking pool in which miscreants could be ducked as a punishment, it is a very early record. In one place, Domesday Book when dealing with the town of Chester [52] more than a hundred years later speaks of a cucking 'chair', but in that case the cucking was apparently into *dung,* since the chair was called a 'dung-chair'. Presumably that pool must have been a pool acting as a cess-pit, or standing alongside a dung-heap, as many village or town pools probably did. No doubt a ducking into such material acted as a much more effective deterrent than the ducking into a seemingly clean village pond which features in more romantic pictures of medieval life. But at least the Hampstead 'scolds' may have been spared that more drastic treatment.

---

were, as it were, labelled in this way, as being earmarked to supply food for them, during the period before the Conquest, were Chiswick and part of Barnsbury. This form of 'earmarking' for a defined purpose appears to reflect (a) the specific purpose for which the land was originally granted to the religious body, or (b) some form of existing dispute, against which the specific earmarking was designed to give a special protection (cf. Raftis *Estates of Ramsey Abbey* 8-10 and 35), or (c) the retention of an estate in the monks' own hands for their own farming, instead of being let out to a farmer-tenant. Willesden was unusual in that by the time of the Domesday Survey the whole of this large manor (15 hides) had been let to the tenant inhabitants collectively, for them to cultivate on their own, without the Canons at that time retaining any part of it under their own management: see *DB Mdx* 3/17 (f.127d); Hoyt *Farm of the Manor* Speculum (1955) 168-9. Other estates of theirs (in St Pancras, Islington, Hoxton and Stanestaple, see DB *Mdx* 3/21, 23, 25, 26, 28) were also held by the tenants, but these were all small estates of 1-2 hides.

[48] As indicated earlier (see page 18), the Canons already held land independently of the Bishop of London, whose seat was at St Pauls; but more than that, individual Canons had already begun to hold lands under what became known as the 'prebend' system (eg. Canon Ralph who held Rugmere after the Conquest, above). Under that system, an individual Canon was assigned various lands or revenues as his 'stipend', for his own support and maintenance.

[49] The Old English in the charter is 'coc cinge pol'

[50] See **Maps O and P**, and page 92, note 28.

[51] As regards another nearby pool, namely the source of the *westwards-flowing* Slade stream, see page 93.

[52] *DB.(Cheshire) f.* 262b: 'cathedra stercoris', literally the chair of dung.

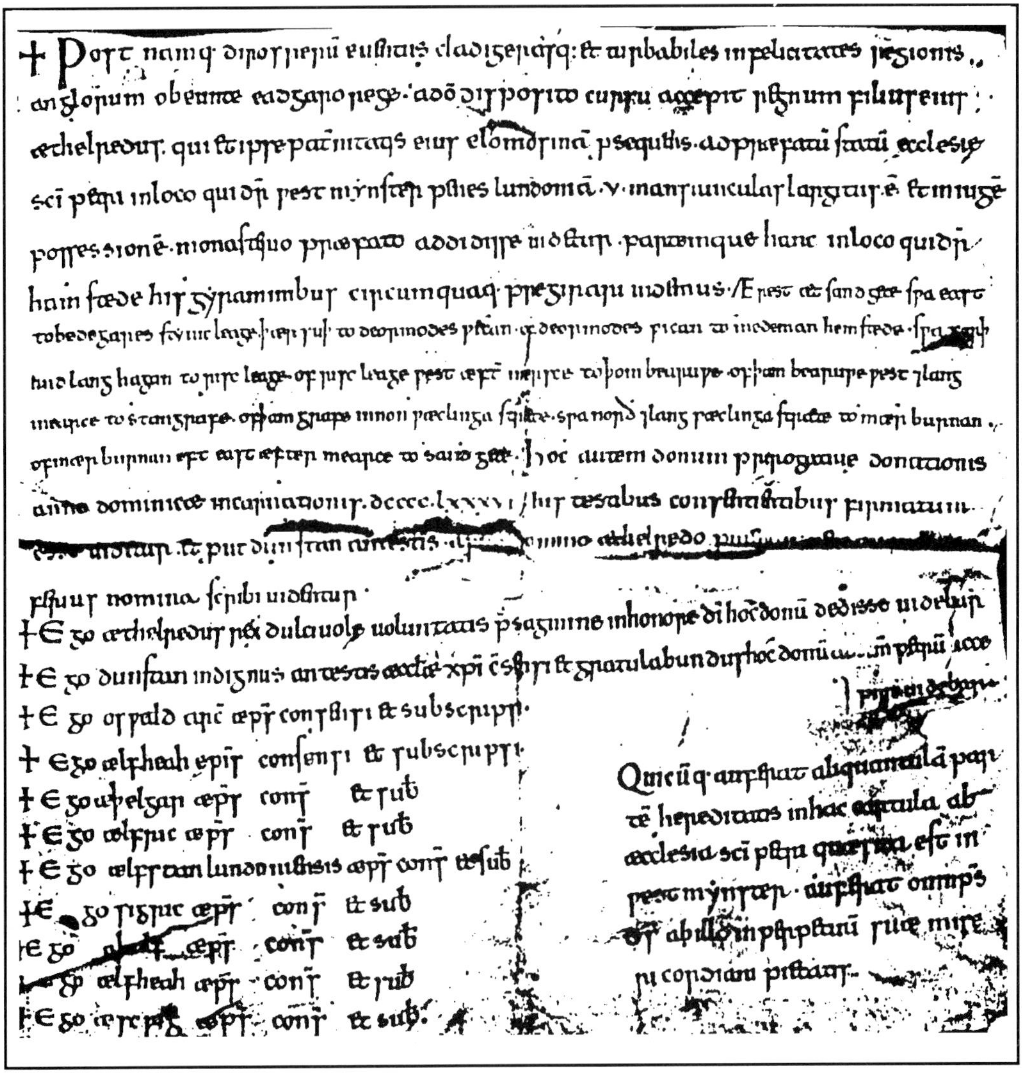

Plate 11. The document written in King Ethelred's reign in or before 988, recording his gift in 986 to the Abbey of five 'little hides' in Hampstead. The 'bounds' of Hampstead in Old English appear in the small script, starting in the sixth line; they are translated in Appendix 2 at page 169. See page 100

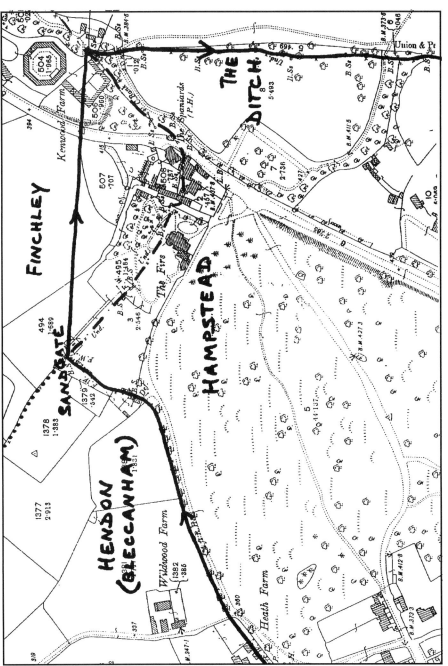

Plate 12. An extract from the 1894 Ordnance Survey, showing (marked-in, in ink) the Hampstead boundary with Bleccanham, Finchley and Tottenhall, in the 'Sandgate', Kenwood and East Heath areas. The first three estates met at Sandgate: from there the Saxon boundary sensibly went 'eastwards', thereby avoiding the hill up to the present-day Spaniards Inn. (The 1894 boundary-line is shown broken.) From the Kenwood farm site, the boundary ran 'southwards', as shown, with a 'track' on the East Heath ridge and (further south) a 'hedge': and possibly a ditch.

See pages 92 and 105

Plate 13. The remains of the great ditch which lies on the old boundary-line between the Westminster Abbey and St Paul's estates of Hampstead and Tottenhall. The ditch was recorded in a document in 1226/7, and a forthcoming survey may help to discover whether it was Anglo-Saxon in origin. The part of the ditch seen at the top lies within the present Kenwood estate, as shown in **Plate 12**, page 110. See page 105

CHAPTER 9

Paddington : between a Road and a River

The name Paddington is an old one, meaning the 'tun' (a farm or enclosure) of 'Padda', no doubt an early resident.[1]

The Descent from Wulfric

In about 998 AD when the Telligraph of King Ethelred [2] recorded those estates which had already come into the possession of the monks [3] in the tenth century, it listed also four other estates in Middlesex which were 'bespoken' for the Abbey but had not yet been received by it. Of these, three (Sunbury, Shepperton and Cowley) were on the south-west and the west boundaries of the shire, but the fourth (Paddington) was probably that part of the wider area now known as Paddington which actually adjoined the great road, Watling Street,[4] just as Hampstead and Hendon did further north. It was described in the Telligraph as a 'praediolum', a little estate, and at that time it still had a life tenant called Wulfric.

Both King Edgar and King Ethelred had had a prominent and 'faithful *minister*' of the name of Wulfric, who owned enormous estates in the Midlands. One cannot say whether these 'two' Wulfrics were the same man, but it is at least possible. The Telligraph records that 'after Wulfric's days', the estate was to revert to the Abbey. Presumably there had been a grant (perhaps by Dunstan, if the much later Westminster tradition were to be relied on [5]) to Wulfric, subject to that condition; or perhaps Wulfric had himself previously owned the land and had made a grant of it to the monks, on the condition that he could continue to live there (or at least to use it) until he died. If the two Wulfrics were in fact the same man, it seems more likely that the estate had been granted to him for life, with reversion thereafter to the Abbey (i.e. the former alternative), because when the '*minister*' (if it is the same man) made his will [6] in about 1002-4 he made no mention of any gift by him to the monks, as piously or smugly he surely would have wished to do, if he had been the person responsible for such a charitable gift to take effect after his death.

---

[1] EPNS *PN Mdx* 132; *VCH Mdx* 9/181. Probably coincidentally, the name 'Pada' is recorded on gold coins of the seventh century, as yet another moneyer: Smart *Moneyers' Names on A-S Coinage* Nomina 3 (1979) 20. Sometimes in its early history 'Paddington' was also spelled with one 'd'.

[2] That is, the material part of it which contained the *factual* detail, see page 63; Sawyer *A-S Charters* No 894; and Appendix 1, page 164.

[3] In the Corridor: Westminster, Lotheresleage, Hendon (the smaller), Bleccanham, Codanhlaw and Hampstead.

[4] Certainly the position of Paddington Wood, which in its time was probably the largest wood in Paddington and later supplied (as Hampstead and Hendon woods did) much timber and brushwood for the Abbey, was situated on Watling Street: see VCH *Mdx* 9/235, and map at *ibid.*180. For Paddington's position, see **Map A**.

[5] In the forged 'Great Charter of Dunstan', Sawyer *A-S Charters* 1293; see Chaplais 'Original Charters' in *A Medieval Miscellany* (Ed. Barnes and Slade) PRS (NS) 36 (1962) 92, and pages 59-61 above. For Wulfric's earlier history, see Stafford *Unification and Conquest* 48, 51 and 159. A third, and later, Wulfric appears as a thegn in Westminster on page 142 below.

[6] Sawyer *A-S Charters* No 1536.

At all events the estate was due to come to the Abbey when Wulfric (whoever he was) died, and presumably it did so, probably by about 1005. According to another later but spurious charter, which did however reflect authentic material,[7] the estate was of only two hides. But Domesday Book makes no mention of Paddington at all, and it is likely that the areas of Paddington, and also Knightsbridge with Westbourne,[8] were (at least by 1086) regarded as part of the new and enlarged Norman manor of Westminster and were included within the Domesday assessment of its thirteen and a half hides.[9]

So it seems that shortly after 1000 AD the small estate of Paddington had been added to the monks' endowment. Although this is the first recorded mention of the district, the name itself is an indication that there was already an earlier settlement there. One cannot say at what date Padda had been one of the former inhabitants.

The Boundaries ?   Map H

There are unfortunately no bounds given for Paddington in any charter, and one can only infer that it was probably that part of the Paddington district which bordered on Watling Street and contained not only the main settlement which later became known as Paddington Green, but also the wood which was known as Paddington Wood.[10] In that position the estate would have lain between Watling Street and the river later called the Westbourne, which on its passage down from Hampstead to the Thames probably formed at this point the boundary between Paddington and the adjoining tract of land. The lower reaches of the river (ie. below the crossing of Watling Street at Kilburn) seem to have had no regular name until comparatively recently, when they received the name of Westbourne. But the adjoining tract of land lying to the west of the river was apparently known at an early date as 'Westburne', meaning 'west of the river', and in due course the name was adopted for the river as well.[11] Since in later records a distinction was drawn between the districts and vills of Paddington and Westbourne, it seems most likely that the first estate received by the monks in Paddington (assessed at only two hides) was restricted to the district east of the river. The district of Westbourne was left to be bracketed probably with Knightsbridge and with it to become part of Westminster during Edward the Confessor's reign.

---

[7] Sawyer *ibid* No 1039; Harmer *Three Westminster Writs* EHR 51(1936) 99. This is the charter, forged in the name of Edward the Confessor, which does not seem to have been fathered onto Osbert de Clare, yet: see also page 90.

[8] For Knightsbridge, see page 71. The three vills of Knightsbridge, Paddington and Westbourne (see text, below) were recognised as included within the parish of St Margarets, Westminster, after that church had been founded in Edward the Confessor's reign, see page 83 above. While Paddington had evidently become part of the Abbey's endowment within the period of about 30 years after its foundation, it is doubtful whether Knightsbridge or Westbourne was, at that time : but see Harvey *WA Estates* 45, and *VCH Mdx* 9/226.

[9] See page 138. It is also significant that in the reference to Paddington in Ethelred's Telligraph (see Appendix 1, page 165) the estate was due to come to the Abbey specifically as part of the Abbey's 'own liberty', suggesting that it was intended to become part of the 'Westminster' estate immediately it came into the monks' possession.

[10] As in Hampstead, so in Paddington a chapel (which was dedicated to St Nicholas) was later built, probably where the still later church stood at the Green. The date when the Paddington chapel was built is not known: it probably was well after the Conquest, rather than before it; it certainly was before 1222, when it was expressly referred to in the Decree issued in the great arbitration between the Abbey and the Bishop of London, see page 83. As regards Paddington Wood, see Note 4 above.

[11] See page 43; Grover EPNS *PN.Mdx* 133; *VCH Mdx* 9/198. For the river's course, see **Map H**. Above the point in the present Kilburn where the river crossed Watling Street, the river was first known as the Kilbourne and only much later as the Westbourne.

CHAPTER 10

Hampstead : People, Village and Lives

The Classes of Society

So far it has been a story of property, of charters, lands and boundaries. But there are other questions to answer. Can one discern any realistic picture of what life itself may have been like before the Norman Conquest, for those who lived and worked in these lands near London? Are the people themselves and something of their lives and surroundings to be seen, however dimly? It was a common saying (at least in the Anglo-Saxon literary world) that for the support of his throne the King needed 'oratores, bellatores and laboratores',[1] those who pray, those who fight and those who work. We have seen something, and will see still more, of those who prayed and those who fought. But it is now the turn of those who worked.

From the time of the early migrations until the foundation and the early endowments of Westminster Abbey, the obligations and rights of peasant classes in 'English' society had been progressively becoming more defined. Already there were more than 400 years of Anglo-Saxon (and, in parts of the country, later Danish) settlement behind them,; and established social patterns had been and were being formed. A once-pioneering society, enjoying considerable freedom, was becoming more structured. More importantly the second wave of wide-ranging attacks in the late tenth and early eleventh centuries by further Danes and Norsemen had made the small men, the peasants and tradesmen who formed the vast majority of the English and existing Danish population, look much more to their kings and lords for physical protection in times of violence. But protection also spelt dependence, and such dependence had to be bought. The price which had to be paid was an increasing subservience to their lords, who in turn were bound to give them defence in return.[2] That somewhat contrived figure the 'free Anglo-Saxon ceorl',[3] like his even more fabled successor the 'Yeoman of England' in later centuries, was to pass into history.

In other ways too, the violence had pointed the way to subservience. From the end of the tenth century, waves of extra taxation were being imposed, both to buy off the Danes with 'geld' and to raise additional money for defence; and (as taxations usually are) these were passed down the line to the small men, who thereby became further indebted, and so in still greater thrall, to their lords.[4] The lords in turn demanded, and obtained, unpaid

---

[1] eg. *EHD* 1/ 919 (King Alfred translating in the ninth century a writer of the sixth century, Boethius) and 928 (Abbot Aelfric, at about the end of the tenth century, see page 129).

[2] Loyn *A-S England* 195-6. But this is not to say that the tendency towards subservience was an entirely new feature. One can trace it back to much earlier periods, eg. when it was arising through previous economic pressures, when a landlord demanded service as well as rent, as a condition of renewing a letting to a freeman, see eg. *Laws of Ine* 67, in Wessex as early as the seventh century, *EHD* 1/406. Even Runciman *Accelerating Social Mobility* P&P 104 (1984) 3-30 does not seem to be inconsistent with this view, see his conclusions at page 21 and 25.

[3] For two views of the 'ceorl', see Campbell *Essays in A-S History* 134-5.

[4] Maitland *DB and Beyond* 323-6; Loyn *A-S England* 305-14

compulsory labour, that dominant badge of service, for the working of their estates: a service which slowly passed into a deeper serfdom, as overbearing lords treated freemen as though they were slaves.[5]

So it is that as the eleventh century began, with a small community of monks now established in their new and fairly primitive monastery at Westminster, most if not all of their unknown tenants in the Corridor estates were probably 'free' peasants who had already fallen or were falling into classes which owed differing degrees of service to the monks. In King Ethelred's Telligraph (998 AD) the tenants are actually, but anonymously, mentioned in a short passage describing that King's gift to the Abbey of the five mansae of land *'in loco qui Hamstede vocitatur a ruricolis'* : 'in the place which is called Hamstede by the country-people'.[6] But this tells us nothing about them, save that they were there.

The Peasant Figures

In the absence of specific records relating to their lives in this region, one has to turn to other contemporary sources, to tell us something of the likely pattern of their days. One rare author, writing perhaps a few years before Westminster Abbey was founded,[7] speaks of the divisions into which working people fell. His record is a short but vivid tract about the management of a rural estate: in view of the cumbersome name by which it has been passed down to us, I will call it more simply the *Estate Guide* [8] The author was clearly involved closely with the estate in question, which lay in the West country and was large and well-organised. He speaks of the classes recognised at that time, from the thegns at the top, down to the slaves at the bottom, with three main categories of working people in between. He goes out of his way to emphasise strongly that wide variations existed in the obligations which people might owe on different estates in other places, because of significant contrasts which might exist between the 'customs' of one estate and the 'customs' of another. Such customs had grown out of particular practices and habits which over long centuries had happened to be followed on different estates; and in time these had come to have the force of very localised 'laws', governing the rights of those who lived in those places.[9]

The anchormen of the *Estate Guide*'s peasant figures were those who were called the 'Geburs', the men who collectively seem to have done most of the work on the author's estate. The *Gebur* was in theory a free man; but (depending on the nature of the local

---

[5] One of King Cnut's laws (c. 1023 AD) refers to overbearing lords (for different reasons) treating freemen as though they were actually slaves: "we will not allow that abuse": *EHD* 1/457. However real slavery was widely accepted.

[6] See page 63 and Appendix 1. This is in the long factual passage in Ethelred's Telligraph which does not suggest forgery. For contemporary scenes of peasant activities, see **Plate 14**, page 133.

[7] Its date, purpose and source have been much debated. For the latest survey of these, see Harvey, P. *Rectitudines and Gerefa* EHR (1993) 1. Following this, I use a mid-tenth century date for the tract's origin, although this is still contentious. The text has come down to us in a subsequently-revised form, but to avoid complication, I will refer to it as though it had all been written at the same time.

[8] *EHD* 2/875; Maitland *ibid*. The original document is in old English, but it carries the weighty title of *Rectitudines Singularum Personarum*, because of a later (and inaccurate) Latin translation of it.

[9] The author seems to draw a distinction between 'the ancient arrangements about the estate' and 'the custom of the district'. Presumably the 'ancient arrangements' were the lord's own arrangements which he had imposed, not matters which gave rise to *rights* on the part of the peasants, as the perhaps even more ancient 'customs' did. The grants of royal lands to both churches and laymen in the tenth and eleventh centuries must inevitably have necessitated changes in estate management and perhaps affected the 'customs' of the lands so granted: cf. Stafford *The Farm of One Night* Ec.HR 33 (1980) 498.

'customs' in his area) long shifts of unpaid work on his lord's lands might be his lot: for example, he might have to work two days every week for the lord; and at the spring-ploughing and sowing, three days a week (such regular duties being called his 'week-work'). In addition he might have many other special duties, at the winter-ploughing or when the winter-folding of pigs, sheep or cattle or the carrying of produce were needed on his lord's lands. Such special duties at different times of the year were known as 'boon-work'. In addition a payment of 'tribute' (in kind, in the form of more obligatory ploughing, or of food) and other exactions in kind at various times of the year would be required of him. But he had rights too, sanctioned by the local 'customs'. As a farmer, he (or an ancestor) had been entitled to receive from his lord a holding, with utensils for his home, tools for his work, and live and dead stock.[10] When not employed for his lord, he and his family were free to work their own land in order to support themselves.

So a mutual dependence between a lord and his man, similar to that under the later Norman feudal system, was already present. In return for his services the man would be entitled to expect protection from his lord, when danger threatened.

Beside the *Gebur* there stood two other serving figures. The first was a smaller but perhaps more versatile man, the *Cotsetla* (later often known as a 'cottar'), a small-holder or cottager ("he is to have 5 acres", the *Estate Guide* says; or sometimes more). The local customs might ordain that he should pay no rent, but should work one day per week for his lord, and three days per week during the busy time of harvest, in addition to other special duties. As his holding was clearly inadequate to maintain a family, he and they were clearly dependent on such other work as he could obtain for pay in kind or in money. Like the *Gebur*, he was already half a serf but yet still in theory a freeman; at least he had to pay a freeman's dues.

The second was a *Geneat,* or 'companion', a superior serving man, who paid rent as a freeman would, and mainly owed personal services to his lord, such as building or fencing a house for him, bearing messages, carrying his goods for him 'far and near' on horseback, providing means of carriage, or acting as his guard. He was in effect a riding-man, a mounted retainer, but he might also have to turn his hand to the tasks of the all-demanding harvest, such as reaping and mowing. In status the *Geneat* had come down in the world, because in earlier Anglo-Saxon times he had been "a real warrior and a person of fairly high rank".[11]

The final class of serving person dealt with by the *Estate Guide* was the *slave*, a figure on whom much of Anglo-Saxon society depended. Slaves had been made of the original Britons; of enemies taken in war; and of those of the Anglo-Saxons' own people who could not or would not comply with their own early laws and found themselves reduced to slavery by legal penalties written into those laws.[12] Even a widespread trade in slaves had

---

[10] On the author's estate, the stock specified for the *Gebur* by custom was 2 oxen, 1 cow, 6 sheep and 7 acres already sown. All of these were to revert to the lord, when the *Gebur* died. In some places, the lord had to supply military arms, and these too reverted: see Whitelock *A-S.Wills 100*. See also Cnut's Laws, EHD 1/465. This reversion of things supplied by the lord was the origin of the lord's right during the later Middle Ages (and even in the centuries after the Dissolution, as a vestigial relic of medieval obligation) to receive a 'heriot' when a customary tenant died. Usually in such later periods the heriot was the best beast held by the tenant, and in the records we shall see the 'reversion' of such animals to the Abbey, when tenants died in Hampstead in the thirteenth and fourteenth centuries, see Vol 2.

[11] Bloch *Feudal Society* (trans. Manyon) 183, cited by Runciman *Accelerating Social Mobility* P&P 104 (1984) 5.

[12] Eg. Laws of Ine (c. 694-700 AD), *EHD* 1/400 : "If anyone steals with the knowledge of all his household, they are all to go into slavery". For A-S slavery, see Pelteret *Slave-raiding and trading* A-S

developed in England. Since the slave's services were unlimited, no specific tasks were assigned to him in the *Estate Guide*. But like the peasants, he had his rights defined for him by the local estate-customs, for example, his food entitlements on the author's estate: each year, for the male slave, there were prescribed '12 pounds of good corn, 2 sheep carcases and one good cow', with special food at the Christmas and Easter feasts. It was often the slave who had the heavy job of a ploughman, and as some recompense in the *Estate Guide* he was entitled to receive a strip of land for ploughing for himself.

One of the main lessons from the *Estate Guide* is that already by the time when Westminster Abbey was founded in the tenth century, the difference between the lord's lands and the tenant's lands, and the distinction between the tenant's 'week-work' and the other special seasonal work which he might be called upon to do (his 'boon-work'), were well established; and this was a century before the Norman Conquest. Both these kinds of compulsory servive continued to exist through most of the subsequent medieval period, within the Westminster Corridor estates as elsewhere, and only began to weaken significantly after the Black Death had killed up to a third of the population in 1349-50.

But one would not expect exactly the same pattern of society to be found in the Corridor estates of Westminster Abbey. The estate described in the *Estate Guide* was somewhere in the West Country, not in Middlesex. It was probably a lay estate, not an ecclesiastical one.[13] It was a place in which there was clearly a strong tradition of firm management, not an estate newly come into the hands of a new group of monks who were themselves probably new to the area. But in spite of these differences, one can begin to discern from the *Estate Guide* some outlines of the life led by the peasants in a Middlesex estate, who were once free and (if they followed the social pattern which prevailed elsewhere) were slowly becoming the serfs which in the end they certainly were at the time of the Domesday Survey. Let us now turn to that.

Hampstead before and after the Conquest   Maps B, K and L
Hampstead presents an interesting example of the Corridor estates, against the general background revealed by the *Estate Guide*. The starting point (although perhaps one should call it an 'end point', if one is considering the Anglo-Saxon period) is the Domesday record itself, which fortunately to some extent looks backwards, as well as at the position in 1086. The past, for the Domesday Commissioners, meant two things: firstly the time *immediately before* the Conquest, 'the time of King Edward the Confessor' (abbreviated throughout the record to 'TRE', from the Latin); and secondly, the point of time *after* the Conquest in 1066, when the Conqueror having taken all the lands of England into his power first granted each estate to a tenant. But the Commissoners' own viewpoint, their 'present', was the period 20 years after the Conquest, when they were completing their survey-reports which, less than one year before, the Conqueror had ordered to be made.[14]

At the time of Domesday the households recorded in Hampstead were those of one

E. 9 (1981) 99; Moore *DB Slavery* A-N S. 11 (1989) 191; and Runciman *ibid* 11-2. The A-S were "avowedly, almost aggressively, slave-owners", Loyn *Governance* 5. For the Church's attitude, see page 131.

[13] But Harvey, P. *Rect. and Gerefa ibid* at page 21 regards the estate as probably one belonging to Bath Abbey.

[14] *A-S Chronicle* 1085; another view is that the Survey took up to twenty months to complete. The king died in 1087 before the reports could be finally edited. The continuing debates as to how the Survey was conducted or put together, as to the real reason why it was ordered, and about the real meaning of some of its phrases or its omissions can be passed-over here.

villein, five *bordars* and one *slave.*[15] Apart from the slave, the class-names of the other tenants have changed from the former English ones described in the *Estate Guide.* Now, ninety or more years after the *Estate Guide,* this is a harsher world with (in other, lay, manors) new and even sterner foreign masters, in which serfdom (as distinct from slavery) has been formally recognised and fresh concepts of obligation have been introduced. In this Norman world the main distinction is that between, on the one hand, the newly named serfs, the *villeins, bordars* and *cottars,* those who are firmly tied to the place where they serve and, on the other hand, the truly free men. Throughout England there are several kinds of free men: but there are no free men of any kind recorded in Hampstead. Possibly there had been no truly free man living in Hampstead before the Conquest: one cannot say.

Of the serfs, the class of *villeins* tended generally to be better off than the *bordars,* but there was no consistency about this: sometimes a *bordar* could be richer or otherwise more fortunate than a *villein* who happened to be at the bottom of his heap. In the case of Hampstead, the single Domesday *villein* was clearly at the top of his small heap, because his own holding was a whole virgate (about 30 acres),[16] while the five *bordars* had to share a virgate between them. There is no neat equation between the classes we have already met in the English *Estate Guide* and these Norman classes. With only about 6 acres apiece, the *bordars*[17] look more like the *cotsetlas* of the *Estate Guide,* who were each to "have about five acres" or more. But in fact it must have been the *bordars* who carried the burden of the work on the monks' estate in Hampstead, just as the *geburs* appear to have done in the estate in the West Country. For the *bordars* the situation must have been bleak, with inadequate land for their support and a workload of free services to provide for the monks. But for the *geneat* there was no equivalent in a small place like Hampstead: if there was anybody superior to anyone else in Hampstead, any leader of the local community, it would no doubt have been the single *villein,* with his comparatively large holding.[18] So there is no tidiness to be found in any comparisons which aim at invariable rules: these class-divisions were rarely clear-cut or consistent.

---

[15] *DB Mdx* 4/ 3 (f.128b). For this purpose one can probably ignore the separate hide there (DB *Mdx ibid* 4/4), which had now been let to the Norman baron Ranulf Peverel, no doubt in knight service, see next page. For the significance of the assessment of 'hides' in DB, see pages 50-1 and 137-8.

[16] See page 51. For the Hampstead entry in Domesday Book, see **Plate 8**, page 86.

[17] S. Harvey 'Evidence for Settl. Study' in *Med. Settlement* (Ed. Sawyer) 197 suggests that in DB *bordars* and *cottars* are broadly synonymous, *except* in a few counties like Middlesex. But in this entry for Hampstead there are no *cottars;* and the *bordars* with about six acres each could equally have been called cottars. 'Cottar' had an English derivation, and 'Bordar' (which did not become popular) a French one, so the juries of the Hundreds employed in the Inquiry could well differ in their use of the terms.

[18] Just as in the thirteenth and fourteenth centuries most of the leaders in the community were, it seems, those villagers who had the largest holdings (the distinctions between the classes having by then become even more blurred), see Vol 2. At least 20 DB villeins in Mdx had as much as a whole hide each, and a few had even more. The Hampstead tenants at the time of Domesday do not reflect the distribution of the classes throughout Middlesex generally, namely *villeins* (1141, about 53%), *bordars* (342, about 17%) and *cottars* (464, about 22%), see Darby (Ed) *DB Geog. of S.E. England* 117-8; Pinder 'Intro. to Mdx. Domesday' 9. The *cottar* was a newly-recognised representative of the 'small men' of the community, namely the man who often had even less land than the *bordar,* or perhaps none at all. But he was potentially the man of the future because, if without land, he was subject to a particularly strong stimulus to develop special skills to earn enough for himself and his family and so often became an independent specialist, such as a blacksmith or a carpenter, or employed such skills as a fulltime paid employee (*famulus*) of the lord. But perhaps significantly there was not even one landless *cottar* in Hampstead, although Middlesex is unique among all the counties in having more cottars than bordars, see Lennard *Bordars and Cottars of DB* Ec. Jo. 61 (1951) 342. For the economic status of Domesday villeins, see Lennard, Ec. Jo. 56 (1946) 244.

Because we have nothing like an *Estate Guide* for the Abbey's estates, we do not know what amount of service the five *bordars* and the *villein* had to perform for the monks at the time of Domesday, still less what their predecessors more than a hundred years before had had to do. But there can be little doubt that some or all of them were expected to do 'week-work' (the regular work each week), and all of them to perform 'boon services' (the extra seasonal work) when called upon to do so. At a much later date they were able to commute some or all of their services for annual payments, as we shall see in due course.[19]

However one can be certain that the pattern of serfdom present in Domesday Book had been inherited from the period before the Conquest, even if the screw had been tightened in the process. On estates which had lost an English lay lord and received a Norman one,[20] the peasants would probably have found that the screw had been tightened on them dramatically. But on a church-estate like Hampstead where the 'lord' remained the same, one would not have normally expected there to have been any great change in the obligations and the treatment of the peasants, even if their theoretical freedom was now formally gone. The English Abbot of Westminster Abbey, Edwin,[21] who had already been in office for about seventeen years before the Conquest, remained in place for up to another five years after the Conquest, so that the monks' general policy as regards administration of any of the Corridor estates should on ordinary expectations have remained much the same.

The Peverel Hide   **Map G**

But it so happens that there is a special record, in the Domesday Survey of Hampstead, of the letting [22] of one of the hides in the manor to the Norman baron, Ranulf Peverel. We find that this Peverel [23] is named as the holder of a hide in Hampstead ("*under* the Abbot"), just as that other baron William Baynard had also been named as the holder (but "*from* the Abbot") of the monks' Berewic in Westminster.[24] But the real significance of this, in the

---

[19] See Vol 2. But much had happened before they were able to commute their services in this way, and the amounts of these later commutations would not be a very reliable guide to the scale of their services at the time of Domesday, still less in the earlier Anglo-Saxon period before the Conquest.

[20] Eg. the lay manors of Eia, Chelsea and Kensington immediately adjoining the Westminster estate on its western side; compare **Maps K and L**. Equally, within the Corridor where WA continued to hold the majority of the land, the lay estate of Lileston, lying between Westminster and Hampstead, gained a new lay lord shortly after Domesday, this time the Norman Otto the Goldsmith, see page 73 above.

[21] See page 159. Edwin survived because he had presumably not taken any ostensible part at the time of the Conquest in opposing the Conqueror, who was swift to act against those who had. It was of course at Westminster that the Conqueror had insisted on being crowned on Christmas Day 1066, a ceremony in which the Abbot no doubt played a part, although it was of course not he whose right it was to place the crown upon William's head.

[22] For the significance of a 'hide', see pages 50-1. It is likely that the possession of the hide by Peverel was by subinfeudation to him, imposing a military obligation on him under the Norman feudal system, by which he was bound to pay to provide a 'knight' (or some unknown fraction or multiple of a knight!) for the Abbey, which in turn was bound to provide for the king a specific number (probably 15) 'knights' when required. See page 142. Holding *sub* (not *de*) the Abbot, Peverel had probably been forced on the Abbey by the Conqueror: cf. the knight imposed on the Abbey at Bury St Edmunds, Douglas *Charter of Enfeoffment* EHR 42 (1927) 245. For the Hampstead record in Domesday Book, see **Plate 8**, page 86.

[23] For more about this enigmatic and intriguing figure in the immediate post-Conquest period, see Vol. 2. At present it is sufficient to say that he had close connections with London, where his "Honor", the so-called 'Honor of London' (i.e. the headquarters of his group of estates, which ranged mainly over East Anglia) was based, and also with St Paul's Church, where he was later buried.

[24] See pages 136 and 142. There was also the unnamed 'knight' who at the time of Domesday held from the Abbey four hides of land in Battersea, across the river Thames, *DB Surrey* 6/1(f.32b). Not many years after Domesday the manor of Hendon was also let in fee-farm to a new tenant, Gunter, a 'man' of the

present context, is that the hide let to Peverel is described in the Survey as "land of the villagers". This indicates that some of the tenants' lands had been appropriated and given to Peverel: this was not an unknown fate for the tenants, since in other places in England lands which formerly in the Anglo-Saxon period had belonged to the peasants had been appropriated since the Conquest, and given to Normans or other unidentified 'knights': eg. this happened frequently in Wiltshire.[25] Again significantly, there is no mention of any remaining villagers on Peverel's hide of land to work it for him, so one can only infer that the services which the five bordars and one villein owed to the Abbot ostensibly on the rest (ie. the other four hides) of the Hampstead estate were probably to be split, by some agreement between the Abbey and Peverel, so that Peverel had someone to work his land for him with unpaid services. Otherwise he would have had to pay for the whole of his work, a situation which no new Norman landlord was likely to have borne.[26]

The appropriation of this land must have had immense consequences for the peasants' situation in Hampstead before the Norman Conquest. Assuming for this purpose that this 'hide' did actually represent an *area* of land,[27] and that this area was something like 120 acres of land, we can see that the peasants in the period *before* the Conquest must have held that additional amount of land between them. Let us assume that about half of this would have been arable,[28] and the other half probably a mixture of open pasture and waste or woodland pasture. If there had been the same number of households there before the Conquest as there were in 1086, it would mean that the six serf households would (on average) each have had an *extra* 20 acres (half of it arable), which would have made a very different picture for them. It would also mean that the Conquest was a disaster for the inhabitants of Hampstead. Due to the Conquest and the consequent introduction of a Norman baron into the quiet Hampstead scene, all or many of the bordars would have been converted from holders of an arguably reasonable amount of land for their own support, to smallholders with obviously too little (five acres) to support their families. As smallholders, they would now be dependent on being able to get paid work to earn their keep.

But *would* there have been the same number of households before the Conquest? Or did something else happen, either at or after the Conquest, to reduce the number of people living in Hampstead? If there had been many more living there before the Conquest, then the sizes of the tenants' landholdings in that period would not have been so dramatically larger than those existing at the time of the Domesday Survey, as I have postulated above. But of course that very hypothesis (of a considerably larger population in Hampstead in the Anglo-Saxon period, with most of the inhabitants in fairly stringent circumstances) would itself be an important conclusion, if verified. And equally, in that case, the *cause* of the reduction of the population to the Domesday figures must itself have been a dramatic and important event for the village.

Abbot, see pages 156-7; and not many years later Chelsea, newly given to the Abbey, was let to the king's Sheriff of Berkshire, William of Buckland, for life, see Mason *WA Charters* No 242.

[25] See *VCH Wilts* 1/83.

[26] For bitter complaints by the English against the effects of the Norman yoke, see *Orderic Vitalis* (Ed. Chibnall) Vol II, Bk IV 203; Vol IV, Bk VII 95.

[27] See pages 50-1. Although the hide may strictly have been a tax assessment, it is probably fair to make this assumption here, since tax and area tend towards one another when the figures are low.

[28] On the basis that the 'land' (ie. the arable) within that hide needed 'half a plough' according to DB, amounting to about 50-60 acres, calculations can be made as to arable, see page 125 below.

The Population   **Maps G and F**

The number of people living in Hampstead at the time of Domesday would probably have been about 50 or below. This total is reached by multiplying the number of households by the average size of a household, and adding some more, for those who may have been missed out in the Survey (as there usually are in any kind of population records). The average size of a household at that time has been much debated, but five is usually accepted now as a fair figure to take. Seven households (assuming that the slave also had a family), with five persons per household, gives a total of 35. With some probable omissions, a final total of up to 50 might be justified.

But can we tease anything out of the Survey about the position *before* the Conquest? As indicated previously [29] one of the main features of the Middlesex Survey is the noticeable decrease between the value attributed to each manor immediately before the Conquest and its value after the Conquest. Middlesex shares this feature with many other counties near London (such as Surrey, Hampshire, Berkshire, Buckinghamshire, Bedfordshire and Hertfordshire), but its own decreases are more particularly marked.[30] The cause of this loss of value is usually ascribed to the devastation created by the Conqueror's forces as they marched on and round London after winning the battle of Hastings; or possibly in the course of subsequent subjugation of reluctant peasantry. Certainly the greatest losses of value occurred on or near the main roads leading towards the City, particularly from the north and west, see **Map G**; and this fits well with the circuitous route round London which the different Norman forces apparently took.[31] It is noticeable that the devastation must have been at its worst towards the outer edges of the county, and that in general it was at its least serious in an arc closer to the City . Hampstead was one of those estates which 'bucked the trend' in that inner arc, because its value very nearly halved (105 shillings before the Conquest, falling to 55 shillings immediately afterwards). This may have been due to something dramatic which perhaps occurred on the main road, Watling Street: or since it is impossible that so prominent a height overlooking London would not have been occupied by the Normans, it may be that there was more local resistance on the hilltop itself than in the lower areas of Hendon or Willesden.

Does the halving of the value of Hampstead mean that the population must have been halved too, eg. by slaughter? One is clearly in the realm of guesswork here, intelligent guesswork, one hopes. It is likely that there was a certain loss of life: or perhaps a loss of residents, by reason of the permanent flight, during the disorders after the Conquest, of any who had previously wished but had been unable to leave, a flight to be followed by a new life elsewhere. But a full halving of the number of inhabitants appears unlikely. If there was devastation, there must have been loss of livestock, of crops, of houses and of woods, as well as loss of life, and all these things must be reflected in the halving of the

---

[29] See page 33.

[30] See the losses in value of the different Middlesex estates depicted quantitatively on **Map G**. For the losses in Bedfordshire, Dr Fowler sought to trace the actual track of different Norman forces working in flying columns, see *Archaeologia* 72 (1921-2) 41-50. The four main areas of damage in Middlesex also suggests a splitting of Norman forces into different columns, moving down the roads towards London, which may have happened after the leaders of the main body of Londoners had surrendered to William at Berkamstead. There was also heavy loss of value at or near the Watling Street gate (Newgate) of London, where the Westminster berewic lay, which suggests strong local resistance in that area from some who disagreed with the surrender.

[31] Stenton *A-S England* 596-7

estate's value. So one can estimate that perhaps there may have been, say, nine so-called 'free' (though in fact serf) households and two slave households in the period immediately before the Conquest, with a grand total of about 75 people in all, ie. 50% more than at Domesday.[32] To put it the other way round, the Domesday figure would represent the loss of one-third from the pre-Conquest figure.

On these assumptions, one could envisage a village before the Conquest of perhaps two villagers holding 30 acres each, and seven others holding as much as an average of about 17 acres each; or some similar combination of figures. This would have accounted for the 180 acres of tenants' land which should have been available at that time. This would be a very different picture from that which appears later in Domesday, when (a) the population had been reduced by about a third, but (b) 120 acres of tenants' land had been appropriated and given to Peverel, leaving at least some and probably most of the residue of the population bereft of the means of supporting themselves. There are, of course, other possibilities and one cannot have any firm assurance about this picture. But, as the historian Maitland said in another context, what better theory have we?

The fact that there were apparently no tenants living on Peverel's hide of land could mean one of two things: either that some of the tenants recorded as living on the Abbot's four hides in 1086 had previously been ousted from the one hide, so as to give Peverel full possession of it; or that there had not been any tenants actually living on that one hide even before the Conquest and that the tenants, while living on the other four hides, had used the single hide ("tenants' land") for their own purposes. If the first of these alternatives were true, it would indicate that some of the Hampstead peasants were being treated even worse, by being evicted as well as losing a great deal of their usable land. If the second alternative were true, it would be consistent with a picture (both before and after the Conquest) of a settlement or settlements spread over the four hides which were retained by the Abbot at Domesday, with their outlying land (the part which came to be taken over by Peverel) being used before the Conquest for agricultural purposes rather than for their own housing.

So where could this land which was taken over by Peverel have been? While we cannot identify it for certain, we know that at all later periods for which there are any records, the area of Belsize had become an identifiable tract which was treated differently from the rest of the manor [33] and became known as a 'sub-manor' of Hampstead. So it may be that Peverel's hide had been in that area too. It is true that in those later times several other parts of the manor (unusually) were let separately to various institutional bodies and to that extent were also treated differently. But in 1259 (the earliest date for which there is a list of the Hampstead tenants and their holdings) there was clearly an area in Hampstead called the 'Hyda', which is probably to be identified with the Peverel hide,[34] and this was clearly at a time when those other parts of the manor had already been let out. This means that at any rate the Belsize area, or rather part of it, is probably the best candidate for the Peverel hide. Further if Peverel's purpose in taking a very small tract near the City of London (the City being the centre of his 'Honor' of estates, and incidentally the place where he was ultimately buried, at St Paul's) was to maintain a foothold there for (say) keeping a house or a produce-farm outside London, it would be difficult to find a

---

[32] However these are fragile calculations, and nothing can be taken as established with any certainty.

[33] See Vol 2.

[34] See VCH *Mdx* 9/95. In many places throughout the country the name Hide or Hyde became attached to a specific area as an early identifying label, and has frequently survived even until now. Other nearby examples are Hyde Park; the area in Hendon which is still known as the Hyde, fronting on to Watling Street; and there are others, in Islington, Tottenham and elsewhere.

better situation than the comparatively high ground of Belsize, overlooking the valley in which the Abbey and London lay, as indeed many great residents of the later Belsize House were to testify in the centuries after the Dissolution. Even the name, which is derived from old French 'Bel Assis' [35] ('beautifully situated', so registering its fine position), has a Norman ring about it, and although it does not appear in any written records until the first half of the fourteenth century, one may ask why such a name *at that time* could have had such a derivation, if it did not reveal some connection with a much earlier Norman occupation, and whether the name was in fact very much older than the surviving records permit us to know.

The main Village and Demesne-farm   **Map O**

As regards the position of the main village [36] during the period before the Conquest, we know that from the second half of the thirteenth century the demesne fields, the lands held at that time by the monks for their own farming,[37] lay south west from the hilltop. From the earliest times the choice of such a position for the main cultivated fields would have made sense, since the ground there was best sited, as the original trees were cleared, to catch the sun's warmth; ample waters from the Westbourne's many sources, with good drainage down the contours, and a spring line, where the London Clay broke clear of the overlying sands, were close at hand; brickearth, and clay for use as daub, were also nearby; and the clay and the sands were well-suited for a combination of heavy and light crops, both wheat and oats.

For both people and early buildings,[38] a main village site just below the last steep crest of the hill was ideal, allowing the north winds to blow over the top. The later manorial farm-centre definitely lay at the junction of the present Frognal and the lane leading to West End (now called Frognal Lane).[39] It also seems that the old buildings on that site as late as 1790 still contained 'a very capacious hall', which was likely to have been a surviving medieval hall.[40] This site was definitely the 'manour-place of Hampstede' which was referred to in the Act of Parliament in 1543, by which authority was given for the springs of Hampstead to be harnessed to supply piped water for London.[41] It is very unlikely that any buildings from the period before the Conquest then survived, but it is not unreasonable to infer that the later manorial farm site had also been the Anglo-Saxon centre. The site would always have been an obvious one, lying adjacent to the most suitable land, with also

---

[35] EPNS *PN Mdx* 112 ; (but the first record of the name was not 1317, but 1334-5, see *VCH Mdx* 9/95).

[36] For the village position and an impression of the lie of the land, see **Plate 15**, page 134. For further possible areas of settlement within the estate, see page 54-5 above.

[37] See **Map O**.

[38] For authentic buildings of a date not later than the first years of the *seventh* century, the reconstructed village at West Stow in Suffolk is probably the most instructive. The Middlesex scene which we are trying to envisage here is of a date about 400 years later. Having regard to the sophistications of that isolated Suffolk village on a river bank in West Stow, a remote spot northwest of Bury St Edmunds, one should not underestimate the degree of civilisation which a place like Hampstead, only six miles from the biggest city in England, may have exhibited, even if the inhabitants were becoming serfs.

[39] Park *Topog. of Hampstead* 125-6; SCL *1762 Manor Map*; SCL.89.3 *Frognal Manor House*.

[40] Park *ibid*.

[41] See also page 45. The geography described in the Act itself makes it clear that the 'manour-place' was the Frognal site. The Bishop of Westminster (for this was just after the Dissolution of the monastery at Westminster and the establishment of a brief Protestant bishopric) also secured the right to convey spring water to the 'manour place', presumably in preference to the stream down Frognal, which was probably suffering from pollution: see the text of the Act quoted in Park *ibid* 73.

a conveniently adjoining stream running down the valley where the present Frognal road runs, and perhaps already feeding a farm pond near the Frognal junction and another pond a short distance down the slope, as it did also in later centuries.[42]

Common Fields   **Map O**

From a very early date some parts of England were being cultivated with the open-field system of communal husbandry, under which the peasants or other landholders owned long individual strips of land, varying from about one quarter to three quarters of an acre, in a 'common field' or fields.[43] The wide rolling spaces which one normally associates with open-field cultivation of this kind did not exist in the terrain of Hampstead, except to some extent on the southwest slopes below the crest, and that was where the demesne fields lay, on the best land. There is no doubt that most of the land in Middlesex, with its heavy woodland or steep contours, did not lend itself to the formation of very large common fields, but did lend itself to the creation of separate fields and closes held by individual owners in scattered hamlets.[44] But the evidence seems to point to a fair amount of communal cultivation in many of the estates in and around the Corridor, and indeed there are clear residual signs that this was the case even in Hampstead. But it is probably impossible to learn when this form of husbandry actually began in the area.

In virtually all the estates surrounding the Corridor of Watling Street it is clear that there had been and were some common fields and that the enclosure of them was a long and gradual process which lasted in some cases right up to the nineteenth century. In some cases the number and size of the fields were extensive, as in Harrow and Willesden: in others the surviving evidence is more limited, as in Hendon, Edgware, Great Stanmore, Finchley and Paddington.[45] It is not possible to say whether these fields were early features: but they must either have been relics of such fields from much earlier times, or they were later progressive importations of forms of common field systems.

In Hampstead itself it appears from the much later Survey of the manor which was carried out by the monks in 1312 that the main fields (at that time called Pyrlegh, Somerlese

---

[42] SCL *1762 Manor Map*; SCL 89.3 *Frognal Manor House*.

[43] See eg. *Laws of Ine* 42 in EHD 1/403 (in Wessex, at the end of the seventh century); Loyn *A-S England* 156 ff; Thirsk *Common Fields* 29 P.& P 3.

[44] In Hampstead in particular many crofts and small holdings can be identified by the time of the thirteenth and fourteenth centuries, see VCH *Mdx* 9/104-111and Vol. 2: but this does not destroy the inference from the evidence that a form of strip-farming had previously been established for some unknown period.

[45] Some of the evidence has been assembled by Garrett *Historical Geography of the Upper Brent* 57-62. In *Harrow* there were ten groups of common fields, each with its own hamlet, when the Enclosure Award was made in 1818; in *Willesden* there were 26 common fields enclosed in 1815; in *Hendon* there were at least four common fields in 1574 (and see Brett-James *Surveys of Hendon* TLMAS 12 (1929) 564); in *Paddington* there were common fields recorded in 1742 (see VCH *Mdx* 9/233); in *Finchley* some fields were still shared in the sixteenth and seventeenth centuries (see VCH *Mdx* 6/64); for *Kingsbury* see VCH *Mdx* 5/72: in *Great Stanmore* the three main field-names were Wheatfield, Beanfield and Fallowfield, see Garrettt *ibid* 59. Further afield in the north-east of the county there is evidence of comparatively early common fields, mostly formed as the woods were cleared collectively: for *Edmonton*, see VCH *Mdx* 5/166-7 (many common fields, dating from at least the twelfth century onwards) and Gray *English Field Systems* 381; and for *Enfield,* see VCH *Mdx* 5/233 (many common fields, dating from the thirteenth century onwards). In *Tottenham* in the fourteenth century there was clear evidence of strip-farming; Moss and Murray *Fourteenth Century Tottenham* TLMAS 24 (1973) 199, and Tottenham Court Rolls (trans. Marcham).

and Homefeld [46]) lay in the same south-western area in which the Anglo-Saxon tenants in an earlier age had probably had to fulfil their obligations of work. There it is clear from the descriptions used that :-

(a) different parts of the fields were assigned (obviously on a rotational basis) to different functions: a part used as arable, a part producing meadow grass, and a part used as pasture. The same division of use in other smaller named fields is also evident;   and

(b) the arable in both Somerlese (then 87 acres) and Homefeld (61 acres) was in 'scattered parcels'. This seems to indicate the strip-farming of fields held then in common. But whether this had been so from a very early period before the Conquest is impossible to say.

Land-Use   Map P

Since most of the Anglo-Saxon boundaries of the estate correspond closely with the boundaries of the manor eight centuries later in 1762,[47] we can be fairly certain that the total acreage of the whole early estate was not much less than the area assessed at that much later date, namely about 2250 acres.The only difference would have been the exclusion of the Codanhlaw area, see **Map P**. Without attempting exactness, let us estimate, say, 1900 acres as the full figure, without Codanhlaw. How much of this would have been used for agriculture, both by the monks and by their tenants, and how much was left as waste? According to Domesday Book, the four-hide manor, which was still held in hand by the Abbey, had '(arable) land for three ploughs', while Peverel's one hide had '(arable) land for a half plough'.[48] A 'plough' in 1086 certainly meant the newer heavy wheeled plough, which had been in general use during the Anglo-Saxon period for well over a hundred years,[49] although the 'scratch-plough' which dated back to Roman and earlier times was still around and may have been of particular service on the Hampstead sands. One plough has been regarded as being able to deal with 100 arable acres in a year,[50] so in 1086 there were about 350 *potential* acres of arable. Of this, it seems that only about 250 acres were actually being cultivated, because there were only two and a half ploughs being used: ie. it was about 27% underused. In view of the halving of the value of the estate in 1066, this figure of 350 acres would mean that for the period before the Conquest one probably has to allow for a higher figure (even accepting that the damage done by the Norman forces is already partly discounted in the 350 figure). Let us say that perhaps 450 acres were thought to be available for arable use (by the monks and their tenants) before the Conquest. But even if the whole of this had been in use in the period before the Conquest, probably a good part of it would have been lying fallow at any one time.

---

[46] See **Map O**. Two of these three names survived in identifiable fields called 'Summer Leys' and 'Purloins' up to at least the eighteenth century, see SCL *Manor Map* 1762, and also beyond. It is reasonable to regard the three fields as being probably of great antiquity *before* 1312 AD: moreover, as indicated above, their known position was the obvious site on the south-west slope below the crest of the hill for early settlers to choose.

[47] See page 105-8.

[48] It did not follow that all that land was in fact being used. Indeed in Middlesex it seems from the Survey that there was considerable underuse of the available land, probably due to the damage caused by the Conqueror's forces twenty years earlier, see Campbell 'Middlesex' in *DB Geog. of S.E. England* (Ed. Darby) 110-3. In Hampstead itself, about 100 arable acres seem to have been uncultivated, which the Commissioners deemed could be cultivated (one plough missing). For some other calculations of cultivation, see Kennedy *Manor of Hampstead* 10-11.

[49] Gimpel *The Medieval Machine* 40-1; Lynn White *Medieval Technology* 41 ff.

[50] Maitland however worked on a basis of 120 acres, see *DB and Beyond* 431-5.

For the group of villagers, this would mean about 100 acres of arable;[51] with about 350 acres for the monks' farm (the same as at the time of the Domesday Survey). But in addition to the arable land, there would have been much else besides, all the pasture (for both the monks' and the tenants' animals), the woods, a heathland area, the usable waste and (in a terrain such as that of Hampstead, where there were many steep slopes and so much swamp and water [52]) various tracts of virtually unusable land. The terrain of the whole estate of Hampstead was (and beneath its modern coverings, still is) extremely diverse, and one can begin to see that the contrast between the comparatively large total area of about 1900 acres for the whole estate and the smaller figure of about 450 acres for the potentially arable land can be largely accounted for. But to try to separate out the figures any more exactly would be to venture even further down the road of speculation.

The woods   **Maps O and P**

There is reason to think that the woods of Hampstead at that time may have taken three forms. Round the top of the hill, on the lightest soil, there was probably much birch and hazel woodland. This was probably the pattern later on in 1312 [53] when there were demesne woods called *Whitebirch* and *Nuthurst*, whose names speak for themselves; the former of which can certainly be identified in the present Viaduct area on East Heath (previously the 'East Park' area), and the latter probably in the Holly Hill and Grove areas of modern Hampstead. These woodland regions may have passed through various changes in their character over the centuries, but it is unlikely that they had previously been cultivated before 1312 and had reverted to woodland.[54] Coppicing, an essential form of management in a society which depended so much on different forms of wood for working, was frequently carried out in Anglo-Saxon times,[55] and one can envisage that any light woods such as the hazels would have been managed in this way.

There was at that time (1312) another wood likely to have contained the lighter varieties of trees, whose name - *Sheppenbrighull* - may indicate its location. In 1762, 450 years later, there were two fields called Great and Little Shepherds Fields, which lay towards the top of the hill on the present Fitzjohns Avenue and also adjoined the Frognal source-stream, and possibly yet another source-stream, of the Westbourne river. Near the fields stood the Shepherds' Well or Conduit, which was one of the main wells supplying the village until at least the 1850s.[56] So the name 'Sheep-bridge-hill' [57] appears to meet all these geographical descriptions; moreover the wood was a commonable wood (ie. available for the villagers) and therefore likely to have been near the main village, which this site

---

[51] ie. 40-50 arable acres (say), out of the 60 acres (or so) which some of them still had in 1086, plus another 50-60 acres (the 'land for half a plough' in the later-appropriated hide which Peverel was given).

[52] Even as late as the thirteenth and fourteenth centuries the 'Fowler' family (often spelt Ffoghler) was much in evidence. To this day, from February each year, wild geese (of a different kind) continue to take their mating flights at dawn between the various waters of the Heath, honking as they go.

[53] See **Map P**. For fuller details of the 1312 Survey of Hampstead, see Vol 2.

[54] They did become cultivated at a *later* date (see the 1762 Manor Map), but that began, it seems, after the Dissolution, when much land belonging to the erstwhile monasteries (including land of the Abbey in Hampstead and elsewhere) was 'on the market' and the 'developers' (such as John Slanning) moved in.

[55] Rackham *History of Countryside* 81.

[56] Barratt *Annals of Hampstead* 2/241; Potter *Hampstead Wells* 13-4.

[57] See its original components in Gelling *PNs in the Landscape* 39, 65 and 170. Moreover the demesne field *Purlegh*, which is in the area of this wood, is based on the ending -*leah*, which denotes an earlier woodland.

was. If the wood was indeed in that location, it would clearly have been on the sandy soil of the Bagshot beds, and for that reason would more probably than not have contained the lighter kind of tree.

Secondly there were some heavy woods of oak and beech, which in part constituted the 'pigwood' recorded in the Domesday Survey, fit for 100 pigs. Probably there had been more areas of heavy woodland in the period before the Conquest, and it may be that they had first suffered during the devastation caused by the Norman armies during the Conquest, and later were being asserted to make way for cultivation. In 1312, when parts of the Abbey's manor of Hampstead were let out to other bodies, the woods of *'Northwood'*, *'Brockhole'* and *'Timberhurst'* standing in the demesne areas retained by the Abbey would probably have been within this category of heavy woodland; *Northwood* growing on and round the present Telegraph Hill (the top of Childs Hill) and spreading down towards the Frognal area; and the latter two woods stretching from the modern South Hill Park area down the south-east slopes of the manor to Chalk Farm below.[58] Since woods rarely disappear entirely unless they are asserted to make room for cultivation or settlement, it seems probable that these were ancient woodlands, maybe antedating even the Anglo-Saxons but certainly given Anglo-Saxon names.

Apart from the six woods already mentioned and shown on **Map P**, we know also of *'Kilburn Wood'*, bordering on West End Lane. From about the twelfth century it was held by the adjoining Kilburn Priory, until the Priory's dissolution in 1536. It was a wood which was still about 36 acres in extent after the Dissolution,[59] and was likely to have been ancient and more extensive woodland long preceding its tenure by the Priory. Since in that position, not far from Watling Street, it was on solid London Clay, it was probably composed mainly of oaks, as the area certainly was at a later time.

Finally there must have been a large amount of woodland in both Belsize and Chalcots, particularly along the southern flank of the estate (ie. south of the demesne fields shown on **Map O**) and also thicker woods in the adjoining northern parts of the estates of Lileston, Tyburn and Rugmere. While the latter woodland, in the adjacent manors, was to survive vigorously and in due course of time to become notorious as St John's Wood, it seems that within the Hampstead boundary over the centuries the woods were probably thinner as the hill ascended and were more quickly asserted to become the cultivated fields shown eventually in the 1762 Map. There is firm evidence of 40-80 acres of wood in Chalcots [60] (with or without 'the wood' specifically mentioned in the Anglo-Saxon bounds near the present Primrose Hill), which we know provided timber and brushwood to its tenants in later centuries, first to the Leper Hospital of St James and, after the Hospital, to Eton College. While the main evidence relates to later periods, it is difficult to believe that the Anglo-Saxons had less woodland, whether to contend with or to make use of.

---

[58] *Northwood* (with two OE. words to its name) is firmly located by many later leases and other references, VCH 9/115-6. For the position of *Brockhole*, see Survey of London 17/126 (field still called Brock Hill in 1761) and **Map O**. Although 'brock' is an OE. word in its own right, meaning 'badger', it could be that the original OE. name was 'throck-holt', meaning a 'managed wood': the demesne wood was firmly stated in 1312 to be a wood "in which neither grazing nor pannage is allowed", and the word 'throck' in its original OE. script looks very like 'brock' and could easily have become corrupted before the fourteenth century. 'Hole' is almost certainly a corruption of OE.'holt', a wood. *Timberhurst* (also composed of two OE. words, meaning timber-hill) probably lay further south from *Brockhole*, on the steeper slope towards Chalk Farm; and it became 'Eastfields' after asserting in the later Middle Ages.

[59] Park *Topog. of Hampstead* 190-1; and SCL Manor Map 1762, which measures the area of the fields on the site of the old wood at nearly the same figure.

[60] 40 acres in 1258, 80 acres in 1312, see VCH *Mdx* 9/99, and Vol 2.

The third and probably the largest 'woodland' tracts must have been the 'waste' areas, ie. mostly scrub and trees interspersed with open spaces (including no doubt a form of heathland area) where rough pasture could be had. Of these there must have been great amounts, and one can say this with some certainty both because of the nature of the very mixed terrain in Hampstead and because there is the balance of 1900 acres to be accounted for to make up the acreage of the estate.

The Day's Work

No modern attempt to depict the day-to-day work of a peasant on a rural estate in the late Anglo-Saxon period could speak more vividly than a description written at that very time. The following brief chronicles of a villager's life, written at a time when the Abbey at Westminster had just been founded, come themselves from a monastic source and therefore reflect the views which some contemporary monks held about their tenants' lives. Abbot Aelfric, a monk who later became best known as the Abbot of Eynsham near Oxford at about the beginning of the eleventh century, was one of the most lucid writers both in simple vernacular English and of course in standard Latin, the lingua franca of the medieval world. Before going to Eynsham, he put together in or shortly after 990 a small teaching guide [61] for the novices in his monastery (at that time, probably the recently founded Cerne Abbey, to which he was sent in 987, to instruct the newly-gathered monks [62]), which included descriptions in both languages not only of "the many and varied activities of a monastic house" but also of the different agricultural occupations of his day, in a question-and-answer form :

Ploughman

Q. *What do you say, ploughman, how do you go about your work?*
A. *Oh Sir, I work excessively hard. I go out at dawn to drive the oxen to the field, and I yoke them to the plough; however hard the winter I dare not linger at home for fear of my master; but having yoked my oxen and fastened the plough-share and coulter to the plough, I have to plough a whole acre or more every day.*
Q. *Have you any companion?*
A. *I have a boy to drive the oxen with a goad-iron, and even now he is hoarse with the cold and his shouting.*
Q. *What else do you do in the day?*
A. *I do a great deal more. I have to fill the oxen's mangers with hay and give them water, and carry the dung outside. It is hard work, because I am not free.*

Shepherd

I drive my sheep at first light to pasture, and I watch over them in heat and cold with my dogs, lest the wolves devour

---

[61] Aelfric *Colloquy* (otherwise Colloquies) Ed. Garmonsway 20-2. See also Knowles *Monastic Order* 61 ff; Godfrey *The Church in A-S England* 332-342

[62] Since the Abbey at Westminster had also recently been founded by then, one would like to think that another Aelfric, with his humanity and wisdom, had had to instruct the newly-gathered monks there, but there is no record of such. Wulfsige, the first Abbot of WA (see page 159) was of a calibre to become both a bishop and a saint in due course, but such incipient quality is not necessarily any guarantee of humanity or wisdom.

> *them, and I lead them back to their fold and I milk them twice*
> *a day, and I move their fold, and in addition I make cheese*
> *and butter, and I am faithful to my lord.*

Oxherd   *Sir, I work much. When the ploughman unyokes the oxen, I*
lead them to pasture, and all night long I stand over them
guarding them on account of thieves, and again at first light I
hand them over to the ploughman well-fed and watered.

Since these brief descriptions (like each of the few contemporary writings of the Anglo-Saxon period which still exist) come from the 'employers' side', we can be certain that they do not represent, either in content or feeling, the views which the peasants themselves would have expressed if they too had been able to put their no-doubt more resonant opinions into some permanent form. But even so, it is to be noticed that the Abbot of Cerne (well known to be a humane and gentle man, even if he was also one of the collective 'lord' of the workers) records both the *fear* of his lord which the ploughman feels, with his obvious anxiety about the results if he "lingered", and (already) the pathos of his wish for *freedom,* while the shepherd, with his prim expression of loyalty towards his lord, is depicted as being careful not to be seen to be expressing any form of complaint. At the very least there could be little better proof of the extent to which the tenants on at least the estates then held by the Abbey of Cerne had been reduced to serfdom, and this moreover from a period clearly well before the writing of these small descriptions.

We cannot of course know whether the position would have been any different on the Corridor estates of the monks of Westminster, either for better or worse. But since Aelfric was writing his *Colloquies* in the decade of the 990s,[63] his text relates to a time not many years after the new Abbey at Westminster had been founded, and it is clear from his descriptions that the relationship between the workmen whom he describes and their lord was already an established one by that date. While the Church from an early date was in general a more humane 'employer' than some of the lay lords,[64] there is little reason to believe that the monks of Westminster would have deliberately foregone any of their rights in relation to the inhabitants of any of their estates, even if they were not as diligent (as they certainly were not, in some of the later centuries), as some other lords may have been, to pursue those rights to extremes.

Another contemporary picture may help us to visualise more detail of Anglo-Saxon rural life. The author of the *Estate Guide*, previously mentioned, may also have been responsible for another early work called the *Gerefa* [65] (which means 'the reeve' in old English). This second work, like the first, was designed to give instruction (in a highly literary form); this time, about the duties and the problems of a reeve whose job it was to

---

[63] The original Colloquies were written before the turn of the century (ie. very shortly after the foundation of Westminster Abbey), but they were 'improved' later by one of Aelfric's former pupils (also called Aelfric, who was called Aelfric Bata, to prevent confusion) after the Abbot's death, but this makes little difference to the conclusion that the serfdom of these tenants was something which had occurred well before the original work.

[64] At least as regards slavery, the Church had for centuries taken a compassionate, if not very effectual, view, encouraging the manumission of slaves, see the details given in *EHD* 1/58-9. As regards the serfs, the Church's attitude was more 'humanity by default' than by conviction as to the principle of freedom.

[65] Liebermann *Gesetze* 453-5; but see Harvey, P. *Rect. and Gerefa* EHR (1993) 12. The text and a translation (as used in the quotations herein) also appear in Cunningham *Growth of English Industry and Commerce*, Appendix B, page 570-5. For the different connotations of 'reeve', see page 144.

manage an estate on behalf of his lord. The kind of reeve in question was a professional employee. The main significance of this guide for our present purposes is the account which it gives of all the varied tasks which the reeve must oversee during the working year. It is these tasks, or most of them on the much smaller estate in Hampstead, which would have fallen to the lot of the peasants to carry out; many of them as part of the free services which they were bound to provide for the monks, but some of them no doubt as paid services, probably paid mostly in kind at that time.

> 'It is most desirable for him [the reeve] to search out how he may promote the estate by farming, when the right time for it comes round.
>
> In May and June and July, in summer, one may harrow, carry out manure, set up sheep hurdles, shear sheep, build up, repair, hedge, build with timber, cut wood, weed, make folds and construct a fish-weir and a mill.
>
> In harvest one may reap ; in August and September and October one may mow, set woad with a dibble, gather home many crops, thatch them and cover them over, and cleanse the folds, prepare the cattle-sheds and also shelters, ere too severe a winter come to the farm, and also diligently prepare the soil.
>
> In winter, one should plough, and in severe frosts cleave timber, make an orchard, and do many things indoors; thresh, cleave wood, put the cattle in stalls and the swine in pigsties, set up a stove on the threshing floor (for an oven and a kiln and many things are necessary on a farm) and moreover provide a hen-roost.
>
> In spring one should plough and graft, sow beans, set a vineyard, make ditches, hew wood for a wild-deer fence; and soon after that, if the weather permits, set madder, sow linseed and woad-seed, plant a garden and do many things which I cannot fully enumerate, that a good steward ought to provide.
>
> He can always find something on the estate to improve; he need not be idle when he is in it; he can keep the house in order, set it to rights and clean it; and set hedges along the ditches, mend the breaches in the dikes, repair the hedges, root up weeds, lay planks between the houses, make tables and benches, provide horse stalls, scour the floor; or let him think of something that may be useful.'

The author of this homily (and only a short part of it has been cited) was obviously indefatigable, not to say officious. Apart from the information which they give us about life in this early period before the end of the Anglo-Saxon era, his little lectures contain an almost ageless catalogue of the kind of jobs which serfs had to carry out for centuries after that period. We will see many of them still being recorded in the accounts of the monks' farm in Hampstead in the thirteenth and fourteenth centuries, at a time when the serfs were still having to carry out some of their services unpaid but had commuted the rest of them for a payment which they had to make to the Abbey annually. By that time several other authors [66] had recently entered the fray with much more sophisticated treatises about how to manage estates, but in the long interval between these Anglo-Saxon writings and those later treatises there is virtual silence,[67] so emphasising the unrecorded timelessness of

---

[66] The best known of these later authors was Walter of Henley, but he was not the first. The first was a Bishop, Bishop Grosseteste, in about the middle of the thirteenth century.

[67] Although there are no more extant didactic writings during this interval, there were many early surveys of other estates which recorded the holdings and obligatory services of the serfs on those estates, but with few mentions of any rights on their part, still less of the professional problems involved in the running of an estate, see *EHD* 2/879 ff.

agricultural life during this period of the Middle Ages.

Finally the Anglo-Saxon author ends his lectures with some illuminating lists of the kind of implements and utensils which the reeve should provide on his estate, if it is to be well managed. Although some of these may have been a little too diverse for a much smaller estate like Hampstead, most of the same or similar equipment must have been there in Hampstead at the same time as the author was writing about his West Country estate; and certainly it was there in later centuries, as the thirteenth and fourteenth documents relating to the monks' farm in Hampstead [68] show : -

"He should provide many tools for the homestead, and get many implements for the buildings : an axe, adze, bill, awl, plane, saw, rim-iron, tie-hook, auger, mattock, lever, ploughshare, coulter; and also a goad-iron, scythe, sickle, weed-hook, spade, shovel, woad-dibble, barrow, besom, beetle, rake, fork, ladder, horse-comb and shears, fire-tongs, weighing-scales, and many spinning implements, such as flax-threads, spindle, reel, yarn-winder, stoddle, weaver's beams, press, comb, carding tool, weft, woof, wool-comb, roller, slay, winder with a bent handle, shuttle, seam-pegs, shears, needle, slickstone."

"One ought also to have coverings for carts, ploughing gear, harrowing tackle, and many things that I cannot now name; as well as a measure, and a flail for the threshing floor, and many implements besides; such as a cauldron, leaden vessel, kettle, ladle, pan, crock, fire-dog, dishes, bowls with handles, tubs, buckets, a churn, cheese vats, bags, baskets, crates, bushels, sieves, seed-baskets, wire-sieve, hair-sieve, winnowing fans, troughs, ash-wood pails, hives, honey-bins, beer barrels, bathing tub, bowls, butts, dishes, vessels, cups, strainers, candlesticks, salt-cellar, spoon-case, pepper-horn, chest, money-box, yeast-box, seats, footstools, chairs, basins, lamp, lantern, leathern bottles, box for soap, comb, iron bin, rack for fodder, fire-guard, meal-ark, oil-flask, oven rake, dung-shovel."

The range of these implements is impressive. Each one of them creates a vivid picture of the kind of activities which the inhabitants of an Anglo-Saxon estate may have had to carry out. We may doubt whether any of the Westminster monks or their own reeves (if they had them [69]) were as professional and indefatigable as this West Country reeve; but then equally one cannot say that they were not. After such an inventory, it is hardly to be wondered at that the author finally gives in and nearly ends with a human touch : "It is toilsome to recount all that he who holds this office ought to think of". But he quickly recovers his relentless style : "but he ought never to neglect anything that may prove useful, not even a mouse trap, nor even, what is less, a peg for a hasp."

If we are to believe our Anglo-Saxon author (and there seems to be little reason for not doing so [70]), there were at least some compensations for the serfs after their hard rounds of

---

[68] Fortunately, among the thirteenth century farm accounts of the monks' manor of Hampstead which themselves contain many scattered details of the kinds of equipment on the manor, there occur two (barely legible) inventories of the implements there.

[69] See page 142-5.

[70] One has of course to remember that he was reflecting the 'employer's' point of view, rather than the 'workers', and that doubtless there were many different angles which *they* would have stressed. But in his *Gerefa*, the same author insists that his reeve should aim to keep the *balance* between the two parties: "the wise reeve ought to know both the lord's land-rights and the folk-rights, even as the counsellors of

work. He lists (in his *Estate Guide*) the free benefits which the various workers are entitled to under the 'customs' of that estate : for example, the woodward is to receive "every tree blown down by the wind"; and the shepherd is to have "twelve nights dung [for his own crops, from the lord's sheepfold] at Christmas, and one lamb from the year's young ones, one bell-wether's fleece, and the milk of his flock for a week after the equinox, and one kid a year old, if he looks after his herd properly".[71] Some similar customary rights were still being observed in Hampstead more than two hundred years after the Anglo-Saxon period, and (having regard to the apparent conservatism of the Westminster administration) it seems likely that they had constituted the custom of the estate during that earlier period too.

And for its ending, the *Estate Guide* lists the happy feasts and rewards of the farm year, at least on the estates with which it deals: extra rations in the winter (customarily at Christmas), special provisions at Easter, the harvest feast for the reaping, a drinking feast for the ploughing, the rewards for the haymaking, the feast for the making of the hayricks, the bonus of one log granted for each load of wood carried, food for the completion of the cornricks; "and many things which I cannot recount". Many of these are also to be seen in succeeding centuries in the records of the Corridor estates of Westminster Abbey.

---

olden days have determined". He has to be both "a faithful reeve" and "a temperate guardian of men".
[71] *EHD* 2/878.

Plate 14. These small drawings, based on illustrations contained in Saxon calendars held by the British Library, show authentic scenes of agricultural life in the eleventh century before the Conquest. They show ploughing, digging and sowing, wood-cutting, shepherding and mowing. See pages 115-7

Plate 15. A view from Hampstead churchyard 'drawn from nature' in 1822, looking south and south-west over part of St. John's Wood (part of the former estate of Lileston) and Paddington, to the Surrey hills beyond the Thames. This was the lie of the land (with surface changes) visible from the main village site in Anglo-Saxon times.

See page 123

CHAPTER 11

Rural Westminster : and Service to the Abbey

Looking back 1000 years

Like their Hampstead estate, the monks' lands in Westminster itself were rural to a degree now difficult to envisage. In the modern City of Westminster, man is now dwarfed by his own creations of stone and brick. But the former 'town' of Westminster was not even recognised as either a 'Cyttie or Burroughe' until an Act of Parliament, to that effect, was passed in 1585.[1] That was 45 years after the dissolution of the Abbey had itself abolished the medieval civil and ecclesiastical power in Westminster, which had resided exclusively in the Abbot. For many centuries by then Westminster had been a comparatively small town, expanding only spasmodically, but hugely, in population when St Edward's Fair was held or the royal Court descended on it. Before that it had been no more than an erstwhile village. The image which we can visualise of this very early settlement, at a range beginning more than a thousand years ago, is that of a small rural community clustered around the Abbey itself and its surrounding fields.

Our mind's-eye picture of that early community may be aided initially by a drawing made many centuries later, a visual extract from one of the first published panoramas, or map-views,[2] of London and Westminster, showing the scene to the west of the City of London as late as 1543-4. Behind the Westminster buildings arrayed along the river bank, the panorama shows the countryside and open space spreading to the top of the Hampstead and Highgate ridge. This drawing was made four years after Henry VIII's final Act of Dissolution of the monastery itself. But the real significance, for our purpose, of this pictorial view (drawn by Anthony Van Den Wyngaerde,[3] an artist from Flanders) is that it was drawn more than 550 years *after* the foundation of the Abbey. So the foundation was already a greater distance backwards in time than the distance forwards, from the date of that scene, to the present day, and this pictorial evidence is that much the more valuable.

Even at that enormous range of years after the foundation of the Abbey, the area which the monks had formerly possessed in their Westminster estate was still a rural locality, with no more than ribbons of buildings (great and small) running along the Strand and the river, around the towering Charing Cross and down the present Whitehall (then King Street) to the Abbey and Palace. Beyond them lay the Westminster fields, with

---

[1] Rosser *Westminster* 226; W.Maitland *London* 2/1348; the Act was 27 Eliz.c.31, 'An Acte for the good Government of the Cyttie or Burroughe of Westmynster'. For the whole of the Middle Ages after the foundation of the Abbey, Westminster (both village or town, and country; excepting only the Palace, when it arrived) had continued to be subject to the sole jurisdiction of the Abbot and Convent (or the Dean and Chapter after the Reformation); it had been known as the Abbot's 'Liberty'.

[2] See **Plate 16**, page 147.

[3] Howgego *Maps of London* 5-6. The map-view is in the Ashmolean Museum, Oxford. Wyngaerde was drawing his picture only four years after a new Protestant Bishopric based on the Abbey had been (briefly) established in place of the Catholic Abbey.

hardly a break before the high ridge beyond.[4] Already by that time two vastly different activities, the Abbey's religious, scholarly and artistic activities and the daily rural operations of ploughing, pasturing and harvest [5] had been carried on alongside one another for more than half a millenium. From such a picture one can begin to infer, however hazily, what the neighbourhood of the Abbey might have actually looked like five or six centuries even earlier.

But fortunately we also have an obviously first-hand, although brief, description in words of the scene round the Abbey. In the early days of January 1066, when Edward the Confessor was being buried in his uncompleted but consecrated Abbey, his first biographer was already at work. He described the locality of the Abbey as "a delightful place, surrounded with fertile lands and green fields, near the main channel of the river which bore abundant merchandise of wares of every kind, for sale from the whole world to the town [London] on its banks".[6] This is the evidence of a man who had actually seen, and could still see, those green fields.

Domesday Westminster   **Maps B, K, L and M**

With the knowledge then that in the course of five hundred years the rural nature of the greater part of Westminster had changed very little, save perhaps in the degree and nature of cultivation, let us now see what Domesday Book tells us about the period *before* the Conquest. The first thing which strikes one is that by 1086 the boundaries of the area called Westminster had grown enormously in size. It had been five mansae (hides) in extent in King Edgar's reign (971); with the further two mansae in their *berewic* or outlying hamlet in Bloomsbury, which was added in King Ethelred's reign.[7] But by the time when the great Survey was carried out, the five hides had grown to thirteen and a half, and the two hides to three.[8] What are the possible explanations for this?

The monks' estate cannot have grown to the south-west. Eia, the well-watered and

---

[4] Several other maps drawn in the sixteenth century amplify the detail of the Wyngaerde panorama. Looking northwards beyond the hamlet of Charing at about the time of the Dissolution of the Abbey, one could still see only the enclaves of buildings at the two Leper Hospitals of St James (across the fields of the present St James's Park) and St Giles (marking that curious swerve still to be seen in St Giles High Street, south of the line of the present New Oxford Street, which was due probably to a marsh then blocking that line, see Davis *University Site* LTR 17 (1936) 31-2). But by 1544, when Wyngaerde sat on the south side of the Thames to draw the western end of his panorama, King Henry VIII was in the process of forming his great hunting park out of the present St James Park, Green Park, Hyde Park and Regents Park, having already bought up all the necessary agricultural fields and taken over St James Hospital (an institution which we will also see playing a part as a tenant of Hampstead land from the thirteenth century, see Vol.2). For an even later impression of the Westminster scene, see **Plate 17**, page 148.

[5] See Mason *A Truth Universally Acknowledged* SCH 16 (1979) 171.

[6] *Vita Edwardi Regis* : see Allen Brown *Norman Conquest* 89 and 80; Barlow *Edward the Confessor* xxii

[7] See page 80.

[8] *DB Mdx* 4/1 and 2 (f.128b). There seems little doubt that the Ethelred grant of two mansae can be identified with part (or all?) of the three hide manor which both Domesday Book and a charter show to have been later granted (shortly before the Survey) to the Norman baron, William Baynard. Baynard was now (by Domesday) a power in both Westminster and London, since he had also by that time inherited the constabulary of the fortress called Baynard's Castle, which the Conqueror had caused to be built by Ralph Baynard (his uncle, see DB *Suffolk* 33/10 (f. 415a)) at the south west corner of the City of London, where the City met the Fleet marsh (or London Fen). See Mason *WA Charters* No 236; Mortimer 'Baynards of B. Castle' in *Studies in Med. Hist.* (Ed. Harper Bill et al.) 241; Robinson *Crispin* 37-40 ; Brooke and Keir *London* 215 ; Douglas *Domesday Monarchorum* 60-2.

'islanded' estate lying between the Tyburn and the Westbourne rivers which we last sighted when it belonged to the Anglo-Saxon royal family,[9] was now in 1086 in the hands of Geoffrey of Mandeville, one of the so-called Companions of the Conqueror and a major landowner in Essex, Middlesex and other counties.[10] Equally Chelsea, which had previously been held by an Anglo-Saxon 'man' (meaning, in fact, a woman, whose name was Wulfwen and whose 'lord' was also royal, namely King Edward the Confessor himself), was now held by Edward of Salisbury, another of the great Norman landowners, who himself held lands in eight other counties and was the Conqueror's Sheriff in Wiltshire.[11] So there was no room for further expansion in that direction.

To the north across Watling Street (that part of it which is the present Oxford Street), the estates of both Lileston and Tyburn had also remained firmly in other hands. Lileston was still, at the time of the Conquest, held by the Englishman Edward, son of Suein; but with his death after the Conquest, his widow had retained the manor, an asset for her new husband-to-be, Otto, the Conqueror's Goldsmith and Die-cutter.[12] Tyburn still remained in the hands of the the nuns of Barking Abbey at the time of the Conquest, but (while remaining a manor of the nuns until the dissolution of their Abbey in 1539) was soon to pass under the physical control (at first) of their baronial tenants the de Veres, yet another of the conquering Norman families.[13] Further eastwards, in the present Bloomsbury area, the Canons of St Pauls continued to hold the two estates of Tottenhall and St Pancras, which each adjoined the Berewic of the monks of Westminster on the north of the present New Oxford Street and from there stretched side-by-side as far as the top of the ridge at Highgate.[14] Yet again there could have been no expansion of the monks' lands in any of those directions, to explain the increase in the size of the Westminster estate in the Domesday Survey.

One possible explanation for the enormous growth in the hidage of the new Westminster 'manor' is that there may have been a dramatic re-rating of the estate for tax purposes. Since the number of hides assigned to a manor was strictly a fiscal rating, and since a low fiscal rating was one way of benefitting a favoured landowner,[15] it could be argued that originally King Edgar might have agreed to an artificially low assessment for the new monastery in the tenth century and that the Normans were doing no more than restoring the balance by setting a more realistic rating for it in their Domesday Survey, a century later. This could be true, but the huge size of the increase suggests that even if

---

[9] i.e to Earl Ralph, Edward the Confessor's nephew, see page 84.

[10] Geoffrey was also the Sheriff of London and Middlesex (a combined shrievalty) and so had great local power both in office and in land: *EHD* 2 / 467 and 1012 ; Round *Mandeville* 151, 347-9 ; *Regesta* 3/275-6 ; Brooke and Keir *London* 194 ; but see Reynolds *Rulers of London* History 57 (1972) 340 .

[11] Ancestor of the first Earls of Salisbury: *VCH Mdx* 1/115. These last two cases are good illustrations of the way in which English landowners had been displaced by Normans, at the gift of the Conqueror: compare **Maps K and L.**

[12] See pages 73 and 103-4.

[13] The de Veres (who seem to have maintained a long and close relationship with Barking Abbey until its dissolution, see Sturman 'Barking Abbey', London Ph.D Thesis (1961) 215 and 288) were to receive the Earldom of Oxford from the Empress Matilda during the civil war 55 years after the Survey, and they reappear later in this story, see Vol 2. For Tyburn's earlier history, see pages 73-4 above.

[14] See **Map B.**

[15] Known as 'beneficial hidation'. In Middlesex, Tottenham was a prime example, with only 5 hides assessed for tax but with well over 1000 arable acres in actual use and a value of over £25 pa. at DB (DB *Mdx* 24). The holder, Countess Judith, was W1's niece, who had married an English earl (since executed).

some more realistic assessment had been made by the Normans, there must also in the intervening century have been a further accretion of land to the monks, in addition to their two earlier estates in Westminster, to explain why the rating had so dramatically changed.

As already indicated,[16] there is reason for thinking that during the century after the new Abbey had been founded, Paddington (under King Ethelred) and Knightsbridge with Westbourne (under King Edward the Confessor) had been added to the monks' possessions. Neither of those two tracts are mentioned separately by name in the Domesday Survey. So both the increased size (fiscal or areal) of Westminster in the Survey, and the absence of Paddington and Knightsbridge from the Survey, seem to combine to confirm for us the picture that those two estates had indeed been granted to the monks in Anglo-Saxon times and that they were now included by the Normans in their increased assessment of the principal Domesday manor of Westminster, with its thirteen and a half hides.[17] Even if that inference were wrong, there is no doubt that the monks were granted each of the two estates (Paddington and Knightsbridge) at *some* early date [18] and that they retained them until the dissolution of the monastery in 1540.

People and Agriculture

So far as the agricultural side of life in Westminster is concerned, the Domesday Book projects a picture of the estate in Anglo-Saxon times which probably differed little in quality from that in any of its other rural manors in the Corridor. But as we shall see, there were distinct differences in the nature of the holdings of the tenants on the estate.

In terms of financial value, Domesday Book records that Westminster with its thirteen and a half hides had been worth only £12 p.a. before the Conquest, as against (say) Hampstead's value of £5 for four hides.[19] The Westminster assessment is surprisingly small, when one considers the comparative merits of the terrains in the two estates. One wonders whether the potential of the Westminster land was not being particularly well realised; or of course whether the Hampstead estate was being very well administered; or again whether the monks' surrounding land was favoured with a low tax-assessment.

At the time of the Survey there were in Westminster eighteen reasonably-landed *villeins,*[20] nine of them each holding a full virgate (of probably about 30 acres) and the other nine each holding half that amount; with one very well-provided tenant holding about 120 acres. Almost as an afterthought, there was also one small 'cottager' (in fact a small-holder) with five acres of his own. After the Conquest the value of the whole estate had fallen from its previous value of £12 to £10, and this suggests that before the Conquest

---

[16] See page 113 and Appendix 1, page 165 (for Paddington); and page 71 (for Knightsbridge).

[17] Harvey *WA Estates* 350 suggests that Chelsea was also included in Westminster's 13.5 hides at Domesday, but this cannot be, because Edward of Salisbury clearly held it at the time of Domesday. There is no doubt that Chelsea did pass into the monks' hands after, but not before, Domesday: see the charter in Robinson *Crispin* 154-5, by which it was leased in about 1116 by the Abbey to yet another important Norman baron, William de Buckland, who was Sheriff of Berkshire.

[18] Harvey *WA Estates* 353. For example Knightsbridge was definitely in the hands of the monks about 30 years after Domesday, since it was named in a genuine list of estates made at the Abbey in about 1117-1121, see *WAM 5670* and page 151 ff. and 156 below.

[19] It was four hides only for this purpose, not five, because of the one hide which had been subinfeudated to Ranulf Peverel and had a separate value; see pages 120 and 123.

[20] For possible settlements in Westminster (other than that round the Abbey), see page 55. As noted on page 50-1, the Domesday record for Middlesex is unique in the amount of detail which it supplies about the 'size' of the actual holdings of the tenants in the manors (even if that detail is not complete).

there may perhaps have been a few more tenants. If, conservatively, one assumes a total of twenty-one well-landed tenants and one cottager before the Conquest, the population of all those who were clearly involved with agricultural life (whether on their own behalf or in the service of the Abbey, or both) would probably have been about 110 (with some extra, for omissions): more than double the population of Hampstead.

Suppliers and Servants to the Abbey   **Map B**
But in addition to this 'agricultural' population, there was also at Westminster, according to the Domesday Survey, an unusual population of 41 real cottagers who each held only their cottage and with it a "garden", and for rental purposes were all combined in one group paying collectively a total of 40 shillings for (specifically) all their "gardens" together. There can be little doubt that this group were of great significance to the life and very existence of the Abbey. While some of these garden-cottagers may perhaps have played some ordinary part in the rural work of the manor, the majority of them (if indeed not all) were part of the more urban scene of Westminster, serving the needs of the Abbey, or perhaps even of the City of London.[21]

In this context it is worth looking at the Domesday description of another - and at that period, a greater - Abbey, the Abbey of St Edmundsbury in West Suffolk, which is much more fully and precisely pictured in Domesday Book than Westminster is. That Abbey (replacing, as perhaps the Abbey at Westminster had, an earlier church) had been founded very late, in 1020 by King Cnut, the first and greatest of the Danish kings. This was about 50 years after the monks at Westminster had received their first endowments from King Edgar. But like Westminster Abbey, the Abbey of St Edmund had also received massive, indeed even more massive, estates from King Edward the Confessor, including full jurisdiction over about a third of the rich county of Suffolk.[22] And by the time of the Domesday Survey, the Abbey at Bury had grown even further in importance and size.

The detailed and illuminating description in Domesday Book [23] of that Abbey's estate in the town of Bury St Edmunds includes the following :-

> "[Also] 75 bakers, brewers, tailors, washers, shoemakers, robemakers, cooks, porters, stewards ; all these daily serve the Saint, the Abbey and the brethren. Besides these, [there are] 13 reeves in charge of the lands, who have their own houses in the same town ; under them [there are] 5 smallholders. [Also]

---

[21] Westminster and Eia, with their alluvial soils near the river, and Chelsea which was on gravel became famous for their market gardens in later centuries, and perhaps these Domesday gardens were the forerunners of such larger-scale enterprises; cf. Rosser *Westminster* 134-5 and Rutton *Manor of Eia* Archaeologia 62 (1910) 49.   A rent of nearly one shilling each for a cottage and garden was high (eg. a good deal higher than some customary tenants in Hampstead were paying 200 years later for both small and larger holdings, after a large amount of intervening inflation) and so suggests some compensating opportunity and ability to earn on the part of the Westminster tenants. Dyer 'Towns and Cottages' in *Studies in Med. Hist.* (Eds. Mayr-Harting and Moore) 96 and 103 also sees these Westminster *cottars* as the beginnings of the borough of Westminster and as servants or minor tenants of the Abbey. For other perhaps comparable cottagers within Middlesex, see also Note 23 below and page 141.

[22] Gransden *Baldwin* A-N Studies (1981) 66. The whole area of more than eight 'Hundreds' in Suffolk had been granted to the Abbey of St Edmund as (in effect) 'Private Hundreds'; cf. page 72-3.

[23] *DB2. Suffolk* 14/167 (f.372a). At Canterbury, DB also recorded a somewhat similar population of 194 smallholders (*bordars*), some of whom may have acted in the same role of servants or servicers for Christ Church, St Augustine's and the town: *DB Kent* ff 3b, 4, 5 and 12. In the manors immediately round London, the total number of cottagers was similarly a large one, more than 250. Other towns in DB had similar groups of cottagers at their door, such as Oxford (with 23) and Warwick (with 100).

34 men at arms, including French and English; under them there are 22 smallholders....... ".

In addition to the above inhabitants, the Abbot *"held 118 men before 1066 for [i.e. to provide] the monks' supplies, and under them 52 smallholders from whom the Abbot could have a certain [amount of] aid".*

This gives us a rare picture of the life surrounding a large Abbey in 1086, and of some of the relationships between the monks and those townspeople who acted as servants in the various capacities listed in this extract of Domesday. There is little doubt that St Edmund's Abbey, with its township, was a larger and more thriving community at this time than Westminster Abbey which had only a small town or village at its gates. The town of Bury surrounding the Abbey had even doubled in value since the Conquest, from £10 to £20, having already grown (as Domesday Book also records) to the extent of an astonishing total of 342 houses built since 1066 on land which had previously been arable land of the Abbey. All this was on a scale which Westminster could not then rival; but in its characteristics, as opposed to size, the comparison is probably a fair one.

There can be little doubt that some or all of the 41 cottagers at Westminster served the Abbey either with produce from their gardens or in the kind of interesting capacities specifically identified at Bury St Edmunds, in providing other food, drink, clothing or special lay services on which the monks depended.

But had any such reservoir of service been there in Westminster before the Conquest, or had it grown up since 1066? The Abbey had been substantially rebuilt and expanded in the two decades before 1066,[24] and the numbers of the monks had grown dramatically from 12 to 80 in the period since the Abbey had been rebuilt before the Conquest.[25] It is clear that this immense revival must have given rise to a growth of new services needed for the royal resting place and its religious guardians. But even before the Abbey's restoration, the community of monks, however reduced it may have become, would have needed service from outside, even if the early monks were required to do much for themselves. It was inevitable that there would begin to grow up round the Abbey, from soon after its foundation in the tenth century, a nucleus of inhabitants whose job or interest it was, not merely to play the part of villagers in an agricultural settlement, but also to provide support in various practical ways for the monks. At the Abbey of St Edmund there was already, even *before* the Conquest, a highly developed pool of suppliers and other workers, who are expressly recorded in the description of that Abbey quoted above.[26]

So one can be sure that some or all of the community of 41 villagers at Westminster who had only their gardens to till at the time of the Domesday Survey reflected an already existing tradition of Abbey-service, which must have grown progressively ever since the Abbey's foundation a hundred years before.[27] If they were wholly or partly engaged in the more urban pursuits of supplying the needs of the monks, they apparently required (or at any rate had been granted) no substantial area of agricultural land to work as well, but depended on what they could earn for their services.

It is also noticeable that, among the very few remaining royal assets in Middlesex, the

---

[24] See pages 68-9.

[25] From 12 to 80 monks, see Flete (Ed. Robinson) *History of WA* 87

[26] DB *ibid.* and see comments in VCH *Suffolk* 1/ 392.

[27] For the many services similarly provided much later in the Middle Ages by Westminster inhabitants, for the benefit of monks, visitors to Westminster (to attend the Palace, the Abbey, the Courts or the Fairs) and Londoners, see Rosser *Westminster* Chap 5, 119-165.

Conqueror himself is recorded in Domesday as 'owning' 30 cottagers of his own, who had to pay him collectively a sum of 14s. 10. 5d. They are referred to without any indication as to where they lived or where they owed their services, save that it was in the Ossulston Hundred. But the description of them in Domesday Book follows immediately after another unusual and hitherto unidentified holding of the king, namely "Twelve and a half acres of Nomansland", the first and only record of any land in Middlesex still held by the king himself.[28] Since it is fairly certain that King Edward the Confessor had established a royal residence at Westminster during his rebuilding of the Abbey, we can probably regard the 30 cottagers 'owned' by his successor as the providers for him of the services necessary for the palace there, comparable with that provided for the monks at the adjoining Abbey by their 41 garden-cottagers.[29] It is also likely that the elusive "Nomansland" was the site or curtilage of the royal residence itself on the banks of the river Thames.[30]

Men-at-arms and Reeves
The Domesday record for the Abbey's estate of Westminster also refers to the existence there of "25 houses of the Abbot's men-at-arms and other men who pay 8 shillings a year". Both of these categories of residents were significant. The name 'men' (*homines*), in this context, clearly had its technical meaning, namely those who had 'commended (ie. pledged) themselves' to serve the Abbot, as 'men' to their 'lord'. Although the Norman feudal system had given rise to fixed military obligations on the part of the ecclesiastical houses (and of course, other principal landholders) to provide specific numbers of men-at-arms for service when required in the Conqueror's army, it is probable that in Anglo-Saxon times as well abbeys of the status of Westminster and St Edmund's had kept similar 'men' close at hand. Such men would have served the dual function of being able to carry arms if required, to deal with any situation which demanded force or even a show of force, and also of performing other more administrative services which their lords might need.[31]

---

[28] For royal generosity in Mdx, see pages 19 and 20. For Nomansland and the cottagers, see DB Mdx 1/1 and 2 (f.127a).

[29] There are also other examples of comparable groups of cottagers in Middlesex, who probably performed similar services. A group of eight cottagers, with 'gardens', and a further 22, without gardens but each holding on average about three acres of land, were to be found on the Bishop of London's main manor at Fulham, possibly performing the same role on behalf of the Bishop and his entourage when he was resident there. Similarly the Canons of St Paul's had 10 cottagers, with on average slightly less than 1 acre each, at Bishopsgate in or just outside the City of London.

[30] For the issue of the 'palace' at Westminster, see page 68. 'Nomansland' has achieved some notoriety among historians as being geographically unidentifiable (eg. Dyer 'Towns and Villages' *ibid* 96 calls it 'mysterious' and places it 'probably near London'). It is the first entry of all in the Middlesex DB. As recorded, it was a strangely small area for any other purpose (only twelve and a half acres), but adequate for an early residence; or at least for the curtilage or land attached to the residence, if the royal building itself was strictly outside the scope of the Survey. The name was subsequently lost. While such a name might have made sense for an early site which (even as a gravel island) was on a shifting river bank and probably had been unused previously, its continued use as a name later for an expanding palace would have become more and more inappropriate and could have been deliberately abolished by a later King. Perhaps significantly the Domesday Survey adds, 'King Edward [the Confessor] held it [Nomansland] similarly'. The Nomansland entry is unique in Middlesex. Moreover the two entries in Domesday Book (Nomansland and the King's cottagers) are *consecutive* entries: there may therefore be a connection. It seems unlikely that the site is to be explained , as Seebohm does, as simply an 'odds and ends' bit of land which was unused at DB. Why should it have the special prominence of the first Middlesex entry? Perhaps the name 'Nanesmaneslande' even implied a warning, 'Keep Off'.

[31] Eg. when Gilbert Crispin, the third Norman Abbot of Westminster, leased the monks' Berewic in the

There is no express mention of any 'reeves' in the brief Domesday description of Westminster, such as those who, as cited above, were "in charge of the lands" of St Edmund's Abbey at Bury and had their own houses in that town. But, as we have seen, the 25 houses in Westminster which are identified in Domesday were quarters not only for military men, but also for lay 'men', who probably served the Abbey in some administrative capacity. Westminster Abbey had a quota of 15 men-at-arms ('knights', as they are usually but anachronistically translated) whom it had to provide for the army under the Norman feudal system.[32]   Some of those who had agreed to act as, or to provide, 'knights' had already been accomodated by the Abbey with other lands [33] before Domesday, for them to hold in return for their services, and so were unlikely to be 'household knights' of the Abbey living in any of the 25 houses.[34] This means that the other lay 'men', who could not have numbered less than ten (i.e. 25 less 15), may in fact have numbered substantially more. Can we justifiably regard some of these lay people as reeves employed by Westminster Abbey, like those employed by the Abbey of St Edmund?

But there is firm evidence that the Westminster monks had had at least one such reeve in their employ before the Conquest, because the Domesday record for one of the two estates in Laleham (in the south-west corner of Middlesex) reveals that *before* the Conquest the 'Reeve of Staines under the Abbot of Westminster' had held that estate in Laleham also.[35] Since Edward the Confessor had earlier given to the Abbey the estate of Staines (an important and valuable place astride the main road and river-crossing to the West), the Reeve was the monks' employee, administering Staines as well as the small two-hide estate in Laleham next door. Whether he did so entirely from Staines or himself had a house at Westminster as one of the Abbey's lay 'men' is not recorded.

But there are other reasons as well for thinking that some of the 25 houses in Westminster housed lay men who acted as reeves on behalf of the Abbey. We do not know for certain what methods the monks of Westminster were using during the period before the Conquest for managing their other lands. Were they for example letting some estates out to 'farmers', i.e. men who took land 'on farm', paying a render for it and themselves receiving the profits of their own management of it? The pattern elsewhere on church estates was that generally at that time monks (or priests) would let out their more

---

present Bloomsbury area to William Baynard in about 1086 (see Note 8 above), the charter provided that Baynard was to furnish the service of one knight and to hold the land 'just as Wulfric Taynus, named the Bordewayte, had held it by better title' (Robinson *Crispin* 38). One may infer that this Wulfric, who as 'Taynus' had clearly been an English thegn, had probably acted as a table-server to the incumbent Abbot from before the Conquest and had provided military assistance as well when needed. It also sounds as if his family forebears (his 'better title') may have provided the same service before him.

[32] Chew *Ecc. Tenants in Chief* 5, 20 ; Harvey *WA Estates* 75.   The quotas established by the Conqueror for the religious houses were notoriously arbitrary and unequal. The quota for St Edmund's Abbey was 40 knights; for St Pauls, 20. On the other hand for Barking Abbey in Essex, the holders of Tyburn manor north of Westminster, William had a special leniency, see pages 73-4 above: he gave it no quota at all (although later the Abbey was often challenged, unsuccessfully, about its claims to this effect).   While the regular feudal system was a Norman introduction, knight service and quotas were not entirely new in England : see Gillingham *Intro. of Knight Service* A-N Studies (1982) 53.

[33] Eg. William Baynard in the Westminster Berewic (see Notes 8 and 31 above) ; an unnamed knight in Battersea (DB. *Surrey* 6/1 (f.32b)); and Ranulf Peverel in Hampstead, see page 119. Later candidates were Gunter in Hendon (see page 156) and William of Buckland in Chelsea (see page 120).

[34] The practice of having military men in or about a church establishment was later frowned on by the Popes and abandoned: Flete (Ed. Robinson) *History of WA* 90

[35] DB. *Mdx* 8/1.

inaccessible lands in this way, rather than try to farm them themselves; but not in the case of estates reasonably near their monastery (or church).[36] If this was the practice at Westminster Abbey, a rural estate such as Westminster itself, adjoining the Abbey, would have been still kept in hand by the monks and managed by them for their own profit through the services of a reeve; and it is likely that the same was true also of estates such as Hampstead and others in the Corridor, in view of their relative proximity and close historical connection with the Abbey. Apparently even Staines at the other end of Middlesex seems to have come into this category.

If it is right that some at least of the other 'men' at Westminster were reeves, this would show that a form of organisation was already established to administer the expanding Westminster estates. The rapid proliferation of the Abbey's lands in Edward the Confessor's time, particularly into the more distant counties such as Worcestershire and Gloucestershire, must have given rise to immense difficulties in their administration. For some of the monks it must also have meant much longer travelling for them to far more distant parts of the country, all of which amounted to a growing interference with the life of secluded devotion to which they were committed.[37]

The swift rise in the numbers of the community of monks, from twelve in (say) 1045 to eighty in the years after the Domesday Survey,[38] may reflect not just the new magnificence of King Edward's 'private Abbey' and mausoleum, but also the more practical requirements of a now large-landowning body. More administration had become needed, and more hands meant lighter work. But it was inevitable that in addition to the extra problems which their growing empire must have imposed upon the monks themselves as a body, other people, laymen, must also have been needed, to assume the more distant duties which the estates entailed and to bring more experienced minds to bear upon the administrative problems.

If this is true of the period shortly before and after the Conquest, it may well be true even of the earlier era after the Abbey's foundation. If indeed the monks numbered only twelve by the time of Edward the Confessor's reign, it is difficult to see how they could have coped, even in that early period when their lands were fewer, with all the problems arising on their estates in the Corridor, let alone their more distant tracts in Hertfordshire, Essex, Sussex, and other parts of Middlesex itself,[39] unless to assist them they had had at least some laymen with previous exposure to the practices of the outside world and past experience as reeves in looking after estates.[40]

---

[36] See Knowles *Monastic Order* 442 and *Religious Orders in England* 1/35. Leases were sometimes for short periods such as a year, but often for one or more lives: see also Lennard *Rural England* 159 ff.

[37] In neither the *Rule of St Benedict* nor the *Regularis Concordia* is any solution prescribed for the problems which would be created for monks by the acquisition of estates. Certain 'journeying' by monks is clearly contemplated in the *Rule*, but 'gadding about' by monks on visits to the properties of their monastery is specifically forbidden by the *Reg. Conc.* The monk's life of devotion must have been difficult (at least in theory) to reconcile with a wide ownership of property. When Dunstan in the tenth century was Abbot of Glastonbury, he put his own brother (who was not a monk) in charge of that Abbey's estates, apparently to free the monks of the need to travel about; Knowles *Monastic Order* 431.

[38] Flete (Ed. Robinson) *ibid* 87. See also page 68-9.

[39] See pages 69-71.

[40] It may be that not all such laymen had yet acquired the expertise of the author of the *Estate Guide'* and the *Gerefa*, described above at pages 115 ff. and 129 ff., who probably had a long tradition of specialisation and training behind him.

In this connection the very name 'reeve' [41] can be deceptive, in covering a range of different grades of employee. At one extreme there were the powerful reeves who were in effect full-time paid officers with a considerable practical expertise, who were employed by the larger landholders to manage one or more of their estates or to hold some other great office.[42]   Such was a 'royal reeve', a man chosen and appointed by the king to manage one or more of the royal estates; or a 'shire-reeve' (originally called a 'scir-man', the name being later converted to 'shire-reeve' and finally the 'sheriff'), who was appointed to act for and to be responsible to the King in a particular shire.[43] Closer home, we have already met other examples of influential reeves, in the men appointed by the Abbey of St Edmunds to adminster its lands,[44] or (in the case of Westminster) the Reeve of Staines.

But at the other extreme there was a much more humble reeve, a villager chosen by his fellow-tenants (at the estate-lord's requirement), to carry out the daily routines of mustering and overseeing those tenants who owed physical services to the lord for the working of the estate. Often a reluctant servant, having a difficult role to play between the lord's stern requirements and his fellow-villagers' interests, this kind of reeve in turn might have an overseer (called a 'serviens' or 'serjeant') appointed over him, who was less of a local man and more of a supervisor from outside.[45] At all events this local reeve was near the bottom of the administrative heap, and we will meet later [46] some of the activities of, and the difficulties met by, such men in their work on the Corridor manors from the thirteenth century onwards.

In that later period of the thirteenth and fourteenth centuries, the monks themselves (whose numbers had by then settled down to 45-50 [47]) had established a more organised system of surveillance and of record-making with regard to their lands and had gained some personal experience of administration and finance. Some of them, and other officials appointed by them, were paying regular visits at that time to the Corridor estates, to oversee, to give orders and to collect profits.[48]   But as regards the much earlier period, both before and after the Conquest, it is difficult to resist the conclusion that most of the administrative problems of the estates must have been dealt with by a body of practical laymen, some of them probably based in Westminster, who were employed as reeves to oversee the procurement, receipt and disposal of the produce of the increasing number of estates and to deal with other questions arising in them. This may have been a fairly rudimentary system in the period before Edward the Confessor's reign, but with the dramatic growth of Abbey landowning during that reign, even the increasing body of

---

[41] The Latin word used at first for all the different kinds of reeve is 'praepositus', a man put in front, or in charge. In due course it came to refer principally to the village reeve. For discussion about the kinds of reeves, see Campbell 'Some agents of the late A-S State', in *DB Studies* (Holt, ed.) 201.

[42] In later times such a man would be given a more important title, such as Steward.

[43] Loyn *Governance* 138-40. The OE title 'gerefa' (reeve) was used in connection with a 'scir' (shire) at least as soon as the shires had been created in the Home Counties, see page 48 above: VI Athelstan (924-939), para. 8.4., *EHD* 1/425-6; Whitelock *A-S Wills* 191.

[44] Yet another example is the author of the *Estate Guide* and *Gerefa*, see Note 36 above.

[45] Practice on different estates varied greatly. Whether or not a serviens (of whom we will see many examples later) was appointed, the village reeve generally had to answer to a lay Bailiff; or in the case of a religious Lord of the manor (as in our case), the Bailiff might be a Monk-Bailiff, see Pearce *Monks of WA* 211.

[46] In Volume 2.

[47] Pearce *Monks of WA* Preface, page x.

[48] See Vol 2. This may sound efficient, but it was still a fairly relaxed system.

monks would inevitably have been swamped without considerable practical help.[49]

Therefore although there had been great changes brought about by efficient administrative methods introduced by the Normans after the Conquest, there is every reason to think that some of the 25 Abbey houses recorded in Westminster in 1086 housed the 'men' who, or whose predecessors, had formed even before the Conquest a kind of early 'civil service' for the Abbey and its expanding territories. It was the Anglo-Saxon period which must have seen this rise of an administrative team in Westminster.

The Meadowland of Westminster   **Maps B and D**

The rural work on the rest of the early Westminster estate surrounded these more urban features near the Abbey. One special aspect of the Westminster agriculture was the large amount of *meadowland* within the estate, which particularly distinguished it from Hampstead, which had none, and Hendon, which in all its 20 hides had only enough "meadow for two oxen", according to the Domesday record. But sufficient meadow to feed up to 11 teams of plough-oxen [50] is recorded for Westminster. In practice this would have meant about 80 oxen, if one assumes that the 10 teams actually at work in Westminster each had a full quota of eight oxen (rather than the smaller, and also recognised, teams of six, four or two). How much meadowland would this mean ? The recording of meadowland in the Domesday Survey was far from consistent, and the measures were variable. One estimate which has been made is that it required three acres of meadow to keep one ox.[51] If that estimate is right, we would be thinking of an area of about 250 acres of meadowland on the estate. Since the area of the Westminster estate itself (*without* the Berewic or Paddington, Westbourne or Knightsbridge) was about 1000 acres, this would mean that about one quarter of that part of the estate was under hay.

Much of this grass would almost certainly have been on the alluvial soil of Westminster, nearest the river. One remembers that description, given above, by the biographer of King Edward the Confessor : 'the fertile lands and green fields which surrounded the Abbey', clearly an account by one who had seen them. That pattern of wide water-meadows along the banks of the river Thames was repeated for most of the other estates bordering the river where the alluvium lay: *Eia* (sufficient for eight teams of oxen; plus an additional income of 60/- from its meadows, a large sum); *Chelsea* (sufficient for two teams); *Fulham* (sufficient for 40 teams); *Chiswick* (for five teams); *Isleworth* (for 20 teams); *Hampton* (for three teams, plus 10/- income); *Sunbury* (for six teams); *Shepperton* (for seven teams); *Charlton* (for four teams); *Laleham* (for five teams); and *Staines* (for 24 teams). In the Domesday Survey of those Middlesex manors which lay further away from the river, the recorded amount of meadowland falls off considerably, as we have already seen in the fairly typical examples of Hampstead and Hendon.[52] It is

---

[49] See page 151 below as regards the system in force only 50 years *after* the Conquest, for the payment of food-renders or money rents which the manors had to provide for the Abbey, and other conclusions which can be drawn for the period *before* the Conquest.

[50] This was the way in which the Domesday surveyors generally recorded the extent of meadowland in Middlesex and the other four counties on the same circuit. On other circuits, meadow was normally recorded in estimated acreages, see Darby *DB.England* 137-9. For the size of plough teams in the *twelfth* century, see Lennard *Demesne Plough Teams* EHR 75 (1960) 193.

[51] Darby *ibid* 138

[52] Curiously, in the huge manor of Harrow, which the Archbishop of Canterbury held, there is no Domesday record of meadow at all, although there were already 49 existing ploughs there for the necessary oxen to pull. But there was 'pasture for the village livestock', *DB Mdx* 2/2 (f.127a), see pages

worth noticing that throughout the Middle Ages until the Dissolution, the hay crop from the meadows of Middlesex was the most valuable crop of all, being sometimes valued at 10-12 times the value per acre of the crops on arable land.[53] Indeed in later centuries, with an ever-growing demand from London and its suburbs for the provisioning of horses and for a year-long supply of meat and milk, the hay-crop became more and more the premier yield, and in some places in Middlesex it became the only crop.[54]

The Westminster Woodland

One other noticeable feature of the Westminster rural scene was that, even as late as Domesday, there was as much pig-wood ('for 100 pigs') in the main Westminster estate, as there was in Hampstead. If one tries to identify where this woodland was within the Westminster estate, one can see that (as one might expect) the riparian lands of Eia and Chelsea had, respectively, no pig-wood, and wood for only 50 pigs, but that further from the river the woodland increases. Lileston had the same quantity as Westminster; Kensington twice as much; and higher up Watling Street Willesden had enough for 500 pigs. Since it appears that Paddington was now being included within the manor of Westminster, the pattern suggests that probably the woodland recorded for Westminster was in fact mainly within the Paddington area.

   Moreover it is clear that (like Hampstead and Hendon) Paddington in later centuries supplied to the Abbey much timber and wood for burning.[55] Since it seems that in later centuries 'Paddington Wood' was in fact in that part of the estate which was near Watling Street,[56] one can infer that perhaps this was where at least some of the Domesday (and the pre-Domesday) pig-wood of 'Westminster' lay. But Paddington Wood, according to a record which shows the size of that wood in 1647, was by that time no bigger than 44 acres. No doubt the earlier demands of the Abbey for both timber and brushwood from Paddington (and the later demands of the Bishopric of London to whom the manor passed after the Dissolution of Westminster Abbey) must have much reduced this wood. It is notoriously difficult [57] (if not impossible [58]) to calculate how much woodland a medieval pig would have required, but it is certain that the pig-wood in Westminster at the time of the Domesday Survey would have been much larger, probably in the range 150-250 acres, than the later (reduced) size of Paddington Wood; and in the century before the Conquest one would expect it to have been larger still.

35-6.

[53] Eg. in 1312 the survey of their manor of Hampstead which the monks carried out shows that the arable land was then worth 4d per acre, while the meadowland was valued at 4/- per acre, see Vol 2.

[54] See Thompson *Hampstead 1650-1964* pp. 9-12; Galloway and Murphy *Feeding the City* London Jo. 16 (1991) 9.

[55] See Vol. 2, and *VCH Mdx* 9/235

[56] See map of Paddington at *VCH Mdx* 9/180.

[57] Darby *DB England* 172-3; Bailey *Hidation of Mdx* 172. One and a half, or two and a half, acres per pig have been calculated as necessary; but with many reservations.

[58] Rackham *History of Countryside* 75-6.

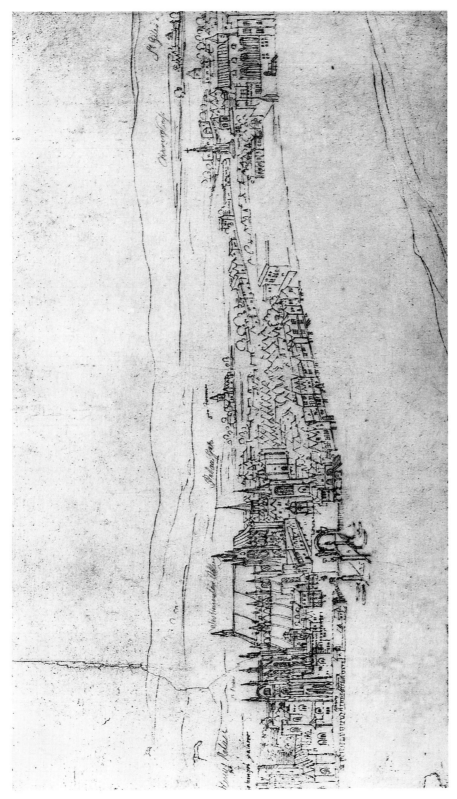

Plate 16. The view of Westminster drawn by Wyngaerde in 1543/4. It shows the narrowness of the built-up area along the river bank, even after more than 550 years had elapsed since the foundation of the Abbey. The villages of St Giles (generally known as 'St Giles in the Fields') and St James's appear as outliers, and beyond lies the long line of the Hampstead-Highgate ridge.   See page 135

Plate 17. A print of an eighteenth-century 'reconstruction', in watercolour, of the earlier rural area of Westminster and St James's. The original watercolour showed the figures as lepers or monks (ie. as though before Henry VIII's purchase of St James's Hospital), but the figures were changed by the later Victorian printmaker to these more politically-correct Elizabethans. The area was still open in 1658.

See page 136

CHAPTER 12

Abbey life : the Corridor contributes

Food-renders and money-rents

While the peasant worked on the land in the Corridor, the monk bowed to his discipline in the Abbey. The main link between the two was the food which the peasant helped both to produce on the endowment estates and to carry to the Abbey for the sustenance of the monks. From their estates in Middlesex and the nearby counties the monks of Westminster certainly began by drawing a weekly 'feorm' or food-render (with or without a money-rent) during the period before the Conquest : and as we shall see below, they continued to draw at least a part of their revenue in the form of a food-render (together with more in the form of money-rents) for a substantial period after the Conquest.[1]

A 'feorm', in its distant origins, was probably derived from the archaic obligation to supply food, which had been formerly owed to an Anglo-Saxon king by a district or region. This render was for the daily support of the king and his retinue, as they reached that district in the course of the king's peripatetic journeys round his kingdom or his own estates. It also seems that when the king granted such land away, to the Church or to a noble or other follower, the obligation went with it.[2] As it had been for the king, so also it was convenient, if not essential, for some of the great lords, who were often peripatetic too on visits to their estates, to receive their renders of food in specified quantities at different places in the course of their journeying. On the other hand a monastery, by definition, was static, even if the Abbot who was often a figure of national importance might sometimes (and indeed often, in later centuries) be on the move on public business or in pursuit of his monastery's interests.[3] And so, in the case of the monastery, the proceeds had generally to come to the lord, not the lord to the proceeds; and (before becoming a mere money-rent) they came in the form of farm produce sufficient for the weekly maintenance of the community of monks.

As already indicated,[4] it is likely that even in the early period before the Conquest the Westminster monks' management of some or all of their nearby Corridor estates was effected through the employment of reeves, rather than by the leasing of them to

---

[1] For example in the first half of the thirteenth century they were still receiving from Gilbert de Hendon, whose family (beginning with the Abbot's 'man', Gunter, shortly after the Conquest, see page 156 below) had held the 'manor of Hendon' from the Abbey for over one hundred years, not only a large rent of £22 but also a yearly render of wheat, grout and oats: WAD f.121b.

[2] See the reference to 'the old feorm', contrasted with later additions to it, in a pre-Conquest survey from the Abbey of Bury St Edmunds, at *EHD* 2/881. Cf. *Laws of Alfred* art. 2, *EHD* 1/409; Stafford *Farm of One Night* Ec.HR 33 (1980) 491.

[3] The early unrecorded obligations of hospitality owed by particular estates to eg. Abbots or other lay 'lords' were sometimes compromised by agreement at much later dates: eg. the Abbot of Westminster at some date not later than 1225 became entitled to specified rights of hospitality at Hendon (see Vol 2) and at Deene in Northants (see Stenton *English Feudalism* 71-2).

[4] See page 142-3.

independent 'farmers'. But, whichever way the management was in fact carried out,[5] the render which was owed was likely to be a render in *kind*, at least in part if not in whole.

When (as was more usual in early Anglo-Saxon times) the only lands belonging to an Abbey were not too distant, it was physically possible for most renders of food from its rural estates to be transported to the Abbey itself. We have already seen that in addition to their work on the lord's land, both those workers the *Gebur* and the *Geneat* had to perform carrying service, which included the provision of the necessary means of carrying the produce to the lord, ie. an ox or horse and cart.

At many monasteries the 'food-render' system can be shown to have been well-established at a very early date, long before the Conquest.[6] Although there is no Anglo-Saxon record which actually shows that the practice was the same at Westminster, there is no reason to think that it was any different. Indeed there is one post-Conquest record which establishes that the practice must have been the same at Westminster, beginning from some earlier date in the Anglo-Saxon period. This was a document [7] made at Westminster in the Norman period, probably between 1117 and 1121, about 30-35 years after the Domesday Survey. It was a list of not only the food-renders and money-contributions which were due each week at that time from the nearer or 'inner' manors of the Abbey, but also some substantial money-rents from the more distant manors.[8]

One can be sure that since at least some food-renders were being received by the monks at Westminster from their inner manors at that time in the twelfth century, they would also have been a regular feature in the previous period before the Conquest, as they had been at other monasteries and churches. The food-render system was a creature of the Anglo-Saxons and indeed, by the time of this document in the Norman period, the practice was already on its way out, as the document itself shows. Since the Norman list is the only detailed evidence which we have about the system at Westminster in any early period, it is necessary to look carefully at it and to extract such evidence as it may have for the previous Anglo-Saxon period.

---

[5] Sometimes a half-way solution for the management was sought, when monks let an estate to one of their own number (presumably when there was at least some ground for regarding that monk as competent to oversee, or procure the supervision of, the farming activities), in the expectation that this would cut out any middle-man profits: see Lennard *Rural England* 157-9. Or again sometimes a letting was made to all of the tenants of a vill where the estate lay, or to a group of them : cf. Willesden, an estate of the Canons of St Pauls, see page 108.

[6] Eg. at Worcester (Hemmings *Cartulary* f.45d); Christ Church, Canterbury (Douglas *Domesday Monachorum* 88 ff); Ramsey (Raftis *Estates of Ramsey* 35-6); Bury St Edmunds (Robertson *A-S Charters* 195-6); St Albans (Robinson *Crispin* 42); and also at the cathedral church of St Pauls (*Domesday of St Pauls*, Ed. Hale, Cam. Soc. 69 (1858) xlviii;).

[7] WAM 5670. See also Robinson *Crispin* 41 ff (with its detailed notes) and Harvey *Estates of WA* 80. It was probably made at that time because, during a 'vacancy' between the death of one Abbot and the delayed election of another, a royal officer was managing the Abbey on behalf of King Henry l, and some record was needed to catalogue the Abbey's entitlements from its manors. Possibly the list was dictated by the King's officer himself, from information supplied to him by officers among the monks. During any such 'vacancy' at a religious house, the King, by 'regalian right' (a right not blessed by canon law), was entitled to step into the shoes of the missing Abbot, to manage the Abbey and to take its profits, until the new Abbot had been elected. The same rule applied after the death of any lay lord and before the formal transfer of estates to his heir, which the king could and did often delay, to his own advantage.

[8] As the document itself says, the more distant manors "would not be able to render" the food-rent, owing undoubtedly to the problems caused by the distances and lack of both communication and easy transport.

The Norman Render-List (c.1120 AD)

The listed weekly produce [9] which the group of 'inner' manors (which included of course the Corridor estates) were obliged to pay to the Abbey consisted of '6 coombs of wheat for bread, and 20 pecks of malt, and 10 pecks of grout, and 3 coombs of oats'; but there was also due (again from the inner manors) a money render of £3. 7s. for the monks' kitchen and '1 mark of silver' (13s. 4d.) for the 'servants' of the monks. The 'malt' was made from barley or other grain prepared by fermentation for making ale, and the 'grout' was a form of coarse meal, also used in the making of a cheap ale.

An earlier historian has argued that the physical quantity of wheat described in this list for the basic food, bread, was inadequate for about 80 monks (as the Abbey's complement was by that time) and for some of the servants, and has suggested that the measurement used for the wheat, a coomb, may have been different in size at that time.[10] But we do not know his calculations, and his conclusion is doubtful. On a recalculation it seems that the six weekly coombs of wheat would have produced about 2500 lbs of bread, which (on the assumption that an average of three lbs of bread was consumed by each man daily) would have been sufficient to feed about 120 people for the week.[11]

In any case, the document also demonstrates that by 1121 there may have been, at an earlier date or dates, some commuting[12] of earlier food-renders for money, or that an additional obligation to pay money as well had by that time been imposed; or both. Either way, this resulted in the inner manors having to pay not only a food-render but also a money-render, expressly for 'the monks' kitchen'. Of course a wheat food-render of such a size would have been more than sufficient for the very early monastery, when there were only about twelve monks.[13] This suggests that the render was then smaller, and was supplemented later. But an additional money-render, as an obligation in a commuted form, may have also been imposed later to provide for the monks, as their complement grew even further. These increases would almost certainly have started contemporaneously with the rebuilding of the Abbey in Edward the Confessor's reign and had certainly continued, after the Conquest, under the Normans. By the time when this document was written the construction of the monks' additional buildings alongside the Abbey itself had been completed,[14] and the monks' complement was full. The weekly money-render of £3. 7s. from the inner manors was a substantial one at that time, and since (as the list records) the Abbey was also entitled to receive, from the more distant manors, an additional and even larger weekly sum, of £8.10s,[15] there was no lack of funds for the monks to be able to

---

[9] For the size of a similar food-render owed to Ramsey Abbey by two of its estates more than a hundred years earlier than the Westminster one, see Raftis *Estates of Ramsey Abbey* 12.

[10] Robinson *Crispin* 43. The 'modern', and probably the ancient, 'coomb' equals four bushels, or half a 'quarter'.

[11] Data for this calculation have been kindly supplied to me by Mr Patrick White of Mount Pleasant Windmill, Kirton-in-Lindsey, Lincs and Dr Kenneth Wright of Nayland, Suffolk. The assumption that an average of three lbs of bread would have been consumed daily by each of the 80 monks and some of their servants (ie. those who received their food from the monastery) is based on the average of four lbs calculated by H.E.Hallam in *Rural England* 65-7 for the ordinary peasant, who had to lead a much more strenuous life and perhaps had to rely more on bread than the monk did. The daily loaf for the monks by about 1500 was less, 2.5 lbs (due to other more palatable food by then ?) Harvey *Living and Dying* 59.

[12] As there had been at other monasteries even before the Conquest, see eg. Raftis *Estates of Ramsey Abbey* 10-11 and Douglas *An A-S Survey from Bury St. Eds.* EHR 43 (1928) 377.

[13] See page 56.

[14] See Gem *The Romanesque rebuilding of WA* A-NS 3 (1981) 55-60; Knowles *Monastic Buildings* 188.

[15] Of course no documents of account existed at the Abbey at such an early date, to record the receipt of

purchase food for themselves.[16]

The geographical distinction which this Westminster list draws between the Abbey's nearer manors and the distant ones is an obscure one. The latter are not identified by name and are simply described as '*longinqua*' (distant), but there is no indication as to where the line is to be drawn between the two groups. Before Edward the Confessor's time, the Abbey's estates were all fairly close, the furthest one being in Sussex and the majority much closer in Middlesex, five of them in the Corridor. But as we have seen, both King Edward and his nobles thereafter granted much more distant estates to the Abbey, particularly in the West Country. Since it was clearly uneconomic, if not in some cases impossible, for food to be brought from such long distances, it may be that the money-rents to the Abbey from those more distant parts had begun at least as soon as those lands were bestowed on the Abbey.[17]

Other special commitments in the Norman List   Maps B and M

In addition to the weekly renders of food and money, the Westminster list goes on to detail other large sums which at least twenty of the Abbey's manors had to contribute annually for certain specific purposes for the monks' support. In most cases the manors in question are identified by name in the document. First let us see what these purposes were and how much was being assigned to them :

	£
For gifts and extra allowances [eg. special food for the sick]	32
For logs (or beams?)	15
For the chamber [the dormitory]	70
For the servants (of kitchen, brewery, garden, vineyard, infirmary, gate)	6.14s
For the 'Maundy' [for its meaning, see below]	4

The first three of these special extras probably reflect aspects of the three basic essentials of the everyday living of the monks, namely food, warmth and clothing. The *food* item was of course additional to both the primary food-render from the inner manors and to such food as was purchased with the special levy of £3. 7s weekly for the kitchen.

---

the various renders. As regards the making of simple administrative documents, it is worth noticing that even about 100 years after DB, when Abbot Samson was elected to the Abbacy of St Edmund's Abbey, he received nothing in writing from his predecessor, save one small sheet on which were recorded (a) the names of the knights of the Abbey, (b) the names of the Abbey manors, and (c) the amounts of the rents due from each 'farm': *Joc. of Brakelond* (Ed. Butler) 29. Nevertheless it is difficult to believe that with their now extensive estates in many parts of the country the monks or their reeves (even with the best of well-developed memories, such as the less sophisticated cultures have fostered) could have kept a check on eg. deliveries without some *physical* record being made. The making of monastic records by notching wooden tallies appears to have started by about the time of this Westminster document in the early twelfth century (Clanchy *Memory to Written Record* 72; Jenkinson *Exchequer Tallies* Archaeologia 62 (1911) 380), and the view has been expressed that such tallies had probably been in use in late Anglo-Saxon times (Lawson 'Edward the Confessor's England' in *A-S England* (Ed. Campbell) 227. But at even earlier times some system of simple marks or scratches at least would have had to be used on, say, barn or mill doors, as has been the agricultural custom over centuries ever since. Although in the Westminster document the money sums are expressed to be weekly dues, it is unlikely that such payments could always have been made weekly, and certainly not from the more distant manors.

[16] Possibly those 41 cottagers with gardens in Westminster were one convenient source of food for sale, see pages 139-40 above.

[17] It is not known whether they had already been paying a money-rent to their previous owners (eg. Pershore Abbey, some of whose lands were appropriated for bestowal on Westminster) or were still paying a food-render to them at the time when the transfers to WA took place.

The £32 represented an additional amount of over 12/- in each week of the year, spent on 'extras', generally for sick or elderly monks or for all or some of the monks on celebratory occasions (birthdays, appointments, anniversaries etc.). In the list these allowances were called 'gifts' (*caritates*) and 'pittances' (*pitanciae*).

The giving of these small extras, mostly in the form of food, seems to have played a marked role in the thinking of the monks, a human touch which perhaps reflects the austerity in their ordinary life (at least in early centuries). The allowances appeared in many of the Abbey records over the centuries,[18] and included little 'presents' (also called *exennia*) which were often in the form of food. For example in later centuries the practice of buying and sending small presents from the Abbey up, or over, the Hampstead hill to monks who were convalescing, or at least 'taking the air', in Hampstead, and to other monks and their companions who were staying at Hendon, is well recorded in the Abbey records; and it is clear from the Norman list that a similar practice went back at least to the early Norman period and probably to Anglo-Saxon times before the Conquest. The 'pittances' too were generally given in the form of food in earlier days; but in later centuries they were often granted as small money allowances (eg.'1d. per day')[19] with which the recipients could buy what they needed.

The entry for '*logs* (or beams)' (*ligna*), for which the Abbey was to receive £15, presents a question. On the one hand, the word '*ligna*' may refer to wood for building, rather than for burning, since it can connote wood of a more substantial size, such as beams or posts. In the period after the Conquest the Normans had been responsible for extensive building projects for new churches and other religious buildings throughout the land.[20] At Westminster, this had meant the completion not only of the massive nave of the new church and of the demolition of buildings in the old sanctuary, but also of the construction of fresh domestic quarters for the monks; none of which Edward the Confessor had completed before he died. Some of this work seems to have taken place before 1084, when the great Norman, Gilbert Crispin, became Abbot of Westminster (1084-1117),[21] but some remained to be completed by him. But by the time that this document was written, all that was in the past and Crispin was already dead.

It seems therefore that the major building projects at Westminster during the Norman period were already over, and that the word *ligna* must have meant the monks' own fuel, the type of wood available not for building but for burning.[22] Moreover if *ligna* had meant some form of building timber, we would have to take note of a surprising absence in the list of any mention of the essential fuel for warmth, upon which the survival of the monks depended.

---

[18] See eg, Pearce *Monks of WA* passim, but particularly 21-4.

[19] Hence our own concept of a pittance as 'a small sum, or small item'; even if the comparative scale has changed somewhat. For the later development of pittances, see Harvey *Living and Dying* 10-11, 43.

[20] 'The Normans revived by their coming the practice of religion which everywhere was lapsing; throughout the land you might see churches rising in every vill, and monasteries in the towns and cities, built in a style unknown before." Wm of Malmesbury *Gesta Regum* (Ed. Stubbs) RS ii. 306 (trans. R. Allen Brown). But for evidence also of pre-Norman church-building, see Gem 'The English Parish Church ... a great Rebuilding?' in Blair (ed) *Minsters and Parish Churches* 21.

[21] Before Crispin became Abbot, the new dormitory with its massive undercroft was finished (some of it surviving, with modifications, to this day), and the cloister, the refectory (a wall of which survives) and the Abbot's chamber were completed during his abbacy (for reasons given by Robinson *Crispin* 35, which Gem *Romanesque rebuilding of WA* A-NS 3 (1981) 38-9 does not cite), together with the locutory (where conversation was allowed). For the undercroft (now a museum), see **Plate 18**, page 163.

[22] This also appears to be the way in which Miss Harvey has interpreted it, see *Estates of WA* 141.

In later centuries the Abbey's Middlesex manors are recorded in great detail as furnishing the major requirements of wood for the Abbey, both for cooking, baking and brewing purposes and for the needs of the monks themselves in their efforts to keep warm in the frigid conditions of their buildings; not to mention their building requirements, which recurred regularly, owing as much to ambitious schemes of improvement as to the effects of frequent destruction by fire during medieval times. Almost without exception, all the cartloads of wood-fuel which was gathered in the Corridor manors during the later thirteenth and fourteenth centuries consisted of *brushwood* . The two words generally used in the records for *brushwood* were 'faggots' (bundles of large brushwood, bound together usually with two withies, giving intense heat to the fire, if only more briefly than logs would) and 'bavins' (similar bundles, but of smaller size and bound usually with one withy). It may therefore be that in the Norman period the word *ligna* suggests that at that earlier time the wood available for this purpose was of a more substantial kind than the brushwood which remained later, after the substantial wood-cutting which had taken place as the centuries went by.

So food, warmth and clothing were the prerequisites for survival. The monks' 'chamber' allowance of £70 appears to be an appreciable one, but the greatest part of this must have been the cost of clothing for the 80 or so monks. The point has been made elsewhere that by as much as 130 years later, in about 1250, the allowance for clothing had only risen to £88,[23] and this after a period of dramatic monetary inflation centred on the end of the twelfth century. But it is right to reply that by that time the number of monks at Westminster had fallen to about 50-60. So the true contrast is between £70 for 80 monks (in c.1120), and at least £88 for 50-60 monks (in c.1250). This equation reflects either the effect of the great inflation, or a substantial increase in the standard of the clothing supplied to the monks; or perhaps the results of both.

The provision made for the *servants* of the Abbey (£6. 14s., in addition to the 'silver 13/4d' already mentioned) reveals the extent to which by about 1120 there was an established complement of lay servants to administer to the needs of the Abbey and its monks, as well as the needs of the many guests and other visitors who came to the Abbey.[24] Back in the tenth century, when the monastic revival was in progress and monasteries were being newly founded or restored, much of the administrative and domestic work was probably done by the monks themselves.[25] But 80 years later, by the time of the Conquest, a system of lay servants had been firmly established in most of the monasteries. With the great increase in the number of monks at Westminster, following the restoration of the Abbey by Edward the Confesssor and the subsequent arrival of the Normans, it is certain that the complement of servants must have grown correspondingly. So now we see, from this list, that there is a group of offices with their own lay staff : the kitchen, the bakery, the brewery, the garden (meaning a kitchen garden and herbarium), the vineyard, the infirmary or sick quarters, and the gatehouse. At Bury St Edmunds in 1086

---

[23] Robinson *Crispin* 44; Thompson *Westminster Customary* (H. Bradshaw Soc.) vol ii. 149. It was £88 "at the least", so it could have been more. As to the Abbey's 'Customary', see page 162 below.

[24] It is unlkely that there were many pilgrims yet at Westminster in spite of the Abbey's growing national importance, since Edward the Confessor had not yet been canonised (not until 1161) : there were other draws there, other relics, but not the prize which Osbert de Clare may already have been eyeing (see page 61). The flood of pilgrims did not come until later, when the Confessor's shrine had become 'one of the sights of medieval England' (Rosser *Westminster* 216).

[25] Knowles *Monastic Order* 439

there had been 75 listed servants in the Abbey, according to the Domesday Survey,[26] already outnumbering the body of monks.[27] By 1120 the number of monks at Westminster (about 80) was larger than the number at Bury,[28] and it is likely that the lay servants at Westminster by this time had grown to a figure which probably exceeded 100. Presumably most, if not all, of them lived in Westminster itself, and if so, the number of the 41 inhabitants labelled as 'cottagers' in 1086 [29] had probably grown accordingly in the 35 years since Domesday.

By the date of our Norman document it seems that already the status of some of servants in the Abbey had become so established that their offices were now hereditary, in the manner which became familiar for so many public and institutional posts during the subsequent centuries of the Middle Ages (and indeed after the Middle Ages).[30] Elsewhere too, only 50 years after this Westminster document was made, another record, relating this time to Glastonbury Abbey, shows similarly that at that Abbey too many of the positions held by servants had already become hereditary.[31] So this pattern among the monasteries was already becoming a familiar one. At Westminster it is likely that such rights in individual families were established at a very early time: at least in the Norman period and perhaps even before the Conquest when Edward the Confessor was reorganising his new Abbey.

The reference in the Norman list to a *vineyard* existing at the Abbey by 1121 reveals a discrepancy. There had been no vineyard mentioned in the Domesday description of the main Westminster estate 35 years before. The only vineyard recorded in Westminster, described as 'newly planted' at the time of Domesday, lay in the smaller Westminster estate, the Berewic in the Bloomsbury area, which had by that time been let to the Norman baron William Baynard. It seems that Baynard, since acquiring the land shortly before about 1085, had planted four 'arpents' [32] of vines in the present Bloomsbury area; but as

---

[26] DB 2 *Suffolk* 14/ 167 (f. 372a). See quotations at pages 139-40 above.

[27] Knowles *ibid*. 440.

[28] In spite of the elaborate establishment at Bury which is revealed in its description in DB, the number of its monks had fallen below that of Westminster by 1121 because of the rapid growth in the complement at the latter during the 65 years since 1050, resulting from the restoration by Edward the Confessor and the further extensions of the Abbey by the Normans since the time of the Conquest.

[29] See pages 139-41.

[30] For example, at about this time (say, 1120), Walter Stantus the father-in-law of William de Wandene had held at least two posts, in the buttery and the vestry of the Abbey (and also certain tenements in the town to which the posts were annexed); and William as his son-in-law was able to claim after the death of his father-in-law that the two posts and the tenements had become rightfully his and his wife's by virtue of her inheritance and his marriage: WAM L and WAD f.87. See also Mason *WA Charters* No 254. Descendants of the same family surrendered the posts back to the Abbey more than a hundred and fifty years later, see Mason *ibid.*, note to No 254. For the Keeperships of the Gate and the Abbot's Prison, which also became hereditary, see eg. WAM 17694.

[31] Knowles *Monastic Order* 440-1

[32] The arpent was a French unit of measurement (probably about an acre in size), which the Normans had introduced, but almost exclusively for vineyards, which they were instrumental in planting at many places in England, see Maitland *DB and Beyond* 375; Round *Essex Arch. Trans.* NS 7/249-51. There were six other vineyards in Middlesex recorded in DB: one possibly in Holborn and one in Kensington, and the other four in the south-west corner of the county. As one might expect, vines were usually planted on estates where the lord had a residence (see Round *VCH Essex* 1/382), and on the same reasoning, probably William Baynard kept a private residence on his Berewic in Bloomsbury (**Map M**). Cf. Count Robert of Mortain with his house at Bermondsey, his 'foothold' near the City. But the Baynards' business address was clearly at Baynards Castle, in the corner of the City wall at the mouth of

far as the Domesday record goes, there was no vineyard reported at that time in the main part of Westminster.[33] But we learn that there was certainly one by 1121, and its position was probably then, as it was later, immediately to the south of the Abbey, in the Tothill area.[34]

The *Maundy* (which is referred to in the Norman document) was the ceremony of washing the feet of a number of poor persons, a duty required of all monks,[35] which was usually followed by the distribution of clothing, food or money. Knightsbridge was one of the two estates which had to contribute 20/- towards the cost of this: although it is likely that Knightsbridge had been granted to the Abbey during the reign of Edward the Confessor, this is probably the first completely authentic reference to Knightsbridge as an Abbey possession.[36]

In addition to the Norman list which we have been considering, there is one other Westminster record of the monks' early requirement of a food-render from a tenant. During his abbacy Gilbert Crispin, who did so much to establish the Abbey on a firm footing, let the manor of Hendon (which in this context probably meant the whole new manor, of a full twenty hides) to 'my man Gunter' for 'one full week of the farm' each year.[37] One cannot say whether this was a repetition of some similar arrangement dating back before the Conquest, with the substitution of the Norman Gunter for an English lessee. Unfortunately the nature of the food to be rendered by Gunter is not recorded, but it is of interest that Gunter's descendant, Gilbert of Hendon, was still paying a food-render over a hundred years later, with an added money rent by that time. By then the render was 36 quarters of wheat, 20 quarters of grout and 40 quarters of brewing oats. Gunter's

---

the Fleet (see page 136); that is, until all their estates were confiscated in 1110-11 on a forfeiture by William Baynard (which involved both 'misfortune and felony': Robinson *Crispin* 39); see too Douglas *DB. Monachorum* 60-2. For Baynard, see also pages 81 and 142.

[33] One possible explanation of this may be that, by its very terms, the entry in DB for the main Westminster manor is specifically limited to the village ('villa') of Westminster, suggesting that it excluded the immediate site and surrounds of the Abbey itself (which in any case would not have been subject to the fiscal assessments which the Survey was designed to assist). On this hypothesis, a vineyard appurtenant and adjacent to the Abbey would probably have been regarded as outside the scope of the Survey, even if it had existed at that time. On the other hand, since it seems to have been the Norman influence which was mainly instrumental in further propagating the vine in England (see VCH *Essex* 1/382), it may well be that it was only when the Abbey fell under the efficient hand of the high-born Gilbert Crispin and the new building programme had been finally completed that thoughts turned to luxuries like vineyards. The attribution of a vineyard to the area of Vine Street by Robinson *Crispin* 44 cannot be right, and in any event seems to arise from confusion between the two Westminster estates.

[34] Tanner *Westminster Topography* TLMAS 16 (1948-51) 238; WAM 17461, 17489.

[35] The *Regularis Concordia* eg. ch. 42 and 63 contain elaborate instructions as regards the carrying out of this duty, on the part of the Abbot downwards.

[36] See pages 71 and 138. Incidentally none of the other Corridor lands appear by *name* among those contributing to these special funds. They presumably were paying the food-render and money-render of the 'inner' manors, but if that were an excuse, why was Knightsbridge (as part of Westminster) included in these 'special payments', and why were eg. Hanwell in central Middlesex, (mistakenly called 'Hanworth' in the Norman list) and Cowley in south-west Middlesex (which were presumably both inner manors, compared with the many remote ones) also included in this special list?

[37] WAD f. 124; Mason *WA Charters* No 241. The date was between 1086 and 1102 AD. The letting was in fee farm, to Gunter and his heirs. Harvey *Gervase and the Fee Farms of WA* BIHR 102 (1967) 135 suggests that the letting was of only three hides (as indeed the main manor had become by the thirteenth century), but it seems to me more likely that the 'manor' so short a time after DB (when the whole of it was held in possession by the Abbot of WA) meant the whole Norman manor, and that the parts of it which became alienated were lost by the Gunter/Gilbert family at a later stage or stages, see Vol 2.

family continued to hold the manor (or at least part of it) until well into the thirteenth century, and during the course of their tenure of it they received many confirmations of their rights over Hendon.[38]

Internal organisation
So already by 1121 AD the monks had reached a stage at which :-

    (a) they had accepted a commutation of part of the 'ancient feorm' due from some of their nearer and older manors, and now looked to an additional money render from them ; and

    (b) they had accepted a complete commutation of any food-renders from their more distant manors ; and

    (c) at least twenty of their estates were already designated by name, to contribute towards special 'funds' for other Abbey services, some of them essential, such as heating and cooking, clothing, and the maintenance of the staff who served in all the domestic offices necessary for the survival and well-being of the monks.

The Abbey had come, later than some religious houses, to rely substantially on cash-dues, rather than just their old food-renders. By this time, an appreciable sum was being received weekly for the purchase of all food other than that conveyed to the Abbey from the nearer manors; and special funds had been allocated for other necessary services. Behind the budgeting which must have determined this apportionment of resources, we can see that there was already a structure of different offices, each dealing with an essential service and its individual complement of staff. Whether the accounting for all these separate purses was sophisticated or not, there was by now an administrative system in place for dealing with the income which the Abbey could expect and which was essential for the support of such a large religious body of monks as the Abbey now possessed.

The creation of this system has been attributed, on the one hand, to the period *after* the refoundation of the Abbey by Edward the Confessor.[39] There can be no doubt that the energies of the Normans had greatly sharpened the efficiency of some features in English administration. It is also true that until the time of this Norman list, made in or shortly before 1121, we have little evidence of the working of administrative methods at Westminster Abbey relating to its estates. On the other hand it is difficult to believe that even the twenty estates (or more) which the monks at Westminster possessed *before* Edward the Confessor became king in 1042 could have been managed without at the very least an embryonic organisation inside the Abbey for dealing with the income derived from them. Certainly such a system, in a developed form, existed in some other monasteries before the Conquest. To test further the existence of such a system at Westminster, one needs to look briefly at the way in which the monastery was organised.

The Abbot and the Prior
Particularly in the Anglo-Saxon period of the tenth and eleventh centuries, the Abbot was the centre of all authority in any Benedictine monastery. In later centuries (as we shall see in relation to Westminster) that centre became more and more divided into two : between the Abbot on the one hand, and a new centre of power, the 'Prior and Convent', on the other. As in other monasteries, the Prior of Westminster and, under him, the body of all the other monks in the monastery (collectively called the 'Convent') came eventually to

---

38 See Mason *WA Charters* Nos 245, 263 and 124, and WAD f.121b. See also Note 1 above.
39 Harvey *Estates of WA* 85; Rosser *Westminster* 4.

possess a quite separate identity, to the extent of (a) their holding in due course their own shared-out portion of the monastery's lands and rents, (b) managing the exploitation of those lands, and (c) then (through separate departments under different officials appointed from among the monks) using and accounting for the produce or proceeds of that exploitation.[40] But if one goes back again to the 'Rule' of St Benedict in the sixth century,[41] one finds that the founder himself was less than enthusiastic about the idea of a divided source of power within a monastery. With some prescience (and certainly some past experience) St Benedict, while allowing the need both for a Prior (or 'Provost') in certain situations and for another senior figure 'the Cellarer', had foretold the 'envies, quarrels, slanders, rivalries, dissensions and disorders' which he regarded as likely to arise bctwccn an Abbot and another major figure of authority such as a Prior, with even some 'serious scandals' also thrown in.[42] In St Benedict's eyes the Cellarer was to be the hub on which the ordinary practical life of the monastery was to turn, but a Prior as a power-figure to rival the Abbot presented great dangers.

By the time of the revised English Code drawn up by Dunstan and his fellow-reformers 400 years later,[43] the position had changed, but was still far from clear. On the one hand, owing no doubt to the close relationship between Dunstan, the other reformers and King Edgar, it was for the first time recognised in that Code that for the election of any Abbot or Abbess the advice and the consent of the King had to be obtained. This was an important change which enabled later kings to interfere more legitimately with the process of election and which came to plague the monks of Westminster on several later occasions. On the other hand, the position of a second figure of authority was left in an ambiguous form. A Prior (still generally called a 'Provost', although the name Prior was also used) was the main candidate.[44] However it was still clear that this did not mean a divided control : any other officer in the monastery was still to be subject to the Abbot, to whom he had to answer. Curiously enough the Cellarer, the wise and busy man of the monastery whom St Benedict had wished to be 'like the father of the whole community', and round whom most of the practical work of day-to-day living seems to have been ordained, was not even referred to in the new English Code.

---

[40] See particularly Vol 2. The ways in which by the thirteenth century the Abbot at Westminster for his part came to differ from the model Abbot prescribed by St Benedict and to allow the rise of the Prior's power were (i) he no longer lived, ate and slept entirely with his 'family' of monks, but lived mainly in his own country house in Eia and at other places where he had rights of 'hospice', including Hendon; (ii) he had acquired many national and other public duties (such as acting, for example, as a Baron of the Exchequer, or in one instance, as Treasurer of England) and administrative powers outside his monastery, which were far greater than those ever contemplated even in the tenth century, when the *Reg. Concordia* was created, let alone the sixth century, when Benedict's *Rule* had been laid down.

[41] See page 56.

[42] *The Rule*, chap. 65. Both dissensions and scandals of this kind there certainly were at Westminster, mainly on two occasions: between Prior Osbert de Clare and two successive Abbots in the twelfth century (see page 61); and Prior Reginald of Hadham and his formidable Abbot, Walter of Wenlock, at the turn of the thirteenth and fourteenth centuries. The latter occurred at a time when records of the management of the Corridor estates were being kept carefully, and have fortunately survived: one can therefore see many of the participants in that dispute appearing in the contemporary records of estate-management relating to Hampstead and other Corridor estates. But the much longer-term struggle between the figures of the Abbot and his Prior-and-Convent, which culminated in a complete and formal division of the Abbey's possessions, including the allocation of specific manors to each party, ranged over the late twelfth, the thirteenth and part of the fourteenth centuries.

[43] See page 58.

[44] Symons (Ed) *Regularis Concordia*.

So at the time when Westminster Abbey was founded in the late tenth century, its Abbot as a figure was still destined to be absolute in his house, subject of course to the revised 'Rule'. In the 95 years between the foundation and the Conquest there were only four Abbots at Westminster. To us they are still relatively shadowy figures, but they were nonetheless real and not mythical.[45] The first, *Wulfsige* (971-997?), had apparently been a Londoner by birth, presumably in part growing up in the city and its neighbourhood, and was now chosen by St Dunstan to lead his new monastery in that same neighbourhood.[46] The second, *Aelfwig* (997-1020?), who was in authority at Westminster during much of the troubled reign and wars of King Ethelred the Unready,[47] was the man who was responsible for procuring from the King the grant of the tract of land in the present Bloomsbury area known as the monks' Berewic.[48] The third, *Wulnoth* (1020-1049?) was said[49] to have become Abbot in 1020 through the 'mediation' of King Cnut (meaning, no doubt, the king's pressure; now made easier by the recent revisions of the monastic Code) and to have been a close confidant and adviser of that King. The last of the Anglo-Saxon Abbots was *Edwin* (1049-1071?) whose abbacy lasted for nearly seventeen years during the reign of Edward the Confessor and then, for about another two or five years,[50] overlapped into the Norman period. During his abbacy the really substantial grants of land to the Abbey were made by King Edward and his nobles, and Edwin must personally have been much involved with not only the King's new building works but also the administrative problems (and the opportunities) which were created by the great increases in the land-holdings of the Abbey.

An early 'sharing of goods' ?   Maps B and M

It is during the lives of one of these Abbots that we can find a small clue as to the monks' adminstration of at least part of the proceeds from their estates. One of the early indications that some form of sharing-out of assets between the Head of a religious house and his 'Community' of monks (or priests) had begun is their acceptance of gifts which had been specially earmarked for *identified* purposes, such as the provision of food specifically for the Community, or for the provision of their clothing. For example at Christ Church, Canterbury (ie.the Cathedral, which in the eighth century was served by secular priests[51])

---

[45] For example there is ample evidence that at least the last three Abbots (of these four) played an active part in attending the royal court, presumably giving counsel and certainly witnessing certain charters, see the texts in Birch *Cart. Sax.* referred to in Sawyer *A-S Charters* Nos 891, 911, 926, 950, 961 (Aelfwig); 959, 974, 1471 (Wulnoth); 1033, 1123, 1125 etc. (Edwin). There also seems little doubt that the first Abbot, Wulfsige, must have been personally close to King Edgar, since Dunstan the King's confidant had chosen him for the post at Westminster; but if the Abbey was founded in 971, he and King Edgar overlapped for only four years before the King's death. Incidentally the fact that Wulfsige in his role as Abbot of Westminster apparently witnessed no (extant) charters for Edgar is more consistent with a late date for the Abbey's foundation than with a much earlier date.

[46] Knowles *Heads of Religious Houses* 76; Brooke and Keir *London* 296. While still Abbot at Westminster, Wulfsige in 992 also became Bishop of Sherborne (another pluralist, like Dunstan, until about 998 or before, when he gave up the abbacy); and eventually became a saint, known as St. Wulfsin.

[47] See page 67.

[48] See page 80. The significance of this grant in the present context is shown in the text and notes below.

[49] *Flete* (Ed. Robinson) 81.

[50] Two: *Flete* 83 and Mason *WA Charters* 9. Five: Robinson (Ed) *Flete* 140; Harvey *WA Estates* 16.

[51] When Dunstan and his fellow reformers later instigated their monastic revival in the tenth century, Christ Church became a monk cathedral, with Benedictine monks serving the Cathedral; just as they did

the special earmarking of gifts of land for the separate benefit of the Cathedral priests makes it clear that as early as that century [52] some division of assets was already taking place between the Archbishop and his community of priests. Similarly at Ramsey Abbey in the Fens (like Westminster, a foundation during the religious revival in King Edgar's reign) the acceptance of various early gifts which had been designated for specific purposes, including the food-supplies of the monks and their clothing,[53] indicates at least the start of the same process at that Abbey.

When the early Abbey at Westminster was founded, it was on a much smaller scale than either Christ Church or Ramsey, and its first cluster of endowments was much more modest than the estates of those other houses. But even among the small group of surviving records at Westminster for this early period, one can see that the monks' acquisition of the Berewic in the Bloomsbury area in 1002 was apparently impressed with the obligation that the land (meaning its produce or other proceeds) should be devoted to the 'maintenance of the brothers'.[54] This appears in the charter of King Ethelred the Unready, already referred to above,[55] which also records the involvement of Abbot Aelfwig in procuring this property from the King by paying him a sum of 100 mancuses of gold. Since the most recent opinion is that this charter can be regarded as 'probably authentic',[56] we seem to have in it a genuine, and probably within the Anglo-Saxon period the only genuine, consignment of a piece of land to the specific cause of the support of the Westminster convent of monks.[57] Since an Abbot is himself identified and indeed named (for the first and only time in the body of any early Corridor charter), it may be that he can specifically be seen as the instigator, at a very early stage of the Abbey's history, of a limited division of assets between himself and his community.

In this, therefore, there is specific support for the more general inference that even the comparatively small cluster of original endowments which Westminster had received demanded at least some embryonic organisation, reflecting the quite separate interests of the 'community' of monks and their superior. This would probably have been necessary to ensure that the food-renders and such money-renders as there may have been in the Anglo-Saxon period were used appropriately for the benefit of the Convent, and that any impressed obligation (such as there was in relation to the Berewic) was performed. So there is good reason to think that at least part, if not all, of the organisational system at Westminster which we have seen detailed in the later Norman list of food-renders and

---

at that time at Winchester, Worcester and Sherborne; Brooks *Christ Church Canterbury* 255-266; Robinson *Early Community at Christ Church* J.Th.S. 27 (1926) 225-40.

[52] Brooks *ibid* 157-160. This conclusion apparently shows that in England the division of assets between the head of a religious house and his 'familia' actually seems to have antedated, if not to have initiated, the fashion which followed on the Continent for this practice of devolution. It is probable that at St Paul's in London there was an even *earlier* division of possessions between the Bishop and the Canons, which we have seen reflected, in a virtually complete form, in their respective holdings round London many centuries later at the time of Domesday : Taylor *Bishop's Estates* 48-52 and *Endowment* A-N Studies 14 (1991) 288; and see **Map B** and page 18.

[53] Raftis *Ramsey Estates* 10-11. See also the similar theme for Peterborough, Winchester, Worcester and Bath : John *The Division of the Mensa* J.Ecc.H. 6 (1955) 143.

[54] WAD f. 77-78. See also the text of the charter printed at Robinson *Crispin* 167.

[55] Sawyer *A-S Charters* No 903. See page 80.

[56] Keynes *Diplomas of Aethelred* 143.

[57] The fact that nearly a hundred years later the monks let the Berewic in fee to William Baynard (see page 81; and Note 32 above) does not mean that it had not earlier been devoted to the monks' support: cf. what happened to Willesden, see page 108.

money-rents had its origins within the last 95 years of Anglo-Saxon (and 'Danish') rule before the Norman Conquest.

The Prior and the Convent

Of the various officers of Westminster Abbey, the *Prior* whose original duties had been mainly disciplinary was destined, as the process of the division of the assets of the monastery advanced further in later centuries, to become more and more powerful. The 'Prior and Convent' came to assume the *undying* 'corporate' role which a religious house played and indeed still plays.[58] In the thirteenth century some of the Corridor manors of Westminster Abbey (together with many others further afield) were formally handed over by the Abbot to the Prior and Convent, who thereafter held them in their own right and administered them or their proceeds. When the first farm-records of the Abbey's manors begin later in that century, we can see the Convent officers visiting their properties on a regular basis, in order to hold manor-courts, to supervise the management of the manor, to collect money profits and to arrange for the collection of special items of produce. Occasionally the Prior himself is to be seen visiting his manors; and even the Abbot himself (by that time, a still more powerful and public figure) descends on one or more of the Prior and Convent's manors for a brief stay of inspection or to celebrate there a holy festival such as Easter. But back in the period before the Conquest the role of the Prior (generally known as the Provost) was a much less distinct one. We hear no name of any Prior at Westminster until after the Conquest, or of any activity on his part.

The Cellarer, and other Officers

One is given the impression that, in spite of his position second to the Abbot, the Prior was then a lesser figure in the administration than the *Cellarer*. For the latter, St Benedict had cast a major role to which a whole chapter of his 'Rule' was devoted.[59] His name indicated his primary function, that of the general caterer for the religious house. But virtually all the practical arrangements in relation to the running of the monastery (extending far beyond the procurement, storage and provision of food and drink) had originally been assigned to him by St Benedict, subject of course to the Abbot's final direction.

But from the fact that the Cellarer (according to the 'Rule') was to have 'assistants', there grew up the other offices whose incumbents (always monks) took over some of his duties. A few of these offices we have seen listed in the Norman document described above: others do not appear in it. The main offices which appear in this history were those held by the *Chamberlain* (for the supply of the monks' clothing, bedding and other personal needs); the *Sacrist* (for the care of the Abbey buildings and church furnishings); the *Kitchener*; the *Granger* [60] (for the storage of grain and other foodstuffs in the granary

---

[58] This division of assets had the enormous practical and legal advantage (which was perhaps a main reason why the move towards such a division was made in the various religious houses) that when the Abbot died and there was a 'vacancy' in the abbacy, enabling the King to step in and claim the so-called 'regalian right' (see page 150) to manage the property and to take the proceeds for the whole period until a new Abbot was appointed, the King's right became limited to the property assigned to the Abbot and did not extend to the share of the property which had been assigned to the composite 'Prior and Convent': see eg. Cal. Pat. Rolls. (1252) 150 and Cal. Close Rolls (1258) 249.

[59] *The Rule*, chap. 31.

[60] The Granger was particularly important in relation, as we shall see, to all the produce which was carried to the Abbey from the nearby manors. According to the *Westminster Customary* (the surviving large book containing the established rules and customs for the conduct of the monks and the administration of the monastery, which was put together in 1266) the Granger ('Granator') was to be "the

and other barns); and the *Infirmarer* (for the maintenance of the sick-room). There were several others, including some which arose in later centuries and will be mentioned below when the need occurs. In later centuries each of these main officers became separately accountable for his own department, and to him a part or parts of the monastery's resources were allotted in order to provide him with enough (at least in theory) to carry out his duties. These officers who ran their own departments became known by the cumbersome title of 'obedientiaries'.

None of these officers at Westminster (other than the Abbot) appear in any genuine document dating back to the period before the Conquest, and it may well be that their organisation was developed much more significantly *after* the Normans had arrived. But it is difficult to see how the various Abbey routines could have been performed before that time without some simple form of devolution of practical responsibility between different officers, even if the principle of full financial accountability had not yet been adopted.

---

assistant and as it were the right hand of the Cellarer", see Thompson (Ed) H.Bradshaw Soc. (1902) ii. 96.

Plate 18. The Undercroft at Westminster Abbey, which carried the weight of the monks' dormitory above it. Work on it must have begun in 1065, if not before, but the large range of monastic buildings probably took another 20-30 years to construct. The sarcophagus, which was inscribed, was Roman, and was found buried on the north side of the Abbey in 1869; a lid, carved with a cross and probably later in date, was on top of it, with a decapitated skeleton of a man inside.

See pages 153 and 24

King Ethrelred's Telligraph

The following is a translation of the factual parts of the Telligraph of King Ethelred (Sawyer *A-S Charters* No. 894; dated 998 AD: see page 63 above), which recount the ways in which the early endowments of the Abbey were acquired. It is not itself a grant of any land, but is in effect a *register* or list of the existing and expected estates. For ease of reference the estates are separately numbered below, but this separation of them does not appear in the Latin. Some freedom in the translation and punctuation has been allowed, in order to clarify the somewhat clumsy Latin. Apart from details in the footnotes below, there are other references, in the text of the chapters above, to the people and places named in the Telligraph, and the page numbers for these references are given below in the translation. All words in square brackets are explanatory and are not in the Latin.   See also **Map B.**

"Nor do we fail to record here the manner in which the estates of that monastery were acquired : -
1. The first endowment was this, an estate of five mansae [hides] of land around the monastery itself [ie. rural **Westminster,** see page 79 above], which father Dunstan bought from my father [King Edgar] for 70 mancuses of gold.[1]

2. Secondly, at the time when my brother, St Edward, obtained the sceptre of the kingdom, a certain soldier named Bryhtmer [2] held an estate of three mansae next to Logereslea [**Lotheresleage**, see page 87 above]. But then, turning all things upside down, Bryhtmer abandoned both his allegiance to his lord, the king, and with it the said estate, and instead chose another man to be his lord. And Dunstan without any delay bought that land from my brother for 30 pounds and granted it to the renowned monastery.

3. Again, when by God's will I obtained the government of the kingdom, I gave to the monastery five mansae in the place which is called Hamstede by the country-people [**Hampstead,** see page 100 above].

4. Again, St Dunstan bought ten mansae from the blessed bishop Ethelwold and another ten from a certain royal soldier called Wulnoth, all for 80 pounds of approved silver, and gave them to the monastery : [this was '**Hendon, the smaller',** see pages 90-91 above].

5. Further, it was again he who bought, for 12 pounds [of silver?], from a certain Eadnoth, the King's officer, three cassati [hides} at the place which is called **Codanhlaw** [see pages 94-6 above], and gave them to the renowned monastery.

6. Also at that time a certain officer of the king called Aelfwine,[3] who lived in Middlesex,

---

[1] The price given in the Westminster charter (Sawyer No. 670) is 120 gold mancuses (3600 pence).
[2]. This man, who is difficult to place, is called Brihtferth in the charter Sawyer A-S Chs. No. 1451, and is there more circumstantially described as a 'hunter' (venator); perhaps a royal huntsman?
3. King Ethelred himself had a *'minister'*, also described as his 'writer' (scriptor), who was called Aelfwine (see Sawyer *A-S Charters* 853; Loyn *Governance* 109; Chaplais 'Royal A-S Chancery revisited' in *Studies in Med. Hist.* (Eds: Mayr-Harting and Moore) 44). But there had also been a *'minister'* of King

was about to journey to the very home of the saintly apostles Peter and Paul, to Rome itself, and being short of money begged a little help from the blessed Dunstan. And Dunstan, lending him 30 pounds of silver, took as a pledge from him eight mansae of land in **Hanwell** [see page 70 above] on condition that on Aelfwine's return from Rome and the repayment of the money to the archbishop, that land should revert to Aelfwine. However when he returned to his home, Aelfwine failed to repay any of the loan; but St Dunstan permitted him to enjoy the land during his lifetime, on condition that after his death the estate should be restored to the said monastery - as indeed happened, so we have heard.

7. Again, St Dunstan bought from Aelfheah, the war-leader,[4] for 200 [mancuses?] of gold ten cassati of land in the place which is called **Sunbury** [see page 70 above] and lent them, in return for a gift bestowed on him, to a widow, Aethelflaed,[5] for her lifetime, on condition that after her death the land should be restored to Westminster.

8. And the estate in **Shepperton** [see page 70 above] is also to be restored to the possession of St Peter at the said monastery after Aethelflaed's death.

9. Again, Aelfhelm Polga [6] for the salvation of his soul granted to the monks living together at Westminster five mansae of land in the place which is called **Brickendon** [Herts, see page 70 above] in the common tongue.

10. Again, Aelfwine [7] my own Steward in Kent gave to the said monastery, for the sake of his own soul and his wife's soul, three cassati of land in the place which is commonly called '**Sillington**' [see page 71 above].

11. And that little estate in **Paddington** [see page 112] is to be restored, after the death of Wulfric, to the said monastery as part of its own 'liberty' [see page 166].

12. Let it also be known that after the death of Aelfric [8] the estate at **Cowley** [see page 70] should be restored to the control of bishop Wulfsin [ie. Wulfsige, the first Abbot of Westminster, see page 159 above]".

Edgar who was called Aelfwine, see Sawyer *ibid.* 761, and he seems a more likely candidate for this reference.

4. The title 'dux' generally meant the Ealdorman of a county, who was the local military leader. This was the famous 'dux', Aelfheah, who had become the Ealdorman of Hampshire in 957 and remained so until his death in 971/2 (see Sawyer *A-S Charters* 639 and 1485).

5. It would be interesting to see this lady as Dunstan's patroness before her death (see page 65 above), but there would be distinct problems of chronology in that. She has been identified as the widow of Ecgferth, a man who had originally bought Sunbury but then lost it in disgrace: Korhammer *Bosworth Psalter* ASE 2. (1973) 184; Brooks *Ch. Ch., Canterbury* 249

6. Aelfhelm did indeed leave Brickendon to the Abbey by his will, Sawyer *A-S Charters* No 1487. He was a royal thegn and a wealthy man, with many lands mainly in East Anglia, owning among other things a long-boat and a stud of horses, see Stafford *Unif. and Conq.* 131-2 and 153-4, and see also Sawyer *ibid.* Nos. 794, 771 and 739.

7. See note 2 above, but no other connection between an Aelfwine as a royal officer and Kent has been found.

8. A common name for this life-tenant, and there is no identifying feature. Prominent Aelfrics of the relevant time were the Abbot of Eynsham (see page 129 above); and the Archbishop of Canterbury (995-1005); and the current Ealdorman of Hampshire.

The Anglo-Saxon Bounds

The following are translations of the various bounds given in charters for Westminster, Hendon and Hampstead. The bounds were all described in Old English, but were contained in charters or other documents written in Latin. Some of the texts are continuous without any form of punctuation, so I have broken them all up into numbered 'steps', in an attempt to simplify their sense.

Some of the geographical features referred-to are capable of clear translation, but are difficult or impossible to identify on the ground. But features which are even incapable of definite translation are given in italics (with or without an attempted translation or identification). The geographical features named in each text, most of which appear on the Maps, are given in bold type, when first mentioned.

WESTMINSTER (see **Maps M and H**, and **Chapter 6**) :-

A. The main Westminster estate granted to WA by Edgar (c. 971 AD)[1]

1. "First, up from the **Thames** along the **boundary-stream** [the Tyburn] to the *pollene* stump [? a pollard; or by a pool ?].
2. So to *bulunga* **fen** [Tothill Fields?].
3. From the fen, following the **old ditch** [Tyburn again], to **Cowford** [the crossing of Piccadilly ?].
4. From Cowford, up along the **Tyburn** to the **wide military-road** [Oxford Street].
5. Along the wide military road to the **old wooden church of St Andrew** [the site of the present church of St Andrew, by Holborn Circus].
6. So into **London fen** [New Bridge St. area, and below St Bride's church].
7. Along the fen southwards to the Thames, to the **middle line of the river.**
8. Along the river 'by land and by strand' to the boundary-stream again."

B. The Westminster 'Berewic', granted to WA by Ethelred (c.1002)[2]

1. "First, from the **mound** [a look-out ? on Tothill Fields ?] to the **Tyburn** river.
2. Northwards along the Tyburn to **Cowford** [the crossing of Piccadilly?].
3. From Cowford to **Watling Street** [Oxford Street].
4. Eastwards along the street to the **dwelling-place** [? St Giles'; a *setle* .]
5. From the dwelling-place to the boundary of the **brethren's croft** [the Berewic].

---

[1] Sawyer *A-S Charters* No 670. It is also to be noticed that this Charter (in its 'grant' passage, not here set out) calls Westminster the 'libertas' of the new Abbey, its first privileged area in which the Abbot was to hold jurisdiction. This is the Latin origin of the former English use of the word 'Liberty' to describe the area of such a jurisdiction. The Liberty came to include not only Westminster, but also Knightsbridge, Westbourne and Paddington (see pages 136-8; and, for Paddington, see also Appendix 1, page 165, where the word 'libertas' appears again).

[2] Sawyer *ibid.* No 903.

6. Thence southwards to the **'old street'**.[3]
7. From the street back to Watling Street [somewhere along Holborn].
8. Along the street to the **old gallows** [the position of Newgate?]
9. Thence to (along?) the **ealdorman's boundary** [the City boundary along the river Fleet?[4]]
10. Thence southwards straight to **Akeman Street** [the Strand].
11. Westwards along the street to **Cyrringe** [Charing].
12. Thence back to the mound."

HENDON (see **Maps N and P,** and **Chapter 7**)

A. Lotheresleage granted by Eadwig to his thegn Lyfing (957 AD)[5]

1. 'These are the land-boundaries at **Lotheresleage** and at **Tunworth** [in Kingsbury].
2. First from the **Tateburn** ['Tata's stream', now Folly Brook, the old boundary between Hertfordshire and Middlesex]; along the boundary to the *withimaere* [withypool? withy-area? withy-border?]
3. Thence along the boundary to the *holen rithe* [hollow streamlet?].
4. Along the streamlet to the **Silk** (river).
5. Thence to the withypool,[6] and so along the boundary to the (enclosed?) **farmstead** ['tunstall'] on **Watling Street.**
6. Along the Street to the **boundary of the people of Tunworth.**
7. West from Watling Street along the boundary to the *liuyssac* [cool oak? pond].
8. Thence along the boundary to the **wicstrete** [Honeypot Lane].[7]
9. Along the (wic)strete as far as the *hredes* **boundary of St Alban** [where Stanmore, held by St Alban's Abbey, begins].
10. Thence along the boundary to Watling Street.
11. South along the street to the **deep trench** [Colin Deep?].
12. Thence to the Silk [river], and so along the boundary to the **apple tree.**
13. Thence to the **boundary stump**, and so eastwards to the Tateburn.

[End of the estate?]

---

[3] For discussion of the suggestion that the present-day 'Old Street', north of the City, used to extend in a curve down to Holborn, see Grimes *Roman and Med.London* 45-6.

[4] This is probably a reference to Ethelred the Ealdorman of Mercia, whose father-in law King Alfred gave to him the custody of the City of London in or after 886, see page 22. The nearby administrative ward of 'Aldermanbury' was also possibly named after him, as was the harbour-wharf, 'Ethelred's Hithe', on the river, later renamed Queenhithe: Dyson *Alfred and Rest. of London* L.Jo.15 (1990) 102 and 109. He clearly had a major part in the revival of the City initiated by Alfred, see page 22.

[5] Sawyer *A-S Chs.* No 645

[6] So there are two references in these bounds to 'withies', in one form or another. In 1597 there was a field in Kingsbury (Tunworth) called Withylands, see map at VCH Mdx 5/52. But it is difficult to equate these features.

[7] See **Map N**. On the line of the *wicstrete* (which was also the Kingsbury-Harrow boundary) there was probably a settled (trading?) area, separated from the line of the Roman road: see Vince *Saxon London* 120-1. A *Roman* road west of the Edgware Road (see O'Neill *Watling St* TLMAS 10 NS/137) is also suggested, but this has little to support it, save perhaps at Edware itself.

14. The **common wood**[8] *hyrth* [belongs? leads?] to Lotheresleage as far as the
King's own wood.[9]

15. Here is the wood which *hyrth* [belongs? leads?] to Tunworth, from *hylfes* [?]
fence to the Silk (river) and up along the Silk
(river) to the *holan rithe* [hollow streamlet ?].

16. Along the streamlet to the **broad-water.**

17. Thence along Watling Street to *hylfes* fence".

B. Lotheresleage, granted to WA by Edgar/Dunstan (972/975 AD)[10]

1. "First from the **old** (enclosed?) **farmstead** ['tunsteall'] on Watling St. to
Edgware.

2. Along the **stony stream** [Edgware Brook?] to the **Silk** (river).

3. And so to the **stream** [Dean's Brook?].

4. Along the stream to **Iccene's ford** and along the ditch as far as the (boundary)
hedge [the Herts-Middlesex boundary, on Barnet Lane].

5. And along the hedge to **Grendel's Gate** [11] [Barnet Gate] following **the King's
boundary** [the Herts-Middlesex boundary] to **Brent** [by Hendon Wood Lane].

6. From Brent along the boundary to the **Tateburn** [Tata's stream].

7. Thence to the **boundary of Hendon** at the **holan rithe** [the hollow streamlet?].

8. Thence to the **Silk** (river).

9. From the Silk (river) eastwards to the old (enclosed?) farmstead."

C. Bleccanham granted to WA by Edgar (c. 971-5)[12]

1. "First at **Sandgate where the three boundaries meet** together [the meeting
point of Hampstead, Finchley and Bleccanham (later Hendon)].

2. From there west, along the **Hampstead boundary** [via. North End] to the
boundary stream [the Kilbourne-Westbourne source on Telegraph Hill].

3. Along the stream to **Watling Street,** and along the street to the **Brent** (river).

4. Up along the Brent to the **ditch-brook** [Mutton Brook?].

5. From the brook to the **crooked aspen-tree.**

6. Thence to the **old** (boundary) **hedge-tree.**

7. From the tree to the triple-boundary at Sandgate."

---

[8] In the charter relating to Chalkhill in Kingsbury (Sawyer *A-S. Chs.* No 1121, see pages 71-2) there is another reference to this 'common wood'. It seems to have lain between the Silk Stream and Watling Street.

[9] See also other references to a royal presence in this area: in the 'King's Boundary' in the next following charter, and in the name 'Kingsbury'. 'Kensal' (of Kensal Green), not far distant, also means the King's wood. For the inference of an earlier royal zone or sector, based on Watling Street, see page 70.

[10] Sawyer *ibid.* No 1451.

[11] Grendel, the monster killed by Beowulf?

[12] Sawyer *ibid.* No 1450. For a possible earlier history, see pages 95 and 24.

HAMPSTEAD (see **Map O** and **Chapter 8**) :-

A. Hampstead granted by Edgar to his thegn Mangoda (? 971-5 AD)[13]

1. "From **Sandgate** south along the **track** to the **foxhanger** [the hill at Chalk Farm].
2. From the hanger west to **Watling Street**.
3. North along the street to the **cucking-pool**
4. From the cucking-pool eastwards to Sandgate".

B. Hampstead granted to WA by Ethelred (986)[14]

1. "First from **Sandgate**.
2. So eastwards to the **wood-clearing** [farm?] **of Bedegar** [near Kenwood Dairy].
3. From there southwards to the **dwelling of Deormod.**
4. From the dwelling of Deormod to **middle-Hampstead** [near South End Green].
5. So onwards along the **hedge** to the **rush-field** [at Chalk Farm].
6. From the rush-field westwards along the boundary [15] to the **wood** [Primrose Hill?].
7. From the wood westwards along the boundary to the **stony-thicket** [?].
8. From the thicket to **Watling Street.**
9. So northwards along Watling Street to the **boundary-stream** [the Kilbourne-Westbourne source from Telegraph Hill].
10. From the boundary-stream eastwards along the boundary to Sandgate".

---

[13] Sawyer *A-S. Chs.* No 805.
[14] BL., *Stowe Charters* 33; Sanders *O. S. Facs.* iii. 34; Sawyer *ibid*. No 1450.
[15] This has also been read as a 'marsh', see Hales *Charters of Hampstead* TLMAS 6 (1890) 560-1.

Useful Dates

Dates of national history

c. 450-600   The Saxon migrations and settlement in the Thames area.

c. 600-735   The Kingdom of Essex dominates 'Middlesex'.

c. 750-850   The Kingdom of Mercia dominates 'Middlesex'.

c. 850-1016   The Kingdom of Wessex dominates 'Middlesex'.
        835-886   Attacks by the Danes in the Thames area: London captured.
        886   King Alfred's treaty with the Danes.   London and its
                    neighbourhood entrusted to Ethelred, Ealdorman of Mercia.
        890-925   War again with the Danes, north of London: the Danes
                    driven north of the Humber.   The creation of 'shires'.
       959-975   The reign of King Edgar. Peace.
    c. 971   The foundation of Westminster Abbey, and start
                 of the Abbey's acquisitions of the Corridor lands.
    978-1016 The reign of King Ethelred (the Unready).
    c. 980-1016 Wars again with the Danes : the Danes finally victorious.

1016-1042   The Danish King Cnut, and thereafter his two sons, rule England.

1042-1066 The reign of King Edward the Confessor.
    c.1050-1066 The rebuilding of most of Westminster Abbey.

1066   The Norman Conquest, and accession of King William I.
1086   The Domesday Survey of England.

****

Dates of the Abbey's acquisitions of the Corridor lands

c. 971	Westminster (the main estate)
971-5	Lotheresleage (part of the later 'Hendon')
971-5	Bleccanham (part of the later 'Hendon')
978-84	Hendon (the 'smaller'; part of the later 'Hendon')
986	Hampstead
c. 1000	Codanhlaw (part of the later 'Hendon')
c. 1000	Paddington
1002	Westminster (the 'Berewic')

1042-66	Knightsbridge and Westbourne
1044-46	Chalkhill
1087-99	Chelsea
1100	Eia

Bibliography

1. Printed sources and Calendars

Babington, C :   Ralph Higden *Polychronicon* RS (1869)
Barlow, F :   *Vita Edwardi Regis* (1992)
Birch, W :   *Cartularium Saxonicum* (1885-99)
Bishop, T & Chaplais, P : *Facsimiles of English Royal Writs* (1957)
Blake, E :   *Liber Eliensis* Camden (3rd ser.) vol. 92 (1962)
Bolton, B :   *The Rule of St Benedict for Monasteries* (transl) (1969)
Butler, H :   *The Chronicle of Jocelin of Brakelond* (1949)
Davis, H :   *Regesta Regum Anglo-Normannorum* I (1913)
Douglas, D :   *The Domesday Monachorum of Christ Church, Canterbury* (1944)
Dugdale, W :   *Monasticon Anglicanum* (eds. Caley, J., Ellis, H. and Bandinel, B. 1817-30)
Robinson, JA   J. Flete *The History of Westminster Abbey* (1909)
Garmonsway, G: *Aelfric's Colloquy* (1991)
Garmonsway, G: *The Anglo-Saxon Chronicle* (trans)
Gibbs, M :   *The Early Charters of St Paul's Cathedral* Camden (3rd) (1939)
Goscelin :   (See Robinson, and Talbot below)
Hale, W :   *The Domesday of St Paul's* Camden vol. 69 (1858)
Hamilton, N :   William of Malmesbury *De Gestis Pontificum Anglorum* RS (1870)
Hardy, TD :   *Rotuli Litterarum Clausarum* (1833-44)
Hardy, W & Page, W : *Feet of Fines for London and Middlesex: a Calendar* (1892-3)
Harmer, F :   *Anglo-Saxon Writs* (1952)
Hearne, T :   Heming *Cartulary of Worcester* (1723)
Lapidge, M & Winterbottom, M : Wulfstan *The Life of Bishop Aethelwold* (1991)
Latham, R :   Bede *The Ecclesiastical History of the English People* (trans, 1990)
Liebermann, F : *Die Gesetze der Angelsachsen* (1903-1916)
Logeman, H :   *The Rule of St Benet* (Benedict) EETS (1888)
Mackie, W :   *The Exeter Book* EETS (1934)
Madox, T :   *Formulare Anglicanum* (1702)
Major, K :   *Acta St. Langtoni* Canterbury and York Society (1950)
Mason, E :   *The Beauchamp Cartulary Charters 1100-1268* (1980)
Mason, E :   *Westminster Abbey Charters 1066-c.1214* (1988)
Plummer, C :   Bede *Opera Historica* (1896)
Riley, H :   Matthew Paris *Gesta Abbatum Monasterii St. Albani* RS (1867)
Robertson, AJ : *Anglo-Saxon Charters* (1956)
Robinson, JA (ed.) : Goscelin 'Life of Mellitus', part-printed in *The History of Westminster Abbey, by John Flete* (1909)
Sanders, W :   *Facsimiles of Anglo-Saxon Manuscripts* (1878-84)
Sawyer, PH :   *Anglo-Saxon Charters: an Annotated List and Bibliography* (1968)
Searle, E :   *The Chronicle of Battle Abbey* (1980)
Sharpe, R :   *Calendar of Letter-Books of the City of London: Book A* (1899)
Stevenson, W : Asser *The Life of Alfred* (1959)
Stubbs, W :   *Memorials of St. Dunstan* RS (1874)
Stubbs, W :   William of Malmesbury *De Gestis Regum Anglorum* RS (1887-9)
Symons, T :   *The Regularis Concordia* (1953)
Talbot, C :   Goscelin's *Life of Wulfsin* (Wulfsige) Revue Benedictine 69 (1959) 68
Thompson, E :   *Customary of St Augustine, Canterbury, and St Peter's, Westminster* (1902-4)
Thorpe, B :   *Diplomatorium Anglicanum Aevi Saxonici* (1865)
Whitelock, D : *Anglo-Saxon Wills* (1930)

Douglas, DC : *English Historical Documents 1042-1189 Vol.2 (1981)*
Whitelock, D : *English Historical Documents c.500-1042 Vol.1 (1979)*

Calendars : *Charter Rolls*; *Close Rolls*; *Inquisitions Miscellaneous*; *Patent Rolls*
Domesday Book (Phillimore Edition) : *Berkshire, Cheshire, Essex, Kent, Middlesex,*
                     Nottinghamshire, Suffolk, Surrey and *Worcestershire*
Victoria County Histories : *Essex* (vols. 1, 2, 3), *London* (vol. 1), *Middlesex* (vols. 1, 2, 3, 4, 5,
                     6, 8 and 9), *Rutland* (vol. 1), *Suffolk* (vol. 1) and *Wiltshire* (vol. 1).
Westminster Abbey Domesday (the main Westminster Cartulary)
Westminster Abbey Muniments : II, III, V, VI, 4786, 4834, 4875, 5670, 12753, 17164, 17461,
                                     17489, 17694, 18265, 25200

2. Secondary Works

A. Books and Theses

Abels, R : *Lordship and Military Obligation in Anglo-Saxon England* (1988)
Anderson, O : *The English Hundred Names: the S-E. counties* (1939)
Archibald, M & Blunt, C : *Sylloge of Coins: BM, Anglo-Saxon Coins* ((1986)
Aston, M : *Monasteries* (1993)
Bardwell, W : *Westminster Improvements* (1839)
Barlow, F : *Edward the Confessor* (1970)
Barratt, T : *The Annals of Hampstead* (1912)
Barron, C : *The Parish of St Andrew, Holborn* (1979)
Barton, N : *The Lost Rivers of London* (1962, 1970)
Bassett, S (ed) : *The Origins of Anglo-Saxon Kingdoms* (1989)
Blair, J : *Early Medieval Surrey: land-holding, church and settlement* (1991)
Blair, J (ed) : *Minsters and Parish Churches: the Local Church in Transition 950-1200* (1988)
Bloch, M *Feudal Society* (trans, 1961)
Blunt, C, Stewart, B & Lyon, C : *Coinage in Tenth Century England* (1989)
Brooke, C & Keir, G : *London 800-1216: the Shaping of a City* (1975)
Brooks, N : *The Early History of the Church of Canterbury* (1984)
Brown, RA : *The Norman Conquest* (1984)
Campbell, J : *Essays in Anglo-Saxon History* (1986)
Chaplais, P : *Essays in Medieval Diplomacy and Administration* (1981)
Cheney, C : *Episcopal Visitation of Monasteries in the Thirteenth Century* (1931)
Chew, HM *Ecclesiastical Tenants-in-Chief and Knight Service* (1932)
Clanchy, M : *From Memory to Written Word* (1979)
Colvin, H : *The History of the King's Works I* (1963)
Cunningham, W :*The Growth of English Industry and Commerce* I (1910)
Dales, D : *Dunstan, Saint and Statesman* (1988)
Darby, H & Campbell, E (eds) : *Domesday Geography of South-East England* (1962)
Darby, H : *Domesday England* (1977, 1986)
Dickinson, H : *The Water Supply of Greater London* (1954)
Doree, S : *Domesday Book and the Origins of Edmonton Hundred* (1986)
Dumville D : *Britons and Anglo-Saxons in the early Middle Ages* (1993)
Dumville D : *Wessex and England from Alfred to Edgar* (1992)
Ekwall, E : *Concise Oxford Dictionary of English Place-Names* (1960)

Ekwall, E :   *English River Names* (1928)
Everitt, A :   *Landscape and Community in England* (1985)
Farmer, A :   *Hampstead Heath* (1984)
Flower, C   *Public Works in Medieval Law*   Selden Soc., vol. 40/ii (1923)
Gelling, M :   *Place-Names in the Landscape* (1984)
Galbraith, VH :   *Studies in the Public Records* (1948)
Galbraith, VH :   *The Making of Domesday Book* (1961)
Garrett, A :   The Historical Geography of the Upper Brent (MA thesis, London Univ. 1935)
Gatty, C :   *Mary Davies and the Manor of Ebury* (1921)
Gelling, M :   *Place-Names in the Landscape* (1984)
Gelling, M :   *The Early Charters of the Thames Valley* (1979)
Gelling, M :   *The Place-Names of Berkshire* EPNS (1973-6)
Gimpel, J :   *The Medieval Machine* (Penguin, 1977)
Godfrey, C :   *The Church in Anglo-Saxon England* (1962)
Gover, J, Mawer, A & Stenton, F.M : *The Place-Names of Middlesex* EPNS (1942)
Gover, J, Mawer, A & Stenton, FM : *The Place-Names of Wiltshire* EPNS (1939)
Gray, H :   *English Field Systems* (1915)
Grimes, W :   *The Archaeology of Roman and Medieval London* (1968)
Grueber, H & Keary, C : *English Coins in the BM: Anglo-Saxon Series* II (1893)
Hart, C :   *The Danelaw* (1992)
Hart, C :   *The Hidation of Cambridgeshire* (1974)
Harvey, B :   *Westminster Abbey and its Estates in the Middle Ages* (1977)
Harvey, B :   *Living and Dying in England. The Monastic Experience* (1993)
Hill, D :   *An Atlas of Anglo-Saxon England* (1984)
Hitchin Kemp, F: *Notes on a Survey of Hendon* (typescript at Barnet Local Hist. Lib.) (1928/9)
Hollister, C   *Monarchs, Magnates and Institutions* (1986)
Howgego, J :   *Printed Maps of London* (1978)
John, E :   *Orbis Terrarum* (1966)
Kennedy, J :   *The Manor and Parish Church of Hampstead* (1906)
Keynes, S :   *The Diplomas of King Ethelred the Unready* (1980)
Knowles, D :   *The Historian and Character, and other Essays* (1963)
Knowles, D :   *The Monastic Order in England* 940-1216 (1963)
Knowles, D :   *The Religious Orders in England* (1948-59)
Knowles, D, Brooke, C & London, V : *The Heads of Religious Houses 940-1216* (1972)
Lawson, M :   *Cnut* (1993)
Lennard, R :   *Rural England, 1086-1135* (1959)
Loftie, W :   *The History of London* (1884)
Lovell, P & Marcham, W : *Old St Pancras*. Survey of London, vol. 19 (1938)
Lovell, P & Marcham, W : *The Village of Highgate*. Survey of London, vol.17 (1936)
Loyn, HR :   *Anglo-Saxon England and the Norman Conquest* (1970)
Loyn, HR :   *The Governance of Anglo-Saxon England, 500-1087* (1984)
Lynn White :   *Medieval Technology* (1964)
Madge, S :   *The Early Records of Harringey* (1938-9)
Maitland, FW :   *Domesday and Beyond* (edition 1987)
Maitland, W :   *The History and Survey of London* (1756)
Mason, M :   *Norman Kingship* (Headstart 1991)
Masters, B :   *Chamber Accounts of the Sixteenth Century* (1984)
Mawer, A and Stenton, FM : *The Place-Names of Buckinghamshire* vol 2 EPNS (1925)
McDonald, J and Snooks, G : *Domesday Economy: a New Approach to A-N History* (1986)
McDonnell, K : *Medieval London Suburbs* (1978)
Megaw, J :   *Introduction to British Pre-History* (1979)
Merrifield, R :   *The Roman City of London* (1965)

Middleton, J   *A View of the Agriculture of Midlesex* (1807)

Mills, A :   *English Place-Names* (1991)

Morris, J. :   *Londinium* (1982)

Napier, A & Stevenson, W : *The Crawford Collection of Early Charters and Documents* (1895)

Ormsby, H :   *London on the Thames* (1928)

Palmer, R :   *The County Courts of Medieval England* (1982)

Park, J :   *The Topography and Natural History of Hampstead* (1814)

Parker, R :   *The Common Stream* (1976)

Pearce, EH :   *The Monks of Westminster* (1916)

Petersson, B :   *Anglo-Saxon Currency* (1969)

Pevsner, N :   *The Buildings of England : Middlesex* (1951)

Pollock, W & Maitland, FW : *The History of the English Law before the time of Edward the First* (1911)

Potter, GW :   *Hampstead Wells* (reprint, 1978)

Potter, GW :   *Random Recollections of Hampstead* (1909)

Rackham, O :   *The History of the Countryside* (1987)

Radford, CR :   *Westminster Abbey before Edward the Confessor* (Occ. Paper No 15, 1965)

Raftis, J :   *The Estates of Ramsey Abbey* (1957)

Ramsay, N, Sparks, M and Tatton-Brown, T : *St Dunstan, his Life, Times and Cult* (1992)

Ridgway, J :   *The Gem of Thorney Island* (1860)

Robinson, JA :   *The History of Westminster Abbey, by John Flete* (1909)

Robinson, JA :   *Gilbert Crispin, Abbot of Westminster* (1911)

Robinson, JA & James, M :   *Manuscripts of Westminster Abbey* (1909)

Rosser, G :   *Medieval Westminster 1200-1540* (1989)

Round, JH :   *Feudal England* (1895, 1964)

Round, JH :   *Geoffrey de Mandeville* (1892)

Sayles, G :   *The Medieval Foundations of England* (1947)

Sheppard, F (gen. ed): *The Grosvenor Estate in Mayfair*. Survey of London, vol.39 (1977)

Smith, A :   *English Place-Name Elements* EPNS (1956)

Somerville, R :   *The Savoy* (1960)

Stafford, P :   *Unification and Conquest* (1982)

Stenton, FM :   *Anglo-Saxon England* (1971)

Stenton, FM :   *Norman London* (1934; and 1970 in DM Stenton *'Essays preparatory to A-S England'*)

Stenton, FM :   *The First Century of English Feudalism 1066-1166* (1973)

Stow, J :   *A Survey of London* (1633)

Stow, J :   *A Survey of London* (ed. Kingsford, C, 1908)

Stow, J :   *A Survey of London* (revised by Strype, 1722)

Sturman, W :   Barking Abbey (Ph.D thesis, London, 1961)

Taylor, P (ed.) :   *A Place in Time* (1989)

Taylor, P :   The Estates of the Bishopric of London (Ph.D thesis, London 1976)

Thompson, FML *Hampstead : Building a Borough 1650-1964* (1974)

Thompson, J :   *Sylloge of Coins: Ashmolean Museum, Anglo-Saxon Pennies* (1967)

Vaughan, R :   *Matthew Paris* (1958)

Vince, D :   *Saxon London: an Archaeological Investigation* (1990)

Vinogradoff, P :   *English Society in the Eleventh Century* (1908)

Whitelock, D :   *History, Law and Literature* (1981)

Whitelock, D, Brett, R & Brooke, C :   *Councils and Synods* I (1982)

Widmore, R :   *An Enquiry into the time of the First Foundation of Westminster Abbey* (1743)

Wilson, D :   *The Bayeux Tapestry* (1985)

Woodruff, D :   *The Life and Times of Alfred the Great* (1993)

Young, C :   *The Royal Forests of Medieval England* (1979)

B. Articles

Abels, R. : 'Bookland and Fyrd-Service in late-Saxon England' *A-N. S.* 7 (1985) 1

Ayton, A and Davis, V. : 'Ecclesiastical Wealth in England in 1086' *SCH* 24 (1987) 47

Bailey, K. : 'The Hidation of Middlesex' *TLMAS* 39 (1988) 165

Bailey, K. : 'The Middle Saxons', in Bassett, S. (ed), *The Origins of Anglo-Saxon Kingdoms* (1989) 108

Banton, N. : 'Monastic Reform and the Unification of Tenth Century England' *SCH* 18 (1982) 71

Baring, F. : 'The Hidation of some Southern Counties' *EHR* 14 (1899) 290

Baylis, C. : 'The Omission of Edgware from Domesday Book' *TLMAS* 11 NS. (1952-54) 62

Bazeley, M. : 'The Extent of the English Forest in the Thirteenth Century' *TRHS* (4th.) 4 (1921) 140

Biddle, M. : 'A City in Transition 400-800', in Lobel (ed) *The British Atlas of Historic Towns: The City of London* Vol 3 (1989) 20

Black, W. : 'Observations on the recently discovered Roman Sepulchre at Westminster Abbey' *TLMAS* 4 (1874) 61

Blackburn, M. and Lyon, S. : 'Regional Die-production in Cnut's Quatrefoil Issue', in Blackburn, M. (ed), *Anglo-Saxon Monetary History* 223

Blair, J. : 'Frithuwold's Kingdom and the origins of Surrey', in Bassett, S. (ed), *The Origins of the Anglo-Saxon Kingdoms* (1989) 97

Blair, J. : 'Introduction: From Minster to Parish Church', in idem. *Minsters and Parish Churches: the local Church in transition 950-1200* (1988) 1

Blair, J. : 'Local Churches in Domesday Book and before', in Holt, J. (ed) *Domesday Studies* (1987) 265

Blair, J.: 'Minster Churches in the Landscape', in Hooke, D. (ed) *Anglo-Saxon Settlements* (1988) 35

Blair, J. : 'Secular Minster Churches in Domesday Book', in Sawyer, PH. (ed) *Domesday Book, A Reassessment* (1985) 104

Braun, H. : 'The Hundred of Gore and its Moothedge' *TLMAS* 7 NS (1937) 218

Brett-James, N.: 'Some Extents and Surveys of Hendon' *TLMAS* 6 NS. (1929) 547

Brooke, C : 'Approaches to Medieval Forgery' *JSArchivists.* 3 (1968) 377

Brooke, C, Keir, G. and Reynolds, S.: 'Henry I's Charter for the City of London' *JSArchivists* 4 (1973) 558

Brooke, C : 'The Central Middle Ages 800-1270', in Lobel (ed) *The British Atlas of Historic Towns: The City of London* Vol. 3 (1989) 30

Brooks, N : 'The Career of St Dunstan' in Ramsay *St Dunstan, his Life, Times and Cult* (1992) 1

Brooks, N. : 'The Creation and early Structure of the Kingdom of Kent', in Bassett, S. (ed) *The Origins of Anglo-Saxon Kingdoms* (1989) 55

Bugden, W. : 'Manor of Chollington in Eastbourne' *Sussex Arch.Collections* 62 (1921) 128

Cam, H :   'The Hundred and the Hundred Manor' in *Liberties and Communities in Medieval England* (1944) 83

Cam, H. :   'The Private Hundred before the Norman Conquest', in Davies, JC. (ed) *Studies presented to H. Jenkinson* (1957) 50

Campbell, J :   'Some Agents and Agencies of the late Anglo-Saxon State', in Holt, J. (ed) *Domesday Studies* (1987) 201

Campbell, J. :   'The Church in Anglo-Saxon Towns', in idem, *Essays in Anglo-Saxon History* 139

Chaplais, P. :   'The Letter from Bishop Wealdhere of London', in Parkes, M, and Watson, A (eds) *Medieval Scribes, Manuscripts and Libraries* (1978) 3

Chaplais, P :   'The Original Charters of Herbert and Gervase, Abbots of Westminster (1121-1157)', in Barnes, P. and Slade, C. (eds) *A Medieval Miscellany* PRS. NS. 36 (1962)

Chibnall, M. :   'Monks and Pastoral Work: A Problem in Anglo-Norman History' *JEcc.H.* 18 (1967) 165

Clarke, P. :   'Anglo-Saxon Harrow and Hayes' *TLMAS* 39 (1988) 177

Corbett, W. :   'The Tribal Hidage' *TRHS* 14 NS (1900) 187

Cowie, R. :   'A Gazetteer of Middle Saxon sites and finds in the Strand/Westminster area' TLMAS 39 (1988) 37

Dales, D. :   'Spirit of the Regularis Concordia', in Ramsay, N, Sparks, M, and Tatton-Brown, T. (eds) *St. Dunstan, his Life, Times and Cult* 49

Darby, H. :   'Domesday Book and the Geographer', in Holt, J. (ed) *Domesday Studies* (1987) 101

Davenport, P :   'Two Middlesex Hundred Moots' *TLMAS* 10 NS (1948-51) 145

Davies, A. :   'The Domesday Hidation Of Middlesex' *HCM* 3 (1901) 232

Davis, E. :   'The University Site, Bloomsbury' *LTR* 17 (1936) 19

Davis, R. :   'Alfred and Guthrum's Frontie'r *EHR* 97 (1982) 803

Dodgson, J.:   'Distribution of the Place-Names -ingas' *Med. Arch.* 10 (1966) 1

Dolley, R and Metcalf, D. :   'The Reform of the English Coinage under Edgar', in Dolley, R. (ed) *Anglo-Saxon Coins* (1961) 136

Douglas, DC.:   'A Charter of Enfeoffment under William the Conqueror' *EHR* 42 (1927) 245

Douglas, DC.:   'Fragments of an Anglo-Saxon Survey from Bury St. Edmunds' *EHR* 43 (1928) 376

Draper, F. :   'The Place-Names Kenwood and Kentish Town' *LTR* 22 (1965) 27

Dudley, M. :   'The Monastic Priest', in Loades, J. (ed) *Monastic Studies* II (1991) 183

Dumville, D. :   'The Treaty of Alfred and Guthrum' in Dumville *Wessex and England from Alfred to Edgar* (1992) 1

Dyer, C.   'Towns and Cottages in Eleventh Century England', in Mayr-Harting, H. and Moore, R. *Studies in Medieval History* (1985) 96

Dyson, T.   'Alfred and the Restoration of London' *LJo* 15: 2 (1990) 99

Dyson, T. and Schofield, J. :   'Saxon London', in Haslam, J. (ed) *Anglo-Saxon Towns in Southern England* (1984) 285

Evans, C. :   'On the Geology of Hampstead', *Hampstead Annual* (1904-5) 74

Farmer, D. :   'The Progress of the Monastic Revival', in Parsons, D. (ed) *Tenth Century Studies* (1975) 16

Feilitzer, O. and Blunt, C. :   'Personal names on the Coinage of Edgar', in Clemoes, P. (ed) *England before the Conquest: Studies in Primary Sources* (1971) 183

Fisher, D. :   'The anti-monastic Reaction in the reign of Edward the Martyr ' *CHJ* 10 (1952) 254

Fleming, R. :   'Monastic Lands and England's Defence in the Viking Age' *EHR* 100 (1965)
                     247

Fowler, G. :   'The Devestation of Bedfordshire and neighbouring Counties in 1065 and 1066'
                     Arch. 72 (1922) 41

Frearson, A. :   'Domesday Book : the Evidence reviewed' *History* 71 (1986) 375

Galloway, J. and Murphy, M. : 'Feeding the City: London and its Agrarian Hinterland' *LJo* 16
                     (1991) 3

Gelling, M. :   'Towards a Chronology for English Place-Names', in Hooke, D. (ed)
                     Anglo-Saxon Settlements (1988) 59

Gelling, M.   'The Boundaries of the Westminster Charters' *TLMAS* 11 NS. (1954) 101

Gem, R. :   'The English Parish Church in the Eleventh and early Twelfth Centuries', in
                     Blair, J *Minsters and Parishes: the Local Church in Transition 950-1200* (1988)
                     21

Gem, R. :   'The Romanesque Rebuilding of Westminster Abbey' *A-N. S.* 3 (1981) 33

Gillingham, J. :   'The Introduction of Knight-Service into England' *A-N. S.* 4 (1982) 53

Golding, B. :   'Robert of Mortmain' *A-N. S.* 13 (1991) 119

Gransden, A. :   'Baldwin, Abbot of Bury St. Edmunds 1065-1097' *A-N. S.* 4 (1982) 65

Gransden, A. :   'The Legends and Traditions concerning the origins of the Abbey of Bury St.
                     Edmunds' *EHR* 100 (1985) 1

Hales, J. :   'Notes on two Anglo-Saxon Charters relating to Hampstead' *TLMAS* 6 (1890)
                     560

Harmer, F. :   'Three Westminster Writs of Edward the Confessor' *EHR* 51 (1936) 97

Hart, C. :   'The Tribal Hidage' *TRHS* (5th) 21 (1921) 133

Harvey, B. :   'Abbot Gervase de Blois and the Fee-Farms of Westminster Abbey' *BIHR* 40
                     (1967) 127

Harvey, P :   'Rectitudines Singularum Personarum and Gerefa' EHR (1993) 1

Harvey, S. :   'Evidence for Settlement Study: Domesday Book', in Sawyer, PH. (ed) *Medieval
                     Settlement: Continuity and Change* (1976) 195

Heslop, T. :   'Twelfth Century Forgeries as evidence for early seals', in Ramsay, N, Sparks,
                     M and Tatton-Brown, T. (eds) *St Dunstan, his Life, Times and Cult* 309

Hills, C. :   'The Archaeology of Anglo-Saxon England in the Pagan Period' *A-S. E.* 8
                     (1979) 297

Hollister, C. :   'The Misfortunes of the Mandevilles', in idem. *Monarchs, Magnates and
                     Institutions* (1986) 118

Honeybourne, M: 'The Fleet and its neighbourhood in early and medieval times' *LTR* 19 (1947)
                     13

Honeybourne, M: 'The Pre-Norman Bridge of London', in Hollaender, A. and Kellaway, W. (eds)
                     Studies in London History (1969) 17

Hooke, D. :   'Early Medieval Estate and Settlement Patterns', in Aston, M, Austin, D. and
                     Dyer, C. (eds) *The Rural Settlements of Medieval England* (1989) 9

Hooke, D. :   'Pre-Conquest Woodland : its Distribution and Usage' *Ag.H.R.* 37 (1989) 113

Hoyt, R. :   'Farm of the Manor and Community of the Vill in Domesday Book' *Speculum*
                     30 (1955) 147

Jackson, E. and Fletcher, E. : 'The Anglo-Saxon Priory Church at Deerhurst', in iidem, "Collected
                     Papers on Anglo-Saxon Churches" (1961)

Jenkinson, H. :   'Exchequer Tallies' *Arch.* 62 (1911) 367

John, E. :   'The Division of the Mensa in early English Monasteries' *JEcc.H.* 6 (1955) 143

Keene, D. :   'Medieval London and its Region' *LJo* 14 (1989) 99

Knowles, D. :   'The Growth of Exemption' *Downside Review* 50 (1932) 201

Knowles, D. :   'The Monastic Buildings of England', in idem *The Historian and other Essays* (1963) 88

Korhammer, P. :   'The origin of the Bosworth Psalter' *A-S E.* 2 (1973) 173

Lapidge, M. :   'The Hermeneutic Style in Tenth-Century Anglo-Latin Literature' *A-S E.* 4 (1975) 67

Lennard, R. :   'The Economic Position of the Bordars and Cottars of Domesday Book' *Ec. J.* 61 (1951) 342

Lennard, R. :   'The Economic Position of the Domesday Villani' *Ec.J.* 56 (1946) 244

Loyn, HR. :   'Boroughs and Mints AD 900-1066', in Dolley, R. (ed) *Anglo-Saxon Coins* (1961) 122

Loyn, HR. :   "Gesiths and Thegns in Anglo-Saxon England from the Seventh to the Tenth Century' *EHR* 70 (1955) 529

Loyn, HR. :   'The Hundred in the Tenth and early Eleventh Centuries', in Hearder, H. and Loyn, HR. (eds) *British Government and Administration* (1974) 1

Loyn, HR. :   'Progress in Anglo-Saxon Monetary History', in Blackburn, M. (ed) *Anglo-Saxon Monetary History* (1986) 1

Mason, E. :   'A Truth Universally Acknowledged' *SCH* 16 (1979) 171

Mason, E. :   'The Donors of Westminster Abbey Charters: c. 1066-1240' *MP* 8:2 (1987) 23

Mason, E. :   'The Mauduits and their Chamberlainship of the Exchequer' *BIHR* 49 (1976) 1

Mason, E. :   'The Site of King-making and Consecration: Westminster Abbey and the Crown in the Eleventh and Twelfth Centuries' *SCH Subsidia* 9 (1991) 57

Mason, E. :   'Westminster Abbey and its Parish Churches', in Loades, J. (ed) *Monastic Studies* II (1991) 44

McDonald, J. and Snooks, G.: 'Were the tax assessments of Domesday Book artificial? The case of Essex.' *Ec. HR.* 38 (1985) 352

Metcalf, D. :   'Monetary History of England in the Tenth Century', in Blackburn, M. (ed) *Anglo-Saxon Monetary History* (1986) 133

Micklethwaite, J.: 'On a filling cistern of the Fourteenth Century at Westminster Abbey' *Arch.* 53 (1892) 161

Mills, P. :   'Excavations at Broad Sanctuary at Westminster' *TLMAS* 33 (1982) 345

Mills, P. :   'Excavations at Cromwell Green in the Palace of Westminster' *TLMAS* 31 (1980) 18

Moore, J. :   'Domesday Slavery' *A-N S.* 11 (1989) 191

Mortimer, R :   'The Baynards of Baynard Castle' in Mayr-Harting, H. and Moore, R. *Studies in Med. History* (1985) 241

Nightingale, P. :   'Some London Moneyers: reflections on the organisation of English Mints in the Eleventh and Twelfth Centuries' *NC* 142 (1982) 34

O'Neill, H. :   'Watling Street, Middlesex' *TLMAS* 10 NS. (1948-51) 137

Page, W. :   'Some remarks on the Churches of the Domesday Survey' *Arch.* 66 (1915) 61

Pelteret, D. :   'Slave raiding and Slave trading in early England' *A-S E.* 9 (1981) 99

Pinder, T. :   'An Introduction to the Middlesex Domesday' in *The Middlesex and London Domesday* (Alecto Edition) (19**)

Prideaux, W. :   'The Westbourne' *N.& Q.* (9th) 8 (1901) 517 and 10 (1902)16

Reynolds, S. :   'The Rulers of London in the Twelfth Century' *History* 57 (1972) 337

Robinson, JA. :   'The Early Community at Christ Church' *J.Th.S.* 27 (1926) 225

Robinson, JA. :   'Westminster in the Twelfth Century: Osbert de Clare' *Ch.QR* 68 (1909) 336

Robbins, R. :   'A Note on Early Finchley' *TLMAS* 18 (1955) 65

Roffe, D. :   'From Thegnage to Barony: Sake and Soke, Title and Tenants in Chief' *A-N S.* 12 (1989) 157

Round, JH. :   'Essex Vineyards in Domesday Book' *Essex Arch. Trans.* 7 NS. (1900) 24

Runciman, W. : 'Accelerating Social Mobility: the case of Anglo-Saxon England' *P.& P.* 104 (1984) 3

Rutton, W. : 'The Manor of Eia or Eye next Westminster' *Arch.* 62 (1910) 31

Scholz, B. : 'Sulcard of Westminster' *Traditio* 20 (1964) 59

Scholz, B. : 'Two forged Charters from Westminster Abbey and their relationship with St. Denis' *EHR* 76 (1961) 466

Searle, E. : 'Battle Abbey and Exemption: the forged Charters' *EHR* 83 (1968) 449

Sharpe, M. : 'The Forest of Middlesex' *HCM* 10 (1908) 7ff and 93ff

Smart, V. : 'Moneyers' names on the Anglo-Saxon Coinage' *Nomina* 3 (1979) 20

Smart, V. : 'Scandinavians, Celts and Germans in Anglo-Saxon England', in Blackburn, M. (ed) *Anglo-Saxon Monetary History* (1986) 171

Stafford, P. : 'The Farm of One Night, and the Organisation of King Edward's estates in Domesday' *Ec.HR* 33 (1980) 491

Tanner, L. : 'Westminster Topography' I. *TLMAS* 10 NS. (1948-51) 234

Tatton-Brown, T.: 'The Topography of Anglo-Saxon London' *Antiquity* 60 (1986) 21

Taylor, H. : 'Tenth Century Church building in England and on the Continent', in Parsons, D. (ed) *Tenth Century Studies* (1975) 141

Taylor, P. : 'The Endowment and Military Obligations of the See of London: a Reassessment of three sources' *A-N S.* 14 (1991) 287

Thorn, F. : 'Hundreds and Wapentakes' in *The Middlesex and London Domesday* (Alecto edition) 33

Waller, J. : 'The Holebourne' 4 *TLMAS* (1874) 97

Waller, J. : 'The Tybourne and the Westbourne' *TLMAS* 6 (1890) 244

Williams, A. : 'Princeps Merciorum gentis: Aelfhere, Ealdorman of Mercia 956-983' *A-S E.* 10 (1982) 143

Williams, L. and Cunnington, W.: 'Dating a Hedgerow Landscape in Middlesex: Fryent Country Park' *The London Naturalist* No 64 (reprint 1986)

Willis, R. : 'History of the Conventual Buildings of Christ Church in Canterbury' *Arch. Cantiana* 7 (1868) 158 ff and 174

Wormald, P. : 'Aethelred the Lawgiver', in Hill, D. *Ethelred the Unready* BAR 59 (1978) 65

Yorke, B. : 'The Kingdom of the East Saxons' *A-S E.* 14 (1955) 1

Index

Numbers in **bold type** refer to the pages of the Plates and their captions. The Maps have not been indexed, because of the duplication of estate-names in them : their subject-matters are to seen in the List of Maps on page 6.

Abbeys 60, 139-40, 149, 158-9, 154 . See also
    Abbot, Estate-management, Prior, WA,
    and other Abbeys by name
Abbots 57, 149, 158-9, 160-1. See also Abbey,
    Aelfwig, Crispin, Edwin, Leofstan,
    Walter of Wenlock, WA, Wulnoth,Wulfsin
Abingdon Abbey 57, 58, 62
Acton 17, 34
Aedwig (king) 87, 167
Aelfgar 73
Aelfgifu 65
Aelfheah (dux) 165
Aelfhelm Polga 165
Aelfric (Abbot of Eynsham) 114, 128-9, 165
Aelfric (A/bp of Canterbury) 165
Aelfric (of Cowley)165
Aelfric, E. of Hants 165
Aelfric Bata 129
Aelfwig (A/WA) 159-60
Aelfwine (Steward in Kent) 165
Aelfwine (of Hanwell) 64-5
Aerodrome Road **97**
Aethelflaed (unknown) 165
Aethelflaed (Dunstan's friend) 65, 165
Aethelflaed (d. of Alfred) 23, 46
Aethelwine (E. of East Anglia) 65
Ailric (of Greenford) 72
Akeman Street 80, 82, 167
Alchester 82
Aldermanbury 68,167
Alderman's boundary 83, 167
Aldwych 21, 47
Alexandra Park 27-8
Alfred (king) 22, 23, 46, 83, 167
Alluvium 26, 27, 139, 145
Alwin Horne (Chalkhill) 71
Anglo-Saxons, passim
Anti-monastic reaction 100
Arbitration (of 1222 AD) 81, 83, 113
Arnulf of Hesdin 36, 52
Arpent of vines 155
Arundel Street 27, 82
Ashford (Mdx) 72
Ashmolean Museum 135
Athelstan (king) 18, 23, 47, 65, 102, 144
Augustine, St 17
Avenue Farm (Hendon) 95
Aybrook Street (Marylebone) 42

Bagshot Sands 28-9, 123, 127
Bailiff 144
Bakehouse 30, 44, 154
Baker Street 27, 79
Balta, Richard of 99
Barking Abbey 42, 67, 73-4, 108, 137, 142
Barnet 18, 168
Barnsbury 33, 39, 108
'Barrow' Hill 107
Bath 58, 82, 70
Bath Abbey 17, 160
Battersea 39, 59, 119, 142
Battle Abbey 62
Bavins 154
Bayeux Tapestry 68, **75, 76**
Baynard, Wm 81, **86,** 103, 119, 136, 142, 155-6,
    160
Baynard, Ralph 136
Baynard's Castle 136, 156
Bayswater 43
Becket, Tho. 34
Beddington 15
Bede 16, 19
Bedegar 106, 169
Bedford 46, 102
Bedfordshire 30, 51, 71, 121
Beech trees 28, 30, 34, 127
Belgravia 27, 43
Belsize, Bel Assis 28, 40, 41, 95, 107, 122, 123,
    127
Benedict, St. 56-8, 143, 158, 159, 161-2
Beneficial hidation 137
Beowulf 168
Berewics (of Staines) 72
Berewic (of WA) 66, 80-2, 88, 107, 119,121, 136,
    137, 141, 142, 155, 159, 160, 166
Berkhamsted 121
Berkshire 121, 138
Bermondsey 59, 103, 156
Berners, Hugh of 39
Birch trees 29, 30, 35, 126
Bishop of London 11, 15, 17, 18, 32, 34, 39, 47,
    54, 65, 73, 83, 106, 107, 113
Bishop of Westminster 123
Blacket's Well 92
Blackheath 82
Blaecca 92
Bleccanham 24, 29, 70, 87, 91-5, 105, **110,** 112
Blechenham family 94
Bloomsbury 27, 81, 107, 136, 137

Boethius 114
Boon-work 116, 117, 119
Bordars 118-9
Borough 46, 47
Borough-Court 47
Boulder Clay 29
Boundaries of shires 18, 31, 47, 52, 54
'Boundary-Ditch' (Hampstead) 105
'Boundary-Stream' (Hampstead) 92-4, 95, 105,
            107-8, 168-9
'Boundary-Stream' (Westminster) 42, 83, 166
Brabazon, Roger of 40
Branch Hill 43
Bread 151
Brent 27, 39, 66, 70, 72, 89, 90, 91, 92, 93, **98,**
    168
Brent Reservoir 66, 89, **98**
Brentford 27, 48, 82, 70
'Bretwalda' 17, 19, 22
Brewhouse 30, 44, 152, 155
Brickearth 27, 28, 123
Brickendon 70, 165
Brihtferth, Bryhtmer 88, 164
Brinkburn Priory 41
British Library **133**
British Museum (site) 81
Britons 16, 116
'Broad military road' see Oxford Street, Holborn
Brockhole, Brock Hill (wood) 127
Brockley Hill 25, 26, 28, **97**
Brook Mews 44
Buckingham 46
Buckingham Palace site 41, 82
Buckinghamshire 17, 30, 52, 71, 121
Buckingham Water Gate 82
Buckland, Wm of 120, 138, 142
'Bulunga Fen' 80, 166
Bury St Edmund's Abbey 67, 72, 119, 139-40, 141,
            142, 144, 149, 150, 151, 155
Burghal Hidage 51
'Burh' 23, 46, 47, 102
Burnt Oak 89

Caen 49
Cambridgeshire 30, 35, 46
Canons of St Paul's 11, 15, 18, 36, 62, 107-8, **111,**
            137, 141, 150
Canterbury 20, 82, 102, 139
Canterbury, A/bp of 15, 17, 18, 21, 57, 58,
            65, 73, 145
Canterbury, Christ Church 34, 44, 60, 139, 150, 160
Cassatus 88
Cathedral monasteries 58, 160
Cattle-thieving 49
Cellarer 158, 159, 161-2
Ceorl 52, 114

Cerne Abbey 128
'Certainty of History' 62, 63
Chalcots (Hampstead) 95, 127
Chalk Farm (Hampstead) 106, 107, 127, 169
Chalkhill (Kingsbury) 69, 71, 168
Chamber (of monks) 152, 154
Chamberlain (of WA) 162
Chamberlain, William the 71
Chapels 66, 99, 113
Charing, 'Cyrringe' 42, 48, 55, 82, 84, 135, 136, 166
Charlton 145
Charters, see special index on page 190
Cheapside 42, 45
Cheddar 69
Chelsea 20, 24, 33, 43, 59, 69, 82, 119, 120, 137, 138,
            139, 142, 145
Chertsey Abbey 57, 62, 67, 73
Cheshire 19
Chester 58, 108
Child family 93
Child's Hill 28, 43, 92-3, 95-6, 105, 127
Chillenden (Kent) 71
Chilterns 16, 21, 37, 38
Chirograph 62
Chiswick 17, 18, 21, 108, 145
Chollington (Sussex) 70
Churches 52, 66, 67, 80, 83, 90, 91, 99, 113, 153
Church estates 11, 12, 15, 17-9, 91
Circuit Commissioners 30
Cistercians 56
City, see London
Clare, Osbert of 61, 69, 90, 91, 94, 113, 154, 158
Clay, see London Clay
Claygate sands 28, 92, 123
Clerkenwell 33
Clothing (of monks) 152, 154
Cnut ('Canute') 23, 35, 66, 67, 72, 102, 115, 139, 159
Codanhlaw 43, 54, 70, 87, 90, 92, 93, 94-6, 105, 112,
            125, 164
Codda 95
Coinage 12, 20, 23, 101-4; and see Die-cutter; Otto
Colchester 46
Colindeep (Hendon) 89, 167
Colne River 16, 17, 47, 69
Commissioners (of DB), see Circuit Commissioners
Common fields 124-5
'Common Wood' (Chalkhill, and Lotheresleage) 168
Commutation of renders 151-2, 157
Conduit Place 44
Coomb 151
Coppicing 34, 126
'Corridor' 19, 66, 69, 70, 73, 84; and see Westminster,
                Hampstead, Hendon, Paddington etc.
Cottagers 27, 138-41, 155
Cotsetlas, Cottars 116, 118
County Hidage 51
Cowford (Piccadilly) 80, 166

Cowhouse Lane/Farm 95, 96
Cowley (Peachey) 69, 112, 156, 165
Covent Garden 83
Coventry Cathedral 62
Cranford 34
Cray River 37
Cressewellfeld (Hyde Park) 43
Cricklewood Lane, see Cowhouse Lane
Crispin, Gilbert 141-2, 153, 156
Crop values 145-6
Crouch End 71
Croydon 16
Cucking Pool 93, 108, 169
'Customs' of estate 115-7
Cyrringe, see Charing

Damage during Conquest 33-4, 121-2
Danes 17, 22-4, 34, 46, 55, 57-8, 59, 61, 67-8, 70, 101,
        114, 161
Danelaw 23
Davies, Mary, of Mayfair 27
Dean's Brook (Hendon) 87, 168
Deene (Northants) 149
Deerhurst Church 80
Denns 34
Deormod 104, 106, 169
Dickers Farm 95
Dies, Die-Cutter 73, 103-4, 137
Diocese of London 15, 16, 17, 47; see also Bishop
Dissolution of monasteries 21, 37
Dissolution of WA 135, 138
Division of assets 18, 108, 160-1
Documents 60-63
Domesday Survey 15, 18-9, 30-6, 38, 50-2, 71, **86,**
        87, 90, 91, 103, 104, 107-8, 113, 117-23, 136-42
Dover 82
Dorset 47
Dunstan 12, 50, 57-60, **64,** 65-6, 67, 79, 88-91,
        94 96, 143, 158, 160, 164-5, 168
'Dux' 101, 165

Eadnoth 94
Ealdorman 47, 65, 73, 165, 167; see also Ethelred
Ealing 16, 17, 20
East Anglia 15, 19, 22, 25, 30, 72, 119, 165
Eastfields (Hampstead) 127
East Heath, (Hampstead)28, 35, 105, **110**
East Park (H. Heath) 28, 29, 35, 126
East-Saxons 16-7, 19, 21, 48, 73
Ebury 27, 84; and see Eia
Edeva, Eideva 104, 137
Edgar (King) **2,** 23, 24, 42, 47, 49, 57-9, 63, 65,
        66, 73, 79-81, **85,** 87-8, 90-2, 94-6,
        100-3, 112, 159, 164-5, 166, 168, 169
Edgware 37, 89, 124, 167

Edgware Brook 168
Edgware Road 25, 82, 167; and see Watling Street
Edith (Queen, and widow of Edward the Conf.) 71, 84
Edmonton 31, 34, 51, 53, 54, 84, 124
Edmund (king) 34
Edward the Confessor 19, 32, 42-3, 56, 60-1, 66-9,
        71-2, **75, 76,** 83-4, 92, 94, 136-7
        141-4, 151-2, 154-5, 159
Edward the Elder (king) son of Alfred 46, 104
Edward the Martyr (king) 88, 164
Edward of Salisbury 137, 138
Edward, son of Suein 73, 104, 108, 137
Edwig (king) 87, 167
Edwin (A/WA) 60, 119, 159
Eia, Eye 26, 27, 33, 38, 41, 59, 71, 119, 136, 139,
        145
'- eia' (suffix) 59
Eleanor of Provence 42
Elstree 28
Elthorne 48, 51, 52
Ely Abbey 30, 58
Enclosures124
Enfield 31, 34, 84, 124
Eorcenwold 73
Epping Forest 22
Ermine Street 32, 33, 34, 35, 36
'Estate-Guide' (Rectitudines) 115-9, 129-32
Estate management 115-7, 129-32, 142-5, 149-
        50, 151-7
Estates, 'reforming' of 53-4
Essex 6-7, 19, 22, 51, 70, 73, 95; see East Saxons
Eton College 127
Ethelbert, king of Kent 17
Ethelred, Ealdorman of Mercia 22, 83, 167
Ethelred the Unready 23, 63, 67, 68, 79, 80-2, 88,
        89, 90, 92, 94, 96, 100, 104, **109,** 112, 113,
        115, 136, 159, 160, 164-5, 166, 169
Ethelwold, Bishop 58, 90, 164
Euston Road 27
Evesham Abbey 57, 58, 62
'Exempt' Abbey 84
Exeter 102-3
Eynsham Abbey 128, 165

Faggots154
Famulus 118
Faringdon Road/Street 39, 40, 79
'Farmers' 142, 149-50
Fauconberg, Eustace of 84
Fens 15
'Feorm' 149; and see Food-rents
'Fences, wood for' 34
Feudal System 19, 119, 141-2
Finchley 18, 27, 28, 29, 34, 54, 92, **110,** 124
Finchley Road 28
Fitzjohns Avenue 41, 126

FitzStephen 34, 37, 38, 39, 42
FitzWilliam, Otto - see Otto the Goldsmith
Fleet River 39-41, 42, 55, 79, 80, 81, 82, 83, 107, 156
Fleet Street 27, 55, 82
Flooding 20, 26, 58-9
Folly Brook 167
Fontenay 41
Fontevrault 41
Fontfroide 41
Fontgombault 41
Food-rents 65, 103, 143, 149, 150-2
'Foothold' near London 12-3, 84, 103, 122-3, 156
'Forest of Middlesex' 21, 36
Forest law 37
Forfeiture of estates 156
Forgery 18, 60-3, 79, 89, 90-2
Fortune Green 54, 96, 105
Fosse Way 32
Fountains Abbey 41
Fowler family 126
Foxhanger (Hampstead) 106, 169
Fragmentation of estates 12, 53-4
Frognal 28, 42, 126
Fryent country park 32
Fulham 17-8, 31, 34, 54, 82, 141, 145

Gallows 83, 167
Ganges 25
Gardens 26, 27, 139-41, 155
Geburs 115-6, 118, 150
Geld (tax) 15, 50-1, 114-5, 137-8
Geneat 116, 150
Geoffrey of Mandeville, see Mandeville
Geological Survey 26, 41
Geology 25-9, 92, 123; see also Gravels,
                    London Clay etc.
Gerefa 129-32, 143, 144; see also Reeve
Gilbert of Hendon 149, 156
'Gillingas' 16
Glaciers 25-6, 29
Glastonbury Abbey 60, 79, 143, 155
Gloucester 69
Gloucestershire 71
Golders Hill 93
Gore Hundred 46, 49, 51-4, 73, 91, 99
Gospel Oak 106-7
Granger, Granator of WA 162
Grant of land, method 61
Gravels 20, 26, 27, 29, 38, 41, 42, 58, 79, 141, 145
Great Charter of Dunstan - see Charters, page 190
Great Charter of Edgar - see Charters, page 190
Great Conduit 42
Great Ormond Street 81
Green Park 27, 41, 82, 136
Greenford 69, 72
Greenwich 21

Grendel's Gate 168
Grossteste (Bishop) 130
Grosvenor Estate 27, 53
Grosvenor, Sir Tho. 27
Grout 151
'Gumeningas' 16
Guthrum 22
Gunter of Hendon 119-20, 142, 149, 156-7

Hackney 45
Hadham, Reginald of 158
Hale, the (Hendon) 54
Hall Road (Hendon) **97**
Halliford 72
Hampshire 71, 121, 165
Hampstead 15, 18, 24, 25-6, 28-9, 31-33, 34-8, 41-3,
        45, 54-5, 59, 63, 66-7, 70, 73, 84, 87, 90, 91-6, 99-
        108, **109, 110, 111,** 112, 117-28,130, **134,** 135,
        138-9, 142, 145-6, **147,** 158, 164, 168, 169
Hampstead Heath 22, 26, 27-9, 35, 40, 45,
                    100, 105-6, 126-7
Hampton 49, 73, 145
Hampton Wick 21
Hamwic 21
Hanger 106
Hanger Lane 34
Hanwell 16, 66, 69, 70, 72, 94, 156, 165
Harefield 32, 50
Harefoot, Harold (king) 66
Harlesden 18, 36
Harmondsworth 20, 61
Harringey, see Hornsey
Harrow 16, 18-21, 25, 27-8, 31, 37, 53-4, 58, 73,
        91, 124, 145
Hastings, Battle of 33, 80
Hatfield Forest 35
Haverstock Hill (Hampstead) 106
Hawthorn 30, 48
Hay 26, 27, 145-6
Hayes 18, 19, 20, 54
Haymarket 27, 79, 82
Hazelwood 30, 35, 126
Heath plants 28, 126; see also Hampstead Heath
Hendon (Anglo-Saxon) 87, 90-1, 94, **97,** 112, 164
Hendon (Norman) 15, 18, 24, 25, 27, 29, 31, 35-8,
        43, 49, 53, 54, 63, 66, 70, **86,** 84, 87-96, **97,**
        98, 99, **110,** 112, 120, 122, 124, 142, 145,
        149, 153, 156-7, 164, 167, 168
Hendon Church 87
Hendon Hill **97**
Hendon Wood 87
Henry I 21, 49, 150
Henry II 21, 36, 82
Henry III 36, 42
Henry VIII 22, 27, 37, 44, 107, 135, 136
Hereditary offices 155

'Herestraet' 80
Heriot 116
Hertford 22, 46
Hertfordshire 17, 18 20, 21, 30, 31, 35, 37, 38, 47, 52, 54, 70, 71, **97**, 121, 165, 168
Hesdin, Arnulf of 36, 52
Hidation of Middlesex 50, 51, 52, 145-6
Hide 31, 50-1, 120, 122, 137-8
Highgate 25-8, 34, 38, 40, 45, 137, **147**
Highwood Hill 26, 28, 87
Hillingdon 32
'hlaw' (suffix) 81, 95-6, 166
'Hlothere' 88
Hodford 95-6
Holcombe Hill 87
Holborn 27, 79, 80, 107
Holebourne 39-40, 42, 45, 79, 81, 83, 156, 166-7
Holliday, Mr 88
Holy Innocents (church) 83
Holy Trinity, Rouen 61
Holly Hill, Hampstead 126
Homefeld (field, Hampstead) 125
Honeypot Lane, Kingsbury 53, 167
Honorius III (Pope) 83
'Honor of London' (Peverel's) 119
Hornsey (Harringey) 18, 34, 54, 71, 106
Horsendon 90
Hospitality 149, 158
Hounslow 36, 49, 51, 52, 53, 73
Housecarls 19, 68
House of Commons 48
Hoxton 18, 108
Humber 15
Hundreds 46, 49-55, 72
Hundred-Court 49-50, 53, 67
Hunting 21-2, 35, 36-7
Huntingdon 46
Hurley Priory 84
Hyda (Hampstead) 122
Hyde (part of Eia) 27, 43, 44
Hyde Park 27, 43, 44, 122, 136

Ice Ages 25-6
Ichnield Way 32
Ickenham 52
Ine (king) 114, 116
Infirmary 44, 152, 153, 155, 162
Inflation 139, 154
Ipswich 21
Isleworth 49, 73, 145
Islington 18, 39, 108
Itinerating kings 69, 149

Judith, Countess 137
Julius Caesar 48

Jumieges 68, **76, 78**

Kensal Green 20, 168
Kensington 27, 28, 33, 119
Kent 17, 19, 37, 40, 47, 71, 139, 165
Kentish Town 40
Kenwood 40, 106, **110, 111**, 169
Kilburn (vill) 43, 54, 127
Kilbourne (river) 43, 113, 168, 169; see also Westbourne
Kilburn Priory 61, 127
Kilburn Wood 127
'King's Boundary' 70, 168
Kingsbury 31, 34, 36, 37, 39, 52, 53, 66, 71, 87, 89, 91, 124, 167, 168
Kingsland Road 32; see also Ermine Street
King's Peace 32
Kingston (Surrey) 70
'King's Wood' (Kensal) 20, 168
'King's Wood' (Kingsbury) 70, 168
Kitchen (of monks) 30, 151, 152, 154
Kitchener of WA 162
Knightsbridge 15, 71, 84, **86**, 113, 138, 156
Knight's service 74, 119, 141-2
'Knights' 38, 119, 142

Laleham 72, 145
La Neyte, see Neyte
Lambeth 59
Lanfranc (A/bp Cant.) 21
Large, Robert (mayor of London) 44
Lay-servants of WA 139-41, 152, 154-5
Lea River 16, 22, 39, 51
'leah' 88, 125
Leases for lives 143
Leofstan (A/St Albans) 37-8
Leper hospitals, see St James, and St Giles
Liberty of WA 135, 165, 166
Lileston 33, 41, 73, 84, 103-4, 107, 108, 119, 127, **134**, 137, 146
Lime trees 29
Lincolnshire 71
Lindisfarne 57
Lisson Grove 73
London 15-24, 25-7, 30, 32-5, 37-48, 52, 55-6, 59, 65, 67-8, 70-1, 73, 80-1, 83, 95, 102-3, 121, 123-4, 135-7, 159, 167
London, Bishop of, see Bishop of London
London Bridge 81
London Clay 25, 27-8, 29, 92, 123, 127
London Diocese, see Diocese of London
London Fen 40, 80, 136, 166
Londonstone 18
London Wall 17-8
'lords' 114, 128-32, 137

Lotheresleage 54, 66, 87, 89-90, 92, 94, **97**, 112, 164, 167
Ludgate Circus 39, 45
Lundenburh 47
Lundenwic 21, 22, 47, 55, 82
Lyfing 87-9, 167-8

Madox, Tho. 101, 103, 191
Maitland, FW. 50, 51, 125
Mall, the 82
Malt 151
Malmesbury Abbey 58
Malmesbury, Wm of 56, 58
Mandeville, Geoffrey of 72, 84, 137
Mangoda 101-4, 169
Manor-Court 161
Manor Map 1762 (Hampstead) 93, 106, 107
'Manour-Place' (Hampstead) 123
'Mansa' (= Hide) 80, 88, 100, 164-5
Marble Arch 25, 48, 49, 52, 53, 82
Market Gardens 26, 139
Marylebone-Euston Road 27, 41
Marylebone Park 37, 107
Matilda (Empress) 137
Matilda (Queen of William I) 49
Matilda (Queen of Henry I) 49
Maudit, Robert 99
Maundy 152, 156
Mayfair 27,41
Mayor's Banqueting House 37
Meadowland 26, 136, 145-6
'men' 19, 141-5
Mellitus (Bishop) 17, 59
Mercia 15-6, 18, 19-21, 22-3, 57, 73, 83, 167
'Middle-Hampstead' 106, 169
Middle-Saxons 16, 20, 21, 46
Middlesex - passim
    common fields 124-5
    damage during Conquest 33, 121, 125
    DB on tenants' holdings 50-1, **86,** 138
    early A-S history 15-24
    geology 25-9
    making of the Shire 46-7
    shire-court 47-9
    WA's early lands in 65-74
    'wheat and beans' 28
    woodland 29-38
Mdx-Herts boundary 17, 18, 20, 21, 31, 47, 52, 168
Midlands 19, 46
Mill Hill 25, 26, 28, 54
Mills 34, 39
'Mimmas', Mimms 16
Minsters 24, 59, 67, 91
Mints 101-2, 103, 104
Mint-towns 102
Mitcham 16

Monasteries
    destruction of 57
    rebuilding of 58
Moneyers 101-4, 106, 112
Monk-Bailiff 144
Monk-Bishop 58
Monk-Cathedral 160
Monk-Priests 91
Monks
    Benedictine 'Rule' 56
    discipline 56, 57-8, 83, 143, 158-9
    numbers 56, 140, 143, 158-9
    organisation 157-62
Mortain, Count Robert of 103, 156
Mucking 16
Muswell Hill 45
Mutton Brook 92, 168

Neasden 90
New Bridge Street 79, 166
Newgate 55, 81, 83, 121
New Minster, Winchester **2**
Newton's map of the Westbourne 92
Neyte, La (Abbot's house) 26, 59
Niger River 25
'Nomansland' 141
Norfolk 21, 30
Norman architecture 68
Norman Conquest 33-4, 73, 87, 117-23, 125
Normans 18, 60-1, 68, 117-23, 136-8, 151-7; see also Feudal System, Norman Conquest
Northants 15, 71
North End (Hampstead) 54, 87, 92
Northumbria 16
Northwood (wood) 127
Nottingham 38
Norwich 21
Nuthurst (wood) 126

Oak trees 28, 29, 30, 34, 35, 127
Oats 38, 123, 151
Obedientaries 162
Offa (K. of Essex) 79, 95
Offa (K. of Mercia) 20, 79
'old gallows' 83, 167
Old Minster, Winchester 58
Ordinance, the Hundred 49-50
Ordinance, the peace-keeping 47
Osbert of Clare 61-2, 69, 89, 90, 91, 94, 113, 158
Oslac (Dux) 101
Ossulston Hundred 46, 48, 51-3, 91, 99
Oswald (Bishop) 58, 73
Oswaldslaw 73
Oswulf, Oswald (of Ossulton) 52
Otto the Goldsmith 73, 103-4, 119, 137

Ouse River 22
Oxendon Hill 53
Oxford 46, 70, 71, 139
Oxford Street 41, 42, 44, 48, 79, 81, 136, 166
Oxherd 129

Padda, Pada 112
Paddington 15, 24, 32, 37, 38, 43, 44, 63, 67, 70,
          71, 82, 84, **86,** 112-3, 124, **134,**
          138, 145, 146, 165
Paddington Wood 113, 146
Palace 13, 68, **75, 77,** 141
Pall Mall 82
Paris, Matthew 37
Parish, the 91, 99
Park Gate 106
Park Lane 53, 82
Parks 27, 41, 44, 107, 136
Pasture 35-6
Penny, silver 20, 102
Pershore Abbey 68, 152
Peterborough Abbey 57, 160
Peverel, Ranulf **86,** 103, 119-23, 125, 138, 142
Piccadilly 27, 41, 80, 82, 166
Pigs 30-1, 127, 146
'Pigwood' 30-5, 127, 146
Pilgrims at WA 154
Pimlico 26, 84
Pittances 152, 153
Placket's Well 92
Platt's Lane 92, 93
Plough 125, 128, 145
Ploughman 29, 128
Pluralism 65, 159
Pond Street 45, 54, 106
'praepositus' 144; see also Reeve
Prebend system 108
Priests 24, 83, 91, 99
Primrose Hill 25, 107, 127, 169
Priors 61, 158-9, 161; see also Osbert of Clare,
          and Reginald of Hadham
Private Hundred 72-3, 139
Proto-Thames 25, 29
Purlegh, Purloins, Pyrlegh (field) 125

Queenhithe 167
Queens, see Edith, Eleanor, Matilda

Ralph, Canon 107
Ralph, Earl 84, 103, 137
Ramsey Abbey 62, 65, 67, 150, 151, 160
'Rectitudines', see Estate Guide
Reeves 129-32, 141-5
'Re-forming' of estates 12, 53-4

Regalian right 150, 161
Regent Street 27, 79
Regent's Park 27, 41, 136
Reginald of Hadham (Prior) 158
'Regularis Concordia' 58, 143, 156, 158-9
'Regulars' 83
Religious revival 23, 57-8
Renders, see Food rents
Rents 138
Revolt of nobles 100
Rivers 16, 17, 20-1, 25-7, 38-45, 58-60, 80, 83
River traffic 59, 82
Roads 25, 32, 33, 37-8, 79-80, 81-3, 166; see also
                              road names
Rocque's map 48, 92,
Romanesque style 68, **78**
Roman roads 80
Romans 16, 17, 24, 48, 80, 81-2, 99-100
Roman sarcophagus **163**
Rome 165
Rouen 61, 68, **78**
Royal grants 19, 20, 53, 70-2, 79-80, 80-81, 88,
                         92, 100, 101
Royal residences 20, 30, 68-9, 141
Royal secretariat 69
Royal titles 23
Royal zone or sector in Mdx 12, 70, 168
Rugmere 18, 33, 34, 36, 107, 127
Ruislip 32
Rutland 15, 71
'Rule' (of St Benedict) 56, 58, 143, 158-9, 161-2

Sacrist of WA 162
St Alban's church (London) 20
St Alban's (Abbey & town) 18, 20, 37-8, 80, 150,
                              167
St Andrew's (Holborn) 5, 80, 166
St Andrew's (Kingsbury) 52, 66, 91
St Augustine 17
St Benedict, see Benedict, St
St Bride's Church 55, 166
St Denis (Abbey of) 60
St Edward (the Martyr; king) 88, 164
St Giles (vill and parish) 37, 79, 81, 83, 136, 147
                              166
St Giles's Hospital 136
St James's Hospital 82, 127, 136, **147, 148**
St James's Park 27, 37, 136
St James's Street 27, 42, 79
St John's Wood 107, 127, **134**
St Margaret's (church) 83, 84, 99, 113
St Margaret's (parish) 83, 84
St Martin's in the Fields 83-4
'St Mary' churches 66
St Mary's Chapel (Hampstead) 66, 99
St Mary's (Hendon) 29, 53, 90, 91

St Mary's (Tyburn) 42
St Mary le Strand 49, 83
St Pancras (estate) 18, 33, 34, 105, 107, 137
St Paul's (cathedral) 15, 17, 18, 19, 62, 65, 105,
    107, 108, 119, 123, 141, 142, 150, 160
St Peter **2**, **85**
'St Peter and St Paul' (Rome) 165
Salisbury, Earls of, and Edward of 137, 138
San(d)ford, Gilbert of 42
Sandgate 92, 105, 106, **110**, 168, 169
Sands, see Bagshot and Claygate
Sandy Heath 28-9
Sandy Road (Hampstead) 92
Savoy 55, 83
'scir' (shire) 47, 144
Scorched-earth policy 33, 121
Secular priests 83, 160
Seine river 68, **78**
Serfs 114-7, 128-9
Serpentine, the 43
'Serviens' 144
Settlements 27, 29, 38, 39, 48, 52-5, 70, 91, 95,
    106
Sheppenbrighull (wood, Hampstead) 126-7
Shepherds Fields (Hampstead) 126
Shepherd's Well 41, 126
Shepperton 16, 70, 112, 165
Sheppey, Isle of 22
Sherborne Abbey 159, 160
Sheriff 48, 84, 137, 144
Shire 17, 46-9, 54
Shire-Court 47, 48-9
Shire-Reeve, see Sheriff
Shooters Hill (Middlesex) 93
Shooters Hill (Surrey) 82
'Sillington' 71, 165
Silk river 39, 89, **98**, 167, 168
Slade stream 93, 108
'Slads', the 93
Slanning, John 126
Slaves 116-7, 121, 129
Sloane Street 43
Soho 83
'Somerlese' (field, Hampstead) 125
Somerset 47
South End (Hampstead) 45, 106
South Hill Park 106
Spaniards Inn (Hampstead) 106, **110**
Speakers' Corner (Marble Arch) 48
Spelthorne 48, 49, 51, 52, 53, 73
Staffordshire 71
Staines 16, 36, 69, 72, 82, 143, 144
Stanestaple 18, 108
Stanmore 31, 37, 38, 53, 91, 124, 167
Stantus,William. 155
Stepney 17, 18, 31, 32, 34, 39, 54, 59, 69
Stoke Newington 18

Stone Cross (Strand) 49
Stow, John 21, 36, 45
Strand 27, 42, 48, 49, 80, 82, 83, 167
Strand Bridge 49
Stratford Place (Oxford Street) 37
Strip-farming 124-5
Subinfeudation 119, 138, 142, 156
Suffolk 17, 30, 67, 91, 139-41,
Sulcard 59, 95
Summerleys (field, Hampstead) 125
Sunbury 66, 69-70, 94, 112, 145, 165
Surrey 16, 21, 22, 25, 71, 91, 121, **134**
Sussex 19, 70
Swiss Cottage 41

Table 1 (well-wooded areas) 31
Table 2 (lightly-wooded) 33
Table 3 (no pasture)36
Tata, Tateburn (Lotheresleage) 167
'Tatewell' (Tothill) 81
Taxation 15, 50-2, 101, 114, 137-8
Teddington 72
Telegraph Hill (Child's Hill) 43, 93, 96, 127, 168-9
Telligraph of Edward the Confessor 94; see
                Charter 1039, page 190
'Telligraph' of Ethelred 63, 67, 79, 89, 90, 94, 96,
                100, 112-3, 115, 164
Templars 93, 104
Temple Fortune 29, 54, 94
Temple (Strand) 83
Tenants-in-Chief 19, 36
Thames River 15, 16, 20, 21, 22, 25, 26, 27, 28,
                29, 32, 39, 40, 41, 42, 43, 45, 58,
                59, 69, 70, 79-83, 166
Thegn 19, 52, 67, 68, 71, 115, 142
Thorney Island 26, 58
'Three boundaries, the' 92, 105, 168
Thurstan 71
Timber 30, 82, 127, 153-4
Timberhurst (wood, Hampstead) 106, 127
Tithes 99
'Totenhala', see Tottenhall
Tothill (Westminster) 81, 156
Tothill Fields 81, 166
Tottenhall (later Tottenham Court) 18, 33, 36, 81,
                105-106, 107, **110**, **111**, 137
Tottenham (Mdx. estate) 31, 34, 124, 137
Tower of London 74
Trafalgar Square 21, 82, 83
Tribal Hidage 20
Tunstall, the (Watling Street) 54, 167,168
Tunworth (Kingsbury) 87, 89, 167-8
Twickenham 20
Twyfords, the (estates) 36
Tyburn Lane 82
Tyburn (estate) 33, 41, 42, 73-4, 84 108, 127, 137

Tyburn (river) 26, 41-2, 43, 44, 59, 74, 79-80, 82, 84, 137, 166

Undercroft of WA 153, **163**

'Vacancy' of an estate 150
Valery, Walter of 73
Vauxhall Bridge 41
de Veres 74, 137
Victoria Park 32
Villagers' activities 115-9, 128-32, **133**, 138-41
Villeins 118-9, 138
Villiers Street 27, 82
Vine Street 156
Vineyards 71, 152, 155-6
Virgate 50, 51, 118

'Waeclingas' 25
Walbrook river 42
Waleys, Henry 42
Waller's map 92-3
Walter of Henley 130
Walter of Valery 73
Walter of Wenlock 158
Waltham half-hundred 51
Waltham Forest 22
Wandene, Wm. of 155
Warren 36
Warwick 139
Warwickshire 71
Wash, the 15, 35
'Waste' 30, 35, 126, 128
Water supply for London 38-9, 40-1, 42, 44-5
for WA 41, 43-4
Watling Street 11, 22, 25, 32, 33, 36, 37-8, 43, 48, 52, 54, 80, 81-2, 87, 89, 93, 95, 105, 107, 108, 112-3, 121, 122, 124, 137, 146, 166-9,
Weald (Middlesex) 25, 31, 87 ff.
Week-work 116, 117, 119
Wells (springs) 39, 42, 44-5, 74, 92
Welsh, the 84
Westbourne (estate) 15, 32, 38, 43, 71, 84, **86,** 113, 145
Westbourne (river) 26, 40, 42-5, 71, 84, 92-4, 96, 105, 113, 123, 126
Wessex 22-4, 46-53, 143; see also Athelstan, Alfred, Edgar etc.
West End (Hampstead) 54, 92
West End (London) 11, 27
West End Lane (Hampstead) 127
West Heath (Hampstead) 28
Westminster Abbey **2, 64,** 85, **109, 163**
Arbitration (1222) 83
A-S Abbots 66, 159

Berewic 66, 80-3, 136, 160-1
buildings 68, 141, 151, 153, 154, 155, 162
commutation 150, 151-2, 157
Dissolution 56, 123, 135, 137
earlier history? 24, 59-60, 95-6
'exemption' from Bp/London 84
food-rents 149-157
forgery 60-3
foundation 23-4, 56-60, 79
'green fields' round WA 136, 145
initial poverty 56-7, 67
internal organisation 157-62
land-acquisition 65-113
land-administration 141-5, 149-51
leases to farmers 142-3
life at 149-62
numbers of monks 56, 140, 143, 154, 155
officers 158-9, 161-2
pilgrims at 154
quota for knights 119, 141-2
rebirth under Edw. C. 68-9
rent-list 51-7
resident 'men' 141-5
servants 139-41, 152, 154-5
site 26, 41-2, 58-9
strategic lands? 70
subinfeudations 119, 138, 142, 156
ultimate wealth 56-7
'vacancy' at 150
water-supply 41, 43-4
W. Customary 154, 162
W. Domesday 62
Westminster, Bp. of 123, 135
Westminster (estate) **85, 86, 147, 148**
Abbot's 'Liberty' 135, 165, 166
acquisition by WA 66, 69-70, 79-80, 83, 164, 166
alluvium 26, 27, 139, 145
Berewic added 66, 80-3
bounds of 79-85, 164, 166-7
early settlements 55
emerges in 10th century 23-4, 57-60
flooding 20, 26, 58-9
garden-cottagers 27, 139-41, 155
'green fields' 136, 145
growth of town 69, 135
lives of tenants 115-9, 128-32, **133,** 138-41
market-gardens 26, 139
meadowland 136, 145-6
'Nomansland' 141
Paddington etc. (added to) 71, 112-3, 136-8
pigwood in 33, 146
'reconstruction' view **148**
royal palace 30, 68, 135, 141
royal secretariat 69
St. Edward's Fair 135
St. Margaret's Church 83-4, 99, 113.

tenantry at DB 139-41
Thorney Island 58-9
villages 55, 138-45
Wyngaerde's view 135
Westminster Lane 82
West-Saxons, see Wessex
West Stow (Suffolk) 123
'wheat and beans' land (Mdx) 28
Whitebirch (wood) 35, 126
'wic' 21, 104, 106
Wicstrete 53, 167
Willesden 18, 31, 34, 36, 90, 108, 121, 124, 146,
          150
William I 18, 19, 21, 33, 36, 61, 73, 104, 121, 141
William II (Rufus) 49
William of Buckland 120, 138, 142
William the Chamberlain 71-2
William of Malmesbury 56-7, 68, 153
Wilton 69
Wiltshire 47, 51, 120
Winchester 2, 58, 69, 75, 102, 103, 160
Withylands (Kingsbury) 167
Wood (brushwood, timber) 29-30, 80, 82, 112, 146,
          153-4
Woodland 28, 29-38, 106-7, 112-3, 126-8, 146
Woolwich 21
Worcester Abbey 57, 67, 73, 150, 160
Worcestershire 51, 56, 68, 71, 73, 143
Wulfred (A/Bp) 79
Wulfric (Paddington) 112, 165
Wulfric Taynus 142
Wulfsin, Wulfsige (Abbot and St.) 128, 159, 165
Wulfwen (Chelsea) 137
Wulnoth (Abbot) 66, 159
Wulnoth (soldier) 91, 164
Wyngaerde, Van der 135, 147
Wytebirche, see Whitebirch

'Yeoman of England' 114
Yeoveney (Staines) 72
York 38.

For the separate index of the Charters referred-to in this book, see next page.

***

The principal Charters relating to the Corridor estates: -

Estate	Number in Sawyer's List	Pages (in this book)
Westminster	670	24, 39, 79, 80, 164, 166
	894	66, 79, 164
	903	80, 81, 160, 166, 167
	1039	81
	1450	39, 79, 80
Lotheresleage	645	25, 87, 167
	894	88, 89, 164
	1039	90
	1451	54, 88, 89, 164, 168
Hendon (the smaller)	894	90, 164
	1039	90
Bleccanham	1039	90
	1450	92, 95, 168
Codanhlaw	894	94, 164
	1039	90, 94
Hampstead	805	101, 169
	1450 (& Stowe Ch. 33)	100, 105-6, 107, 169
Paddington	894	112, 113, 165
	1039	113
Knightsbridge	1039	71
Chalkhill	1121	71, 168
Chelsea	-	20 (for A-S charters *before* WA's holding)

Some of the group forged at Westminster, mostly by Osbert de Clare: -

	(pages)
Sawyer No 774 ('Great Charter of Edgar')	89, 90, 96
1293 ('Great Charter of Dunstan')	89, 90, 91, 94, 96, 99, 112
1043 ('First Charter of Edward the Confessor)	69, 90, 99
1040 ('The Widmore Charter')	90, 99
1295 ('grant' of the smaller Hendon by Dunstan)	91

Sawyer No 1039 (which has never been fully printed) is included in the top group, because (like No. 894, the Telligraph of Ethelred) it is probably a curate's egg, partly good and partly bad.

Other charters (mostly about other estates in Middlesex) are referred-to on the following pages: -
16, 17, 20, 22, 24, 59, 63, 70, 72, 91, 91, 101, 104, 112, 159, 164, 165

A fine sentiment for the historian

"It is not my part to determine whether the present Collection be likely to be of Use or Ornament to the Publique. Others must judge of That."

Thomas Madox *Formulare Anglicanum*, 1702 AD

*****